D0679315

Global e-Commerce

Are the Internet and e-commerce truly revolutionizing business practice? This book explodes the transformation myth by demonstrating that the Internet and e-commerce are in fact being adapted by firms to reinforce their existing relationships with customers, suppliers, and business partners. Detailed case studies of eight countries show that, rather than creating a borderless global economy, e-commerce strongly reflects existing local patterns of commerce, business, and consumer preference, and its impact therefore varies greatly by country. Paradoxically, while e-commerce is increasing the efficiency, effectiveness, and competitiveness of firms, it is also increasing the complexity of their environments as they have to deal with more business partners and also face greater competition from other firms. This incisive analysis of the diffusion and impact of e-business provides academic researchers, graduates, and MBA students with a solid basis for understanding its likely evolution.

KENNETH L. KRAEMER is Professor at the Paul Merage School of Business and at the Donald Bren School of Information and Computer Science, University of California, Irvine. He is also Director of the Center for Research on Information Technology and Organizations (CRITO) and Director of the Personal Computing Industry Center (PCIC).

JASON DEDRICK is Co-Director of the Personal Computing Industry Center and Senior Research Fellow at CRITO, University of California, Irvine.

NIGEL P. MELVILLE is Assistant Professor of Business Information Technology at the Stephen M. Ross School of Business, University of Michigan.

KEVIN ZHU is Associate Professor at the Rady School of Management, University of California, San Diego.

Global e-Commerce

Impacts of National Environment and Policy

Edited by

KENNETH L. KRAEMER

JASON DEDRICK

NIGEL P. MELVILLE

KEVIN ZHU

CAMBRIDGE UNIVERSITY PRESS
Cambridge, New York, Melbourne, Madrid, Cape Town, Singapore, São Paulo

Cambridge University Press
The Edinburgh Building, Cambridge CB2 2RU, UK

Published in the United States of America by Cambridge University Press, New York

www.cambridge.org
Information on this title: www.cambridge.org/9780521848220

First published 2006

Printed in the United Kingdom at the University Press, Cambridge

A catalogue record for this publication is available from the British Library

ISBN-13 978-0-521-84822-0 hardback
ISBN-10 0-521-84822-9 hardback

Contents

Figures

Tables

Boxes

Notes on contributors

Roman Beck is Assistant Professor at the Johann Wolfgang Goethe University, Institute of Information Systems in Frankfurt, Germany. As a political economist he worked for two years at the Institute for Rural Development Studies on different research projects about the impacts of infrastructure on economic developments. He coordinated the research project "IT Standards and Network Effects" funded by the German National Science Foundation. His research focuses on the role of IT in creating new business models, the diffusion of IT innovations, and the role of externalities and network effects on the adoption of new standards, especially among SMEs. He publishes on a wide array of topics in the field of IT standards such as EDI, Web EDI, and m-commerce. His academic research has been published at several international IS conferences and proceedings and in academic journals such as *EM-Electronic Markets*, *Wirtschaftsinformatik*, *JGIM*, *Information Polity*, and *CAIS*.

Eric Brousseau is Professor of Economics at the University of Paris X, France and Director of EconomiX, a joint research center between the CNRS (French National Science Foundation) and the University of Paris X. He is also co-director of the GDR TICS (Research Consortium "Information Technologies and the Society") of the CNRS. His research agenda focuses on the economics of institutions and the economics of contracts, with two main fields of applications: the economics of intellectual property rights and the economics of the Internet and digital activities. On this last issue he works on digital business models, on the development of e-commerce and e-markets, and on the governance of the Internet and of the information society.

Bruno Chaves is Research Engineer for Economics at the University of Paris X, France at EconomiX. His research focuses on economics of online coordination systems. He is also webmaster for various research organizations.

Tain-Jy Chen is Professor in the Department of Economics at National Taiwan University, and former President of Chung-Hua Institution for Economic Research. His research interests are in international trade and industrial development.

Jason Dedrick is Senior Research Fellow at CRITO at the University of California, Irvine. His research is focused on the globalization of information technology and the economic impacts of IT at the firm, industry, and national levels. He is now working on a multi-country study of the adoption and impacts of electronic commerce, as well as a study of global knowledge networks in the personal computer industry. Mr. Dedrick is co-author, with Kenneth L. Kraemer, of *Asia's Computer Challenge: Threat or Opportunity for the United States and the World?* (Oxford University Press, 1998). He is also author of numerous journal articles, book chapters, and other publications.

Satoshi Hamaya is Senior Research Analyst at the Center for Economic Research at the Fujitsu Research Institute in Japan. His key research interests focus on Internet business in Japan, electronic commerce, and IT business strategies and governance. His major publications include "Internet Business White Paper 2002" co-authored and edited, "The Diffusion and Utilization of E-Commerce: The Comparative Characteristics of Ten Countries and Regions," and "Outsourcing for Sustainable Competitive Advantage: Information Systems."

John L. King is Dean and Professor at the School of Information at the University of Michigan. His research over the past two decades has concentrated on the relationship between technical and social change, and especially on IT-related changes in highly institutionalized production sectors such as transport, financial services, health care, criminal justice, and government. He has served as Professor at the University of California at Irvine, as Editor-in-Chief of the INFORMS journal *Information Systems Research*, as Marvin Bower Professor at Harvard Business School, as Board Member for the Computing Research Association, as Fulbright Distinguished Chair of American Studies at the University of Frankfurt in Germany, and as a senior scientific advisor to the Computer and Information Science and Engineering Directorate, and the Social, Behavioral, and Economic Research Directorate at the US National Science Foundation.

Wolfgang Koenig is Professor of Information Systems at Johann Wolfgang Goethe University, Institute of Information Systems in Frankfurt, Germany. From 1995 to 2000 he headed an interdisciplinary research program sponsored by the German National Science Foundation on "Competitive Advantage by Networking – the Development of the Frankfurt and Rhine–Main Region." Since the end of 2002 he has chaired the "E-Finance Lab Frankfurt am Main," a joint research program with Accenture, Bearing Point, Deutsche Bank, Deutsche Postbank, Finanz IT, IBM, Microsoft, Siemens, and T-Systems. Since October 2004, he has been Dean of the faculty of Economics and Business Administration. Moreover, he serves as Editor-in-Chief of the leading mid-European IS journal *Wirtschaftsinformatik*. He is a member of the board of external directors of several companies. His research interests are in standardization, networking, and e-finance. His research has been published in academic journals such as *EM-Electronic Markets*, *Wirtschaftsinformatik*, *JGIM*, *JISeB*, *JITSR*, and *CAIS*.

Kenneth L. Kraemer is Professor of Management and Computer Science at the Paul Merage School of Business and the Donald Bren School of Information and Computer Science at the University of California, Irvine, where he has been since 1967. He is Director of CRITO and PCIC. He was also Director of the NSF Industry–University Cooperative Research Center (I/UCRC – CRITO Consortium) from 1997 to 2003. He holds the Taco Bell Chair in Information Technology for Management and has held the Shaw Professor Chair in Information Systems at the National University of Singapore (1990–1991). He was elected a "Fellow" of the Association for Information Systems in 2003. His research spans thirty-nine years in information technology management: social and organizational implications of IT, national policy for IT production and use, contributions of IT to productivity, IT in developing countries, and the dynamics of the IT industry and offshore sourcing. He has published over 175 papers in scholarly journals such as *Management Science*, *Information Systems Research*, *MIS Quarterly*,

Organization Science, *Journal of Management Information Systems*, *Communications of the ACM*, *Computing Surveys*, *Telecommunications Policy*, *Policy Analysis*, *Public Administration Review*, and *The Information Society*. His books include *Computers and Politics*, *People and Computers*, and *Datawars* (Columbia University Press, 1982, 1985, 1987), *Modeling as Negotiating* (Ablex, 1985), *Wired Cities* (G. K. Hall, 1987), *Managing Information Systems* (Columbia University Press, 1989), *The Information Systems Research Challenge* (Harvard Business School, 1991), *Asia's Computer Challenge: Threat or Opportunity for the United States and the World* (Oxford University Press, 1998), and *Global E-Commerce* (Cambridge University Press, 2006).

Kalle Lyytinen is Iris S. Wolstein Professor at Case Western Reserve University. He currently serves on the editorial boards of several leading IS journals, including *Journal of AIS* (Editor-in-Chief), *Journal of Strategic Information Systems*, *Information and Organization*, *Requirements Engineering Journal*, *Information Systems Journal*, *Scandinavian Journal of Information Systems*, and *Information Technology and People*, among others. He is an AIS fellow (2004), and the former chairperson of IFIP 8.2. He has published over 150 scientific articles and conference papers and edited or written ten books on topics related to system design, method engineering, implementation, software risk assessment, computer-supported cooperative work, standardization, and ubiquitous computing. He is currently involved in research projects that look at the IT-induced innovation in software development, architecture and construction industry, design and use of ubiquitous applications in health care, high-level requirements model for large-scale systems, and the development and adoption of broadband wireless standards and services, where his recent studies have focused on South Korea and the USA.

Nigel P. Melville is Assistant Professor at the Stephen M. Ross School of Business, at the University of Michigan, where he researches and teaches innovation with information and information technology. Previously, he was the Students in Free Enterprise Sam Walton Fellow and Assistant Professor of Information Systems at the Carroll School of Management, Boston College. He earned his Ph.D. in management from the Graduate School of Management at UC Irvine. His papers have appeared in *MIS Quarterly*, *Information Systems Research*, and *Communications of the ACM*. Prior to earning his Ph.D., he worked as a new product development engineer for Motorola, as a technical editor in Osaka Japan, and co-founded a customer relationship management software company. He is a member of the Association for Computing Machinery and INFORMS. He earned an M.S. in electrical and computer engineering from UC Santa Barbara and a B.S. in electrical engineering from UCLA.

Juan J. Palacios is Professor of Economics and Head, Transnational Studies Program at the Department of Political Studies, University of Guadalajara, Mexico. Professor Palacios is a member of Mexico's National Research System (SNI) and of the Information and Communication Technology Innovation Program for E-business and SME Development (ICT-4-BUS) Program Advisory Council of the Inter American Development. His research interests include the PC industry and e-commerce in Mexico, and he has published articles on topics such as "Impacts of liberalization and economic integration on Mexico's computer sector," "Globalization and e-commerce: environment and policy in Mexico," and "The development of e-commerce in Mexico: A business-led passing boom or a step toward the emergence of a digital economy?" He is also author of *Production Networks and Industrial Clustering in Developing Regions. Electronics Manufacturing in Guadalajara, Mexico* (2001, Mexico: Unversidad de Guadalajara).

Dennis S. Tachiki is Professor at the faculty of Business Administration and Graduate School of Business Administration at Tamagawa University in Tokyo, Japan. He has been a consultant for the Japanese Ministry of Economy, Trade and Industry, and for the Machine Tool Industry Association, on e-commerce and industrial competitiveness. His current research focus is on the diffusion of technology across the production networks of multinational corporations in the Asia-Pacific region. He has co-edited *Regional Strategies in a Global Economy* and *Pathways to Innovation.*

Zixiang (Alex) Tan is Associate Professor at the School of Information Studies at Syracuse University in New York. His research and teaching interests include policy and regulation, industry restructuring, global competition, and application deployment in the ICT sector, with a geographic focus on China and Asia.

Paulo Bastos Tigre is Economist MSc in Production Engineering, and D.Phil. in Science and Technology Policy. Presently he is Professor of Industrial Organization at the Institute of Economics of Rio de Janeiro Federal University, Brazil. He was visiting research fellow at the University of California Berkeley (1997), University of Brighton (1994), and Université de Paris XIII (1996), and has served as consultant and advisor to several national and international institutions related to technology development. He has been conducting research in technology development issues for twenty-five years, especially in the field of economics of information and communications technologies. These include the development of the computer and software industry in developing countries, electronic commerce, strategies and policies for the telecommunications industry, regulations, and international agreements for trade in services.

Rolf T. Wigand is Maulden-Entergy Chair and Distinguished Professor of Information Science and Management at the University of Arkansas at Little Rock. He is the immediate past Director of the Center for Digital Commerce and the Graduate Program in Information Management at Syracuse University. Mr. Wigand researches information management, electronic commerce and markets, IS standards, and the strategic deployment of information and communication technology. His research interests lie at the intersection of information and communication business issues, the role of newer IT, and its strategic alignment within business and industry. His research has been supported by the National Science Foundation, the German National Science Foundation (DFG), the Volkswagen Foundation, the International Social Science Council, Rome Laboratory, and others. He is an editorial board member of almost thirty academic journals, book series, and yearbooks, and the author of five books and over 110 articles, book chapters, and monographs.

Ouyang Wu is Division Head of the Department of Policy and Planning under State Council Informatization Office in the People's Republic of China. He moved to this position after he finished his research project organized by CRITO. Some of his publications include "Deregulating Telecommunications in the US," "What Can We Learn from the Reform of Telecommunications in the US?" "Convergence in China: Barriers in the System, Business and Management," "Some Issues in the Process of Restructuring the Chinese Telecommunications Market," "Cable Networks, Electronic Commerce and Social Informatization," "Opportunities and Challenges for Non-State Owned Enterprises in China Telecommunications Market," "ITA: The Trade Framework in Information Age," and so on. He has visited Canada and the Netherlands as a visiting scholar and worked as an affiliate researcher for a year for the Program on Information Resources Policy at Harvard University.

Sean Xu is a doctoral candidate at the Paul Merage School of Business, University of California, Irvine. His research interests include IT assimilation and usage by firms, organizational/economic impacts of IT and e-business, the diffusion of network technologies, and economics of network standards. His work has been published or accepted for publication in *MIS Quarterly*, *Journal of Management Information Systems*, *European Journal of Information Systems*, and *Electronic Markets*. He won two Best Paper Awards at the International Conference on Information Systems in 2002 and 2003, and a Best Paper Award at the America's Conference on Information Systems in 2004.

Kou Yukawa is Senior Research Associate at the Center for Economic Research at the Fujitsu Research Institute in Japan. He is also a Visiting Researcher at Tokyo University. His key research interests include Internet business and cluster of Internet companies, especially the Bit Valley phenomenon in Japan. Two of his main English publications are "Internet Companies in Japan after the Collapse of the Internet Bubble – an Analysis of Internet Companies and Their Cluster" and "A Cluster of Internet Companies in Tokyo: Review of Bit Valley."

Kevin Zhu is Associate Professor at the Rady School of Management, University of California, San Diego. His research falls in the intersection of economics, technology, and management science, with a focus on economics of information systems, technology diffusion, business value of IT, and strategic adoption of technology standards.

His work has been published in *Management Science*, *Information Systems Research*, *MIS Quarterly*, *JMIS*, and the *European Journal of Information Systems*. He was recently awarded the prestigious Faculty Early Career Development (CAREER) Award by the US National Science Foundation – the highest honor bestowed by the US government on outstanding young scholars who are most likely to become academic leaders of the twenty-first century. He has won the Best Paper Award, two years in a row, at the International Conference on Information Systems (ICIS).

Introduction

KENNETH L. KRAEMER,
JASON DEDRICK, AND
NIGEL P. MELVILLE

Motivation

The new millennium coincided with an explosion in the use of the Internet for commercial purposes. Dot.com companies in the United States such as Amazon and eBay led the way, creating online services where none had existed before. Recognizing the value of e-commerce, traditional companies also jumped online, including Wal-Mart in retail, Cisco in networking, Dell in the PC industry, and Charles Schwab in banking. In just a few short years, a company without a website was considered passé and the Internet was becoming mythologized: "A few years from now business economists may include the Internet in the Schumpeterian Hall of Fame, as an economic innovation of the same magnitude as the steam engine and the assembly lines of yore" (DePrince Jr. & Ford, 1999). Radical changes toward online business models were widely believed to be ushering in a "new economy" requiring new competitive strategies, business models, and even a new economics.

Given the major role played by the United States in developing the Internet and fostering its commercialization, other nations voiced concern that it would dominate e-commerce, spreading US culture and economic influence via electronic networks. The Internet compresses time and space, making it easier for companies to expand beyond regional boundaries. Commerce emerges as a powerful force beyond the control of individual countries, with a corollary being that the relevance of differences between countries diminishes. Taking this argument to the extreme, some predicted the emergence of a borderless global economy. In his treatise on strategies for the new economy, Kenichi Ohmae (2001, p.5) argues that "the idea of Japan or America as economic aggressor is simply a 'cartographic illusion' – a misperception derived from the false idea that national borders represent lines of true political autonomy." Powerful global production networks and the rise of offshore outsourcing would appear to be consistent with this view of a borderless global economy. The Internet may indeed be driving a shift toward a global marketplace, with significant ramifications for supply chains, business processes, customer service, and the basis of competition.

In times of rapid change, historical perspective is lacking. What is reality and what is hype? And how can we systematically distinguish between the two? Anecdotes and case studies have been the primary means of examining the impact of the Internet on societies, markets, and economies, painting detailed portraits of particular organizations and events. Exposing rich phenomena in context helps understand the "how" and "why" of e-commerce. However, their application to other contexts is limited. What happens in one country or region may not happen in another. The impact of back-office e-commerce operations may be different than customer-facing websites. Processes particular to one industry such as finance differ from those in others such as manufacturing. This leads to differences in how the Internet and e-commerce are applied, resulting in varying performance impacts.

A systematic analysis of the impact of the Internet and e-commerce across firms, industries, and economies is necessary to separate hype from reality. We focus on understanding the topographical patterns of e-commerce across diverse economies and industries in order to assess the evolution of e-commerce (transformational versus incremental change), the extent of US hegemony, and the extent to which globalization diminishes the power of nations, shapes local economies, and re-aligns national cultures. This book addresses these and other issues by reporting the results of a major research program using country case studies, secondary data, and survey data collected across ten economies, three industries, and small and large firms.

The research program, which is called the Globalization and E-Commerce (GEC) project, was supported by grants from the Information Technology Research (ITR) Program of the US National Science Foundation. Our research focused on understanding how differences in national environments and policy influenced the diffusion and impacts of e-commerce in a global context. Consequently, we examined diffusion in ten economies, including both developed and developing ones. Within each economy we further studied the three industry sectors most shaped by the early diffusion of e-commerce – manufacturing, distribution, and finance – and both small and large firms within these sectors. Among the various studies that comprised the GEC Project, we gathered secondary data on forty economies, historical case study data on ten economies, and original survey data on 2,139 firms across the ten case study economies (the USA, Brazil, China, Denmark, France, Germany, Japan, Mexico, Singapore, and Taiwan). We refer to this latter survey data throughout the book as the "GEC Survey" or "global sample."

The value propositions of the research program described herein are four fold. Given varying approaches to managing and controlling national economies, varying levels of technological infrastructure, and diverse national, business, and consumer cultures, we might expect significant variation in how e-commerce is adopted, how it diffuses, and how it impacts firms, industries, and countries. The first value proposition is thus to provide an enhanced and systematic understanding of the relationship between national environments and policy and the use and impacts of e-commerce. Findings also improve understanding of variation in e-commerce use and impacts across manufacturing, finance, and retail industries, as well as across large versus small and medium-sized organizations. Such results inform the decisions of policymakers who seek to develop and shape e-commerce applications to fit their specific contexts with maximal benefit. Results also assist researchers in their quest to unearth structural patterns in how technology is diffused and used, and its effects.

The second value proposition is to provide insights for firms, industries, and global e-commerce markets. Analysis of the GEC Survey data reveals substantial opportunities for the application of e-commerce to fit local contexts. Results described herein underscore, however, that a one-size-fits-all approach is not advisable. Only by carefully understanding the historical antecedents of information technology application as well as the prevailing business and cultural conditions can e-commerce application be successful.

The third value proposition is to serve as a benchmark for future studies. One motivation for the current research program was a lack of cross-country analyses of e-commerce application using systematic survey data. Having undertaken this colossal task, it is our hope that this research program, as documented herein, will serve as a rigorous scientific benchmark for future studies of national and global Internet and e-commerce trends. To this end, the editors have attempted to be completely transparent in describing and interpreting not only the findings of the various studies but also the methodology used to derive them.

The final value proposition is to provide a snapshot in time to preserve the early facts of the e-commerce and Internet revolution. So much has been written about the Internet and e-commerce by pundits, essayists, economists, business researchers, and others. Unfortunately, however, intermingled with excellent studies and useful insights is a monumental collection of hyperbole. This book, therefore, is a counterbalance of sorts, enabling future generations to assess studies of the Internet, e-commerce, and globalization and draw their own conclusions about what really happened – or didn't happen.

Research approach

The approach of the research described in the following chapters was to bring together academic experts to develop a common research protocol, conduct country and international analyses, and share findings at annual meetings. The research protocol was developed to achieve multiple objectives. The first was to create a team culture to facilitate knowledge development, sharing, and cross-fertilization of ideas. Second, a common survey instrument had to be developed that applied to diverse economies spanning Asia, the Americas, and Europe. Moreover, it had to be translated into multiple languages, independently checked for alignment with the original, and piloted in each country. Third, we had to collect secondary data that were comparable across countries with which to better understand their socioeconomic environments and e-commerce diffusion over time, as a way of providing perspective for our cross-sectional survey. Finally, to complement both the GEC Survey and the secondary data and to obtain a granular understanding of the Internet and e-commerce within each country, we chose to develop case studies for each country, including specific industries and/or firms. These case studies were written by local experts.

We developed several partnerships to carry out the work. First was our partnership with the academic experts in each country who signed on for the four-year effort. Second was a partnership with the International Data Corporation (IDC) of Framingham, Massachusetts. The company helped develop the survey questionnaire, secure translations into multiple languages, check the questionnaire translations with its in-country staff, oversee conduct of the survey by the international survey firm Market Probe, and review the survey results. We chose IDC because it has experience working in many countries, conducts its own surveys in several countries, and has experts in e-commerce in each of the countries in this study. Third was a partnership with Empirica, GmbH in Germany for data and analysis related to projects sponsored by the European Commission's Information Society Technologies (IST) Directorate General. These projects – ECATT, Project Star, SIBIS, eBusiness Watch – provided additional data useful for special firm-level, cross-country analyses that complemented the basic GEC analyses.

Organization of the book

The book comprises ten chapters and three appendices. The first chapter is an introduction, while Chapters 2 through 9 are individual country analyses. Chapter 10 summarizes the findings from the firm-level, cross-country analyses. Appendix I describes data-collection details and the questionnaire, Appendix II provides statistic measures by sector and size, while Appendix III provides statistic measures by country. A thumbnail portrait of each chapter follows.

1. Introduction

Looking across all countries in the study, we must conclude that e-commerce is diffusing in an evolutionary fashion, in contrast to the hyperbole of radical change. Factors promoting adoption and diffusion include globalization, economic liberalization, and appropriate public investment in information infrastructure such as telecommunications and the Internet platform. Consistent with this finding, there is significant national diversity in e-commerce adoption, particularly in downstream marketing, sales, and other customer-oriented activities. However, there is convergence in upstream activities, which is driven by the increasing importance of global production and distribution networks in the world economy. Finally, the idea of US hegemony is a myth. The influence of the United States on e-commerce developments is diminishing as other nations draw on their own cultures and technological infrastructures and local firms develop tailored business models and applications that fit their specific needs.

2. *United States*

Despite early experiments which were quite transformative, the development of e-commerce in the United States has been evolutionary rather than revolutionary, and its impacts have been changes in degree more than in kind. Many key e-commerce technologies and business processes were developed in the United States within the Silicon Valley model. However, it is only one dimension of e-commerce diffusion in the USA. A much larger share of e-commerce activity is characterized by a pattern of "adaptive integration," in which existing firms incorporate the new technologies and business models offered by the Internet to extend or revamp their existing strategies, operations, and supply and distribution channels. Increasingly, e-commerce is just part of the broader evolution of commerce.

3. *France*

France took an alternative path to the Internet and e-commerce. It was late to the Internet because of its early adoption of Minitel and electronic data interchange (EDI) in the early 1980s. Both were earlier forms of e-commerce that were made obsolete by the rapid, global adoption of Internet-based e-commerce in the mid-1990s. The French-specific path for e-commerce has been shaped by the unique characteristics of the French economy and innovation system. The large established firms have not been well adapted to the decentralized process of innovation at the heart of the Internet revolution, and few French start-ups were able to develop in the Internet sector. French firms, especially in finance and retail but also in manufacturing, were well entrenched with their customers and had no reason to change. Combined with a highly regulated economy, development of e-commerce has been confined largely to dominant firms that were driven to go online in the late 1990s in response to international competition, especially within European Community markets.

4. *Germany*

Slow to the Internet initially, Germany has become a fast follower in adopting Internet-based e-commerce innovations. Though extensive use of established technologies such as EDI and electronic funds transfer (EFT) may have delayed adoption, Germany has since caught up on most measures of use. German firms choose applications carefully based on their proven track records of success in other countries. Two salient factors driving adoption of e-commerce in Germany are the international orientation of its economy and the dynamism of its small and medium-sized enterprises (SMEs).

5. *Japan*

Japan's unique industrial landscape – its interlocking networks of firms (*keiretsu*), highly interwoven political economy (iron triangle), and distinctive business culture – has led to a somewhat insular business environment slow to the Internet. Despite this, Japan is comparable with other economies along various e-commerce measures. Analysis of the Internet and globalization in Japan illustrates that even in the absence of global drivers, local factors can drive e-commerce diffusion and impacts. Japan's convenience stores and i-mode applications also illustrate how the unique characteristics of national economies can be reinforced by the use of the Internet and e-commerce, rather than washed away into a global melting pot.

6. *China*

The use of e-commerce and the Internet in China is a study of contrasts. There is wide geographic inequality, yielding a digital divide of sorts between rich coastal regions and relatively poor interior areas. Coastal regions have much better infrastructure and many more Internet users than others. Moreover, larger enterprises have larger IT budgets and better-trained staffs than small and medium-sized enterprises, and are more capable of engaging in e-commerce. However, they tend to be more conservative than smaller, more entrepreneurial companies which lack the financial and human resources to engage in e-commerce. Thus, there are only a few islands of success linked to foreign multinationals, despite active government promotion to local enterprises. Overall, given its large population and islands of Internet success, China appears poised for future growth in e-commerce adoption and diffusion.

7. *Taiwan*

Taiwan is unique in that it has characteristics of both a developing economy – slowly developing legal framework, low rate of IT spending, low number of IT professionals within firms – and a developed economy – highly developed, modern, and global manufacturing sector, as well as a high literacy rate. Given its role in global manufacturing supply chains, the most salient driver of e-commerce in Taiwan appears to be international competitive pressure, especially in manufacturing, where e-commerce is becoming a competitive necessity. However, until inequalities and concerns over rule of law, security, and privacy are mitigated, the development of e-commerce in Taiwan will be mixed.

8. *Brazil*

Brazil's large size and its considerable geographic distance from global production networks create a relatively inward-oriented economy. Local factors have thus driven e-commerce, especially the need for financial efficiency because of historically rampant inflation and low gross domestic product (GDP) per capita. Disproportionate wealth distribution impedes widespread adoption of consumer-oriented e-commerce. Overall, Brazil illustrates the importance of local versus global forces in driving e-commerce, shows how the financial sector can lead in e-commerce adoption, and reveals the innovation of large firms relative to small firms in the use of e-commerce.

9. *Mexico*

Mexico's socio-economic environment, which is similar to that of many Latin-American countries, has a large impact on e-commerce diffusion. Its highly skewed income distribution, traditional shopping culture, skewed size distribution of firms, low level of technological development of firms, and relatively informal business culture have created a complex e-commerce growth pattern that varies by industry and size of firm that can best be described as "islands of innovation" within a slowly developing e-commerce environment.

These islands occur mainly in selected manufacturing sectors where Mexico serves as a production platform for many foreign multinationals, as illustrated by its famed *maquiladoras* along the border with the United States, and special trade zones within the country at key places like Guadalajara, Mexico City, and Monterrey. These production hubs, along with a strong financial sector, are the most dynamic and modern segments of the economy, and have traditionally led in the use of IT, as well as in the use of the Internet for e-commerce. In contrast, SMEs lag large firms in e-commerce, though evidence suggests that the gap may be narrowing. Overall, the story of e-commerce in Mexico is one of strong global finance and manufacturing sectors driving moderate use of e-commerce.

10. Global diffusion and convergence of e-commerce

This chapter integrates a number of firm-level cross-country analyses focused on understanding e-commerce as a technical innovation within the context of the larger literature on the diffusion of innovations. It summarizes what we know from the study overall regarding the environmental, organizational, and technological factors that influence e-commerce adoption, the nature and extent of e-commerce diffusion and use, and the business value that firms derive from e-commerce.

Acknowledgments

This research has been supported by grants from the US National Science Foundation (CISE/ISS/ITR and DST, grant numbers 0085852 and 0132911, respectively) and by the European Information Society Technologies Programme of the European Commission (ECATT, Project Star, SIBIS, and eBusiness Watch projects). Part of the data was provided by Empirica, GmbH, Bonn, Germany. Any opinions, findings, and conclusions or recommendations expressed in this material are those of the authors and do not necessarily reflect the views of the National Science Foundation or the European Commission.

We are especially grateful to Rosalie Zobel of the European Commission and Suzanne Iacono of the National Science Foundation who created the opportunity for this research by encouraging international cooperation, bringing together researchers at the European Commission's Conference on E-Work and E-Commerce in Venice, Italy in 2003, and supporting the research generally.

We acknowledge the following academic research participants, many of whom are chapter authors in this book but without all of whom this project would not have been possible. They worked with us over four years and were patient with the many rewrites requested by the project leaders.

Brazil: Paulo Bastos Tigre, Country Expert. Professor and Director, Institute of Industrial Economics, Federal University of Rio de Janeiro.

China: Zixiang (Alex) Tan, Associate Professor, Syracuse University. Ouyang Wu, Country Expert. Secretary General, Center for Information Infrastructure and Economic Development, Chinese Academy of Social Sciences.

Denmark: Niels Bjorn-Andersen, Country Expert. Professor, Director of Center for Electronic Commerce, Copenhagen School of Business. Kim Viborg Andersen, Assistant Professor, Copenhagen School of Business.

France: Eric Brousseau, Country Expert. Professor, University of Paris X and Director, Department GIFT (Globalization, Innovation, Firm, Territory) of FORUM (Research Center from the CNRS # 7028). Director of the GDR Technologies de l'Information et de la Communication et Société (CNRS Research Consortium on "Information and Communication Technologies and the Society"). Bruno Chaves, University of Paris X.

Germany: Wolfgang Koenig, Country Expert. Professor, Johann Wolfgang Goethe University, Institute of Information Systems, Frankfurt University. Rolf Wigand, Researcher. Professor, University of Arkansas at Little Rock. Roman Beck, Researcher, Johann Wolfgang Goethe University, Institute of Information Systems, Frankfurt, Germany.

Japan: Dennis Tachiki, Country Expert. Professor, Faculty of Business Administration, Tamagawa University. Satoshi Hamaya, Research Fellow, Fujitsu Research Institute. Kou Yukawa, Senior Research Associate, Fujitsu Research Institute.

Mexico: Juan J. Palacios, Country Expert. Professor and Director, Strategic International Studies Unit, Centre for Strategic Development Studies, University of Guadalajara.

Singapore: Poh-Kam Wong, Country Expert. Professor, Director, Centre for Management of Innovation and Technopreneurship, National University of Singapore.

Taiwan: Tain-Jy Chen, Economic Expert. Professor, Department of Economics, National Taiwan University and Chung-Hua Institute for Economics.

United States: John Leslie King, Country Expert. Dean and Professor, School of Information, University of Michigan. Vlad Fomin, Researcher. Kalle Lyytinen, Professor, Case Western Reserve University. Sean Xu, Researcher, University of California, Irvine.

We also wish to acknowledge our outside research partners. At IDC, these were John Gantz, Research Director, and Carol Glasheen, Alan J. Farias, and Amy White of IDC's Global Research Organization. At Market Probe, it was David Pantano who managed the survey effort. At Empirica, GmbH, it was Werner Korte, Karsten Garies, and Hannes Selhofer, who cooperated in several ways: consulted with us on the design of questionnaires, provided us with access to secondary data collected by the European Commission projects, commented on drafts of papers, co-authored papers, and supported our efforts generally.

The UCI team

Kenneth Kraemer and Jason Dedrick conceived the project, secured funding, organized the international team, managed the project throughout, and worked with the country experts and the UCI team in conducting the country analyses, the cross-country analyses, and the firm-level analyses. Kevin Zhu, Sean Xu, Jennifer Gibbs, and Eric Shih worked on the cross-country firm-level analyses. Debora Dunkle worked on survey design, questionnaire design, survey management, data management, data analysis, and substantive engagement throughout the project. Nigel Melville helped develop this book, including editing, re-writing, and organizing the chapters as well as co-authoring Chapter 1. Kenneth Kraemer, Jason Dedrick, Nigel Melville, and Kevin Zhu have put together this book through various collaborations.

We also wish to acknowledge the CRITO support team. Kathy Honda provided project coordination throughout the entire project and edited all project manuscripts, special issues of scholarly journals, and this entire book. We are most grateful for her commitment, dedication, and competence. Carolyn Davidson provided project website creation and maintenance. Terri Pouliot, Jane Chun, and Tanya Nguyen provided administrative support to the local and international research teams.

Kenneth L. Kraemer
Jason Dedrick
Nigel P. Melville
Kevin Zhu

References

DePrince Jr., A. E. & Ford, W. F. (1999). A Primer on Internet Economics. *Business Economics*, 34, 42–48.

Ohmae, K. (2001). *The Invisible Continent: Four Strategic Imperatives of the New Economy*. New York: Harper Perennial.

1 *Globalization and national diversity: e-commerce diffusion and impacts across nations*

KENNETH L. KRAEMER,
JASON DEDRICK, AND
NIGEL P. MELVILLE

Introduction

In recent years globalization has become the subject of fervent debate, intensified by the spread of low-cost information and communications technologies (ICTs), particularly the Internet. On the one hand, cross-border flows of capital, labor, and information may be leading to convergence in how economic activities are organized, reducing the role of the state and its ability to control and guide its own economic development. There are fears that globalization is causing serious economic dislocation as competition intensifies and trade imbalances grow. On the other hand, culture, history, regulation, and other local factors may limit economic convergence, preserving national differences and creating unique capabilities and comparative advantages.

The spread of low-cost ICTs, particularly the Internet, accelerates the convergence process by facilitating cross-border information flows and coordination of economic activities. Excitement about the Internet's potential for improving quality of life and bolstering overall economic health is, however, tempered by concern over its potential for worsening the perceived threats of globalization.

The United States has played a key role in developing Internet technologies and applying them to create new models of e-commerce – uses of the Internet for business activities such as buying, selling, and providing support for products and services in the firm's value chain. US firms have been supported in these efforts by favorable government policies, a largely deregulated telecommunications market, a dynamic venture capital market, and positive attitudes toward information technology. US companies have used the Internet to create new businesses, transform old ones, and coordinate global production networks. However, despite the positive effect on productivity and corporate profits, shifting production and job dislocation have engendered concern in the USA over the impacts of the current phase of globalization that is intensified by the Internet and e-commerce (Engardio et al., 2003; Roach, 2005).

Outside the USA there is substantial variation in the extent to which different economies support and promote e-commerce. Some businesses are using the Internet to reach new markets and coordinate with global production networks; others hardly use e-commerce at all. Likewise, sophisticated consumers have tapped the Internet to buy products that might be unavailable or expensive locally, while others do not buy online. Given wide variation in economic development, culture, history, technological innovation, and other local factors, untangling the worldwide e-commerce dynamic is no simple task. Combined with the significant potential of the Internet and e-commerce to support economic growth, there is a need to better understand the global forces driving Internet diffusion, how those forces are channeled by national environments and policies, and the economic impacts of the Internet and e-commerce.

The present volume analyzes e-commerce in eight economies: Brazil, China, France, Germany, Japan, Mexico, Taiwan, and the USA. It is a product of the Globalization and E-Commerce (GEC) project of the Center for Research on Information Technology and Organizations (CRITO) at the Paul Merage School of Business, University of California, Irvine. Case research was conducted by twenty distinguished scholars who are expert in the macroeconomic, technological, and cultural dimensions of each economy. Primary data were collected via a common survey of 2,100 firms across 10 economies. The goal was to develop understanding of how e-commerce is unfolding within firms broadly, and within each country.[1] Synthesizing primary survey data and secondary data sources, each author has examined the role of local and global factors in shaping e-commerce diffusion. Taken together, the studies advance understanding of the globalization and convergence debate, providing new empirical evidence with which to examine fundamental questions.

This introductory chapter serves two purposes. First, we provide the necessary conceptual and empirical background to enable a reading of any chapter in any order. To this end, we describe the theory

[1] Singapore and Denmark were also included in the GEC project – see country studies for details (Andersen et al., 2003; Wong and Ho, 2004).

and conceptual framework and briefly review the research methodology (details can be found in Appendix I). Second, we provide a cross-country analysis of the results of the GEC Survey regarding the driving forces, diffusion, and impacts of e-commerce across the economies and firms in the study. We also synthesize findings across individual cases.

Theory and conceptual framework

Diffusion of innovations

We adopted the theory and framework of Berger & Dore (1996), and of much innovation diffusion research, which asks what environmental and policy variations influence innovation outcomes in different national contexts (Nelson, 1993; Rogers, 1995; King et al., 1994; Boyer, 1996; Boyer & Drache, 1996; Freeman & Soete, 1997; Talukdar et al., 2002). One view is that the global flows of goods, capital, people, and technology are leading to convergence across countries in the organization of economic activities (Bell, 1973; Ohmae, 1990; Womach et al., 1991). Another view is that the impact of these forces on individual countries will vary according to the economic, political, and social context of the country, and as a result there will remain significant national differences in economic organization (Berger & Dore, 1996; Boyer, 1996; Boyer & Drache, 1996; Wade, 1996; Dedrick & Kraemer, 1998).

It is commonly assumed that Internet-based e-commerce is a globalizing force moving all countries and industries toward greater convergence (Cairncross, 1997; Adam et al., 1997; Kenney & Curry, 2000). This is supported by the fact that much e-commerce is driven by global production networks led by multinational corporations and facilitated by open trade regimes, global competition, and global telecommunications networks. However, both theory and prior research (Porter, 1986; Bartlett & Ghoshal, 1989; Globerman et al., 2001) suggest that there might be differences along the value chain. Upstream activities such as design, engineering, and manufacturing are considered more likely to converge toward common practices, as they involve more standardized processes and can be optimized globally to achieve economies of scale. Downstream activities are considered inherently more likely to diverge across countries, as they involve tailoring products and services to local consumer preferences, business practices, languages, and cultures.

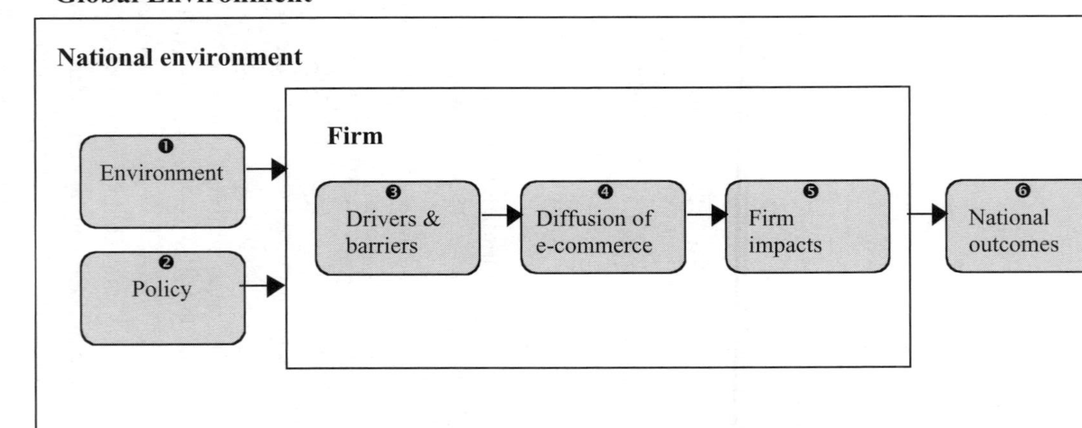

Figure 1.1 Conceptual framework
Source: CRITO GEC Survey, 2002

We would thus expect to find more convergence in e-commerce that involves upstream activities in the value chain, as well as in business-to-business (B2B) e-commerce interactions, both of which are defined by common business processes and standards. By contrast, we would expect greater divergence in downstream sales and marketing activities, and in business-to-consumer (B2C) transactions, as these activities must be tailored to local conditions. We examine this proposition via the following conceptual framework.

Conceptual framework

The innovation we are studying is Internet-based e-commerce, or simply e-commerce. We define e-commerce as the use of the Internet to conduct or support business activities along firm and industry value chains.[2] Depending on the industry, these activities may include research and development (R&D), design and development, procurement, operations/manufacturing, marketing and sales, logistics, and support activities such as infrastructure, human resources, finance, and value chain coordination. We posit that the diffusion and impacts of e-commerce use are driven by environmental and policy factors of the local economy, which are in turn shaped by the global environment (Figure 1.1, Table 1.1). The three primary dimensions of the framework – global environment, national environment, and the firm – as well as their respective sub-dimensions were derived from the previous literature on innovation diffusion and e-commerce (Rogers, 1995; Swanson, 1994; Tornatzky & Fleischer, 1990; Cooper & Zmud, 1990; Fichman, 2000; Ramamurthy et al., 1999; Dasgupta et al., 1999; Gibbs et al., 2003; Zhu & Kraemer, 2005).

At the global environment level, processes such as globalization of production and markets, trade liberalization, multinational corporation (MNC) strategies, technical innovation, and global competition are driving all countries and industry sectors toward the adoption of Internet and e-commerce innovations. In addition, there is a global flow of information about "best practices" or effective e-commerce

[2] This broad definition is similar to the way some people define e-business. For example, Mesenbourg (2001) defines e-business as "any process that a business organization conducts over computer-mediated networks" and e-commerce more narrowly as "the value of goods and services sold over computer-mediated networks." There is little uniformity of definition in the academic or practitioner literature.

Table 1.1 *Conceptual framework*

Concepts	*Variables*
Global environment	Global production networks, global markets, technical innovation, trade liberalization, global competition, MNC strategies, e-commerce movement.
National environment	
1. Environment	Wealth, industry structure, information infrastructure, consumer preferences, social/cultural factors, business practices.
2. Policy	Telecommunications diffusion and cost, infrastructure investment, openness to trade and investment, regulatory and legal environment, e-commerce promotion.
Firm	
3. Drivers and barriers	Drivers: external, internal operational, and strategic drivers. Barriers: economic, institutional, cultural, legal and privacy barriers.
4. E-commerce diffusion	Level of Internet use; use for online sales, procurement, and services; use with distribution channels.
5. Firm impacts	Organizational performance: sales, efficiency, cost, competitiveness. Competitive environment: number of distribution channels, suppliers, and competitors, competitive intensity.
6. National outcomes	Diversity versus convergence in e-commerce diffusion and impacts.

Source: CRITO GEC Survey, 2002
Note: See Appendix I for details on data collection and the survey instrument

models produced by the IT industry, consultancies, academics, and the business press. We refer to this as the global e-commerce movement.

Factors in the national environment may constrain or enhance innovation outcomes contributing to national diversity in e-commerce diffusion and impacts (Gibbs et al., 2003). The environment itself includes wealth, industry structure, information infrastructure, financial systems, human resources, social and cultural factors, and consumer preferences. Wealth, in particular, is an important differentiator of innovation outcomes between developed and developing countries (Gibbs et al., 2003). National policy comprises liberalization of telecommunications and IT markets, development of information infrastructure, investment in human capital, and regulations such as consumer protection and intellectual property rights protection. National outcomes refer to the aggregate level of diffusion and impacts within and across different economies. E-commerce is expected to exhibit divergence in downstream activities and convergence in upstream activities within an economy. Diffusion patterns also are expected to exhibit greater diversity than convergence across economies; for example, between developed and developing countries.

Firm-level factors include drivers and barriers, e-commerce diffusion, and impacts. Drivers of e-commerce diffusion include external factors such as pressure from competitors, customers, and suppliers; operational factors such as cost reduction and better coordination; and strategic factors such as entering new markets. Barriers to e-commerce diffusion include cultural factors such as the desire for face-to-face interaction and concerns about privacy and legal protection, and economic factors such as Internet access costs and the cost of setting up an e-commerce site. E-commerce diffusion refers to the extent of adoption and use by firms and consumers, the volume of transactions and services carried out online, and patterns of e-commerce use. The latter refers to the sectors/activities where e-commerce is used in an economy, what companies are involved, and how services are delivered. Impacts refer to the effects of e-commerce on firm performance and on the competitive environment.

Research methodology

The research was carried out using a ten-country cross-sectional survey and historical case studies. Secondary data were collected to supplement primary data and case studies, as well as to enable cross-country analyses to validate findings using a larger set of economies. In addition, three workshops were held to review and discuss findings from each country, and to plan ensuing phases of the project.

Survey

The survey was designed on the basis of an extensive literature review, interviews with IT managers, and discussions with country managers

Table 1.2 *GEC Survey sample*

	Manufacturing	*Wholesale/Retail*	*Banking/Insurance*	*Total*
Small (25–249 employees)	364	357	365	1,086
Large (250+ employees)	379	344	330	1,053
Total	743	701	695	2,139

Source: CRITO GEC Survey, 2002

from the International Data Corporation. What follows is a brief description of the survey – Appendix I provides a complete discussion.

To ensure a broad representation of both developed and developing economies, the survey was conducted in the United States and nine other countries (Brazil, China, Denmark, France, Germany, Japan, Mexico, Singapore, and Taiwan) during 2002 (Table 1.2).[3] The sample was stratified by firm size and country, with sites selected randomly within each size cell. Establishments were equally distributed across three industry sectors that are considered leading users of the Internet and e-commerce – finance, manufacturing, and wholesale/retail distribution. The sample frame was obtained from a list representative of the entire local market, except in China where the sample focused on the more economically dynamic regions of Beijing, Shanghai, Guangzhou, and Chengdu. About 200 establishments were surveyed in each country except in the USA, where 300 were surveyed.

Respondents were screened by the question "Do you use the Internet to buy, sell, or support products or services?" The final sample thus represents firms actually using the Internet for business, rather than the full population of firms in each country. The final dataset contains 2,139 valid cases (Table 1.2). Most respondents were CIOs, CEOs, IS directors, or business managers, i.e., the people most involved in key decisions about e-commerce adoption and use.

Case studies

In addition to the survey, several papers were prepared for each economy by a country expert or team. These papers examined in detail the

[3] We use data from all ten countries for the analysis in this chapter, although only eight case studies are included in this volume.

environmental and policy factors influencing e-commerce adoption, the nature of e-commerce use, and the impacts of e-commerce. Complementing the firm-level data from the surveys, these analyses provided rich qualitative and quantitative information at the economy level.

Secondary data analysis

We also collected data from a variety of secondary sources, which were used in the country cases and in special analyses such as studies of the determinants of e-commerce diffusion in larger samples of firms (Zhu et al., 2004) and in a larger sample of forty countries (Shih et al., 2004, 2005). The secondary sources included IDC's e-commerce market model, the European Commission's ECATT, SIBIS, and eBusiness Watch surveys, and CRITO's global database (Appendix I). These analyses support findings from the GEC global sample and provide an insight into additional variables and issues not included in the global sample. The results of these analyses are incorporated in this chapter as appropriate. Detailed results of the cross-country studies are presented in Chapter 10.

Findings

Global environment

The global diffusion of e-commerce is a process driven by a variety of forces. These include the strategies of MNCs, the growth of trade and foreign investment, international trade liberalization regimes such as the World Trade Organization, the development of global production networks, the creation of a low-cost global information and communications infrastructure, and an "e-commerce movement" driven by the IT industry and opinion leaders. These forces are felt by all countries to varying degrees, but are more prominent in shaping diffusion in economies that have open trade and investment regimes, have more firms that are part of global production networks, and have more firms engaged in global competition.

Multinational corporations

MNCs are powerful global institutions that drive the diffusion of new technologies and business practices in two ways. First, they bring resources, including capital, knowledge, and their own IT-based business practices, wherever they operate and diffuse these resources to their employees and to local firms with which they do business (Coe et al., 1997). Second, MNCs bring competition to local markets, placing pressure on local firms to adopt these technologies and business practices in order to survive (Grossman & Helpman, 1993).

MNCs also drive e-commerce diffusion through their coordination of global production networks/commodity chains. Production in manufacturing industries such as autos, electronics, textiles, and toys has extended across national borders and become increasingly globalized or regionalized (Ernst, 2003; Dedrick & Kraemer, 1998). During the last two decades, these global networks have expanded into developing regions of Asia-Pacific, Latin America, and Eastern Europe. Retail and wholesale industries have also become globalized with department, discount, and specialty retail stores regionalizing their operations and creating vast commodity chains to supply them with goods from around the world (Gereffi, 1999). Financial institutions, which were among the first to go global, have begun to globalize their back-office operations in recent years, with call centers, IT services, software production, and business process outsourcing (BPO) moving to diverse locales such as India, Ireland, Israel, Russia, the Caribbean, and the Philippines (Dossani & Kenney, 2004). Other services industries are following these trends as they seek to exploit markets for goods and labor.

Participation in these global markets is an important driver of e-commerce as the industry networks that serve them rely heavily on telecommunications and IT-enabled processes for coordination and collaboration. For example, within the computer and electronics industries, some countries have domestic firms that participate in these global networks as suppliers or subcontractors (e.g., Taiwan, Korea, Malaysia, the Philippines) or serve as production platforms for subsidiaries of MNCs (e.g., Singapore, Ireland, Scotland, China), while others such as the USA and Japan are coordinators of such networks. Although the roles differ, the integration of countries into global production networks often involves the adoption of e-commerce as a condition for participation (Ernst, 2003; Dedrick & Kraemer, 2004).

Indeed, our analysis of the GEC Survey data indicates that more highly global firms engage more extensively in e-commerce (Gibbs et al., 2003). The level of globalization is defined in terms of organization structures (establishments in multiple countries, headquarters abroad), percentages of sales and procurement abroad, and pressure

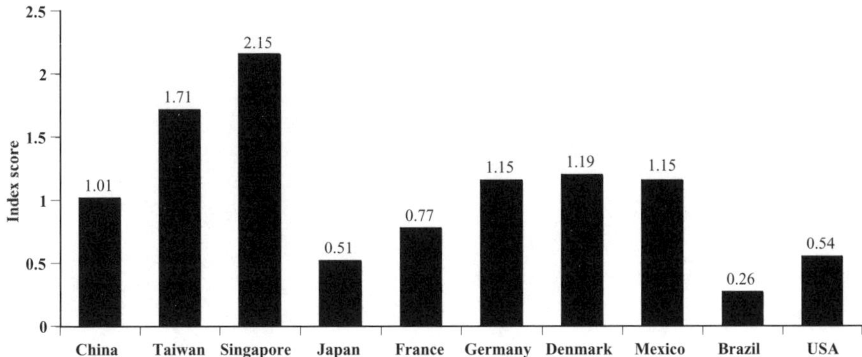

Figure 1.2 Degree of globalization of firms in each economy
Source: CRITO GEC Survey, 2002

from international competition. Based on this, we would expect countries whose firms are highly globalized to be more active in adopting e-commerce.

Among the economies in our survey, those rated highest on an index of globalization are Taiwan and Singapore, whose small economies are highly integrated into global networks (Figure 1.2). These two also have the highest ratio of online sales to GDP (Figure 1.3), while less global economies such as Brazil, Japan, and the USA are below the trend line.

E-commerce movement

A phenomenon that we call the e-commerce movement is another significant driver of e-commerce. This movement obtained its initial impetus as a new driver of economic growth from the information superhighway strategy promoted by the Clinton–Gore administration (Kraemer & King, 1996), and was adopted by a number of other countries in the form of national information infrastructure plans (Kahin & Wilson, 1997). The rapid growth of the Internet made parts of these plans obsolete, but their emphasis on deregulation and private-sector leadership remained. Within the private sector, the IT industry saw new market opportunities and began preaching to its customers about the potential benefits of electronic markets. The movement has been fostered by venture capitalists, business media, industry associations, academics, and governments. The movement was hyped beyond reality

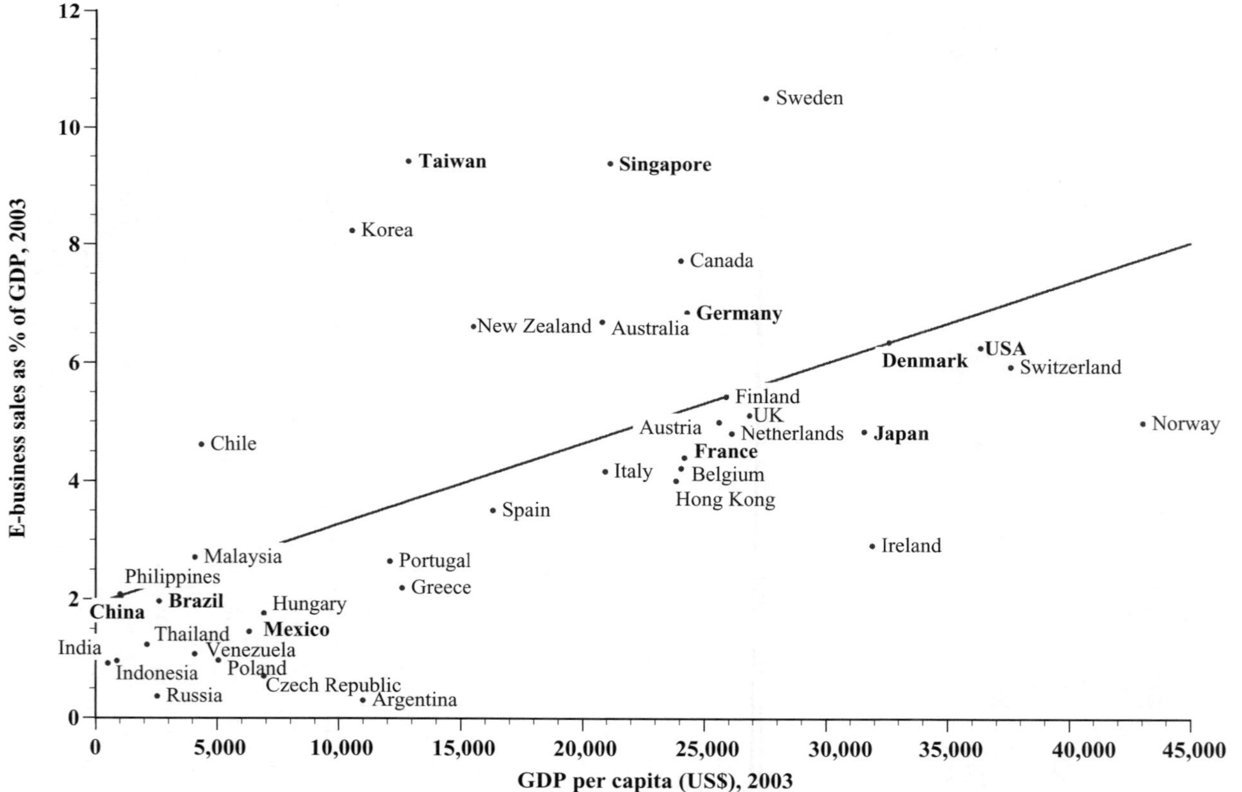

Figure 1.3 E-commerce diffusion and wealth
Source: CRITO GEC Survey, 2002 secondary database

during the dot.com boom, then was widely discredited in the ensuing bust. However, in the aftermath of the boom and bust, the evidence suggests that there are sustained IT-driven productivity gains for many firms and countries (Zhu et al., 2004; Phan, 2003). Also, the excess physical capacity (e.g., fiber optic networks) installed during the boom years has left in place a high-quality, low-cost infrastructure even after many of its builders have disappeared.

International policies

Institutions such as the World Trade Organization (WTO), the International Telecommunications Union (ITU), and the World Intellectual Property Organization (WIPO) have been instrumental in creating more open rules and effective regulations for trade, investment, telecommunications, and intellectual property. The WTO has extended global trade rules to include services, such as financial services and telecommunications, helping to provide a better technical and financial infrastructure to support e-commerce. Liberalization of other IT-related services might provide more impetus to the globalization of e-commerce, but WTO negotiations on services have been unsuccessful in recent years.

The ITU has promoted telecommunications liberalization and the expansion of telecommunications, and wireless and Internet services to developing countries. Lower costs and greater diffusion of telecommunications and the Internet have facilitated the global expansion of e-commerce and also supported IT-enabled business strategies such as offshore outsourcing.

Under the WTO, agreements on the trade-related aspects of intellectual property rights (TRIPS) set common international rules for intellectual property protection. These are important in building the necessary confidence for intellectual property holders to provide more content online, and to encourage greater production of intellectual property worldwide. However, in the area of intellectual property rights (IPR), lack of enforcement remains a big problem in many countries (Gibbs et al., 2003).

In sum, the global forces described here tend to drive convergence across countries. MNCs try to standardize internal practices worldwide and push their suppliers and partners to align processes and technologies with those of the MNC. Countries that sign WTO and other agreements are forced to accept global norms that reduce differences in

Table 1.3 *Macroeconomic indicators, 2002*

	USA	*Germany*	*France*	*Japan*	*China*	*Taiwan*	*Brazil*	*Mexico*
GDP in US$bn	10,417	1,976	1,410	3,979	1,237	281	452	637
GDP per capita US$	36,006	24,051	24,061	31,407	989	12,509	2,641	6,432
GDP growth (annual percent)	2.43	0.18	1.21	0.32	8.00	3.60	1.50	0.73
GFDI (percent of GDP)	2.43	5.36	8.02	1.43	4.69	n.a.	4.44	2.45
Trade (percent of GDP)	23.63	67.05	52.07	21.00	54.77	99.98	29.41	56.38
Income distribution: richest 20%: poorest 20%	9.0	4.7	5.6	3.4	8.0	n.a.	29.7	16.5

Source: World Bank, 2004

national policies. Global production and distribution networks rely on ICTs to improve coordination, shorten time-to-market, cut inventory, and reduce errors. In many industries there is convergence to common or compatible software tools, communication protocols, and business practices.

National environment

Environment

Just as global competition is a key factor driving all countries toward adoption of e-commerce, market forces are the key determinant of e-commerce diffusion within countries. The United States is the largest economy with the highest GDP per capita and an annual growth rate of 2.43%. It is also largely a domestic economy as trade accounts for less than 25% of GDP (Table 1.3). Thus, it has an economic environment and level of wealth that is favorable to the use of e-commerce. Japan, Germany, and France also have relatively large economies and high GDP per capita, but low economic growth. Japan's economy is insular whereas trade accounts for more than 50% of GDP in France and Germany. Although large and wealthy, the low growth of Japan and Germany in particular might be less favorable to experimentation with new technologies. France also would be less favorable to experimentation, but, as we will see later, for other reasons (Chapter 3 and Brousseau & Kraemer, 2003). China, which has the largest economy of the developing countries but the lowest GDP per capita because of its equally large population, is the fastest growing economy at 8% per year. More than half of its GDP is based on trade which suggests that it might be open to external influences such as the e-commerce movement, and might learn from foreign MNCs. Taiwan has the smallest economy but healthy growth and is almost totally dependent on foreign trade, which suggests that it would be the most open to MNC influences to adopt e-commerce. Brazil and Mexico's large income inequality is likely to be a key factor retarding the use of e-commerce.

The information infrastructure in countries is related to wealth, and as shown in Table 1.4, there is considerable variation in the infrastructure of countries in the study. In absolute terms, the USA has the largest installed base of PCs, phones, Internet users, and broadband users. However, other developed countries (Denmark, France, Germany, Japan, Singapore) also have relatively large installed bases.

Table 1.4 ***Technology indicators, 2002***

	USA	*Germany*	*France*	*Japan*	*China*	*Taiwan*	*Brazil*	*Mexico*
Main phone lines per 1,000 pop.	645.8	650.4	568.9	557.9	166.9	583.3	223.2	146.7
Cell phone subscribers per 1,000 pop.	488.2	716.7	647.0	636.1	160.9	1064.5	200.6	254.5
Cable subscribers per 1,000 pop.	255.0	250.0	57.5	183.0	75.0	206.7	n.a.	24.3
Internet hosts per 1,000 pop.	399.9	31.4	23.3	72.6	0.1	96.6	12.9	n.a.
Internet users per 1,000 pop.	551.4	411.6	313.8	448.5	46.0	382.5	82.2	98.5
IT as percent of GDP	3.9	3.1	3.5	2.7	1.7	1.8	2.5	1.1
PCs per 1,000 pop.	658.9	431.0	347.1	381.9	27.6	395.7	74.8	82.0
Software piracy rate (percent)	0.23	0.32	0.43	0.35	0.92	0.43	0.55	0.55

Source: World Bank, 2004

It is mainly the developing countries of Brazil, China, and Mexico that are low in the installed base for e-commerce and likely to remain so for some time into the future given their large size, the cost of extending the infrastructure, and the still high cost (except for China) of Internet use. Yet, even in these countries, the installed base is greater in large urban, industrial areas than in the rest of the country, which means that the necessary information infrastructure is likely to be available for these markets. The rapid growth of cell phones in all countries also creates opportunities for e-commerce that delivers new kinds of information and services to broader populations.

As the foregoing suggests, it is generally the case that new technologies are adopted first and most intensively by richer countries, which have the financial resources to invest in these technologies, the human resources and infrastructure to support their use, and higher wage rates that make it worthwhile to introduce labor-saving technologies (Caselli & Coleman, 2001; Shih et al., 2004).

Figure 1.3 illustrates this point, showing the relationship between online sales as a percent of GDP (diffusion) and GDP per capita (wealth) for forty countries, including the GEC Survey economies. There is a positive and significant relationship between wealth and diffusion, indicating a large gap in e-commerce activity between developed and developing countries. Yet there is considerable variance even among developed countries, which suggests that other factors besides wealth must explain country differences. Research from the GEC project has identified a number of national factors that go beyond wealth in explaining differences among countries in the level of e-commerce transactions. These include investment resources, industry structure, competitive pressure, information infrastructure, payment mechanisms, and rule of law (Shih et al., 2005; Zhu & Kraemer, 2002; Zhu et al., 2004, 2005).

Policy

Liberalization of telecommunications, financial services, and transportation services in many countries has been an important driver of Internet diffusion and e-commerce. In fact, the Organization for Economic Cooperation and Development (OECD) found a strong early link between the degree of competition in telecommunications and Internet diffusion across its member countries (OECD, 1996). In a related study, we found that lower telecommunications costs and greater use of credit cards (associated with greater competition in financial services) are associated with higher levels of e-commerce (Shih et al., 2004, 2005; Zhu et al., 2004). Likewise, deregulation of the trucking and airlines industries in the USA and elsewhere was a precursor to the rapid growth of cargo and courier services that are critical to supporting e-commerce (Fomin et al., 2003).

In addition, many governments have developed national plans for encouraging Internet and e-commerce use. They have implemented e-government policies that require use of the Internet for government procurements, offered incentives or subsidies to help smaller firms go online, and promoted extensive use of the Internet for government information and services. However, our research shows that government promotion has had limited effects on the diffusion of e-commerce in most countries. In fact, fewer than 10% of interviewees in the GEC Survey said that government promotion was an important driver of e-commerce in their firms. Nevertheless, the research shows that other types of government regulation, such as privacy protection, can be critical to supporting e-commerce. Concern for privacy and data security is the most significant policy barrier reported by firms in the survey (Table 1.6). This is especially important in developing countries, as discussed in Chapter 10.

We also find evidence in country-level data that respect for the rule of law is an important indicator of e-commerce use (Shih et al., 2005). For instance, higher credit card penetration is an important driver of e-commerce in countries where the rule of law is strong, but has no impact where it is weak. The implication is that even if people have credit cards, they will hesitate to use them to purchase online unless they feel that they have adequate guarantees of privacy and protection against fraud.

Firm-level findings

Drivers of e-commerce use

The GEC Survey asked executives what factors were important determinants in their decision to go online. We found that the strongest drivers of e-commerce use are the desire to expand markets for existing products and services, to improve coordination with customers and suppliers, and to enter new markets (Table 1.5). These motivations are consistent with the messages of the e-commerce movement

Table 1.5 ***Firm drivers to e-commerce use***

Percent indicating driver is a significant factor	*Global*	*Rated #1 by*
To expand market for existing product or services	47.9	USA, Germany
To improve coordination with customers and suppliers	43.7	France, Singapore, Brazil, Mexico
To enter new businesses or markets	42.0	Taiwan
Customers demanded it	36.9	Japan, China
To reduce costs	35.7	Denmark
Major competitors were online	31.3	
Suppliers required it	22.3	
Required for government procurement	15.2	
Government provided incentives	8.3	

Source: CRITO GEC Survey, 2002

Table 1.6 ***Firm barriers to e-commerce use***

Percent indicating barrier is a significant factor	*Global*	*Rated #1 by*
Concern about privacy of data or security issues	44.2	All but three
Inadequate legal protection for Internet purchases	34.1	
Need for face-to-face customer interaction to sell our products	33.8	Denmark, France
Costs of implementing an e-commerce site	33.6	
Customers do not use this technology	31.4	
Finding staff with e-commerce expertise	26.5	Germany
Our level of ability to use the Internet as part of our business strategy	24.8	
Business laws do not support e-commerce	24.2	
Making organizational changes	23.9	
Prevalence of credit card use in the country	20.3	
Taxation of Internet sales	16.5	
Cost of Internet access	15.1	

Source: CRITO GEC Survey, 2002

which claims that the Internet allows firms to tap into new markets without having to make costly investments in physical facilities, and to create a seamless supply chain that could respond quickly to changes in supply and demand conditions.

The survey clearly shows that firms are more likely to respond to customer pressure (36.9%) than to supplier pressure (22.3%), suggesting that e-commerce adoption is pulled rather than pushed through the value chain. In the case of manufacturers as well as distributors, "customers" are other businesses, whether other manufacturers, distributors, or retailers. In global value chains, small and medium-sized businesses frequently are suppliers to larger domestic manufacturers, which in turn are suppliers to large branded customers. In industries such as computers, electronics, and automobiles, large MNCs have forced suppliers to adopt e-commerce technologies as a requirement for doing business (Chapter 7; Chen, 2003). For retailers and many financial services companies, the customer is the final consumer, who may desire the convenience of online sales and services in addition to existing channels.

Among other external factors, competitive pressure was a relatively important driver of demand, cited by 31%. Government promotion and incentives had little impact, suggesting again that e-commerce is mainly driven by market forces. However, the impacts of government policy were greater for developing countries, where there may be fewer resources or market incentives to go online. Again, this was confirmed by the firm-level cross-country analysis (Chapter 10).

Different drivers are more important in some countries than others, as Table 1.5 shows. But at the broader level, there was a consistent focus on either market expansion or coordination in all economies, which reflects the nature of the Internet as a widely available open network that can be used either to reach new customers at a relatively low cost, or as a flexible underlying platform that can support a variety of value chain configurations.

Barriers to e-commerce use

The GEC Survey also asked respondents what they saw as barriers to e-commerce use. Here, a somewhat surprising response was that the biggest barriers were concerns over privacy and security of data as well as inadequate legal protection for Internet purchases (Table 1.6).

This may have been due in part to the newness of e-commerce and the fact that both businesses and consumers were still getting comfortable with the relatively anonymous online transactions involved. But it also clearly reflected the need for an effective legal and regulatory environment, reinforcing the country-level findings discussed above (Shih et al., 2005; Zhu & Kraemer, 2005). Among the three industries studied, concern about privacy and security was ranked number one by all industries, but was highest in the financial sector, where this barrier was cited by 62% of firms.

Interestingly, privacy and security concerns were rated the number one barrier in all countries except the three European countries, where stronger privacy protections have been enacted (Table 1.6). Such protections were once criticized in the USA as inhibiting e-commerce by creating unnecessary burdens on business, but now it appears that they may actually create a more conducive environment for online business.

The number three barrier was the need for face-to-face customer interaction. This reflects firms' perceptions of customer preferences and the fact that the Internet is not a replacement for personal interaction in many cases. Even in the USA, where mail order and other direct marketing businesses are well established, the need for face-to-face interaction was cited by 42% of respondents as a significant barrier.

Diffusion of e-commerce

A general finding from the research is that Internet and e-commerce use has spread widely in both developed and developing countries. There is a broad acceptance that the technology is valuable and that both firms and countries cannot afford to be left behind or left out. Even a country such as China, with elevated control over the flow of information, seeks only to place limits on how the Internet is used, not to prevent its use (Chapter 6). Singapore, which still bans satellite TV dishes, places only limited controls on Internet use. Everyone is aware of the economic importance of being connected.

Extent of e-commerce use

E-commerce is still in its early stages. However, it is growing rapidly – e-commerce sales are equivalent to nearly 10% of GDP in some countries.[4] Surprisingly, while the USA leads in total e-commerce sales, it is no longer the leader relative to GDP (Figure 1.4). Instead, the small trading economies of Singapore and Taiwan have become the

[4] These figures should be interpreted cautiously, as e-commerce revenues are based on sales and can involve double counting, while GDP is based on value added.

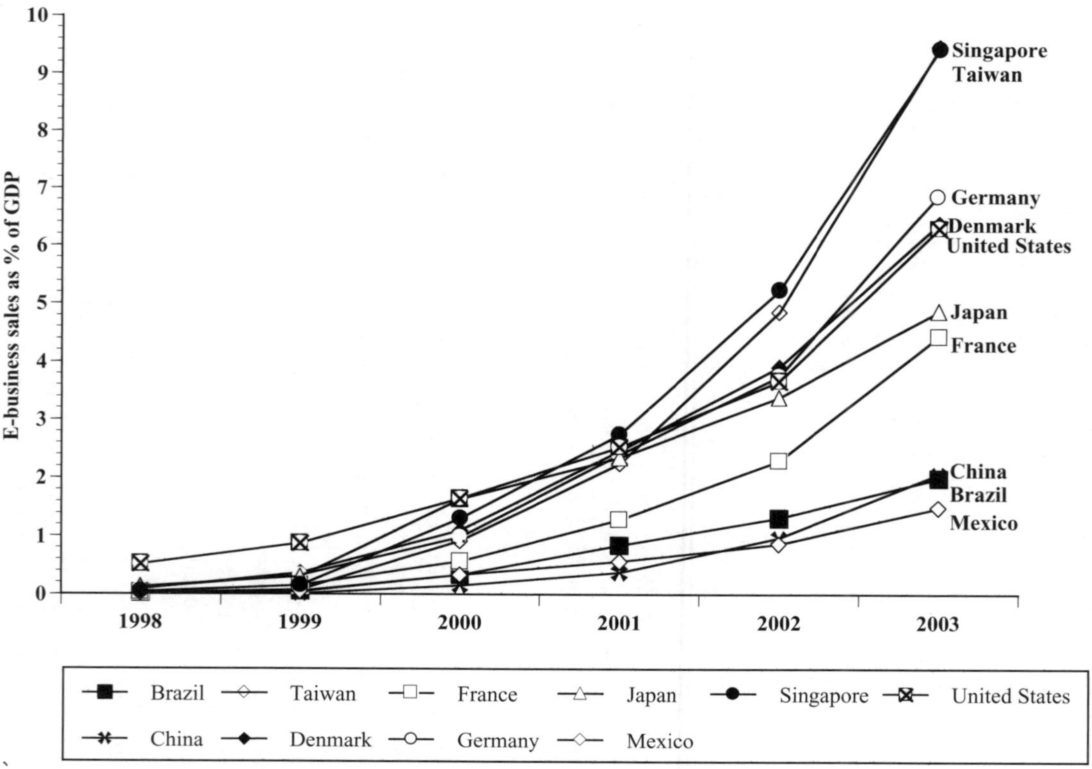

Figure 1.4 Internet-based e-commerce diffusion, 1998–2003
Source: IDC, 2004

most active in online sales, due in large part to their roles in the global production networks of the computer, electronics, textile and apparel, and toy industries. In addition, these are two places where aggressive government promotion may be having an impact (Wong & Ho, 2004; Chen, 2003).

The next group of countries includes Germany, Denmark, and the USA (Figure 1.4). Germany is the central hub for business in the European Union, while Denmark is a small open-trading economy (Koenig et al., 2003; Andersen et al., 2003), and both have a relatively high proportion of internationally oriented businesses. Lagging behind among the developed countries are Japan and France. Both have more domestically oriented firms, and both were relatively late to adopt Internet-based e-commerce. In both France and Japan, businesses had already made large commitments to electronic data interchange[5] systems and were slower to adopt B2B technologies (Chapters 3, 5; Brousseau, 2003; Tachiki et al., 2004). This is consistent with the notion of path dependencies and our firm-level research which shows that firms that had already adopted EDI were less likely to adopt e-commerce than those with no EDI (Zhu et al., 2006). The final group is the developing countries of Brazil, Mexico, and China. In these cases, the leading firms are actually quite aggressive in adopting the Internet according to our survey, but there remain large segments of the global economy in which IT is barely used.

Diffusion of e-commerce uses among firms

Moving to the firm level, the character of diffusion is indicated by the percentage of firms using e-commerce for different purposes. The GEC Survey shows that firms make multiple uses of the Internet for

[5] Electronic data interchange is the interorganizational, computer-to-computer exchange of business documentation in a standard, machine-processable format. In general, EDI standards include the data standard (format of messages) and the communication protocol. EDI typically transmits data over private networks or value-added networks (VAN) (Emmelhainz, 1993). EDI systems represent the first generation of e-commerce and have been adopted in a variety of industries since the 1970s (Iacovou et al., 1995; Riggins et al., 1994). In the last decade, the Internet, facilitated by the development of open standards such as the Transmission Control Protocol/Internet Protocol (TCP/IP) and eXtensible Markup Language (XML), has become the preferred platform for e-commerce because of its greater flexibility, ease of use, and lower cost. For a more detailed description and analysis of EDI and the Internet as platforms for e-commerce, see Zhu et al., 2006.

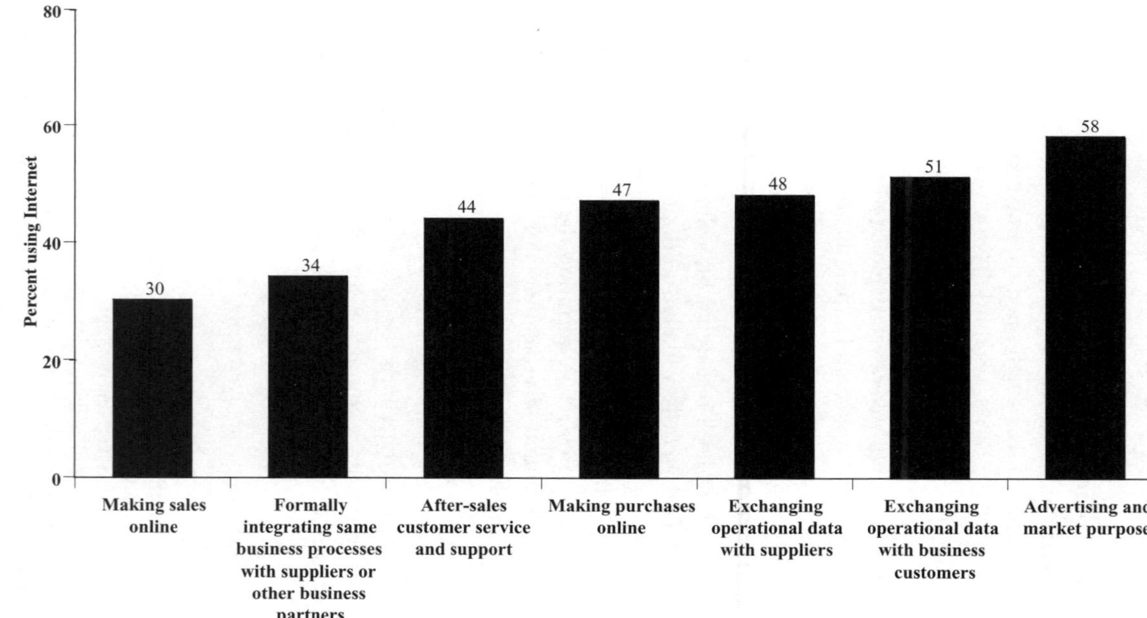

Figure 1.5 Firm uses of e-commerce
Source: CRITO GEC Survey, 2002
Note: Pooled results across all GEC economies

business, but, surprisingly, online sales is the lowest use (30%). Nearly twice as many firms use the Internet for advertising and marketing (58%) as for online sales (Figure 1.5). Similarly, more firms use the Internet to buy (47%) than sell. More firms also use the Internet for coordination (exchanging operational data (48–51%) and integrating business processes (34%) with suppliers and business customers) than for sales. Even customer service and support (44%) attracts higher use than online sales.

The low percent of firms using the Internet for sales is surprising given that expanding markets and entering new markets are major drivers of e-commerce use (Table 1.5). The findings indicate that e-commerce is much more than just sales, whether to consumers or to other businesses. E-commerce includes activities internal to the firm and to its entire value chain, from suppliers to business partners, to customers. This is in marked contrast to perceptions created by media coverage of well-known e-commerce firms like Amazon.com and eBay – namely, that e-commerce is mainly about consumer sales. The relatively large proportion of firms engaged in these other activities indicates that online selling requires these other activities as complements, if not prerequisites. That is, selling online requires advertising and marketing to attract customers, procurement of products to sell, information exchange with suppliers, and after-sales service for customers. In addition, firms may use the Internet to drive sales to traditional outlets rather than compete with those outlets by selling online.

The GEC Survey also indicates that the pattern of e-commerce use is different for more global firms than for more local firms (Figure 1.6). The use for customer-oriented activities, such as advertising and marketing, online purchases, and online sales is similar for both groups. However, global firms use the Internet for supply chain coordination and information sharing with suppliers and business customers more than local firms. They also are more likely to use the Internet to formally integrate some of their business processes (e.g., procurement, sales, operations) with their partners. In addition, global firms are more likely to use the Internet for after-sales customer service and support.

The emphasis on customer service and support by global firms suggests that they add value to their products through use of the Internet for service enhancements such as order tracking, online customer support, and various tools (Chapters 2, 7; Chen, 2003). Integration

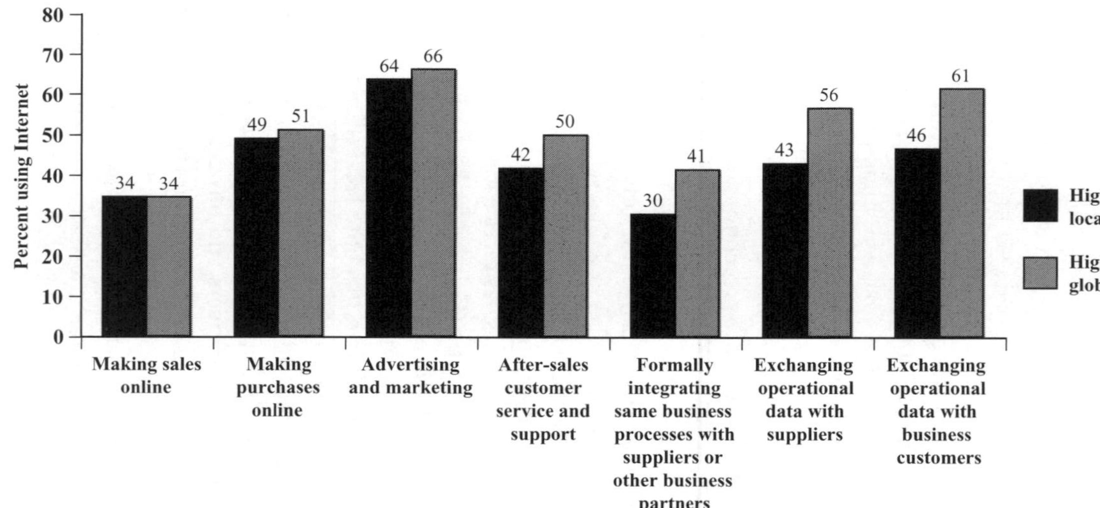

Figure 1.6 Use of e-commerce by high global and high local firms

Source: CRITO GEC Survey, 2002

Note: High global is top 25% of firms in degree of firm internationalization; low global is bottom 25%

of business partners also differs according to the degree that firms are global. These differences reflect the fact that global firms operate internationally in production chains where the Internet can reduce geographic and time boundaries and enable better coordination, integration, and efficiency in response to global competition. In contrast, local firms operate within a country or region and focus mainly on local markets where they have a physical presence and engage in e-commerce as another distribution channel to respond to initiatives by local competitors.

The use of e-commerce for different activities varies by economy, but the pattern is not a simple divide between developed and less developed countries (Figure 1.7). Rather, it is related to endogenous features of the economy and its global linkages. A substantial proportion of firms in the developed countries of Germany, Denmark, and the USA are engaged in online sales and purchases. They also have formally integrated their processes with suppliers and business partners, indicating substantial use of the Internet for supply chain coordination. The high proportion of firms engaged in all three uses in Germany reflects the intensive diffusion of e-commerce among German firms, where both large and small firms have been characterized as fast followers in technology adoption (Chapter 4; Koenig et al., 2003). In contrast, the high proportion of firms engaged mainly in online purchasing in Brazil, Denmark, Mexico, and the USA indicates a more focused use on procuring inputs for production (Palacios, 2003; Palacios & Kraemer, 2003).

The developed economies of Japan and France are much less engaged in any of these e-commerce activities, probably because both Japan and France have been late to the Internet. Japan has been slow because "it is not always clear to Japanese managers that e-commerce represents a better business model than their existing style of management" (Tachiki et al., 2004). France has been late to the Internet due to the existence of EDI, Minitel, and other B2C and B2B pre-Internet technologies, which performed some functions similar to those provided on the Internet (Brousseau, 2003). Singapore shows greater uptake of business process integration, which reflects its position as a production platform for foreign multinationals.

Diffusion of B2B and B2C e-commerce

We distinguish between diffusion of B2B and B2C e-commerce, since the two types of transactions have distinct characteristics. B2B

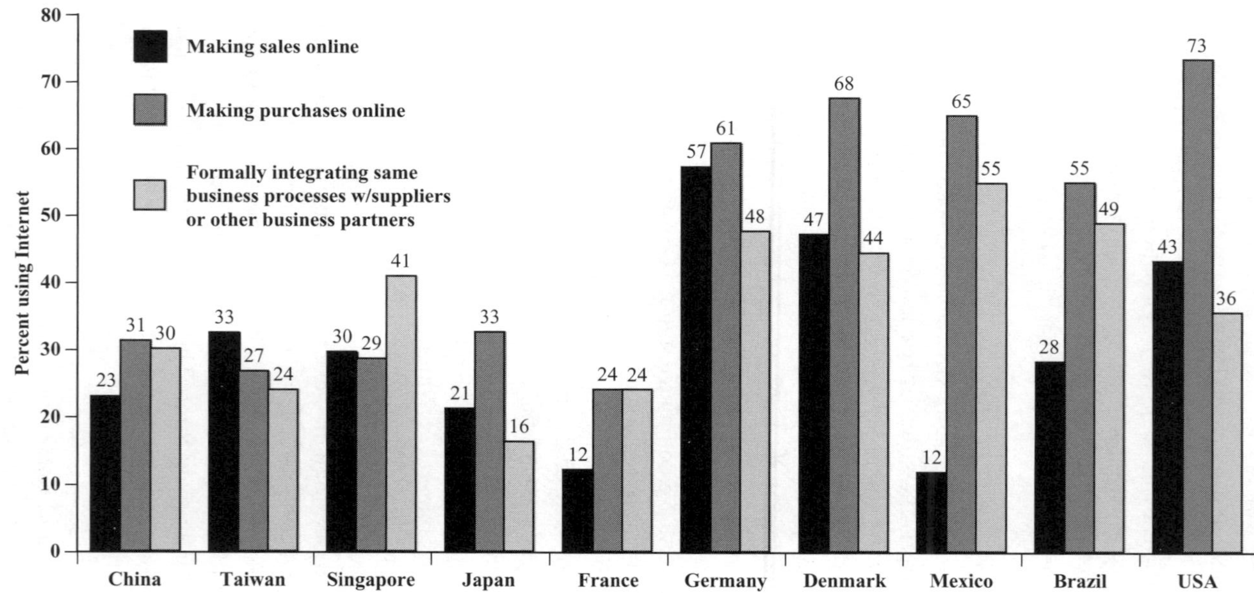

Figure 1.7 E-commerce uses across economies
Source: CRITO GEC Survey, 2002

Table 1.7 ***B2B and B2C sales and services***

Firms doing online sales	
Percent B2B only	12.9
Percent B2C only	7.1
Percent both B2B and B2C	15.0
Firm online sales as percent of total sales (among firms selling online)	
B2B	15.2
B2C	18.6
Firms doing online services	
Percent B2B only	23.1
Percent B2C only	12.9
Percent both B2B and B2C	33.3

Source: CRITO GEC Survey, 2002

transactions involve two firms, both of which are attempting to achieve some kind of performance goals such as increasing sales and profits, reducing costs, or improving productivity. In such a case, there is presumably a willingness to adopt common technologies and business practices to achieve such results, even within the context of different national business practices. B2C transactions, by contrast, involve selling to consumers, who may have much more varied utility functions and less willingness to change their purchasing behavior just to reduce transaction costs. For instance, consumers who want to try on a garment before purchasing it are unlikely to buy online unless the merchant makes it very easy to return unsatisfactory merchandise. Even then, the consumer may enjoy the shopping experience, or simply may find it more convenient to go to a store and come home with the merchandise in hand.

While the level of B2B and B2C e-commerce is increasing over time among economies, direct selling on the Internet is still in its infancy among individual firms. The GEC Survey indicates that about 35% of the firms engage in online sales over the Internet (Table 1.7). About twice as many firms engage in B2B online sales (12.9%) versus B2C online sales (7.1%), and a substantial proportion engage in both (15%). Among firms selling online, the percent of online sales of all sales is low: 15.2% (B2B) and 18.6% (B2C).

In contrast to online sales, online services are provided by twice as many firms (69.3%). These services range from product catalogs to product reviews, product specifications, product configuration, technical support, customer service, bill paying, account information, and research/planning tools. This variety of services reinforces the point made earlier in the discussion of e-commerce uses, namely that e-commerce is more than sales.

B2B and B2C in highly global and highly local firms

Given the differences in the nature of B2B and B2C transactions and participants described earlier, we would expect to find considerably more local variation in B2C e-commerce than in B2B. The findings from both case studies and the GEC Survey confirm these expectations.

The GEC Survey found that high global firms (the top 25% in terms of having establishments abroad, buying and selling abroad, and facing foreign competition) are more likely to engage in B2B including both B2B sales and B2B services (Figure 1.8). Meanwhile, high local firms (bottom 25% on the same indicators) are more likely to engage in B2C, especially in terms of providing services to consumers online. The two groups were equally likely to engage in B2C sales, which implies that any advantages or greater motivation local firms have in the consumer market do not make a difference in terms of actually selling online. Instead, the big difference is in B2C services, where local firms were significantly more likely to conduct business online.

One explanation for this surprising finding might be that highly global firms (over half of which had foreign headquarters) provide fewer services overall to consumers, and that they are more likely to outsource the services they provide in other countries rather than providing them directly. If this is the case, the difference is simply explained by the fact that local firms are more service-oriented, not that they have a higher proclivity for providing those services online.

However, it may be that for any given level of consumer services, local firms are more likely to provide them online. The reasons could have to do with better ties to local supply chain partners. Two examples are product availability information and order tracking, both of which are common services offered on B2C websites. Providing these services online requires integration with warehouses, distribution centers, and shipping companies to track inventory and shipment information. This

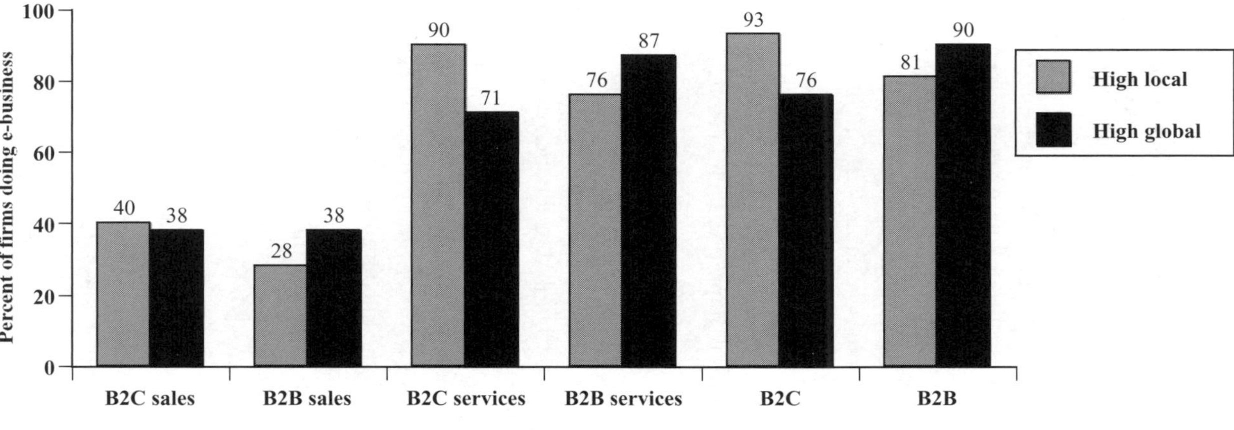

Figure 1.8 B2B and B2C e-commerce in high local and high global firms
Source: CRITO GEC Survey, 2002
Note: Final two categories indicate aggregate use of B2C and B2B

may be easier for local firms that have well-established relationships with local partners.

Global firms might also see less payoff or competitive advantage in providing online services to consumers. Knowledge of B2C is less transferable from country to country, and it is expensive for firms to gain local knowledge. Global firms may be deterred from providing B2C services by challenges due to national differences in language, culture, consumer behavior, and government regulations, which may be especially important in the often highly regulated financial sector.

These survey findings are reinforced by case studies showing heavy use of B2B technologies such as EDI, extranets, and supply chain management applications by globally oriented firms in industries such as automobiles and electronics (Chapters 2, 7; Chen, 2003; Tachiki et al., 2004). Yet local retailers and financial services firms are leaders in many countries in providing a wide range of services to consumers, taking advantage of their knowledge of the local market and existing distribution infrastructures (Chapter 5; Tachiki et al., 2004).

B2B and B2C differences among economies

Looking at Figure 1.9, it is apparent that relative to B2C, more firms are engaged in B2B sales and services in economies that are strongly tied to international trade and global production networks. Singapore, China, and Taiwan are production platforms for MNCs, with which their firms share information and collaborate intensively in carrying out their role in global supply chains (Wong, 2003; Chen, 2003; Tan & Wu, 2002). Similarly, Germany's *Mittelstand* firms are heavily engaged in international trade within the European continent (Koenig et al., 2003; Andersen et al., 2003). In contrast, even though the USA, Mexico, and Brazil engage in international trade, they are largely "domestic economies" and so there is no difference in the proportion of firms engaged in B2B or B2C transactions.

Sectoral differences in B2B and B2C e-commerce

As indicated in the conceptual framework, we expected that global networks drive B2B e-commerce as they define common business processes and standards for integration, whereas local competition drives B2C e-commerce as local characteristics lead to diverse approaches. We find support for this proposition by looking at differences across industry sectors and comparing manufacturing firms, which are upstream in

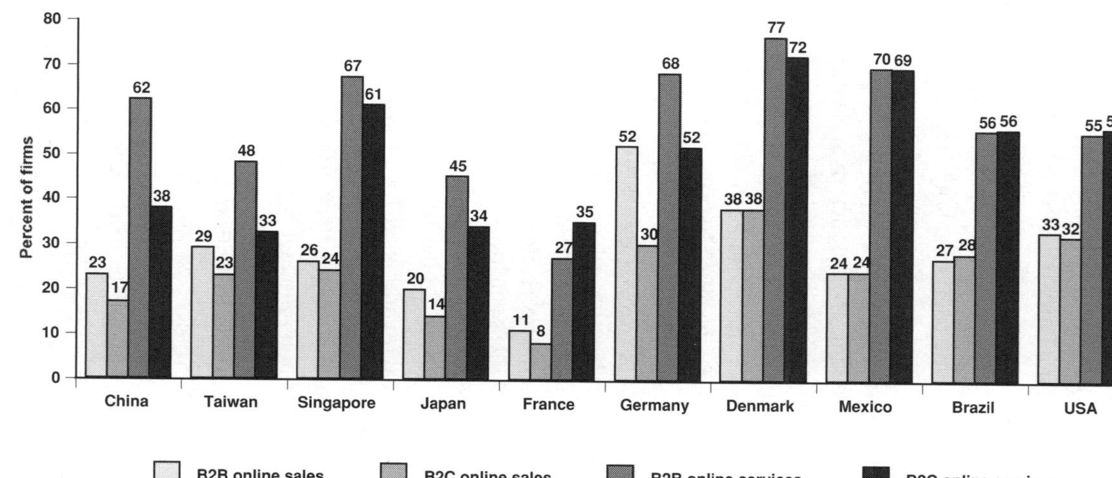

Figure 1.9 Firms engaged in B2B and B2C by economy
Source: CRITO GEC Survey, 2002

the value chain, with wholesale/retail distribution, which are further downstream.

We found considerable convergence among countries in the use of e-commerce to coordinate the supply chain and to gain efficiencies (lower cost, lower inventories) in the manufacturing sector. Manufacturers tend to adopt similar technologies and business practices regardless of national origin, as they strive to maintain or enhance linkages to global production networks. A more important difference is between large and small manufacturers. In some countries, both large and small firms are likely to use e-commerce technologies; for instance, Germany's mid-sized firms are often leaders in technology adoption (Chapter 4; Koenig et al., 2003). But in other countries, smaller manufacturers do not have the IT infrastructure or experience to adopt e-commerce, and risk being replaced by foreign suppliers which do (Chen, 2003; Andersen et al., 2003). As a result, governments in economies such as Taiwan have taken steps to help SMEs develop these resources and link up electronically to their larger customers.

In contrast to manufacturing, the use of e-commerce in the retail sector is closely tied to the structure of distribution and consumer shopping habits in each country. In France, a few large department stores control distribution and absorb new e-tailers; in Taiwan and Japan, the dense network of convenience stores provides a solution for consumers' preference for dealing in cash and seeing products before paying for them; in the USA, the broad use of credit cards and the tradition of buying from mail-order catalogs helped to pave the way for online innovators like Amazon. In fact, over 70% of retail e-commerce in the USA is conducted by non-store retailers such as catalog companies, direct marketers, and online-only merchants (US Census Bureau, 2004).

While the manufacturing and distribution sectors are at opposite ends of the value chain for physical goods, the financial sector has an entirely different value chain handling flows of money, securities, loans, and insurance policies. The focus of the country studies in this research was mainly on retail services, in which competition is local or national due to regulations that limit the scope of firm activities and differences in consumer habits in handling financial transactions. For instance, US consumers still use cash and checks extensively, while Europeans are more likely to use debit cards. There is widespread use of automated teller machines (ATMs) and other forms of automation in developed countries, but those technologies are accessible only to the higher-income population in developing countries.

This sectoral comparison confirms previous theories that B2B e-commerce supports upstream activities and tends to be more global, whereas B2C supports downstream activities and tends to be more localized (Globerman et al., 2001; Porter, 1986), as well as arguments for the advantage of local presence for B2C e-commerce (Steinfield et al., 1999; Steinfield & Whitten, 1999). It appears that e-commerce results in both global convergence and national diversity.

Impacts of e-commerce diffusion

Organizational performance

Firms in the survey report a wide range of impacts from going online. Intangible benefits such as improvements in customer service, internal efficiency, coordination, sales area coverage, and competitive position are reported more frequently than more tangible benefits such as staff productivity gains, increased sales, and cost reductions (Figure 1.10). This may reflect the difficulty of measuring impacts and linking them directly to Internet use.

While firms do report benefits from going online, in some cases consumers may have gained at the expense of firms, as they have the ability to gather information and search for lower prices online, even if they end up buying in a store. For instance, car shoppers can gather extensive data about new cars, including dealer invoice prices, which improves their bargaining position and reduces the information advantage previously enjoyed by dealers.

Firms that operate more globally achieve more benefits than firms that operate locally on every dimension surveyed (Figure 1.11). This may be because they can amortize their investments in e-commerce over a wider customer base, or because their global experience gives them an advantage in using the technology to greater effect. One of the biggest differences between high and low global firms is the number reporting increased international sales. This suggests that the Internet can help international firms to increase their international business, but is rarely a means for non-international firms to become international. It also refutes the notion that the Internet removes barriers to entry to foreign markets, or that most firms can sell globally without developing a physical presence in those markets.

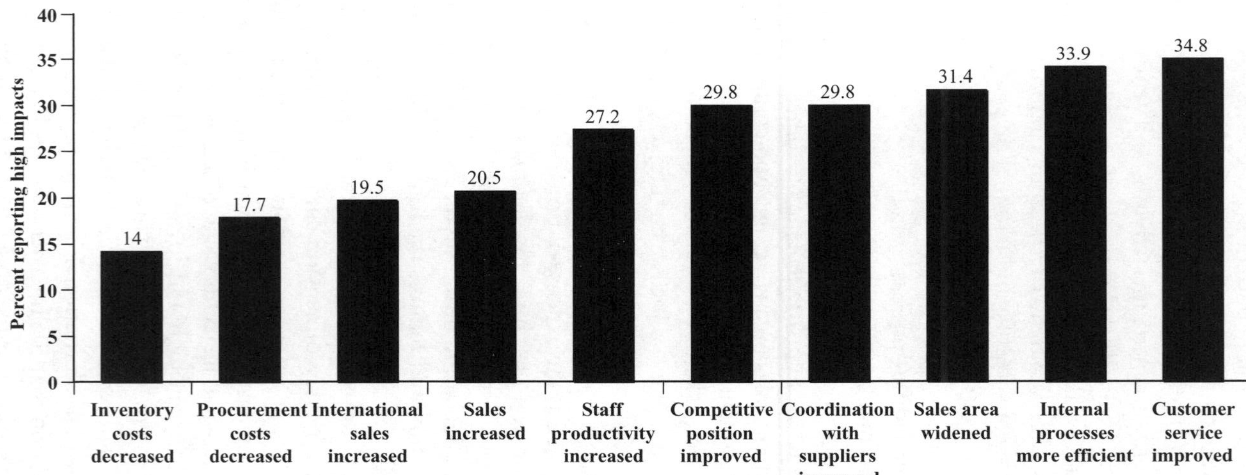

Figure 1.10 Firm impacts from e-commerce
Source: CRITO GEC Survey, 2002

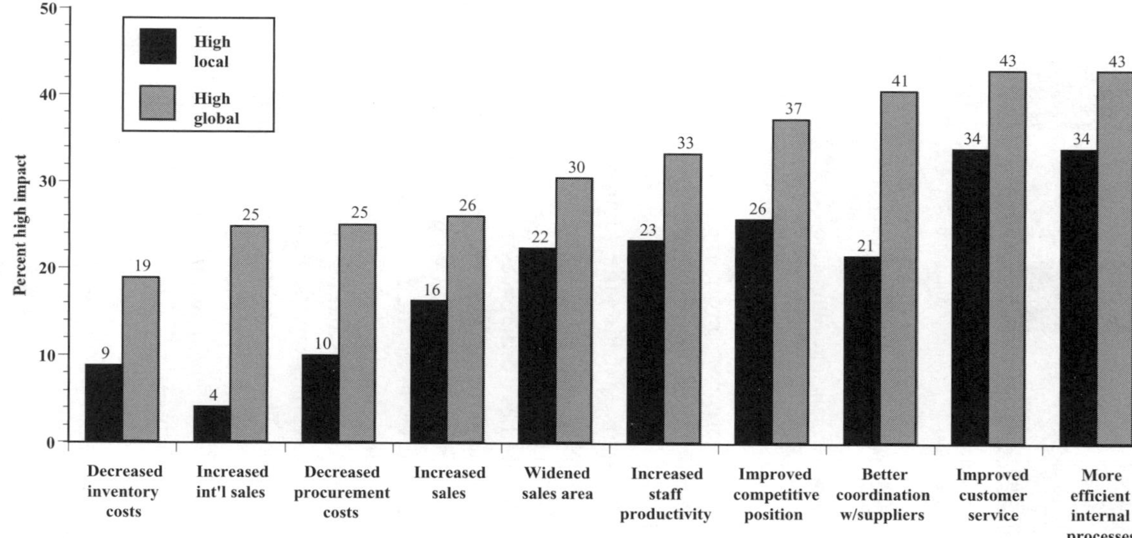

Figure 1.11 Performance impact differences between high global and high local firms
Source: CRITO GEC Survey, 2002
Note: High (low) global is top (bottom) 25% of firms in degree of firm internationalization

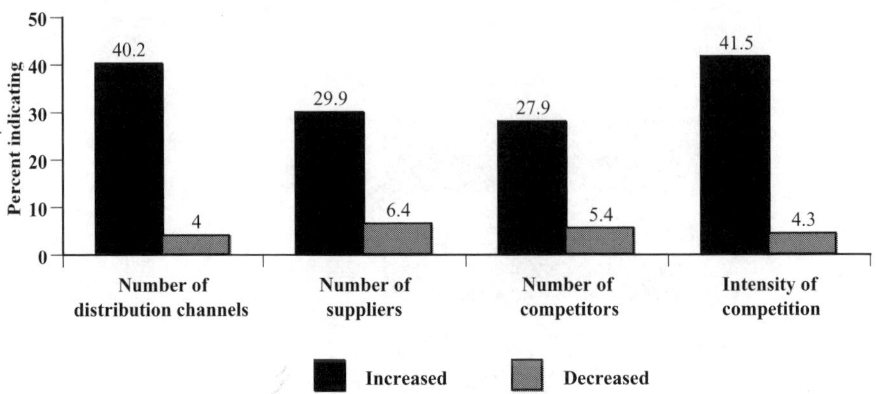

Figure 1.12 Impact on value chain and competition
Source: CRITO GEC Survey, 2002

There are marked differences across the countries in terms of reported impacts. For instance, Figure 1.10 shows 20.5% of firms reported increased sales. However, this figure ranges from 36% in Mexico to just 1% in Japan. Likewise, the number of firms reporting improved coordination with suppliers ranged from 14% in Germany to 51% in Mexico (see individual chapters).

One interpretation of these differences is that the impact of e-commerce is related to the nature of use. The most vivid case is Japan, where 34% reported better coordination with suppliers, but only 1% reported higher sales. This reflects the fact that Japanese firms have concentrated on improving supply chain efficiency more than online selling, which Tachiki et al. (2004; Chapter 5) attribute to the nature of Japan's industry structure with its *keiretsu* industry groups and its complex distribution channels. The pattern is reversed in Germany, which had already applied EDI throughout the supply chain, even down to midsized firms. German firms were aggressive in using the Internet for coordination, yet given their earlier investment in EDI, they may have been reluctant to make additional investments in supplier coordination through the Internet (Chapter 4; Zhu et al., 2006).

Competitive environment

Use of the Internet for business also shows significant impacts on firms' competitive environment (Figure 1.12). Far more respondents reported increased numbers of competitors and suppliers than reported a decrease. The same is true for intensity of competition and for the number of competitors that businesses face (Figure 1.12). Taken together, these findings indicate that firms are operating in increasingly complex environments, with more competition and more value chain partners. The Internet and e-commerce may be driving some of this increased complexity, but conversely, adopting e-commerce may be a response to greater complexity arising from factors such as deregulation and globalization.

Summary and conclusions

The mantra of the dot.com bubble years was "the Internet changes everything." After the crash, a more common sentiment was that the Internet had not changed much of anything. Many new online retailers were founded but only a few, such as Amazon and eBay, survived. Meanwhile, traditional retail firms learned to use the Internet as an additional channel. While B2B e-commerce involves large volumes of transactions, the highly touted B2B exchanges disappointed investors, as both buyers and sellers were hesitant to join. Finally, many technology suppliers crashed, along with their plans to become rich by selling the picks and shovels of the Internet gold rush.

Though the Internet revolution didn't quite happen as expected, the growth of e-commerce transactions continued throughout the dot.com crash, reaching over $1.6 trillion in 2003 (IDC, 2004). The Internet is becoming firmly entrenched in consumers' buying habits, at least as a source of information and, increasingly, for actual purchases. For businesses, it is becoming inconceivable not to have a website, and most firms are moving to use the Internet to improve internal efficiency and coordinate with customers and suppliers, as well as to buy and sell online. In many cases, the result is a reinforcement of existing business relationships, but at the same time there are examples of more transforming effects. For instance, eBay claims that over 430,000 individuals are using its platform to earn a significant share of their income, creating a national and even international marketplace for craftspeople, artists, collectors, and entrepreneurs (Kampert, 2004).

Another example of more dramatic change is the role that e-commerce technologies have played in enabling the global relocation of knowledge activities such as R&D, software development, call centers, product design, and back-office financial and legal work. Collaboration technologies and the dramatic reduction in international telecommunications costs made it economically feasible to take advantage of low-cost skilled labor in places such as India, Ireland, Israel, China, and the Philippines.

To summarize, e-commerce has been driven by a combination of broad global forces tempered by national environments and firm-level business imperatives. Adoption has been quite rapid in developed countries, while the more globally oriented sectors in developing countries have been quick to follow. The technology has been used more for coordination than for transactions, but transaction volumes have been growing steadily. The impacts of e-commerce so far have been more incremental than revolutionary, but it must be remembered that commercial use of the Internet is less than a decade old, and we may be seeing just the beginning of the types of transformations that will be apparent in coming years.

Distilling our findings, we identify four key themes: 1) global trends, 2) evolutionary diffusion, 3) national diversity in e-commerce, and 4) the myth of US hegemony in e-commerce.

Global trends

Common factors that influence diffusion and adoption of e-commerce can be found at the global, national, and firm levels. At the global level, these include liberalization of trade, investment, and telecommunications, as well as the "e-commerce movement," an intellectual movement that has carried both faith in technology and knowledge of its use around the world. The other major force behind diffusion of e-commerce is the continuing expansion of multinational corporations and the global production and service networks they coordinate. These firms employ advanced technologies wherever they go, require their business partners to adopt technologies and business practices, and indirectly put pressure on local companies to adopt e-commerce in order to be able to compete with them.

At the national level, we identified several common technological and economic factors that influence diffusion, including wealth, information infrastructure, and credit card use (Gibbs et al., 2003; Shih et al., 2004; Zhu et al., 2004). We also found that some of these factors are strongly moderated by the rule of law, which is apparently critical to the willingness of firms and individuals to engage in online transactions (Shih et al., 2005). The case studies reported in

Chapters 2 to 9 confirm that the absence of a strong rule of law is a significant barrier to e-commerce. However, both case studies and survey results show that mere government promotion has limited impact on diffusion.

At the firm level, our survey results show that the biggest drivers of e-commerce use were desire for market expansion and improved value chain coordination. The most important barrier was concern about privacy and security issues, followed by inadequate legal protection for Internet purchases. This reinforces the national-level findings that e-commerce drivers are economic in nature, while barriers are more institutional or legal.

As for how firms are actually using the Internet for business, secondary data show that B2B transactions dwarf B2C, both globally and in all countries (IDC, 2004). Survey data show similar results at the firm level. They also show that the most common applications of e-commerce are for communication with customers and value chain coordination, while online selling is the least common use.

An important differentiator among firms in both intensity and nature of e-commerce use was their level of globalization. Highly global firms do more business online overall than more local firms. However, there was no significant difference in terms of selling, buying, or marketing. The biggest difference was in activities related to value chain coordination. It appears that global firms face more pressure to coordinate their geographically dispersed value chains and support global customers. Local firms are as likely to buy and sell online, and actually provide more services to consumers online.

The most significant impacts of e-commerce are improvement in customer service, coordination with suppliers, more efficient internal processes, and expansion of firms' sales area. In the area of impacts, the global/local split is most dramatic. Highly global firms report greater benefits on every indicator of sales, efficiency, and coordination, perhaps because they are able to achieve economies of scale from their e-commerce investments, or because their broader experience with IT enables them to utilize the Internet more effectively.

Evolutionary diffusion

The dot. com boom created high expectations for the scope, depth, and immediacy of the impact of e-commerce on business and economies. It was widely believed that e-commerce would quickly diffuse throughout firms, industries, sectors, and entire economies. It was expected that e-commerce would penetrate deeply into business processes, enabling radical transformation of business models and new supply chain configurations.

The reality of e-commerce has been very different. Significant change is observed within certain narrow industry segments, such as book retailing in the USA and mobile commerce in Japan. However, the overall diffusion and impact of e-commerce is better described as a gradual process, adapting and changing into more complex and improved forms in stages.

This evolutionary process becomes even more understandable when considering the switching costs associated with existing technologies and the need for broad institutional change to employ e-commerce effectively. France had a long and successful history of EDI for B2B and Minitel for B2C. Thus, when Internet-based e-commerce applications became available, there was slow adoption due to existing methods which were viewed as being adequate. In China, heavy investment in IT infrastructure and the Internet was counterbalanced by incompatible institutional infrastructure and firm business processes. The result has been a gradual diffusion of e-commerce in China, focused in wealthier, internationally oriented coastal regions, where organizational complements have been faster to emerge.

National diversity in e-commerce

While there is a good deal of convergence across countries in terms of drivers, barriers, uses, and impacts of e-commerce, we also found evidence of national divergence and diversity in the survey, and especially in the country cases. To generalize, we found that upstream activities in the value chain tended toward global convergence, while downstream activities show more national and even local diversity.

For instance, case studies show that firms in almost all countries tend to use older technologies such as EFT and EDI in support of upstream business processes such as financial transaction clearing, supply chain management, and just-in-time inventory systems. Firms with no EDI are adopting newer Internet-based technologies to lower costs and increase flexibility in such processes, and the firms with EDI are gradually incorporating Internet-based B2B as an extension or substitute for EDI.

For downstream activities such as retailing and consumer financial services, there are real differences across national economies in how much e-commerce is used and the form that it takes. These differences can be explained by differences in consumer behavior, social norms, or industry structure. For instance, shoppers in places such as France, China, and Japan have been less willing to buy products sight unseen, or to pay for them in advance with credit cards. They also are used to making daily shopping trips to local stores. So in those countries, online buying has been slower to catch on, and transactions often are handled through local convenience or department stores and paid for with cash on delivery. In the USA, consumers are more familiar with long-distance shopping over the phone, and as a result online purchases are generally paid for by credit card and delivered by courier to the customer's home.

Other examples of national diversity in consumer-oriented e-commerce include the success of the i-mode and other mobile Internet services in Japan (Chapter 5; Tachiki et al., 2004) and the emergence of strong local content suppliers in Brazil to satisfy demand for local language and cultural content (Chapter 8; Tigre, 2003; Tigre & Dedrick, 2003). From Europe to Asia, especially in China, use of mobile data communications such as short messaging service (SMS) has run well ahead of the USA. In fact, it has been reported that the simple business of downloading ring tones reached $2.5 billion worldwide in 2003, mostly outside the USA (Schoenberger, 2004). These examples reflect differences in consumer preferences, regulatory environment, and industry structure.

Myth of US hegemony in e-commerce

Many countries have harbored concerns about US influence over the Internet, fearing that globalization will bring a loss of national economic control and the invasion of US culture. The Internet was invented in the USA, built on the English language, and in its earlier days had an individualistic frontier culture that was very American. Some US firms saw e-commerce as a way to lower barriers to entry and compete in new international markets, a possibility that was not so attractive to incumbent national firms in those markets.

After all the hype and fear, the evidence shows that the Internet and e-commerce have become dominated less over time by US companies and business practices. The dot.com boom and bust in the USA did have echoes in a number of other countries, but within the context of their own entrepreneurial traditions and supported mainly by domestic investors. In addition, other nations have not been content merely to imitate US approaches to e-commerce but have developed strategies suited to their own economic and social context.

Concluding remark

Internet-based e-commerce has been neither the boon that many had hoped for nor the bane that others had feared. It has largely reinforced existing institutions and relationships at the firm, industry, and country levels. It has exhibited both convergence upstream and divergence downstream in firm value chains. It has also exhibited considerable divergence across countries, and between developed and developing countries. While Internet growth has been phenomenal in all countries, e-commerce growth has been and will continue to be much slower. Thus, e-commerce is marked by evolution rather than transformation. It is precisely this evolutionary character of e-commerce which points to the need for continual monitoring and analysis of its use and impacts over the longer term. Hopefully, this book will serve as a benchmark and a motivation for such efforts.

References

Adam, N., Awerbuch, B., Stonim, J., Wegner, P., & Yesha,Y. (1997). Globalizing Business, Education, Culture Through the Internet. *Communications of the ACM*, 40(2), 115–121.

Andersen, K. V., Bjorn-Andersen, N., & Henriksen, H. Z. (2003). Globalization and E-commerce: Environment and Policy in Denmark. *Communications of the Association for Information Systems*, 12, 218–275.

Bartlett, C. & Ghoshal, S. (1989). Managing across Borders: New Strategic Requirements. *Sloan Management Review*, 28, 7–17.

Bell, D. (1973). *The Coming of Post-industrial Society*. New York: Basic Books.

Berger, S. & Dore, R. (Eds.) (1996). *National Diversity and Global Capitalism*. Ithaca, New York: Cornell University Press.

Boyer, R. (1996). The Convergence Hypothesis Revisited: Globalization but still the Century of Nations? In S. Berger & R. Dore (Eds.), *National*

Diversity and Global Capitalism. Ithaca, New York: Cornell University Press, 29–60.

Boyer, R. & Drache, D. (Eds.) (1996). *State Against Markets*. London: Routledge.

Brousseau, E. (2003). E-commerce in France: Did Early Adoption Prevent its Development? *The Information Society*, 16(1), 45–57.

Brousseau, E. & Kraemer, K. L. (2003). Globalization and E-commerce: The French Environment and Policy. *Communications of the Association for Information Systems*, 10, 73–127.

Cairncross, F. (1997). *The Death of Distance*. Cambridge, MA: Harvard Business School Press.

Caselli, F. & Coleman II, W. J. (2001). Cross-country Technology Diffusion: The Case of Computers. *The American Economic Review*, 91(2), 328–335.

Chen, T. J. (2003). Globalization of E-commerce: Environment and Policy of Taiwan. *Communications of the Association for Information Systems*, 12, 326–353.

Coe, D. T., Helpman, E., & Hoffmaister, A. W. (1997). North-South R&D Spillovers. *The Economic Journal*, 107(440), 134–149.

Cooper, R. B. & Zmud, R. W. (1990). Information Technology Implementation Research: A Technological Diffusion Approach. *Management Science*, 36(2), 123–139.

Dasgupta, S., Agarwal, D., Ioannidis, A., & Gopalakrishnan, S. (1999). Determinants of Information Technology Adoption: An Extension of Existing Models to Firms in a Developing Country. *Journal of Global Information Management,* 7(3), 41–49.

Dedrick, J. & Kraemer, K. L. (1998). *Asia's Computer Challenge: Threat or Opportunity for the United States and the World?* New York: Oxford University Press.

Dedrick, J. & Kraemer, K. L. (2004). *Impacts of Information Technology on the Organization of Economic Activities: A Study of the Personal Computer Industry*. Irvine, CA: CRITO, University of California, Irvine.

Dossani, R. & Kenney, M. (2004). The Next Wave of Globalization: Exploring the Relocation of Service Provision to India. Working paper, Palo Alto: Asia/Pacific Research Center, Stanford University.

Emmelhainz, M. A. (1993). *EDI: A Total Management Guide*. New York: Van Nostrand Reinhold.

Engardio, P., Bernstein, A., & Kripalani, M. (2003). Is Your Job Next? *Business Week*, 50–60.

Ernst, D. (2003). The New Mobility of Knowledge: Digital Information Systems and Global Flagship Networks. Working paper, Honolulu: East West Center.

Fichman, R. G. (2000). The Diffusion and Assimilation of Information Technology Innovations. In R. W. Zmud (Ed.), *Framing the Domains of IT Management: Projecting the Future Through the Past*. Cleveland, OH: Pinnaflex Publishing, 105–127.

Fomin, V. V., King, J. L., McGann, S. T., & Lyytinen, K. J. (2003). Globalization and Electronic Commerce: Environment and Policy in the US. *Communications of the Association for Information Systems*, 10(8), 276–325.

Freeman, C. & Soete, L. (1997). *The Economics of Industrial Innovation* (3rd Ed.). London: Pinter.

Gereffi, G. (1999). International Trade and Industrial Upgrading in the Apparel Commodity Chain. *Journal of International Economics*, 48, 37–70.

Gibbs, J., Kraemer, K. L., & Dedrick, J. (2003). Environment and Policy Factors Shaping Global E-commerce Diffusion: A Cross-country Comparison. *The Information Society*, 19(1), 5–18.

Globerman, S., Roehl, T. W., & Standifird, S. (2001). Globalization and Electronic Commerce: Inferences from Retail Brokering. *Journal of International Business Studies*, 32(4), 749–768.

Grossman, G. M. & Helpman, E. (1993). *Innovation and Growth in the Global Economy*. Cambridge, MA: MIT Press.

Iacovou, C. L., Benbasat, I., & Dexter, A. S. (1995). Electronic Data Interchange and Small Organizations: Adoption and Impact of Technology. *MIS Quarterly*, 19(4), 465–485.

International Data Corporation (IDC) (2004). *Internet Commerce Market Model*. Framingham, MA.

Kahin, B. & Wilson, E. (1997). *National Information Infrastructure Initiatives: Vision and Policy Design*. Cambridge, MA: MIT Press.

Kampert, P. (2004) Entrepreneurs Find It's a Pleasure Doing Business on eBay. *Chicago Tribune*. From www.siliconvalley.com/mld/siliconvalley/living/9328940.htm

Kenney, M. & Curry, J. (2000). Beyond Transaction Costs: E-commerce and the Power of the Internet Dataspace. Working Paper, Berkeley, CA: Berkeley Roundtable on the International Economy, University of California, Berkeley, July 11.

King, J. L., Gurbaxani, V., Kraemer, K. L., McFarlan, F. W., Raman, K. S., & Yap, C. S. (1994). Institutional Factors in Information Technology Innovation. *Information Systems Research*, 5(2), 139–169.

Koenig, W., Wigand, R. T., & Beck, R. (2003). Globalization of E-commerce: Environment and Policy in Germany. *Communications of the Association for Information Systems*, 11, 33–72.

Kraemer, K. L. & King, J. L. (1996). Order Without Design: NII in the United States. *Information Infrastructure and Policy*, 5(2), 135–168.

Mesenbourg, T. (2001). Measuring the Digital Economy. Discussion Paper, Bureau of the Census. From www.census.gov/eos/www/papers/umdigital.pdf

Nelson, R. R. (Ed.) (1993). *National Innovation Systems: A Comparative Study*. New York: Oxford University Press.

Ohmae, K. (1990). *The Borderless World: Power and Strategy in the Interlinked Economy*. New York: Harper Perennial.

Organization for Economic Cooperation and Development (OECD) (1996). *Information Infrastructure Convergence and Pricing: The Internet*. Paris: Committee for Information Computer and Communications Policy.

Palacios, J. J. (2003). The Development of E-commerce in Mexico: A Business-led Passing Boom or a Step toward the Emergence of a Digital Economy? *The Information Society*, 19(1), 69–80.

Palacios, J. J. & Kraemer, K. L. (2003). Globalization and E-commerce: Environment and Policy in Mexico. *Communications of the Association for Information Systems*, 11, 129–185.

Phan, D. D. (2003). E-business Development for Competitive Advantages: A Case Study. *Information and Management*, 40(6), 581–590.

Porter, M. E. (Ed.) (1986). *Competition in Global Industries*. Boston, MA: Harvard Business School Press.

Ramamurthy, K., Premkumar, G., & Crum, M. R. (1999). Organizational and Interorganizational Determinants of EDI Diffusion and Organizational Performance: A Cause Model. *Journal of Organizational Computing and Electronic Commerce*, 9(4), 253–285.

Riggins, F. J., Kriebel, C. H., & Mukhopadhyay, T. (1994). The Growth of Interorganizational Systems in the Presence of Network Externalities. *Management Science*, 40(8), 984–998.

Roach, S. (2005). The New Macro of Globalization. Global Economic Forum, Morgan Stanley, June 6. Taken from www.morganstanley.com/GEFdata/digests/20050606-mon.html

Rogers, E. (1995). *Diffusion of Innovations* (4th Ed.). New York: Free Press.

Schoenberger, C. R. (2004). Cell Phone Rings Equal Bling Bling. *Forbes.com* Retrieved March 9, 2004, from www.forbes.com/2004/02/17/cz_cs_0217ringtones_print.html

Shih, C., Dedrick, J., & Kraemer, K. L. (2005). Rule of Law and the International Diffusion of E-commerce. *Communications of the ACM*, 48(11), 57–62.

Shih, C., Kraemer, K. L., & Dedrick, J. (2004). *An Extended Accelerator Model of Country-level Investment in Information Technology*. Irvine, CA: CRITO.

Steinfield, C., Mahler, A., & Bauer, J. (1999). Electronic Commerce and the Local Merchant: Opportunities for Synergy Between Physical and Web Presence. *Electronic Markets*, 9(2).

Steinfield, C. & Whitten, P. (1999). Community Level Socio-Economic Impacts of Electronic Commerce. *Journal of Computer Mediated Communication*, 5(2). From www.ascusc.org/jcmc/vol5/issue2/steinfield.html

Swanson, E. B. (1994). Information Systems Innovation among Organizations. *Management Science*, 40(9), 1069–1092.

Tachiki, D., Hamaya, S., & Yukawa, K. (2004). Diffusion and Impacts of the Internet and E-commerce in Japan. From http://crito.uci.edu/pubs/2004/GEC3Japan.pdf

Talukdar, D., Sudhir, K., & Ainslie, A. (2002). Investigating New Product Diffusion across Products and Countries. *Marketing Science*, 21(1), 97–114.

Tan, A. Z. & Wu, O. (2002). Globalization and E-commerce: Factors Affecting Diffusion in China. *Communications of the Association for Information Systems*, 10, 4–32.

Tigre, P. B. (2003). Brazil in the Age of Electronic Commerce. *The Information Society*, 19(1), 33–43.

Tigre, P. B. & Dedrick, J. (2003). Globalization and E-commerce: Environment and Policy in Brazil, *Communications of the Association for Information Systems*, 10, 189–217.

Tornatzky, L. & Fleischer, M. (1990). *The Process of Technological Innovation*. Lexington, MA: Lexington Books.

US Census Bureau (2004). *2002 E-commerce Multi-Sector Report*. Washington, D.C.: Department of Commerce.

Wade, R. (1996). Globalization and Its Limits: Reports of the Death of the National Economy are Greatly Exaggerated. In S. Berger & R. Dore (Eds.), *National Diversity and Global Capitalism*. Ithaca, NY: Cornell University Press.

Womach, J. P., Jones, D. T., & Roos, D. (1991). *The Machine that Changed the World: How Japan's Secret Weapon in the Global Auto Wars Will Revolutionize Western Industry*. New York: Harper Perennial.

Wong, P. (2003). Global and National Factors Affecting E-commerce Diffusion in Singapore. *The Information Society*, 19(1), 19–32.

Wong, P. & Ho, Y. P. (2004). E-commerce in Singapore: Impetus and Impact of Globalization. From http://crito.uci.edu/pubs/2004/Singapore_GECIII.pdf

World Bank (2004). *WDI Online*. From http://publications.worldbank.ord/WDI/

Zhu, K. & Kraemer, K. L. (2002). E-commerce Metrics for Net-Enhanced Organizations: Assessing the Value of E-commerce to Firm Performance in the Manufacturing Sector. *Information Systems Research*, 13(3), 275–295.

Zhu, K. & Kraemer, K. L. (2005). Post-adoption Variations in Usage and Value of E-business by Organizations: Cross-country Evidence from the Retail Industry. *Information Systems Research*, 16(1), 61–84.

Zhu, K., Kraemer, K. L., & Gurbaxani, V. (2006). Migration to Open-Standard Interorganizational Information Systems: Network Effects and Path Dependency. *MIS Quarterly*.

Zhu, K., Kraemer, K. L., Xu, S., & Dedrick, J. (2004). Information Technology Payoff in E-business Environments: An International Perspective on Impacts of E-business in the Financial Services Industry. *Journal of Management Information Systems*, 21(1), 17–54.

Zhu, K., Kraemer, K. L., Xu, S., Korte, W., & Gareis, K. (2005). Extending the Theory of Diffusion Innovations to Explain E-business Adoption by Firms – Innovation, Context, and Fit. Working paper, Irvine, CA: CRITO.

2 *The United States: adaptive integration versus the Silicon Valley model*

JASON DEDRICK,
KENNETH L. KRAEMER,
JOHN L. KING, AND
KALLE LYYTINEN

Introduction

E-commerce in the United States has been shaped by the economic, social, and policy environment in which it developed, and in particular by the unique business patterns of the US high-tech industry sector. Many key e-commerce technologies and business processes were developed in the United States and the so-called Silicon Valley model – venture capital funding, entrepreneurial start-ups and spin-offs, and close ties to university research (e.g., Kenney, 2003) – has been the locus of much of the investment, innovation, hype, and despair associated with Internet-based e-commerce. Firms in the Silicon Valley model include many survivors of the dot.com era that are leaders in highly visible segments of B2C e-commerce, such as book and music retailing, online auctions, web portals, travel services, and online stock trading.

But the Silicon Valley model is only one dimension of a rich and complex pattern of e-commerce diffusion in the USA. A much larger share of e-commerce activity is characterized by a pattern we call "adaptive integration," whereby existing firms incorporate the new technologies and business models offered by the Internet to extend or revamp their existing strategies, operations, and supply and distribution channels. Adaptive integration is the dominant pattern for business-to-business e-commerce in most major industries, including manufacturing, wholesale trade, banking, insurance, and transportation, and B2B dominates B2C e-commerce by far.

Given a full decade since Internet-based e-commerce emerged on the US business landscape, it is becoming clear that early predictions that the Internet would eliminate barriers to entry, radically alter distribution channels, destroy previous sources of competitive advantage, and create a "new world of low-friction, low-overhead capitalism" (to quote Bill Gates, 1995, p. 158) may have overreached. The overestimation of e-commerce impacts is partly a reflection of unrealistic expectations about the ability of people and organizations to change as rapidly as Internet technology has changed. But just as importantly, it reflects gradual integration of the Internet by established businesses to reinforce their competitive position and strengthen their business relationships.

The development of e-commerce in the USA has thus been evolutionary rather than transformative, and its impacts have been changes in degree more than in kind.[1] At the national level, e-commerce has grown steadily, and now exceeds $1.67 trillion annually (US Census Bureau, 2005b). At the firm level, GEC Survey data and other empirical evidence illustrate widespread adoption of the Internet for a variety of business functions, leading to improved efficiency and increased market reach. However, e-commerce so far is being used mostly to support existing value chain relationships rather than for restructuring procurement or distribution channels. Similarly, industry studies suggest that e-commerce is being applied mostly within existing market relationships rather than to create new marketplaces.

Over time, the possibility remains that major changes in kind will occur when e-commerce reaches a sufficient scale. These changes in kind can be illustrated only by particular examples thus far, but they suggest what the future of e-commerce might hold. On the B2C side, companies such as Yahoo! and Google have created highly successful advertising-driven businesses, eBay has become a virtual market for thousands of consumers and small businesses, and Amazon has evolved from an online bookstore to an e-commerce platform for major brick-and-mortar retailers. On the B2B side, the computing industry has been transformed by the success of Dell Inc. (Kraemer & Dedrick, 2005; Dedrick & Kraemer, 2005), which has used the Internet to dramatically increase the reach and scope of its direct sales model. But these examples are few thus far.

With this general background, we now summarize the specific findings of the US case study.

[1] This is in contrast to other books on e-commerce in the USA, which suggest that it has been transformational (BRIE-IGCC E-conomy Project, 2001; Dutton et al., 2005). We argue that transformations may yet occur, but for the most part are rarely seen.

- *Adaptive integration is the dominant model.* The Silicon Valley model of e-commerce development is only part of the tapestry of e-commerce that has evolved in the USA. Adaptive integration, whereby existing firms incorporate technology as an extension of their existing strategies and business models, is actually the dominant pattern.
- *US environment is favorable to e-commerce development.* The US environment has been generally favorable for firms to develop Internet-based e-commerce. The USA is the world's largest single market, united by common laws, language, currency, and business practices. Its IT firms were leaders in creating the key technologies of the Internet, and its businesses, universities, and other organizations were leaders in adopting IT and the Internet. Consumer adoption of PCs was relatively high, and consumers were accustomed to remote purchasing from earlier catalog and telesales experience. The national transportation and distribution system was geared to direct package delivery, and couriers such as FedEx and UPS were Internet innovators. The open, competitive telecommunications and Internet service provider markets lowered access costs. The availability of venture capital and a well-established initial public offering market provided capital to support Internet-oriented innovation with new business models and services.
- *The government's role was to build infrastructure and get out of the way.* The US government was largely a cheerleader for e-commerce. However, it played a broader role through support for defense and university projects, which created the Internet and provided a cadre of professionals and technicians to build out the Internet and develop e-commerce applications. The government's early deregulation of telecommunications created competition and lower costs, and its resistance to Internet taxation was effectively a subsidy to e-commerce. However, failure to create competition in local telecoms or cable TV markets may have slowed broadband adoption, and the government has been slow to deal with issues such as information privacy and security, spam, and online fraud.
- *The United States is the leader in readiness and diffusion.* The USA leads globally in readiness and diffusion of e-commerce, but the actual level of online sales is only around 2% of total US retail sales. However, online sales continue to grow, and e-commerce levels are significantly higher in industries such as manufacturing, where EDI use is much higher. In terms of total sales, B2B e-commerce is

much larger than B2C, with manufacturing and wholesale distribution dominating B2B sales.

- *E-commerce impacts have been positive though different from many expectations and reinforcing of existing relationships.* E-commerce has led to greater firm efficiency, better customer service, and improved supply chain coordination, but has had less impact on sales. Firms perceive e-commerce as enhancing their competitive position and expanding their distribution networks, but also increasing the number of competitors and intensity of competition they face. The pattern of e-commerce use and impact in the USA has primarily reinforced and extended existing inter-firm relationships rather than transformed them, consistent with the adaptive integration thesis.

Country background: environment and policy

A distinctive mix of environment and policy factors has led to a unique pattern of e-commerce in the United States. Since the USA was the leader in adopting e-commerce, is the largest user, and is the source of many of the underlying technologies of the Internet, it has become the default pattern against which other countries are compared and contrasted.

The US model of e-commerce

The Silicon Valley model is often pointed to as the unique element of the US experience with the Internet and e-commerce. Although there are various definitions, the model is perhaps best described as the emergence of new, dedicated Internet firms, supported by venture capital, that were established to define and occupy the new economic space represented by the commercialization of the Internet (Kenney, 2003: 70).[2] There is no question that the innovative firms that were created in Silicon Valley were important experiments and contributed much to the

[2] Cohen et al. (2001) define the Silicon Valley model as "a set of social institutions (research universities, venture capitalists and specialized law firms) and market institutions (flexible labor market, incentive compensation, financial capital, high-skilled people from around the world) that make it possible for an entrepreneurial company to bring innovations to market quickly and at scale." Kogut (2003) defines it as "The embrace within a region of institutions – venture capital financing, equity markets, fluid labor markets for global talent, fiscal policies which lower the costs of starting and operating a business and proximity of university and research institutes – that promote new firm innovations."

development of e-commerce in the USA. However, by itself, this model is an incomplete and misleading representation of the unique pattern of e-commerce development in the USA. Early successes and impacts of the Silicon Valley model do not reflect the more widespread and rich impacts associated with the US pattern of e-commerce development. Consequently, we address two key questions in this chapter.

Research questions

The first research question is: *What is the pattern of e-commerce development in the USA?* We argue that the Silicon Valley model of venture capital-funded start-ups is only part of the e-commerce story. It deals with the dot.coms and the beginning period of Internet and e-commerce development, which was focused mainly on B2C. Icons such as Amazon, eBay, Yahoo! and Google were venture capital funded and fit the model. However, the e-commerce story is more complex than venture capital, start-ups, and regional innovation focused on retailing to consumers. It is set in a national context of favorable environmental conditions, *laissez innover*,[3] government policy, and widespread technology readiness, and involves the adaptive integration of the Internet by traditional companies, largely to conduct B2B commerce and to coordinate national and global value chains.

The second question is: *What are the impacts and implications of the US pattern of development?* It was expected that e-commerce would have dramatic effects on both firm distribution channels and supply chains. As suggested by some, "the theory underlying B2C e-commerce was that the elimination of the costs of store and sales employees and the use of a more efficient supply chain due to taking customers' orders directly should allow online firms to sell at a discount" (Kenney, 2003). These lower costs would pull customers away from traditional retailers, essentially disintermediating them in the consumer marketplace. The theory underlying B2B e-commerce focused more on creating highly efficient and transparent markets that would transform the structure of industry value chains. The empirical evidence, however, shows that

[3] *Laissez innover*, which is from McDermott (1967), means freedom for technological innovation. As we use the term, it refers to the lack of significant government control over technology, allowing the providers and users to take advantage of the opportunities that technology provides. The primary emphasis is constant technological innovation that is mirrored and reinforced by institutional innovation in business, government, and society.

Table 2.1 *Macroeconomic indicators, 1998–2002*

	1998	*1999*	*2000*	*2001*	*2002*
GDP in US$bn	8,720.20	9,206.90	9,810.20	10,065.27	10,416.82
GDP per capita US$	31,691.71	33,038.22	34,760.33	35,277.37	36,123.23
GDP growth (annual percent)	4.32	4.14	3.78	0.25	2.43
GFDI (percent of GDP)	4.43	6.09	5.63	3.40	2.43
Trade (percent of GDP)	23.87	24.19	26.31	24.13	23.63
Income distribution: richest 20%: poorest 20%					9.0

Source: World Bank, 2004

such transformative impacts have been rare, and that e-commerce more often has had the impact of reinforcing existing relationships.

Environment

The US economy is large, with a GDP in 2002 of $10.4 trillion, or $36,100 per capita (Table 2.1). However, it is mainly a domestic-oriented rather than a globally oriented economy. Trade (imports plus exports) accounts for just 24% of GDP. Manufacturing (19.6% of GDP), distribution (18%), and finance (31%) are the largest industries, representing over two-thirds of the economy (United Nations, 1999). Small and medium-sized enterprises dominate the economy in terms of number of firms (98%), but large firms account for about one half of total economic output (Small Business Administration, 2002).

The data in the GEC Survey reflect these trends. Overall, US firms are domestically oriented – only 8% of procurement spending and 5% of total sales is from abroad (Table 2.2). Also, 78% of firms reported a low level of competition from abroad. It is mainly the manufacturing firms that have establishments abroad (36%) and have substantial sales (12%) and procurement (13%) from abroad. Manufacturing firms are also by far the most affected by competitors abroad (35% reporting high degree). Large firms are much more likely than SMEs to have establishments abroad (46% versus 20%), yet the difference in international sales, procurement, and competition is much narrower. To summarize, US manufacturers are highly international, while the

Table 2.2 *Internationalization of US firms*

	Establishment size		*Sector*			*Total*	
	SME	*Large*	*Mfg.*	*Distrib.*	*Finance*	*US*	*Global*
Percent of companies with establishments abroad*	20	46	36	21	13	23	24
Percent of companies with headquarters abroad*	5	8	9	5	3	5	8
Mean percent of total sales from abroad*	5	8	12	3	4	5	12
Mean percent of total procurement spending from abroad*	8	8	13	9	1	8	20
Degree affected by competitors abroad (percent)*							
Low	80	70	45	86	96	78	68
Moderate	9	14	20	8	4	10	16
High	11	16	35	6	0	12	15

Source: CRITO GEC Survey, 2002
Note: *Indicates statistically significant difference between the USA and the global sample at .05 or greater

distribution and finance industries are much more domestically oriented. Large firms are somewhat more international than SMEs.

The US environment has been highly favorable for firms to develop Internet-based e-commerce. The USA is the largest single market in the world, providing scale for new ventures and extending existing businesses. The market is united by common laws, a common language, a common currency, and common business practices, making it easier to do business. It has a payment medium in the form of credit cards, which were widely used by consumers and could easily be employed for e-commerce transactions.

The capabilities needed for e-commerce had also been developing in the USA for decades. The country's IT firms were world leaders in developing computers, and the US government, universities, and

Table 2.3 *Technology infrastructure, 1998–2002*

	1998	*1999*	*2000*	*2001*	*2002*
Telecommunications					
Main phone lines per 1,000 pop.	654.97	660.24	664.49	670.63	645.81
Cell phone subscribers per 1,000 pop.	252.08	309.57	389.02	450.76	488.15
Cable subscribers per 1,000 pop.	244.08	246.57	246.24	256.18	254.97
Internet					
Internet hosts per 1,000 pop.	111.05	191.31	286.29	372.87	399.88
Internet users per 1,000 pop.	308.09	366.96	440.62	501.49	551.38
IT					
IT as percent of GDP	4.14	4.29	4.48	4.23	3.89
PCs per 1,000 pop.	451.65	507.27	572.10	625.01	658.88
Software piracy rate (percent)	0.25	0.25	0.24	0.25	0.23

Sources: IDC, 2003b; IPR, 2003; ITU, 2004; World Bank, 2004

non-IT firms were world leaders in using computers. The IT industry created and aggressively promoted new technologies needed to support the Internet and e-commerce. In addition there was a pool of skilled and ambitious people ready to start or join new companies during the initial Internet gold rush. The business and social culture encouraged such risk taking, even treating unsuccessful ventures as valuable learning experiences rather than shameful failures.

On the demand side, US customers were oriented to online buying as consumers had experience with remote purchasing through catalogs or over the phone. Most were experienced in using computers at work or at home. Many had used email, bulletin boards, or proprietary online services such as AOL or Prodigy, and they were quick to embrace the web – once graphical browsers such as Mosaic, Netscape, and Explorer were introduced.

On the supply side, US businesses had long made heavy investments in information technology, which provided the infrastructure for Internet-based e-commerce (Table 2.3). They had developed extensive internal IT systems and often were already doing business electronically via EDI and EFT systems. Most were receptive to Internet-based trading systems (Mesenbourg, 2001). Leading IT firms such as Cisco, Dell, IBM, Intel, Oracle, and Sun moved quickly to adopt the Internet to improve their operations and touted their success to stimulate demand for their products, creating a virtuous cycle.

In addition to its IT infrastructure, the USA had a national transportation and distribution system that was geared to small package delivery to businesses and households via the US Postal Service and private couriers such as UPS, Federal Express, and DHL. These were integrated with a global transportation system that permitted products to be drop-shipped quickly from assembly plants or distribution hubs to retailers and even consumers. Freight forwarding and logistics companies handled the paperwork and managed transportation to reduce shipping and inventory costs (King & Lyytinen, 2005).

Finally, the relatively open US telecoms market and the rapidly changing computer and telecoms technologies created many new market opportunities, which were seized upon by entrepreneurs aided by venture capital. The largest concentration of firms commercializing the Internet was in Silicon Valley, but other clusters emerged in San Francisco, Seattle, and New York City. These firms were joined by others – law firms, accounting firms, employment agencies, executive search firms, and investment banks – specializing in services to small entrepreneurial firms. Together, they created a business ecology which accelerated the growth of new Internet-related businesses and also supported adaptation by traditional businesses (Kenney, 2003).

Government policy

The US government played an important role in the development of the Internet and its underlying technologies. The Internet itself grew out of government projects, first supported by the Department of Defense as ARPANET and later by the National Science Foundation (NSF) as NSFNET, which connected government contractors, research institutes, and universities. When the Internet was commercialized in 1995, there was already a large number of academic, government, and business institutions experienced in using it. The USA had a large system of research universities, supported by federal and state funding, with world-class engineering and computer science departments that produced scientists and engineers. It also had leading research laboratories in large companies such as AT&T, IBM, and Xerox. Its liberal immigration policy attracted many of the best foreign scientists and engineers. Together, these institutions created a large talent pool available for innovation and entrepreneurship (Kenney, 2003).

Finally, the United States had a well-developed telephone system with uniform rates and usage rules as a result of the AT&T government-regulated monopoly. The federal government deregulated telecoms earlier than most industrialized nations, which promoted competition, drove down the cost of bandwidth, and encouraged greater use of telecoms and the Internet. But true competition in local service was arguably slowed by the Telecoms Act of 1996, which left local phone and cable monopolies in place. Today, broadband costs are much higher in the USA than in places like Korea, and broadband penetration has been slower.

US policy toward the Internet and e-commerce over the past decade was shaped largely by the Clinton–Gore National Information Infrastructure (NII) initiative of 1993 (Kraemer & King, 1996). While the NII initiative preceded commercialization of the Internet, and actually had little to say about the Internet, its principles have largely defined the US policy framework. The NII defined the role of government to include promotion of private-sector investment and technological innovation, universal service, intellectual property protection, privacy and security protection, e-government, and promoting competition in telecommunications. Actual operation of the Internet was transferred from the NSF to a group of Internet backbone providers, while various technical issues were largely managed by international non-profit organizations such as the Internet Engineering Task Force and the Internet Corporation for Assigned Names and Numbers (ICANN).

The US government did not favor particular technologies or standards for telecoms or data communications (unlike Europe with Global System for Mobile Communications (GSM) for wireless and national EDI standards). However, the USA was the first major economy to widely adopt the TCP/IP protocol standards of the Internet in spite of previous official endorsement of the competing OSI suite (Kahin, 1997). US firms built proprietary standards such as Internet Explorer, Cisco's Internet Operating System, and Adobe's PDF on top of the open standards of the Internet.

Policies that perhaps most affected e-commerce in the USA involved taxation, privacy, and intellectual property. By banning specific taxes on online transactions, the federal government in effect subsidized

Table 2.4 *Information infrastructure, 1995–2002*

Economy	*PCs per 1,000 people, 1995*	*PCs per 1,000 people, 2002*	*Telephone mainlines per 1,000 people, 2002*	*Cell phone subscribers per 1,000 people, 2002*	*Internet users per 1,000 people, 1995*	*Internet users per 1,000 people, 2002*	*Broadband households per 1,000 people, 2001*	*Internet total monthly price ($ per 20 hrs use), 2002*
Brazil	17	75	223	201	1	82	8	27.99
China	2	28	167	161	0	46	1	10.14
Denmark	271	577	689	833	38	513	n.a.	17.62
France	135	347	569	647	16	314	35	14.15
Germany	178	431	650	717	18	412	30	14.10
Japan	120	382	558	636	16	449	54	21.12
Mexico	26	82	147	255	1	98	n.a.	22.63
Singapore	202	622	463	791	29	504	117	11.04
Taiwan	98	396	583	1,064	12	382	110	n.a.
USA	328	659	646	488	76	551	96	14.95

Sources: ITU, 2004; OECD, 1996 (data not available for non-OECD countries in study); World Bank, 2004

e-commerce, but also left a confusing patchwork of state sales taxes based on whether firms had a physical presence in a state. As the GEC Survey will show, online vendors opposed strong privacy protection, and privacy regulations remained weak; privacy concerns are much more prevalent in the United States than in Europe. Intellectual property concerns drove the adoption of the 1998 Digital Millennium Copyright Act (DMCA), which was strongly supported by the entertainment industry. The DMCA put strong restrictions on the sale and use of technologies that could be used to make illegal copies of copyrighted software and published works. The success of online music (and later movie) sharing networks such as Napster and Kazaa have led the entertainment industry to take legal action against both file sharers and companies that provide file-sharing technologies, and even to target Internet service providers.

E-commerce readiness

Technology penetration

When the Internet was first commercialized in 1995, the United States had a far greater installed base of PCs and more Internet users relative to population than other countries in the GEC Survey (Table 2.4). By 2002, however, countries such as Denmark and Singapore had closed the gap, while in cell phone use the USA fell behind most other countries in the group. Internet access costs were in the middle of the pack, while broadband penetration fell behind Singapore and Taiwan (and more dramatically behind Korea and Canada, among non-survey economies).

In absolute terms, however, the USA still has the largest installed base of PCs, Internet users, and broadband users. This large installed base encouraged firms to invest in websites and associated IT capabilities to provide information, entertainment, and online shopping services to consumers. Thus, the adoption of the Internet and e-commerce was facilitated by the earlier diffusion of personal computers and local area networks at work and personal computers and modems in the home. Broadband via cable modem and digital subscriber line (DSL) increased the speed with which content could be downloaded from the Internet and engendered a switch to flat-rate user pricing due to competition among the networks.

Table 2.5 *Use of e-commerce technologies in US firms, 2002*

	Establishment size		*Sector*			*Total*	
Percent using . . .	*SME*	*Large*	*Mfg.*	*Distrib.*	*Finance*	*US*	*Global*
Email	100	100	98	100	100	100	99
Website	78	90	85	76	86	80	74
Intranet*	53	78	52	58	57	56	64
Extranet	26	44	30	29	26	29	33
• accessible by suppliers/ business partners	14	36	20	16	16	17	21
• accessible by customers	14	26	19	14	18	16	18
EDI	39	65	58	38	37	43	44
• over private networks	15	30	26	17	5	17	19
• Internet-based	8	9	12	7	10	8	8
• both	15	26	19	13	23	16	16
EFT*	62	65	54	60	82	63	43
Call center*	38	56	48	35	48	41	32

Source: CRITO GEC Survey, 2002
Note: *Indicates statistically significant difference between the USA and the global sample at .05 or greater

To summarize, the United States led other countries on many broad dimensions of Internet and e-commerce development. Broader environment and policy factors help to explain why it was well positioned to adopt e-commerce. An important question then is: "To what extent did this broad national readiness translate into e-commerce readiness and diffusion in firms, and with what impacts?"

Firm-level readiness

Although the US economy is a global leader and rapid adopter of e-commerce infrastructure, at the firm level there is surprisingly little difference in the use of e-commerce technologies between US firms and those in other countries (Table 2.5, Figure 2.1).[4] This is especially

[4] The exception is electronic funds transfer, which is more widely used in all sectors of the US economy than the global sample (Figure 2.1).

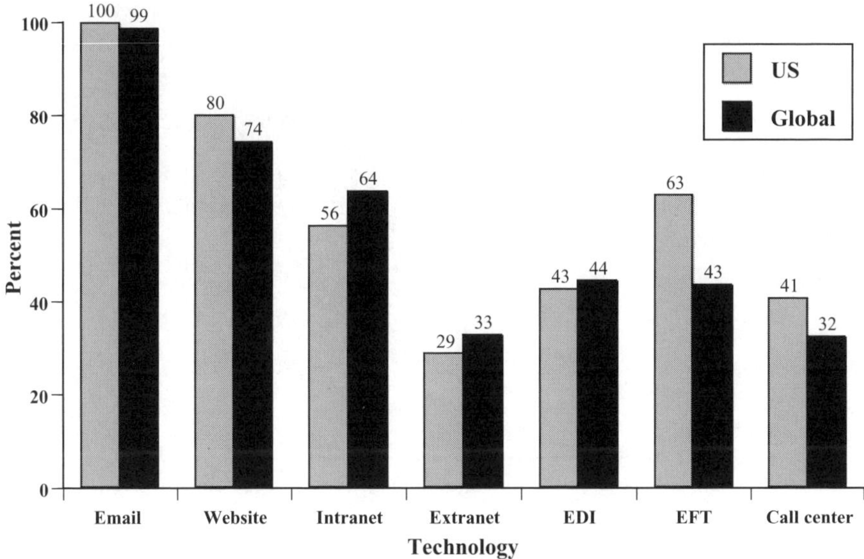

Figure 2.1 Use of e-commerce technologies: US and global firms
Source: CRITO GEC Survey, 2002

surprising given that the global sample includes developing countries such as China, Brazil, and Mexico. However, it should be noted that the survey sample is not representative of entire national economies but just of firms in three sectors that are using the Internet for business. Therefore, the survey data are best seen as comparing US firms to their peers in other countries, rather than comparing the US as a whole to the world.

Among US firms, email usage is virtually universal, and nearly 80% have a website. Intranets are less common (56%), and extranets are used by only 29% of firms. This reflects the varying complexity of these uses, which ranges from very low for email, to quite high for extranets, which require coordination with external partners and sophisticated user interfaces. More large firms than small ones use all of the technologies, and especially the more complex ones. This may be due to their deeper IT capabilities as well as their ability to achieve economies of scale and recoup their initial development costs. Use of Internet-based technologies across industry sectors is similar. Among pre-Internet

Table 2.6 *Investment in IT by US firms, 2002*

	Establishment size		*Sector*			*Total*	
Percent using . . .	*SME*	*Large*	*Mfg.*	*Distrib.*	*Fin.*	*US*	*Global*
PCs per employee	.68	.53	.59	.60	.93	.66	.82
IT employees as percent of total employees	5.51	3.59	3.42	4.90	.04	5.25	9.12
IS operating budget as percent of 2001 revenue	11.08	8.51	6.98	12.94	8.96	10.73	7.75
Web-based spending as percent of IS operating budget	14.61	18.25	13.43	14.63	19.24	15.08	14.89

Source: CRITO GEC Survey, 2002; weighted sample

technologies, manufacturing leads in EDI use, and financial firms are leaders in EFT (Table 2.5).

In general, the pattern of adoption reflects the cost and complexity of implementing different technologies, the internal capabilities of the firms, and to some extent the nature of the task performed by the firm (e.g., EFT for finance). These findings are consistent with diffusion of innovation theories, such as Tornatzky and Klein (1982), Rogers (1995), and Zhu et al. (2003).

IT investment

The resources for developing e-commerce infrastructure in US firms are modest, with only 15% of total IS budgets spent on web-based applications (Table 2.6). Although IS budgets as a percent of firm revenues are greatest in the distribution sector, finance firms spend proportionately more of their IS budgets on web-based applications than those in distribution or manufacturing. Large firms also spend proportionately more than smaller firms. In addition, while large firms spend proportionately more of their IS operating budget on web-based applications, SMEs overall spend proportionately more of their revenues on IS.

Table 2.7 *Enterprise integration strategy, 2002*

Extent to which Internet applications are electronically integrated with . . .	*Establishment size*		*Sector*			*Total*	
	SME	*Large*	*Mfg.*	*Distrib.*	*Finance*	*US*	*Global*
Internal databases/information systems							
Percent little to none	55	40	58	55	37	53	53
Percent some	13	27	21	14	14	15	24
Percent a great deal	32	33	21	31	49	32	24
Those of suppliers/business customers							
Percent little to none	66	75	71	66	65	67	72
Percent some	16	16	14	20	9	17	18
Percent a great deal	18	9	15	14	26	16	10

Source: CRITO GEC Survey, 2002

Enterprise integration

On another dimension of e-commerce readiness – enterprise integration – US firms have integrated their internal and external information systems with the Internet more fully than the global sample (Table 2.7, Figure 2.2). Almost one-third of US firms (versus 24% of global firms) have highly integrated the web with their internal systems and 16% (versus 10% of global firms) have highly integrated their external systems.

The data concerning enterprise integration among firms show that US firms lead other countries' firms in this measure of readiness. They lead in the extent of integration (percent a great deal) of the Internet with their enterprise systems and with the information systems of their suppliers and business customers (Table 2.7). Relatively speaking, then, US firms are more ready for e-commerce than their foreign counterparts, although the gap in integration is not large. Interestingly, about twice as many SMEs report that their applications are integrated with suppliers/customers as do large companies. This could reflect the demands of flagship firms in their value chains, as well as their need for IT integration to protect their position in the value chain and offset their lack of market power (Ernst & Kim, 2001).

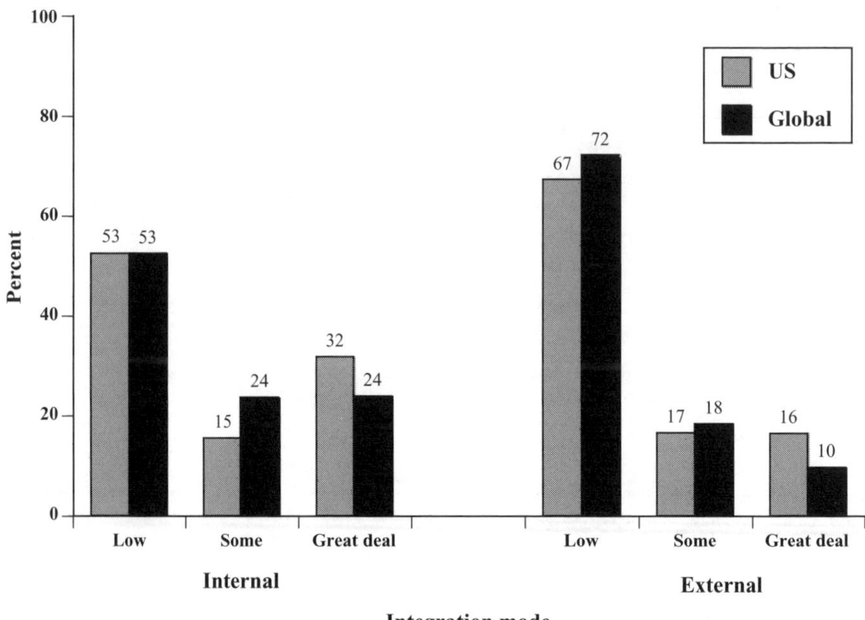

Figure 2.2 Enterprise integration in US firms, 2002
Source: CRITO GEC Survey, 2002

Drivers and barriers to e-commerce

It was difficult for US firms to ignore the combination of greed and fear that marked the Internet boom of the late 1990s. The desire to somehow catch the dot.com magic, or to avoid being "Amazoned" out of business, motivated firms to evaluate and experiment with the Internet and e-commerce. Beyond this point, however, more standard business concerns came into play. The evolution of B2B and B2C e-commerce was driven by a combination of firms' internal strategic and operational goals, and external pressure from customers, suppliers, and competitors.

At the same time, firms faced a variety of potential barriers, ranging from limitations in their own capabilities and those of their business partners, to concerns over legal and regulatory issues. On many of these items, perceived barriers were lower in the USA than in other countries, thanks to the generally favorable environment and policy factors

Table 2.8 *Drivers of e-commerce*

Percent indicating driver is a significant factor	*Establishment size*		*Sector*			*Total*	
	SME	*Large*	*Mfg.*	*Distrib.*	*Finance*	*US*	*Global*
Customers demanded it	34	42	35	34	42	36	37
Major competitors were online	31	46	30	28	56	33	31
Suppliers required it*	18	23	22	19	14	19	22
To reduce costs	32	40	36	30	36	33	36
To expand market for existing product or services*	48	61	52	45	62	50	48
To enter new businesses or markets	38	47	45	39	34	39	42
To improve coordination with customers and suppliers	38	63	51	38	43	42	44
Required for government procurement*	10	6	13	8	5	9	15
Government provided incentives*	4	1	4	4	0	3	8

Source: CRITO GEC Survey, 2002
Note: *Indicates statistically significant difference between the USA and the global sample at .05 or greater

discussed previously. Still, the GEC Survey illustrates some significant concerns, especially around privacy and security.

Drivers

The chief factors driving e-commerce among US firms are the desire to expand markets, to enter new businesses or markets, and to improve coordination in the value chain (Table 2.8, Figure 2.3). These are the same among all firms, and reflect the fact that e-commerce is a market-driven phenomenon. Consistent with US policy to let the private sector implement e-commerce, government regulation and incentives were not important drivers for adoption. They were somewhat more important

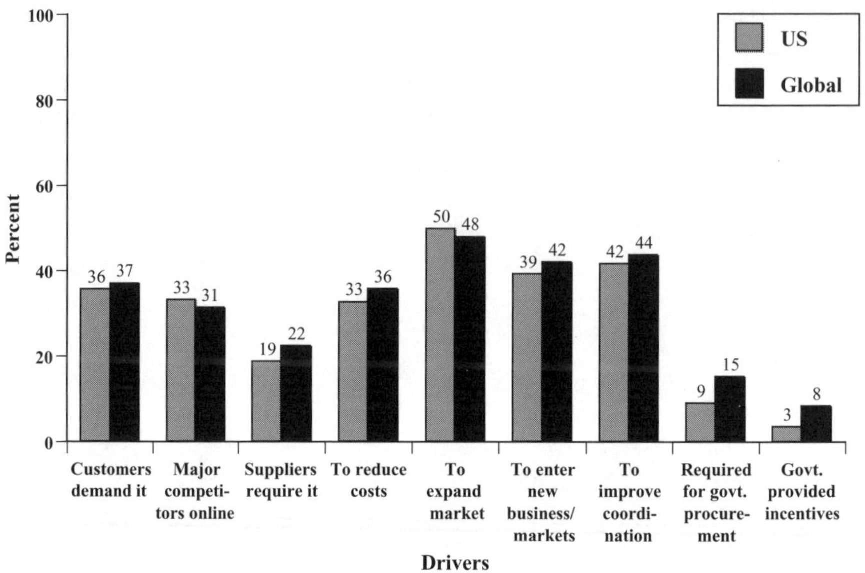

Figure 2.3 Drivers for Internet use for e-commerce, 2002
Source: CRITO GEC Survey, 2002

in the global sample (Figure 2.3), and particularly among developing countries (see chapters on Mexico, China, and Brazil).

Manufacturers and large firms are driven mostly by the desire to expand markets and improve value chain coordination. This is consistent with the earlier finding that manufacturing firms and large firms in the USA are more internationally oriented and seek growth while also needing to improve coordination within their global supply chains. These supply chains include not only their subsidiaries but often overseas suppliers and business partners (Sturgeon, 2002; Gereffi, 2001).

Financial firms are driven by the fact that their competitors are online, as well as by the desire to expand markets. This may reflect the fact that their business is fundamentally based on information transactions, which creates vulnerabilities if competitors offer such transactions in a convenient manner online, but also creates the possibility for expanding markets without necessarily making investments in physical infrastructure (although market expansion in some segments of the financial sector, e.g., banking, is limited by government regulation). The distribution sector is also driven by the desire to expand markets. In this case, the Internet gives wholesalers and retailers a new channel for marketing and advertising, and also the option of selling directly online in areas where they do not have a physical presence.

Barriers

The generally favorable environment for e-commerce development is reflected among firms in the global sample. In particular, the USA has a strong rule of law and financial protections for businesses and consumers, in contrast to other countries, particularly China, Mexico, and Brazil. Cross-country analysis of the GEC Survey data has shown that the general environment for commerce in a country is more important to the level of e-commerce development than specific laws supporting e-commerce (Shih et al., 2005).

The chief barriers to e-commerce development among US firms are concerns about privacy and security, the need for face-to-face interaction in commercial transactions, and the cost of implementing e-commerce (Table 2.9, Figure 2.4). The greatest concern, expressed by 47% of the US firms, was privacy and data security. This suggests a failure of US policy to successfully engage these concerns of firms both as regards to their transactions with other firms as customers or suppliers and to their transactions with consumers. It also suggests failures of US policy to adequately protect consumer privacy and security as firms are likely reflecting views garnered from consumers. Privacy and security concerns are high in developing countries, but are much lower in the three European countries, reflecting the strong privacy protections put in place by the European Union. It is likely that such concerns have increased in recent years as businesses and consumers have become more aware of various forms of online fraud, such as "phishing" for confidential information, as well as highly publicized security breaches by hackers.

Diffusion of e-commerce

The diffusion of e-commerce can be better understood when viewed at the national level and then the firm level using the GEC Survey data. A common way of categorizing e-commerce is to distinguish between B2B

Table 2.9 *Barriers to e-commerce*

Percent indicating statement is a significant obstacle	*Establishment size*		*Sector*			*Total*	
	SME	*Large*	*Mfg.*	*Distrib.*	*Finance*	*US*	*Global*
Need for face-to-face customer interaction	43	32	43	38	54	42	34
Concern about privacy of data or security issues	48	42	49	41	67	47	44
Customers do not use the technology	27	28	18	32	21	27	31
Finding staff with e-commerce expertise	24	22	23	26	21	24	27
Prevalence of credit card use in the country*	18	7	13	19	11	16	20
Costs of implementing an e-commerce site	32	25	27	31	39	32	34
Making needed organizational changes*	14	21	20	13	13	15	24
Level of ability to use the Internet as part of business strategy	21	19	19	22	20	21	25
Cost of Internet access*	12	2	4	12	14	11	15
Business laws do not support e-commerce*	9	2	4	9	10	8	24
Taxation of Internet sales*	16	6	6	21	0	15	16
Inadequate legal protection for Internet purchases*	12	8	12	11	15	12	34

Source: CRITO GEC Survey, 2002

Note: *Indicates statistically significant difference between the USA and the global sample at .05 or greater

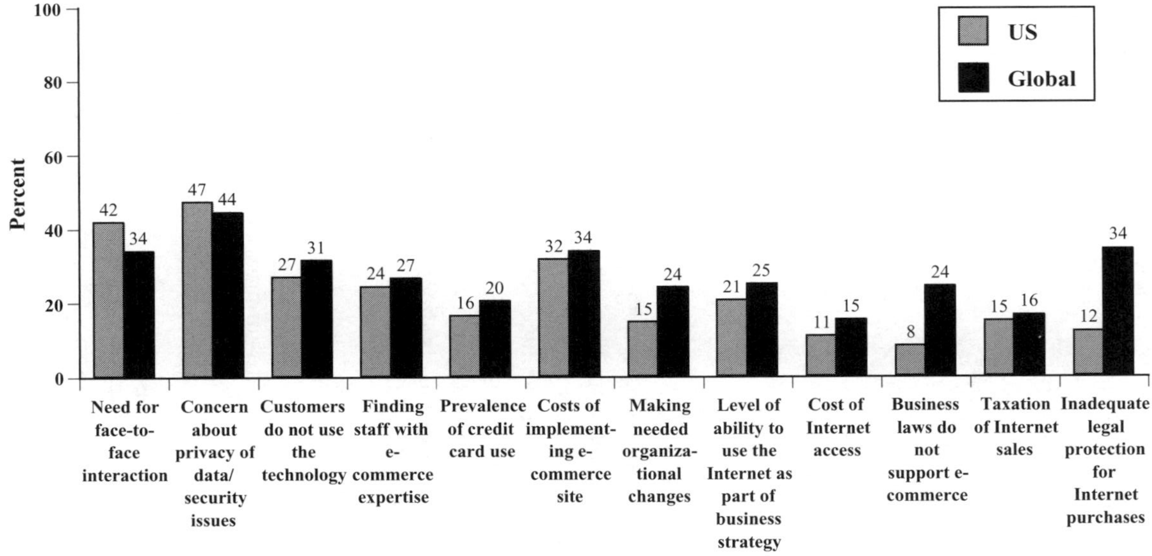

Figure 2.4 Barriers to Internet use for e-commerce (percent indicating barrier is a significant obstacle)
Source: CRITO GEC Survey, 2002

Table 2.10 *US shipments and e-commerce, 2002 (billions of dollars)*

	Value of shipments, sales or revenue	*E-commerce*	*E-commerce as percent of total sales*	*Percent distribution of e-commerce sales*
Total	14,675	1,157	7.8	100
B2B	6,582	1,072	16.2	92.7
Manufacturing	3,840	752	19.6	65.0
Merchant wholesale	2,742	320	11.7	27.7
B2C	8,093	85	1.1	7.3
Retail	3,230	44	1	3.8
Selected services	4,863	41	0.9	3.5

Source: US Census Bureau, 2004
Note: Includes EDI

and B2C transactions. In terms of total sales, B2B clearly dominates B2C e-commerce. B2B e-commerce accounted for 92.7% of total e-commerce whereas B2C accounted for only 7.3% in 2002 (Table 2.10). This partly reflects the large volumes of commerce conducted over existing EDI networks, but even in terms of Internet-based e-commerce, IDC reports that B2B accounts for about 85% of total sales (IDC, 2003a).[5] This is consistent with (although lower than) reports from the US Census Bureau (2004, 2005a).

B2C e-commerce

There was a proliferation of start-up firms between 1995 and 2000, which were intended to replace physical stores with online sales and services. Many of these firms, which were supported by exuberant venture capital and IPO funds, burned through their funding and eventually went out of business when the dot.com bubble burst in 2001. Some were bought out for large sums prior to the bust (e.g., Geocities, Excite), while others were picked up cheaply afterwards.

[5] Due to differences in definitions and data-collection methods, it is difficult to make meaningful comparisons of data from different sources. For instance, the US Census Bureau (2004) includes EDI, while IDC (2003a) does not. Also, there are different definitions as to what qualifies as an e-commerce transaction, e.g., whether payment must be made online or not.

However, the dot.coms stimulated traditional retail firms to act. Both Barnes and Noble and Borders developed online sales to counter the Amazon threat, as did others in the retail industry such as Wal-Mart, Target, and Office Depot, in reaction to Amazon and others. This pattern was repeated by traditional firms in other sectors when potential dot.com challengers moved into music, videos, toys, consumer electronics, computer games, wine, etc.

In the post-bubble era, there has been consolidation in B2C e-commerce, led by the two dominant pure Internet firms which had built a strong customer base and robust IT capabilities that could be leveraged by others. Amazon has relationships with the online businesses of major retailers such as Borders, Target, Nordstrom, Land's End, and many others, ranging from running the online business (Borders) to "powered by Amazon" (Target) to "featured" retailer relationships (Land's End, Office Depot). At the other end of the spectrum, eBay is the dominant platform for thousands of small businesses to do business online as well as for its more familiar consumer-to-consumer (C2C) sales. In fact, eBay's own survey claims that 430,000 people now earn a significant part of their income by selling on eBay (San Jose Mercury News, 2004).

E-commerce accounts for less than 2% of total retail sales but has captured a larger share of some specialized consumer-oriented businesses such as travel reservations, where it was 24.1% of total revenue in 2002 (US Census Bureau, 2004). This type of information-based service is a good fit for the Internet, as transactions can be handled entirely online. In the financial sector, new firms emerged in the online stock trading market (eTrade), but online banking was largely an extension of the traditional banking sector, with little impact from pure-play online banks. So far, the more significant use of the Internet by consumers has been for information gathering. Many consumers would not go to a car dealer or electronics retailer without at least checking the Internet for product reviews and price information, which is available from retailers, manufacturers, and independent websites such as ConsumerReports.com, Cars.com, or Edmunds.com.

Retail e-commerce in the United States is growing slowly but steadily, despite the collapse of the dot.coms. For example, retail e-commerce was 1% of total retail sales in 2002 compared with 0.7% in 1999, and reached 1.9% in 2004 (US Census Bureau, 2005b).

Non-store retailers – namely catalog firms and online firms (US Census Bureau, 2004) such as Lands' End, Spiegel, eBay, uBid,

Table 2.11 *Top twenty US Internet retailers, 2000*

Rank	*Company*	*Online sales ($)*	*Existing*	*Start-up*
1	eBay	3.5–3.7bn		•
2	Amazon.com	1.7–1.9bn		•
3	Dell	1.1–1.3bn	•	
4	Buy.com	700–800m		•
5	Egghead.com	500–600m	•	
6	Gateway	500–600m	•	
7	Quixtar	400–450m		•
8	uBid	275–325m		•
9	Barnes and Noble	275–325m	•	
10	Cyberian Outpost	200–250m		•
11	Value America*	200–250m	•	
12	MicroWarehouse	200–250m	•	
13	Office Depot	175–200m	•	
14	eToys.com	150–175m		•
15	Lands' End	150–175m	•	
16	The Spiegel Group	150–175m	•	
17	Fingerhut	150–175m	•	
18	CDW	150–175m	•	
19	JCPenney	150–175m	•	
20	Gap	125–150m	•	

Source: National Retail Federation, 2000 in Fomin et al., 2003
Notes: Sales to US customers only. *Ceased retail operations

Amazon.com, and Buy.com – account for 75% of retail e-commerce. Most are not pure Internet companies however, as the definition used by the Census Bureau includes the online sales of traditional retailers if they operate a separate e-commerce unit (such as BarnesandNoble.com). Of the top twenty firms in online sales in 2000, more than 65% were existing companies rather than start-ups (Table 2.11). This reinforces the idea that e-commerce is an extension of existing patterns rather than a disruption.

B2B e-commerce

Shortly after new firms emerged in B2C, they also emerged in B2B, including online exchanges that were expected to change the structure of supply chains in many industries. Some exchanges succeeded, or at least grew, such as Covisint in the auto industry, but most failed (e.g., Ventro – previously Chemdex – in the life sciences and medical equipment industries). Helper and MacDuffie (2003) observed that fewer than 20% of the 1,000 B2B exchanges that existed in 2000 would survive in any form. The problems leading to failure were the unwillingness of firms to make information available to competitors, customers, or suppliers; power issues and lack of trust among members of the exchanges; inability to achieve standards that facilitated interoperability; and inability to attract enough guaranteed participation to achieve scale and liquidity (Helper & MacDuffie, 2003; Kenney, 2003).

Unlike B2C, in which Internet start-ups played a key role, the largest and most visible B2B users were traditional firms in the manufacturing and distribution sectors that already used EDI with their business partners, e.g., Intel, Cisco, Dell, GM, and Ford. In some cases they have migrated transactions from EDI to the Internet because of its open standards, lower cost, greater flexibility, and ease of use. They also created business networks that were private exchanges but used the technology of the public exchanges. For instance, a company called Viacore now hosts private exchanges using RosettaNet standards for several major electronics companies.

As of 2002, e-commerce represented 19.6% of the total value of manufacturing shipments and 11.7% of wholesale trade (US Census Bureau, 2004). The percentages were similar for 2003 (US Census Bureau, 2005a). E-commerce in the manufacturing sector was dominated by the transportation equipment industry, which accounted for 40% of all e-commerce in the sector in 2002. Automakers are heavy users of EDI with their suppliers and dealers, and e-commerce accounted for 48% of their revenues.

EDI still accounts for a significant share of B2B e-commerce (for instance, 86% of merchant wholesale e-commerce, US Census Bureau, 2004), but it is now being moved from costly private networks to the web and complemented by newer web-based tools using XML, RosettaNet, and other standards to automate inter-firm processes. This has increased the speed and accuracy and lowered the cost of exchanging data across firms, improving supply chain efficiency. It also has led to widespread adoption of e-commerce technologies by suppliers of lead firms, which require their suppliers to do business electronically.

The other large segment of B2B e-commerce is accounted for by wholesale trade. Wal-Mart, the $250 billion retailer, runs its own B2B exchange with suppliers and requires them to adopt specific technologies (e.g., bar coding, EDI, XML) and conform to process requirements such as vendor-managed inventory that use these technologies (McKinsey Global Institute, 2001). B2B exchanges also have been developed to link wholesalers to retailers, such as Worldwide Retail Exchange and Global Net Exchange.

The B2B side of the financial sector has long been heavily dependent on IT for clearing banking transactions, processing insurance claims, and handling stock trades. The use of e-commerce by loan aggregators such as Fannie Mae and Freddie Mac is helping to support a consolidation in the mortgage brokerage industry (Markus et al., 2003)

Firm level

At the firm level, the GEC Survey shows "making sales online" is generally the lowest use of the Internet by firms in all surveyed economies (Table 2.12). This is also true for the USA, although larger firms and the distribution sector make considerably greater use than small firms or the manufacturing and finance sectors. Consistent with US global leadership in e-commerce, the percent of US firms doing online sales is considerably larger than the global sample (43% vs. 30%).

In contrast to the low use of online sales among US firms, the survey data show that 64% of all firms are using the Internet for advertising and marketing, 56% for after-sales service and support, and 54% for exchanging data with suppliers and business customers. This pattern exists among all three sectors, and is generally higher than the global sample (Table 2.12). It is consistent with the argument that the Internet is primarily a vehicle for exchanging information rather than making sales, at least so far.

Online sales and procurement

The GEC Survey data indicate that only 43% of US firms sell online, while 73% purchase online. Likewise, only about 5% of US firms' total sales are online, whether B2C or B2B (Table 2.13), but manufacturing firms buy 11% of their direct goods for production online, distribution firms buy 11% of their goods for resale online, and firms in all sectors buy around 20% of their supplies and equipment online

Table 2.12 ***Uses of the Internet, 2002***

Percent using the Internet for . . .	*Establishment size*		*Sector*			*Total*	
	SME	*Large*	*Mfg.*	*Distrib.*	*Finance*	*US*	*Global*
Advertising and marketing purposes*	62	78	71	57	81	64	58
Making sales online*	42	55	28	52	32	43	30
After-sales customer service and support*	54	66	58	55	56	56	44
Making purchases online*	72	80	77	71	76	73	47
Exchanging operational data with suppliers	41	55	46	42	41	43	48
Exchanging operational data with business customers*	52	65	65	47	64	54	51
Formally integrating the same business processes with suppliers or other business partners	35	41	38	34	36	36	34

Source: CRITO GEC Survey, 2002
Note: *Indicates statistically significant difference between the USA and the global sample at .05 or greater

(Table 2.13). The heavier use of the Internet to purchase than to sell is consistent with the argument that adoption and use are inversely related to the complexity of the activity. It is possible to purchase online with little more than a credit card, while selling online involves a greater investment in technology, marketing, and delivery processes.

In terms of online sales and procurement, the USA clearly leads the global sample. This reflects the greater willingness of US firms and consumers to conduct transactions online, even though they are not much more likely to use the Internet to exchange information. This may be explained by the earlier evidence that the USA has a relatively good infrastructure, as well as the legal and regulatory environment, to support online transactions.

Online services

As many as one-third of US firms provide online services of some kind (B2C, B2B, or both), but the percent of total services conducted online

Table 2.13 *Firm online sales and procurement*

	Establishment size		*Sector*			*Total*	
	SME	*Large*	*Mfg.*	*Distrib.*	*Finance*	*US*	*Global*
Online sales							
Mean percent of total consumer sales conducted online (all establishments)*	5	4	5	5	6	5	4
Mean percent of total business sales conducted online (all establishments)	5	6	2	7	3	6	4
Online procurement							
Mean percent of money spent for direct goods for production is ordered online (all establishments)	9	14	11			11	8
Mean percent of money spent on goods for resale is ordered online (all establishments)	11	4		11		11	7
Mean percent of money spent on supplies and equipment for doing business is ordered online (all establishments)*	19	20	17	19	23	19	8

Source: CRITO GEC Survey, 2002
Note: *Indicates statistically significant difference between the USA and the global sample at .05 or greater

is small, at 7% for consumer services and 14% for business services (Table 2.14). Within manufacturing, sales-oriented services lead, with product specifications provided by 81% of the firms and product configuration by 51%. Service and technical support are provided by 56% of the firms, but order tracking and account information are provided by 20% or less. This emphasis on sales-oriented services is consistent

Table 2.14 *Online services, 2002*

	Establishment size		*Sector*			*Total*	
	SME	*Large*	*Mfg.*	*Distrib.*	*Finance*	*US*	*Global*
Type of online service							
Percent B2B only	19	30	36	17	10	20	23
Percent B2C only	23	15	12	22	36	22	13
Percent both B2B and B2C	33	45	36	34	36	35	33
Mean percent of total consumer services conducted online	8	5	4	8	13	7	8
Mean percent of total business services conducted online	14	12	21	11	30	14	11
Percent of manufacturing websites which support							
Product configuration	54	43	51			51	55
Order tracking	18	26	20			20	22
Service and technical support	58	51	56			56	54
Product specification	82	79	81			81	80
Account information	14	19	16			16	17
Percent of wholesale/retail distribution websites which support							
Gift certificates and/or registry	19	56		23		23	21
Product catalog	58	84		61		61	70
Product reviews	54	64		55		55	49
Individual customization	34	58		37		37	21
Account information	36	36		36		36	22
Percent of banking and insurance websites supporting . . .							
Online services such as filing applications, filing claims, paying bills, transferring funds	52	61			53	53	54
Access to account information	61	76			62	62	57
Online tools such as research tools, planning tools, etc.	63	64			63	63	52

Source: CRITO GEC Survey, 2002

Table 2.15 *How firms use the Internet to sell products and services*

Percent indicating Internet used to . . .	*Establishment size*		*Sector*			*Total*	
	SME	*Large*	*Mfg.*	*Distrib.*	*Finance*	*US*	*Global*
Address new markets only	10	2	12	8	5	8	15
Address traditional distribution channels only	46	39	50	47	20	45	44
Compete directly with traditional distribution channels	25	50	24	25	60	29	27
Replace traditional distribution channels	20	9	15	19	15	18	13

Source: CRITO GEC Survey, 2002

with the strong role that marketing and advertising play in firm motivations for using the Internet.

The same pattern holds in distribution where the emphasis is on product catalog and product reviews. In contrast, the banking and insurance sectors within finance are more transaction oriented, providing planning tools, account information, and services related to paying bills, transferring funds, or filing applications and claims.

Distribution strategies

A major issue which firms face as they contemplate selling online is channel conflict, which is the risk that by competing with existing distribution channels they will simply cannibalize sales and alienate their own sales channel. Fear of channel conflict and lost sales has long inhibited PC makers such as HP, Compaq, and IBM from shifting to a direct sales model to compete with Dell (Dedrick & Kraemer, 2002). When retailers have sufficient market power, they may use that power to restrict their suppliers' online sales. For instance, Home Depot is said to prohibit many suppliers from competing with it by selling online.

US firms in the survey most often use the Internet to address existing distribution channels (45%), but a significant number (29%) compete directly with their traditional channels or replace those channels with the Internet (18%) (Table 2.15). A few (8%) use the Internet only to reach new markets and thus avoid problems of channel conflict. Interestingly, large firms are more likely to compete directly with

Table 2.16 *Participation in an Internet-based trading community, 2002*

	Establishment size		*Sector*			*Total*	
	SME	*Large*	*Mfg.*	*Distrib.*	*Finance*	*US*	*Global*
Percent who have heard of the concept of an Internet marketplace*	71	81	78	69	77	72	80
Of those who have heard . . .							
Percent participating as a buyer only*	13	19	19	8	53	14	7
Percent participating as a seller only*	31	40	39	32	6	32	12
Percent participating as both a buyer and a seller*	47	29	35	50	31	45	17
Percent not participating*	9	12	7	11	11	10	64

Source: CRITO GEC Survey, 2002
Note: *Indicates statistically significant difference between the USA and the global sample at .05 or greater

their traditional channels, perhaps reflecting their greater market power. Among the sectors, financial services firms are much more likely to compete with their traditional channels, which are often their own outlets (e.g., banks) or agents (insurance companies), both of which are captive channels which cannot just switch to another supplier.

Internet trading communities

US firms show a very different pattern from the global sample in their participation in Internet-based trading communities. While more global firms had heard of such communities (80% versus 72%), only 36% of global firms were participating in them, compared with 90% of US firms[6] (including 45% which participate as both buyers and sellers) (Table 2.16). This suggests that US firms are much more comfortable with the trading community concept, which has antecedents in

[6] These numbers have been calculated by adding all three categories of "percent participating" in Table 2.16.

popular buyers' clubs. Also, the US data could include firms which buy or sell surplus items on eBay, Overstock.com, or similar exchanges. Other evidence suggests that firms are not buying much of their manufacturing inputs or goods for resale, i.e., their "bread and butter," in such exchanges.

The overall picture is one of widespread but cautious adoption. Firms are more likely to use the Internet to buy items such as office supplies or equipment than to purchase more strategic items such as manufacturing inputs. While the majority of firms use the Internet for purchasing, it accounts for only a small share of total volume. The same is true at a lower level for online sales. The data also indicate that US firms are using the Internet and e-commerce to reinforce their existing business relationships, or to extend their business into new markets, rather than to disrupt their value chains or disintermediate business partners such as wholesalers or retailers. This cautiousness stands in contrast to the "revolutionary" rhetoric that surrounded the Internet and e-commerce in earlier times.

Impacts of e-commerce

The relatively low penetration of e-commerce into overall commerce and the pattern of adaptation of e-commerce into existing business processes and practices suggest that the impacts so far would be mainly reinforcing and negligible. There is some support for this view, but the pattern of impacts is actually richer and more nuanced.

National impacts

When the Internet and e-commerce investment is considered at the national level as part of the exuberant IT investment that occurred from 1995 to 2000, it is likely that it also contributed to the exceptional gains in productivity and economic growth that were witnessed during the period (Jorgenson, 2001). Because the investment was greater in the USA than in other countries, the impact was also greater (Daveri, 2000). Thus, Internet- and e-commerce-induced spending reinforced the existing contribution of IT investment to the US economy. A study by Litan and Rivlin (2001) estimated the likely productivity impact from the Internet across eight industry sectors which account for about 70% of the nation's GDP. While admittedly speculative, the study estimates that the impact of the Internet over five years could translate into an annual contribution of 0.2–0.4% to the baseline trend of productivity growth.

From another perspective, billions of dollars were invested in startups that went broke, so the dot.com boom and bust clearly had costs for the economy as well. Interestingly, overinvestment in Internet infrastructure led to disaster for firms building out the infrastructure (such as companies like Cisco and Sun), but also drove down bandwidth costs to a level that now is a boon to Internet service and content providers and their customers.

Firm-level impacts

Much of the literature on the Internet and e-commerce has emphasized their potential impact on firm competitiveness. Consequently, market growth and keeping up with competitors have been major motivators for firms to invest in e-business. Less emphasis was initially placed on the benefits to firm efficiency but these impacts have also come to the fore as firms have gained experience.

Sales impacts

Consistent with the national and firm-level online sales outlined earlier, few US firms report high impact on increased overall sales (24%) or international sales (9%) (Table 2.17). However, 40% report high impact on improved customer service and 36% report their sales area has widened. Also consistent with the pattern of gradual growth of online sales, it is possible that the widened sales area and improved customer service will translate into increased sales in the future as businesses and consumers become more accustomed to Internet transactions.

The global sample has twice the percent of firms reporting increased international sales, which reflects the relatively low level of globalization of US firms. Among US firms, manufacturers were twice as likely as the other sectors to report increased international sales, again reflecting the greater international orientation of that sector. Surprisingly, there was no significant difference between large and small firms on this measure.

Table 2.17 *Impacts of doing business online, 2002*

Percent indicating high impact	*Establishment size*		*Sector*			*Total*	
	SME	*Large*	*Mfg.*	*Distrib.*	*Finance*	*US*	*Global*
Sales impacts							
Customer service improved	39	48	40	40	41	40	35
Sales area widened*	35	39	39	35	35	36	31
Sales increased	22	34	26	26	16	24	21
International sales increased*	9	10	14	7	8	9	20
Efficiency impacts							
Staff productivity increased	31	32	29	29	39	31	27
Coordination w/suppliers improved	28	35	33	27	33	29	30
Internal processes more efficient	26	38	35	23	36	28	34
Procurement costs decreased	12	14	18	9	18	13	18
Inventory costs decreased	10	14	6	11	18	11	14
Competitive impacts							
Competitive position improved	32	44	37	32	32	33	30

Source: CRITO GEC Survey, 2002

Note: *Indicates statistically significant difference between the USA and the global sample at .05 or greater

Efficiency impacts

A similar proportion of US firms report high impact on different measures of efficiency, including increased staff productivity (31%), improved coordination with suppliers (29%), and more efficient internal processes (28%). Thus, while e-commerce is often seen as a sales and marketing tool, its impacts on efficiency are greater than its impact on sales. These higher impacts are all consistent with the pattern of use seen earlier where firms emphasized adaptation and integration of the technology into existing business processes and practices.

Real cost reductions in procurement (12%) and inventory (11%) were reported by far fewer firms. This appears to be related to the

Table 2.18 *Association between external integration and costs*

	External integration			
Extent procurement costs decreased (%)	*Low*	*Medium*	*High*	*Total*
Not at all	62	49	29	55
Somewhat	22	38	40	27
A great deal	16	13	31	18
Extent inventory costs decreased (%)	Low	Medium	High	Total
Not at all	74	50	49	66
Somewhat	16	29	35	21
A great deal	10	21	16	13

Source: CRITO GEC Survey, 2002

nascent level of inter-firm integration in the global sample because other research indicates that firms which are more integrated with partners in their value chains show considerable cost and inventory reductions (Dedrick & Kraemer, 2005; McKinsey Global Institute, 2001). This is also the case among US firms that are more integrated, as firms with higher levels of external integration are more likely to report that procurement and inventory costs declined a great deal (Table 2.18).[7]

Firm competitiveness

The GEC Survey indicates that one-third of US firms reported a high impact when stating that their competitive position improved as a result of using the Internet for business. More large firms than small firms report this impact, and more manufacturing firms report this particular impact although sector differences are not large. On an international comparison, only a slightly higher share of US firms than global firms reported that their competitive position improved.

Given the multiple impacts of e-commerce on efficiency (process, staff, coordination, cost) outlined above, one would expect that firm efficiency has been a major contributor to the improved competitive position of the US firms. And indeed it has, but it appears that increased sales, and particularly improved customer service, have also been salient. That is, both sales and efficiency impacts are strongly

[7] The correlation between "external integration" and "procurement costs decreased" = .27 and with "inventory costs decreased" = .22 and is statistically significant (US firms). The result is similar for the global sample.

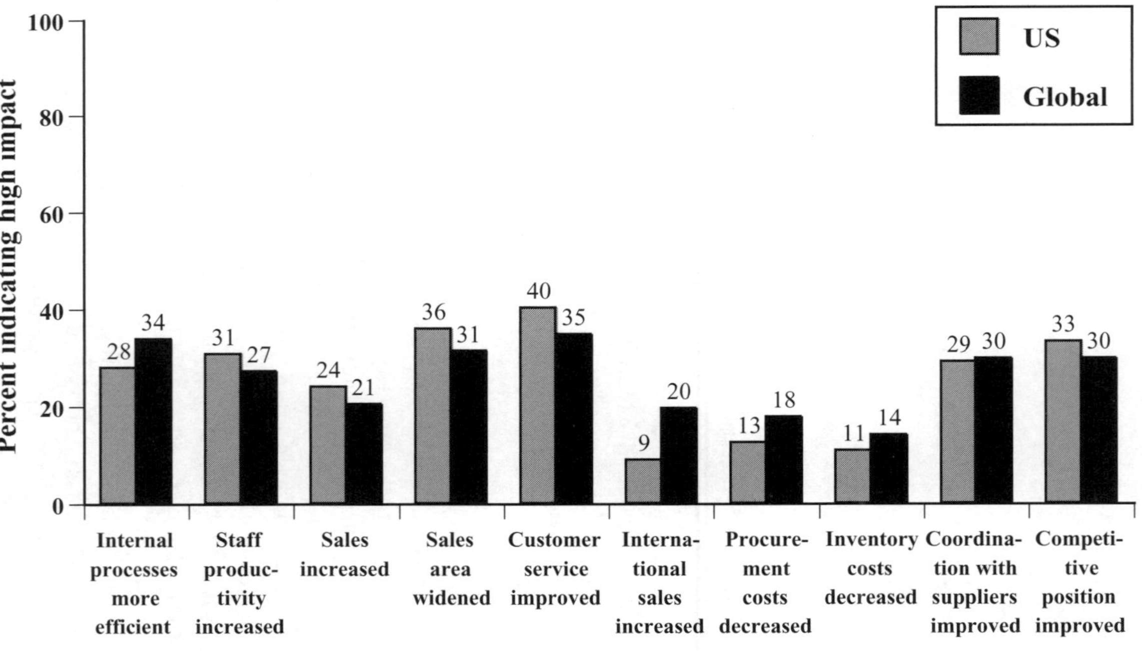

Figure 2.5 Impacts from use of the Internet for e-commerce
Source: CRITO GEC Survey, 2002

related to firm competitiveness. The correlation of sales with improved competitive position is 0.678 and efficiency is 0.426; together they explain 58% of the variance in the US sample (see Figure 2.5).

Impacts on number of suppliers and customers

There has been a debate in the academic literature as to whether e-commerce would lead firms to increase or decrease their number of business partners. Malone et al. (1987) predicted a shift from internal production to more market relationships with more firms. Clemons et al. (1993) argued that firms would outsource more production but use a smaller number of suppliers to reduce transaction costs. At the firm level, there are examples of firms drastically reducing the number of front-line suppliers (e.g., Dell and Cisco have streamlined their supply base) and distributors (Compaq went from thirty-nine to four distributors; Apple eliminated most of its retail relationships).

The GEC Survey data clearly show a trend toward a greater number of both distribution channels and suppliers (Table 2.19). While most US firms reported no change, 45% reported an increase in distribution channels, while only 5% reported a decrease, and 34% reported an increase in suppliers, while only 12% reported a decrease. This suggests that the Internet is reducing transaction costs (e.g., finding, negotiating with, and monitoring partners) and expanding the scope of firms' business networks. At the same time, firms also reported a greater number of competitors (29% increased versus 12% decreased) and intensity of competition (38% increased versus 5% decreased). Thus, as firms expand their reach, they also find more competition, or competition finds them.

The result is that firms are operating in a more complex world, in terms of both their own networks and their competitive environment. Whether this is caused by the Internet, or the Internet is a response to dealing with greater complexity, is unclear; probably both are true. One factor behind the increased complexity is the ongoing process of economic globalization which has increased the opportunities for new markets and new relationships in distribution and supply, while also increasing the number of competitors and the intensity of competition among firms. Support for this interpretation is provided by the fact that manufacturing firms are the most likely to report an increase in number of suppliers and in intensity of competition, and as seen earlier, the manufacturing sector is the most global of the three.

Table 2.19 *Changes in firms' environment since using the Internet*

	Establishment size		*Sector*			*Total*	
Percent indicating . . .	*SME*	*Large*	*Mfg.*	*Distrib.*	*Finance*	*US*	*Global*
Number of distribution channels*							
Increased	46	42	49	44	44	45	40
No change	48	57	45	49	56	49	56
Decreased	6	1	6	6	0	5	4
Number of suppliers*							
Increased	34	35	48	29	34	34	30
No change	54	57	41	59	56	54	64
Decreased	12	8	11	12	9.7	12	6
Number of competitors*							
Increased	28	34	30	28	28	29	28
No change	61	53	55	61	62	60	67
Decreased	11	13	14	11	10	12	5
Intensity of competition*							
Increased	37	45	52	32	38	38	42
No change	59	48	43	63	58	57	54
Decreased	5	7	6	5	4	5	4

Source: CRITO GEC Survey, 2002

Note: *Indicates statistically significant difference between the USA and the global sample at .05 or greater

Conclusion

At both the national and firm level, it is clear that the US pattern of e-commerce development is distinctive. The Silicon Valley model is an important early pattern, but it is neither a complete description of the US experience, nor the dominant pattern. The US pattern is best characterized as adaptive integration in which firms adapt those uses of the technology that best fit with their existing business processes and inter-firm relationships.

Specific features of the US pattern include widespread adoption of open Internet standards; new business models such as portals (Yahoo!), the online mall (Amazon), and online auctions (eBay); and private exchanges formed by industry consortia or flagship firms. Many of these have been extended abroad through US companies or through local companies adopting these features.

E-commerce must be judged as still relatively immature in the United States. Using comparable datasets at both the country and firm level, the USA leads other countries in information infrastructure, e-commerce uses, and B2B and B2C sales. However, e-commerce sales as a percent of total sales are a small percentage at both the national and firm levels.

As might be expected given how e-commerce "fits in" with existing business practices, it has not fundamentally changed the way business is done, at least not yet. Existing structures for commerce are more efficient, transparent, responsive, and competitive, as illustrated by the impacts on efficiency, customer satisfaction, supply chain coordination, and the competitive position of US firms. E-commerce has not resulted in widespread disintermediation as firms see the Internet more as a complementary channel than as a substitute for traditional channels. In addition, it has not dramatically changed the supply chain; rather, it has been incorporated into existing relationships in firms' value chains.

E-commerce has not dramatically changed the nature of consumption either. It has put more power in the hands of consumers in comparison shopping for features and price and has increased convenience for some consumers and businesses. However, most shopping is still conducted in stores, not online. Most consumers still apparently want to try on clothing, inspect produce, or listen to a stereo system before purchasing. Given the widespread presence and convenience of major retail chains and shopping centers, it is still easier and faster to get in the car and go to a store than to place an order online and wait several days for delivery. B2C e-commerce should continue to grow as consumers become more accustomed to shopping online and retailers improve their service and reliability, but it is unlikely to empty the parking lots of Wal-Marts and shopping malls around America as was once feared.

The bigger story of e-commerce is happening upstream in the supply chain, where it is invisible to the average consumer except perhaps in the form of lower prices. B2B e-commerce is already very large in the USA, mostly because of existing EDI networks that handle large volumes of transactions. With the Internet, however, the other 98% of US firms that could not afford to implement EDI have the potential for conducting B2B e-commerce, which could lead to new opportunities for SMEs as well as serious risk for those which are not able to adapt. For larger firms, Internet technologies such as XML are less costly and more flexible than EDI, and will encourage more widespread e-commerce use. The fact that the auto industry accounts for nearly half of the B2B e-commerce volume in the manufacturing sector suggests that there are many other sub-sectors with plenty of room for growth.

When we consider why e-commerce has not had the expected impacts, there are several obvious and less obvious explanations. First, it is now clear that expectations were overblown and unrealistic. Second, e-commerce has proved to be more difficult to implement, given the size of the US economy, the state of infrastructure development nationally and within firms, and the extent of organizational, buyer, and seller learning that has to occur for e-commerce to take off. An important question, therefore, is whether there is reason to believe that e-commerce will have transformative impacts when it reaches scale – when a majority of businesses, governments, and households are using the Internet for commerce.

The answer to this question will probably vary by industry sector. For instance, the direct sales model for PCs has been around since Dell and Gateway entered the business in 1984–1985, yet it never captured more than 10% of the market until Dell began selling online in 1995. Since then, Dell has grown to a 30% market share in the USA, and other PC makers have increased their direct sales. A byproduct has been the disappearance of several of the largest distributors and many retailers, not to mention PC makers. Other factors were involved as well, but it is not unrealistic to credit the Internet as playing a major role in the transformation of the PC industry. Yet there has been no radical change in the upstream supply chains of the PC industry, even though e-commerce has been applied quite extensively between PC makers and suppliers; here the technology was used to augment existing relationships.

In other industries, there are serious obstacles to major change. For instance, state regulations requiring consumers to purchase automobiles through local dealerships prevent any radical change in the way cars are sold and distributed. Banking regulations limit the activities of banks across state lines. The need for face-to-face interaction limits the role and impacts of e-commerce in many service industries. Also, the cost of implementing e-commerce is not a one-time investment, as additional costs are borne as new business partners are added. So, while firms on average increase their number of business partners when they go online, there may be a tendency to consolidate and focus this investment as more e-commerce encompasses more complex processes that require richer links between firms.

As we have illustrated throughout this chapter, and as Helper and MacDuffie's (2003) analysis of B2B in the auto industry demonstrates, businesses adapt the technology to fit their existing practices and relationships. Thus, independent B2B exchanges, which threatened existing relationships in industries, failed to develop, whereas private exchanges led by a flagship firm or industry consortia are succeeding because the implications for ownership and control are clear. These exchanges also do not threaten firms' power the way public exchanges can. A public exchange allows buyers and sellers to see information from both competitors and business partners; this information can be used to negotiate as well as to set competitive strategy, and while everyone would like to have more information available for their own use, firms are loath to reveal their cost and supply information to others.

There are also examples of changes in kind that might be emerging that do not show up in national accounts or in the type of survey conducted by the GEC. For instance, we earlier cited an eBay report that over 430,000 people are making some or all of their living selling on eBay, including individuals and small businesses in remote parts of the country. With eBay providing the platform for marketing, selling, and payment, an individual or small business can realistically operate online with limited technological skills and investment. This is a step toward the original promise of the Internet, i.e., that it would reduce the importance of location and distance and allow individuals to reach a national or even international market online. Such a trend is no threat to Wal-Mart or Toyota, but it is an opportunity for individuals with an entrepreneurial bent.

It also has possible implications for rural areas and smaller cities that have lost jobs as farming has died and factories have moved offshore, followed more recently by the call centers that were supposed to be their salvation. Those places will never likely attract the so-called "creative class" (Florida, 2002), or develop the kinds of dynamic industry clusters seen in Silicon Valley and elsewhere. But they also do not suffer from the negative externalities found in technology hubs such as traffic congestion and steep housing prices, and for many they offer social benefits of strong community ties. While eBay might not lead to the revitalization of rural America, it does provide an alternative to people in those places who may be more creative than they are given credit for. All of this points to the need for tracking e-commerce over time to determine the nature and extent of the changes that are actually occurring.

References

BRIE-IGCC E-conomy Project (2001). *Tracking a Transformation: E-commerce and the Terms of Competition in Industries*. Washington, D.C.: Brookings Institution Press.

Clemons, E. K., Reddi, S. P., & Row, M. C. (1993). The Impact of Information Technology on the Organization of Economic Activity: The "Move to the Middle" Hypothesis. *Journal of Management Information Systems*, 10(2), 9–35.

Cohen, S. S., Delong, J. B., Weber, S., & Zysman, J. (2001). Tools: The Drivers of E-Commerce. In The BRIE-IGCC E-conomy Project, *Tracking a Transformation: E-commerce and the Terms of Competition in Industries*. Washington, D.C.: Brookings Institution Press, pp. 3–26.

Daveri, F. (2000). Is Growth an Information Technology Story in Europe Too? Working Paper, Parma, Italy: Universita di Parma, September 12.

Dedrick, J. & Kraemer, K. L. (2002). Globalization of the Personal Computer Industry: Trends and Implications. Working Paper, Irvine, CA: CRITO.

Dedrick, J. & Kraemer, K. L. (2005). The Impacts of IT on Firm and Industry Structure: The Personal Computer Industry. *California Management Review*, 47(3), 122–142.

Dutton, W. H., Kahin, B., O'Callaghan, R., & Wyckoff, A. W. (Eds.) (2005). *Transforming Enterprise: The Economic and Social Implications of Information Technology*. Cambridge, MA: MIT Press.

Ernst, D. & Kim, L. (2001). Global Production Networks, Knowledge Diffusion, and Local Capability Formation: A Conceptual Framework. Working Paper, Honolulu, HI: East–West Center.

Florida, R. (2002). *Rise of the Creative Class*. New York: Basic Books.

Fomin, V. V., King, J. L., Lyytinen, K. J., & McGann, S. T. (2003). Diffusion and Impacts of E-Commerce in the United States of America: Results from an Industry Survey. Working Paper, Irvine, CA: CRITO.

Gates, B., Myhrvold, N., & Rinearson, P. (1995). *The Road Ahead*. New York: Viking.

Gereffi, G. (2001). Shifting Governance Structures in Global Commodity Chains, with Special Reference to the Internet. *American Behavioral Scientist*, 44(10), 1616–1637.

Helper, S. & MacDuffie, J. P. (2003). Suppliers and Intermediaries. In B. Kogut (Ed.), *The Global Internet Economy*. Cambridge, MA: MIT Press, 331–380.

International Data Corporation (IDC) (2003a). *EIM-Country View*. Framingham, MA.

International Data Corporation (IDC) (2003b). *Internet Commerce Market Model v.8.3*. Framingham, MA.

International Planning and Research Corporation (IPR) (2003). *Eighth Annual Business Software Alliance (BSA) Global Software Piracy Study, Trends in Software Piracy 1994–2002*. Washington, D.C.: Business Software Alliance.

International Telecommunication Union (ITU) (2004). *World Telecommunication Indicators Database* (8th Ed.). Geneva, Switzerland.

Jorgenson, D. (2001). Information Technology and the US Economy. *American Economic Review*, 91(1), 1–32.

Kahin, B. (1997). The US National Information Infrastructure Initiative: The Market, the Web and the Virtual Project. In B. Kahin & E. J. Wilson III (Eds.), *National Information Infrastructure Initiatives: Vision and Policy Design*. Cambridge, MA: MIT Press, 150–189.

Kenney, M. (2003). The Growth and Development of the Internet in the United States. In B. Kogut (Ed.), *The Global Internet Economy*. Cambridge, MA: MIT Press, 70–108.

King, J. L. & Lyytinen, K. (2005). Automotive Informatics: Information Technology and Enterprise Transformation in the Automotive Industry. In W. H. Dutton, B. Kahin, R. O'Callaghan, & A. W. Wyckoff (Eds.), *Transforming Enterprise: The Economic and Social Implications of Information Technology*. Cambridge, MA: MIT Press, 283–313.

Kogut, B. (Ed.) (2003). *The Global Internet Economy*. Cambridge, MA: MIT Press.

Kraemer, K. L. & Dedrick, J. (2005). The Role of Information Technology in Transforming the Personal Computer Industry. In W. H. Dutton, B. Kahin, R. O'Callaghan, & A. W. Wyckoff (Eds.), *Transforming Enterprise: The Economic and Social Implications of Information Technology*. Cambridge, MA: MIT Press, 313–335.

Kraemer, K. L. & King, J. L. (1996). Order Without Design: NII in the United States. *Information Infrastructure and Policy*, 5(2), 135–168.

Litan, R. E. & Rivlin, A. M. (2001). Projecting the Economic Impact of the Internet. Papers and Proceedings of the One Hundred and Thirteenth Annual Meeting of the American Economic Association. *American Economic Review*, 91(2), 313–322.

Malone, T. W., Yates, J., & Benjamin, R. I. (1987). Electronic Markets and Electronic Hierarchies. *Communications of the ACM*, 30(6), 484–487.

Markus, M. L., Steinfield, C. W., & Wigand, R. T. (2003). The Evolution of Vertical IS Standards: Electronic Interchange Standards in the US Home Mortgage Industry. Proceedings of the ICIS Pre-conference MISQ Special Issue Workshop on Standard Making: A Critical Research Frontier for Information Systems. Seattle, WA, December 12–14, 80–91.

McDermott, J. (1967). Technology: The Opiate of the Intellectuals. In A. H. Teich (Ed.), *Technology and the Future*. New York: St. Martin's Press.

McKinsey Global Institute (2001). *US Productivity Growth 1995–2000: Understanding the Contribution of Information Technology Relative to Other Factors*. Washington, D.C.

Mesenbourg, T. L. (2001). *Measuring Electronic Business*. Washington D.C.: US Bureau of the Census.

Organization for Economic Cooperation and Development (OECD) (1996). *Information Infrastructure Convergence and Pricing: The Internet*. Paris: Committee for Information Computer and Communications Policy.

Rogers, E. M. (1995). *Diffusion of Innovations* (4th Ed.). New York: Free Press.

San Jose Mercury News (2004). EBay Offering Loans for Small Businesses, May 7, 1F, Business Section.

Shih, E., Kraemer, K. L., & Dedrick, J. (2005). Rule of Law and the International Diffusion of E-Commerce. *Communications of the ACM*, 48(11), 57–62.

Small Business Administration (2002). Small Business Share of Economic Growth, *Small Business Research Summary*, No. 211. Washington, D.C.: SBA, 1–2.

Sturgeon, T. J. (2002). Modular Production Networks: A New American Model of Industrial Organization. *Industrial and Corporate Change*, 11(3), 451–496.

Tornatzky, L. G. & Klein, K. J. (1982). Innovation Characteristics and Innovation Adoption-Implementation: A Meta-Analysis of Findings. *IEEE Transactions on Engineering Management*, 29(1), 28–45.

United Nations (1999). *National Accounts Database*. New York: United Nations, Statistics Division.

US Census Bureau (2004). *2002 E-commerce Multi Sector Report*. Washington, D.C.: Department of Commerce.

US Census Bureau (2005a). *2003 E-commerce Multi Sector Report*. Washington, D.C.: Department of Commerce.

US Census Bureau (2005b). *Quarterly Retail E-Commerce Sales, 4th Quarter 2004*. Washington, D.C.: Department of Commerce. From http://www.census.gov/mrts/www/data/pdf/04Q4.pdf

World Bank (2004). *WDI Online*. From http://publications.worldbank.ord/WDI/

Zhu, K., Kraemer, K. L., & Xu, S. (2003). E-business Adoption by European Firms: A Cross-Country Assessment of the Facilitators and Inhibitors. *European Journal of Information Systems*, 12(4), 251–268.

3 France: an alternative path to Internet-based e-commerce

ERIC BROUSSEAU AND
BRUNO CHAVES

Introduction

The French-specific path for e-commerce is shaped by the characteristics of the country's economy and innovation system. The French national system of innovation is led by large established firms that are not well adapted to the decentralized process of innovation at the heart of the Internet revolution. This has hindered the development of e-commerce as innovation has occurred only in industries where dominant firms were driven to go online in response to national and international competition. Also, the central government used to play a powerful role in the economy, and has more influence over technology adoption choices than in other countries.

As a result, technologies tend to be widely adopted only when supported by big companies, as in the case of EDI, or by government, as in the case of videotext. France was an early adopter of e-commerce in the 1980s in both the business-to-business and the business-to-consumer segments based on EDI and videotext (marketed as Minitel) technologies, respectively (Brousseau, 2001, 2003; Brousseau & Kraemer, 2003). As a result, when the Internet became available for commercial application in the mid-1990s, French consumers and firms did not perceive it to be advantageous compared with existing technologies, delaying adoption of Internet-based e-commerce.

The diffusion of Internet-based e-commerce was inhibited by the adoption of these earlier technologies and the switching costs associated with moving to Internet-based options. Also, the presence of efficient physical distribution channels limited the adoption of online shopping. Finally, overall Internet adoption was low relative to France's size and wealth, as the lack of network externalities (due to low adoption) reduced the incentive for consumers and businesses to go online.

Over time, however, the impressive wave of innovation that accompanied the worldwide development of the Internet altered business and government perceptions. By 1998, France's migration to the Internet was assured when a new government launched a pro-active policy in favor of Internet adoption. This wide-ranging program aimed to enable the country to catch up with other developed countries in Internet use and in the development of related technologies. Thus, the combination of early adoption of e-commerce using older standards and late adoption of Internet-based e-commerce – an early–late adoption path – is the defining feature of France's e-commerce development.

The unique factors that characterize the French economy and its modes of innovation have driven a unique pattern of e-commerce use. First, B2C e-commerce has been dominated by major retailers which deliver goods via their existing distribution channels rather than cannibalize sales via competing channels; yet, they are the dominant e-tailers in France as well. Pure-play e-retailers are mainly foreign subsidiaries, though some French e-tailers compete successfully for niche markets. Likewise banks have been slow to develop online services that could compete with existing branches and ATMs. Second, French firms, especially those in manufacturing, have implemented technologies that support coordination rather than online transactions (sales, procurement). Third, French adopters have tended to integrate their web applications more tightly into existing internal information systems than firms in other countries.

Given these patterns of use, the impacts of e-commerce are relatively constrained. The most substantial impacts are in improved internal processes and inter-firm coordination, rather than increased sales or lower procurement costs. Also, the Internet has had limited impact on the number of trading partners or the intensity of competition faced by French firms, compared with their counterparts in other countries. Overall, then, the French economy and its innovation system have led to a unique pattern of e-commerce adoption, which has in turn shaped its impacts.

Taken together, the results of our study illustrate the interaction of environmental and policy factors in shaping the overall adoption of e-commerce in France and, more particularly, the adoption of the Internet and e-commerce in French firms. Specific results are summarized as follows.

- *An early–late adoption path is the dominant model.* France was an early adopter of e-commerce based on the early technologies of EDI and videotext in the 1980s and a late adopter of Internet-based e-commerce in the late 1990s.

- *The French environment was unprepared for Internet e-commerce.* The centralized innovation system and national government of France were at odds with the decentralized, entrepreneurial nature of the Internet and were slow to recognize its importance as a platform for e-commerce. Preference for face-to-face transactions, late adoption of PCs and the Internet among households, and switching costs for business limit the potential network economies and therefore limit business investment.
- *France lags other developed countries in readiness and diffusion.* It is characterized by a low level of Internet use for e-commerce in comparison with other developed countries. Use for coordination with supplier and business partners occurs mainly through traditional EDI technology. Where use occurs, it is oriented toward coordination within the firm and between the firm and its business partners. It is also tightly integrated with existing operational systems rather than with external, market-oriented systems such as websites for online sales and customer relationship management.
- *E-commerce impacts have been positive but limited.* The impacts of e-commerce have mainly been to increase internal efficiency and inter-firm coordination rather than to increase online sales or the competitive market position of firms.

Collectively, these results indicate that the digital economy followed a French-specific path that led to a lower level of development and use of Internet-related technologies than would be expected for a country at its state of development. This pattern is due to specific features of its environment and policy, readiness for e-commerce, the lack of significant drivers for e-commerce, and the existence of particular barriers to adoption and use. The next sections elaborate on these features before showing the pattern of use and impact that evolved from them in France.

Country background: environment and policy[1]

France and its economy in context

France is a member of the European Union and a nation with a rich history and cherished traditions. The population of France (metropolitan)

[1] This focuses on the analysis of the French sample, but occasionally brings in other data and the results of comparative analysis of France, Germany, and Denmark

Table 3.1 *Demographics and macroeconomic indicators, 1998–2002*

	1998	*1999*	*2000*	*2001*	*2002*
GDP in US$bn	1,451.95	1,443.71	1,305.40	1,309.81	1,409.60
GDP per capita US$	24,863.06	24,628.22	22,165.54	22,128.63	23,714.10
GDP growth (annual percent)	3.40	3.21	3.79	2.10	1.21
GFDI (percent of GDP)	5.18	11.51	16.56	11.23	8.02
Trade (percent of GDP)	49.58	49.62	55.86	54.27	52.07
Income distribution: richest 20%: poorest 20%			5.60		

Sources: OECD, 1996; World Bank, 2004

is approximately 62 million, with an annual growth rate of 0.6%. The country's 2002 GDP was $1.4 trillion, or $24,000 per capita.[2] France is also a very internationally oriented economy. For example, trade accounts for 52% of GDP and foreign direct investment (FDI) is 8% of GDP (Table 3.1). Indeed, French FDI is the highest among the countries in the study. Thus, the French economy is quite international (The Economist, 2005) and potentially open to foreign competition.

The data in the global sample reflect this internationalization of firms in the French economy. For example, 21% of total procurement spending and 15% of total sales among French firms are from abroad (Table 3.2). These and other measures of internationalization (especially total sales from abroad) are higher than the average for the global sample.

Within France, the manufacturing sector is the most international, followed by distribution and then finance. For example, 27% of firms in manufacturing have establishments abroad, 19% of the firms have headquarters abroad, and 22% of the firms' total sales are from abroad, compared with far less for the other sectors (Table 3.2). Moreover, it is the manufacturing sector that is most affected by global competition as 39% of the firms report a high degree of competition from abroad, compared with 7% or less for finance and distribution. Again, however,

using the GEC survey data (Brousseau & Chaves, 2004). This comparison with two countries that have similar levels of development and that belong to the European Union provides richer understanding of the French-specific path of development.

2 More recent French figures (2004) place GDP at €1.5 trillion, or €25,000 per capita.

Table 3.2 *Internationalization of French firms, 2002*

	Establishment size		*Sector*			*Total*	
	SME	*Large*	*Mfg.*	*Distrib.*	*Finance*	*France*	*Global*
Percent of companies with establishments abroad	22	53	27	23	12	23	24
Percent of companies with headquarters abroad	7	22	19	4	4	7	8
Mean percent of total sales from abroad	14	30	22	14	9	15	12
Mean percent of total procurement spending from abroad	21	19	14	25	6	21	20
Degree affected by competitors abroad (percent)							
Low	72	41	34	80	90	71	68
Moderate	17	23	27	16	3	17	16
High	11	36	39	4	7	12	15

Source: CRITO GEC Survey, 2002

French firms appear less affected by competitors from abroad than the global sample. This could be a mechanical effect of the size of the country, which is a large economy relative to the average size of the economies in the global sample.

Generally speaking, the French economy has been internationalizing, liberalizing, and opening to foreign competition over the last two decades. As a result, business decision-makers are aware of what is happening abroad and seek to implement similar business processes in France. Therefore, France should be a country where e-commerce would develop quickly as it did in many other countries with the same level of wealth. Why it did not is an interesting and important story.

Environment

Several environmental factors have developed in France that should favor the development of e-commerce. The French production system

Table 3.3 *Technology infrastructure (comparable to other economies), 1998–2002*

	1998	*1999*	*2000*	*2001*	*2002*
Telecommunications					
Main phone lines per 1,000 pop.	583.90	578.07	577.10	573.49	568.92
Cell phone subscribers per 1,000 pop.	191.96	365.62	493.31	605.33	647.00
Cable subscribers per 1,000 pop.	44.19	48.10	51.29	54.59	57.52
Internet					
Internet hosts per 1,000 pop.	8.75	21.03	19.06	13.29	23.29
Internet users per 1,000 pop.	63.43	91.60	143.65	263.77	313.83
IT					
IT as percent of GDP	3.17	3.36	3.59	3.72	3.47
PCs per 1,000 pop.	232.20	267.47	304.28	328.60	347.10
Software piracy rate (percent)	0.43	0.39	0.40	0.46	0.43

Sources: IDC, 2003; IPR, 2003; ITU, 2004; World Bank, 2004

is now composed of firms and industries whose organization is flexible and networked. It should allow the implementation of e-business and e-commerce practices. Innovation capabilities have been reinforced, especially in the internal IT infrastructure of firms. Moreover, France benefits from digital skills in terms of both IT production and use. It has a tradition of producing efficient telecommunications equipment and services, as well as software. It also experienced early diffusion of online services (Minitel), both in businesses and in the public domain.

Infrastructure

A national infrastructure for e-commerce also is apparent. France benefits from excellent logistics, package delivery, payment systems, and legal and business services, which are required for e-commerce.

It has also developed the national IT infrastructure to support these other infrastructures. Telephone and broadband continue to expand gradually, while mobile service has more than tripled in subscribers (Tables 3.3 and 3.4). The number of Internet users (Table 3.3) and Internet households (Table 3.4) has increased six fold. At the same time, Internet access devices, such as PCs, that permit individuals and firms to engage in e-commerce have almost tripled (Tables 3.3 and 3.4). Most of the barriers that made Internet access scarce and costly

Table 3.4 *Technology infrastructure (France only), 1998–2004*

	1998	*1999*	*2000*	*2001*	*2002*	*2003*	*2004*
Cell phone penetration rate (all population), percentage[(a)]	19	34	49	62	64	69	73
Percentage of households with PCs[(b)]	19	23	28	32	37	41	45
Percentage of households with Internet access[(b)]	na	6	12	18	23	28	31
Percentage of households with high-speed Internet access[(c)]	na	na	na	na	8	12	14
Percentage of households with Minitel[(b)]	22	18	16	14	13	13	12

[(a)]Source: ART, *Observatoire des Mobiles* 1997–2004
[(b)]Source: INSEE, Enquêtes sur les Conditions de Vie des Ménages de 1996 à 2004 (Heitzmann & Dayan, 2004) and (Frydel, 2005)
[(c)]Source: Médiamétrie, *L'Observatoire des Usages Internet*, 2004

have now been removed. For example, the monthly cost of Internet use is among the lowest of the countries in the study. Overall, French spending on IT as a percent of GDP (3.5%) is similar to that of other developed countries.

Industry structure

The structure of French industry presents a mixed environment for e-commerce as regards firm size, industry sector, and IT use within firms and sectors. French industry is divided between large internationalized firms and many smaller, local companies. While there are dense webs of smaller companies active on the global market in many other countries, this is not the case in France (Brousseau & Kraemer, 2003). Large companies are more internationalized, more high-tech, and more modern than the vast network of small domestic companies that are their suppliers. The large companies employ more skilled workers, use IT more intensively, and are managed using business practices similar to most of their global competitors. In contrast, the smaller French firms often do not go international and do not feel the necessity to use IT intensively (The Economist, 2005). Those that use IT intensively generally work with large clients that pressure them to go digital. For example, the automotive industry extensively implemented EDI in the late 1980s and pressured its suppliers to do likewise (Brousseau, 2001; Boyer & Freyssenet, 2002).

These features vary somewhat by industry as some sectors are mostly composed of small firms (intermediary goods and consumption goods), while others are more concentrated and dominated by large firms (large equipment and automotive). The latter are more likely to go digital than the former because large firms are generally more digital and they tend to spur their competitors/partners in the industry to adopt IT.

The historical evolution of different industry sectors in France has had a strong effect on the different paths of diffusion among the finance, distribution, and manufacturing sectors. The finance sector has suffered from the historically strong state intervention in the economy which protected banks and other financial institutions from both global and local competition. Concentration in the banking sector over the last decade has enabled some to go international but they are still considered weak internationally. More precisely, French banks manage long-term relational interactions with their business clients and with customers. They therefore compete on quality rather than on price. As a result, they are often weak competitors on all the markets where competition is based on price and where clients use the services of several banks (Bertrand et al., 2004; Boutillier et al., 2004; De Bandt & Davis, 2000; European Central Bank, 2004).

Retail finance and banking in particular is strong as it remains a proximate activity where local reputation, physical presence, and deep knowledge of customers matter. French banks have dense webs of local branches and ATMs that provide efficient services to the public. The banks cooperate to provide a low-cost and efficient debit/credit card system, "*Carte Bleue*," which supports payments. They also have provided online banking through Minitel. Consumers are not encouraged to change financial service providers and are not used to doing so. Thus, while financial services are easy to digitize, this sector has had little pressure to develop Internet-based e-commerce until recently.

The French retail industry imported US marketing methods linked to superstores and specialized outlets and adapted them to the organization of European markets. The French government supported these efforts because it considered modern marketing channels a means of reducing inflation by cutting intermediary fees and increasing competition. These efforts enabled several French companies to become international leaders in the retail industry. Paradoxically, this retail strength hindered the development of e-commerce in France. Competition in the domestic market drove retailers to serve local markets well, with differentiated goods and services and widely distributed outlets tailored to the character of each urban market. Thus, there have been few opportunities for e-retailers to compete with traditional retailers, except in niche markets such as music CDs, rural markets not served well by retail outlets, and women executives in the Paris region.

Moreover, the large distribution companies are engaging in e-retailing to preempt the pure-play Internet firms. Among the thirty online sellers that were profitable in 2001, twenty were subsidiaries of large firms, either retailers (Alapage, Fnac.com, Darty.com, etc.) or transportation companies (sncf.com) (Brousseau, 2001). Less than ten were pure players. Given these features of the French retail distribution system, one would expect B2C e-commerce to be less developed in France than in other countries.

Manufacturing firms in France have limited ability to develop online selling (B2C). For example, it is complex to sell tangible products online because it increases many logistics costs. Moreover, complex and differentiated products are seldom sold online since they often require inspection by the client and consultancy services by the seller. In addition, since efficient distribution channels exist in France, there are few incentives for the manufacturers to bypass them by going online. This hinders the development of B2C. In B2B, the inter-firm relationships among French manufacturing firms are long term and cooperative rather than competitive. Thus, the emphasis is on information systems that enable coordination and collaboration among firms within a value chain, and the preference has been for proven technologies rather than experimental approaches more oriented toward settling deals online such as the Internet.

As indicated above, there are few pure-player e-commerce firms in France. Those that exist are either subsidiaries of US pure players like Amazon, eBay, or Yahoo!, or small independent firms organized on a craft shop model. For example, with the online distribution of computers and related products, a set of very small discounters compete with larger sites, like those of the specialized retailers or those of the computer manufacturers, by aggressively discounting outdated products. While these sites tend to develop strong price competition in a very specific niche of the market, their sales volumes are marginal. They are often operated by small, independent entrepreneurial firms that do everything on their own, from the design of their website to making deliveries. For most players, which are traditional firms, e-commerce remains an experimental field considered to be complementary to their traditional activities. Most players take positions in e-commerce in order to watch what is going on, to incrementally invest in the required knowledge and assets, and to be ready if Internet-based online selling develops suddenly.

Government policy

The French national government, which has a strong influence in business and the national economy, was late to recognize the importance of the Internet, but when it did, it implemented a widespread program to boost the development of a French information society and digital economy in the late 1990s. This policy was reinforced by European Union (EU) policy aimed at sustaining the development of a unified and dynamic European digital arena (Brousseau, 2002).

Part of the reason for its lateness was that the government was preoccupied with preparation for the deepening of the integration of the European economy following the major treaties signed among the EU members in the 1990s. France had to adapt its economy and its industry to an increasingly competitive and global environment. Since the state played a strong role in an economy that was not widely open to competition, a wide set of reforms took place between the mid-1980s and the late 1990s. Most organizations became more flexible by outsourcing non-core activities and by implementing modular principles of organization. French companies went more international as well.

This new business climate favored the adoption of e-business and e-commerce practice by the end of the 1990s. With the restructuring achieved, in 1998 the French government launched a widespread program called PAGSI – the Government Action Program for the Information Society (Comité Interministériel pour la Société de l'Information, 1998). It targeted seven areas: developing Internet access, stimulating IT use in education, developing content and services, encouraging technological innovation, stimulating IT use within business and society, developing a legal framework for digital networks, and facilitating e-commerce. This program was to enable France to catch up with other developed countries in Internet use and e-commerce and in the development of new technologies. Since 1998, the government has furthered the deregulation of telecommunication services, reshaped the legal framework to adapt to digital technologies, promoted IT training and innovation, and developed e-government (Brousseau & Kraemer, 2003; see also the French Government website at www.internet.gouv.fr [accessed 21 May 2005]).

As mentioned above, these policies were both a component of, and aligned with, the year 2000 e-Europe initiative of the European Union that promoted the development of a strong digital economy (European Commission, 1999). An intensive effort for legislation and inter-member benchmarking occurred to stimulate member states to align on the most advanced states. The Commission and the Council of the EU tried to stimulate development of a dynamic digital industry in Europe through specific support programs for R&D and development of content. Programs were also developed to boost the adoption by business and government of digital technologies and the new methods of work and business enabled by them.

While the European and the French policies impacted the adoption of digital technologies and e-commerce development significantly, they were insufficient to really enable France to catch up. The bursting of the Internet bubble further slowed the pace of diffusion. Nevertheless, France is now adopting digital technologies and related practices using the Internet as a platform for e-commerce.

E-commerce readiness

As indicated earlier, France's national IT infrastructure is less developed than that in countries with similar levels of economic development. This is also true for Internet technologies used in households and firms.

Household use of the Internet

French households are significantly lower users of the Internet than many other Europeans (Table 3.5). According to a 2003 survey, 50% of the French public had never used the Internet as recently as 2002, although this was down from 70% in 2000 (GfK/SVM Sciences et Vie Micro, 2003). Although French households are continuing to embrace PCs and Internet access, this effort is insufficient to enable the French to catch up with European leaders as yet. While the majority of French now use cell phones, enabling them to access newer e-commerce services, the level of mobile use is also lower than in other major

Table 3.5 *The digitization of the European population, 2002*

	Germany	*Belgium*	*Spain*	*France*	*Italy*	*UK*
Internet users (millions)	24.6	3.5	5.7	10.2	21	21.6
Share of population with Internet access (percent)	30	44	29	29	38	43
Share of the above with high-speed access to the Internet (percent)	21	25	25	23	21	14
Monthly time online per user	15h04	5h55	9h49	9h42	8h00	8h00
Share of population with a cell phone (percent)	65	70	75	62	89	75

Source: Le Journal du Net, www.journaldunet.com/chiffres-cles.shtml (accessed July 2003)

European economies. Without broader diffusion of Internet technologies in France, it is unlikely there will be much consumer demand for B2C e-commerce.

Business use of Internet technologies

The same low adoption of the Internet applies for business users. French firms are significantly behind the global sample in the use of e-commerce technologies such as websites, extranets, and Internet-based EDI (Table 3.6). However, intranets and especially standard EDI over private networks are used far more in France than in the global sample. We will say more about this in sections below.

Among industry sectors, firms in manufacturing are generally highest on the use of all e-commerce technologies (Table 3.6). This is consistent with our earlier analysis regarding the greater propensity of the manufacturing sector to adopt the Internet for e-commerce over finance and distribution.

The foregoing relationship between the low level of technology diffusion among households and the low willingness of firms to invest in e-commerce-related technologies also applies to mobile commerce. French citizens are less equipped with cell phones than other Europeans and therefore French firms are less likely to develop m-commerce applications (Table 3.7).

Table 3.6 *Use of e-commerce technologies, 2002*

	Establishment size		*Sector*			*Total*	
Percent using . . .	*SME*	*Large*	*Mfg.*	*Distrib.*	*Finance*	*France*	*Global*
Email	98	100	92	100	97	98	99
Website	54	80	60	52	58	54	74
Intranet	68	86	64	71	59	68	64
Extranet	14	53	31	8	28	15	33
• accessible by suppliers/ business partners	11	31	20	8	17	12	21
• accessible by customers	11	24	20	8	18	11	18
EDI	43	74	64	36	44	43	43
• over private networks only	30	47	29	32	18	30	19
• Internet-based only	5	4	15	0	13	5	8
• both	8	23	20	4	13	8	16
EFT	30	38	24	33	26	30	43
Call center	22	48	22	23	18	22	32

Source: CRITO GEC Survey, 2002

Table 3.7 *Content/services to mobile customers, 2002*

	Establishment size		*Sector*			*Total*	
Percent providing or planning to provide mobile content or services	*SME*	*Large*	*Mfg.*	*Distrib.*	*Finance*	*France*	*Global*
Already available	8	13	9	8	9	8	14
Plan to add within the next year	14	20	11	16	7	14	18

Source: CRITO GEC Survey, 2002

The French bias toward traditional technologies and standards

As mentioned previously, the delayed adoption of Internet-based e-commerce in France was due to the earlier adoption of alternative technologies for e-commerce. This can be seen clearly in the case of

Table 3.8 *EDI use among selected European economies (percent)*

		France	*Germany*	*Denmark*
	YES	45	67	68
	EDI over private networks	70	46	24
Use EDI?	Internet-based EDI only	11	15	30
	Both	19	39	46
	NO	55	33	32

Source: CRITO GEC Survey, 2002

EDI where most French firms are users of only standard EDI,[3] and few are users of Internet-based EDI or both standard and Internet EDI (Table 3.6). This is further highlighted in the international comparison in Table 3.8, which shows that in 2002, 70% of French EDI users relied on traditional EDI, while the figures were lower by far in Germany and Denmark. French reliance on the EDI standard has continued, although there is beginning to be a shift in the platform used to exchange data. In 2003, 41% of firms used the EDI standard for exchanging data with customers and suppliers. However, 38% were using it over private networks, 38% over the Internet, and 24% over both.[4]

Since France was an early adopter of standard EDI, firms have considerable experience with the technology, appear to be satisfied with it, and have little incentive to switch to the Internet. It is likely that French firms did not switch to the new platform as the German and Danish firms did because with fewer Internet adopters, the positive returns were lower. A shift may be occurring now.

The lack of greater Internet use in France is important because online sales have been found to be positively correlated with adoption of various Internet technologies, but negatively correlated with the use of standard EDI (Brousseau & Chaves, 2005; Zhu et al., 2006).[5]

[3] Traditional EDI refers to the use of EDI standards (proprietary or open) over private networks. Internet EDI refers to the use of EDI standards over the public Internet. Internet, or Internet-based exchange, refers to the use of XML standards over the public Internet.

[4] These data are constructed from the e-Business Watch survey (European Commission, 2003).

[5] This has to be balanced by the fact that in our survey, online sales refers to sales over the Internet only. Since several alternative platforms were used in

That is, what differentiates online use among firms is not the use of digital technologies per se, but the type of technology used. Proprietary technologies such as EDI tend to reinforce traditional relationships among firms that are already collaborating, while standard, open technologies appear more likely to support market exchanges which require public platforms such as the Internet, since market relationships are more flexible. Prior investments in proprietary technologies, even though more expensive than newer technologies, seem to be a barrier to the use of the newer, more open set of technologies because of sunk costs and switching costs.

At the same time, the global sample points out that French firms tend to use digital network technologies to fuel their existing business processes, especially their internal processes, by enhancing the integration among their applications and the coordination processes with traditional business partners, rather than increasing their sales by developing new marketing channels and new business partners. This French-specific behavior, as compared with Danish and German firms, also explains why EDI technologies are used more intensively in France than in the other economies.

The French "financial connection"

French firms are less intensive users for most of the IT covered in the survey, but there is one type of technology which has a wider gap than the average: electronic funds transfer. Although use of EFT is low in all sectors, the genesis of this pattern is directly linked to the history of French banking. In the 1970s French banks developed a computer-based system to manage clearing among the banks. While efficient, the system was not aimed at reconciling payments with commercial transactions (and related documents such as bills or order of payments). Despite the request from business users to develop a system that would support the management of single payments, the banks did not change the system until the late 1990s. This clearly hindered business customers from relying on the inter-bank information systems to manage electronic payments. Table 3.6 clearly shows that France is using EFT

France – Minitel for B2C and EDI for B2B – the online sales are underestimated; obviously there is a positive correlation between the use of Internet technologies and Internet sales.

Table 3.9 *Enterprise integration strategy, 2002*

Extent to which Internet applications are electronically integrated with . . .	*Establishment size*		*Sector*			*Total*	
	SME	*Large*	*Mfg.*	*Distrib.*	*Finance*	*France*	*Global*
Internal databases and information systems							
Percent little to none	50	41	53	46	57	49	53
Percent some	18	33	10	23	18	19	24
Percent a great deal	32	26	37	31	25	32	24
Those of suppliers and business customers							
Percent little to none	81	78	71	84	86	81	72
Percent some	14	14	14	15	11	14	18
Percent a great deal	5	8	15	1	3	5	10

Source: CRITO GEC Survey, 2002

less than the global sample and it is also using it less than the finance sectors of Germany or Denmark (Brousseau & Chaves, 2004).

Enterprise integration

As shown in Table 3.9, French Internet applications are more integrated to internal information systems than the global sample. This is due primarily to the very high rate of integration in manufacturing (37%), and to a lesser extent in the distribution industry (31%). In contrast, the level of integration of Internet applications with suppliers' or business customers' information systems is low. Manufacturing is the notable exception, where 15% of the firms indicate their Internet applications are electronically integrated with those of suppliers and business customers compared with 5% for all sectors in France (Table 3.9). Thus, even though the use of EDI technology predominates in France and in manufacturing (Table 3.6), there are some segments within manufacturing that have made a move to the Internet in their inter-firm relationships.

Looking at the data more broadly, Table 3.9 indicates that French firms integrate their internal databases and information systems more deeply than the global sample. This suggests another reason for the low level of Internet use among firms other than lateness to the Internet.

Compared with what happened in many countries, the French did not primarily develop websites as show-windows before seeking to integrate them with their business operations or to coordinate with their business partners. From the beginning, they considered Internet applications as part of their enterprise information systems. These more integrated Internet interfaces take longer to develop and interconnect with business partners' information systems. Thus, partly because French firms were late to the Internet, they learned from others' experience and integrated Internet applications more fully from the start. Ironically, this also is likely to have slowed diffusion.

To summarize its readiness for e-commerce, France is characterized by a low propensity to use B2C Internet technologies, but ranks high in the use of the B2B technologies, especially in the manufacturing industries. France's path of adoption is linked to the slow migration of the former technological base (traditional EDI) to the new Internet standards such as TCP/IP, XML, and RosettaNet. This slowness now appears related to three explanations. First, the switching costs of changing the installed base. Second, France being a late adopter, the increasing returns of adoption are lower than in economies where the uses of the Internet and e-commerce are more developed. Third, the French tendency to tightly integrate systems, which takes longer to do, increases costs and delays adoption. There may be other factors as well, which can be seen as we next consider drivers and barriers to e-commerce.

Drivers and barriers to e-commerce

As indicated earlier, the French national environment did not create strong drivers for the adoption of the Internet as a platform for e-commerce, but it did create barriers. French consumers and firms felt that they already had adequate platforms in Minitel and EDI. The Internet was new, its future uncertain, and there were switching costs in a move to the Internet. But, some French firms were driven by the need to restructure themselves for global competition within the new rules of the European Union. This created strong incentives to improve their internal systems and, at least in manufacturing, to develop better linkages with firms abroad in their value chains. These features of the environment are strongly reflected in firm perceptions of drivers and barriers to e-commerce.

Table 3.10 *Drivers for Internet use, 2002*

Percentage of individuals indicating driver as a significant factor	*Establishment size*		*Sector*			*Total*	
	SME	*Large*	*Mfg.*	*Distrib.*	*Finance*	*France*	*Global*
Customers demanded it	14	25	15	14	14	15	37
Major competitors were online	22	23	24	20	32	22	31
Suppliers required it	10	13	5	11	10	10	22
To reduce costs	18	22	16	19	21	18	36
To expand market for existing product or services	21	30	24	19	34	22	48
To enter new businesses or markets	20	22	22	19	23	20	42
To improve coordination with customers and suppliers	42	36	37	44	33	41	44
Required for government procurement	15	20	10	15	27	15	15
Government provided incentives	9	2	2	12	7	9	8

Source: CRITO GEC Survey, 2002

Drivers

Fewer French firms in the global sample are driven to use the Internet for motivations similar to firms in the global sample. For example, market drivers such as market expansion, entering new markets, or meeting customer demands are a motivation for twice as many firms in the global sample as in the French firms (Table 3.10). A similar relationship exists for efficiency considerations (reduce costs). Two motivations distinguish French firms.

The first is improving coordination with customers and suppliers. The highest proportion (41%) of French firms indicates this is a driver, and they are basically on par with the global sample. This motivation is consistent with a changing environment that required French firms to get their own houses in order, and those of their key business partners. It also is supported by French firms' tendency to implement intranets and EDI systems (as shown in the previous section). The low implementation of extranets is consistent with the lateness of firms to the Internet given other available alternatives. Inter-firm systems, whether EDI or

Internet based, are complex to implement since they have to link the business processes and information systems of multiple partners and previous investments in EDI no doubt slowed the use of extranets.

The second distinguishing driver is government influence. We have indicated previously the large role that government plays in French business. This is illustrated in Table 3.10 by the fact that government requirements and incentives are the only drivers for Internet use that are equal to (or slightly higher than) the global sample. This confirms the continuing major influence of the French government in business and industry, and its essential role in the digitization of the society (even though governmental drivers are the weakest drivers in France).

In an analysis comparing France, Germany, and Denmark, we found that firms can be characterized by four contrasted patterns of motivations for Internet and e-commerce use (Brousseau & Chaves, 2004).[6] The distribution of these patterns across the three economies shows several things, which reinforce the analysis above. First, French indicators of the digitization of the economy and the society are not lower because French users are less intensive users of digital technologies, but because there are fewer users in France. Second, there are fewer users in France because there are fewer incentives to adopt the new technological base since the low rate of adoption generates low positive network externalities for new users, who therefore delay adoption. France is also characterized by a high proportion of firms that use the Internet only because they are required to do so by the government.

Barriers

As was the case with drivers, French companies do not identify the same barriers to e-commerce as firms in the global sample (Table 3.11). Surprisingly, the main difference does not lie in the low propensity of

[6] Pattern 1 can be labeled "inert," since these firms do not seem to be pushed by any of the nine drivers to use the Internet. Pattern 2 firms are "adaptive" in the sense that the adoption of the Internet and related business methods is constrained (or stimulated) by clients and competitors. Pattern 3 firms are "pro-active" in that they adopt the Internet because they identify opportunities to increase sales or exploit new market opportunities. Pattern 4 firms use the Internet because they are "influenced by government."

Table 3.11 *Barriers/difficulties, 2002*

Percent indicating statement is a significant obstacle	*Establishment size*		*Sector*			*Total*	
	SME	*Large*	*Mfg.*	*Distrib.*	*Finance*	*France*	*Global*
Need for face-to-face customer interaction	47	43	36	51	38	46	34
Concern about privacy of data or security issues	19	47	24	15	45	20	44
Customers do not use the technology	31	19	27	34	17	31	31
Finding staff with e-commerce expertise	21	11	6	24	27	20	27
Prevalence of credit card use in the country	14	19	19	12	14	14	20
Costs of implementing an e-commerce site	22	26	20	24	12	22	34
Making needed organizational changes	22	25	19	24	19	22	24
Level of ability to use the Internet as part of business strategy	16	17	18	16	11	16	25
Cost of Internet access	6	13	11	4	6	6	15
Business laws do not support e-commerce	24	30	21	24	35	24	24
Taxation of Internet sales	20	12	13	24	16	20	16
Inadequate legal protection for Internet purchases	39	28	16	47	35	39	34

Source: CRITO GEC Survey, 2002

consumers to use the Internet, although it is the third highest barrier cited by French firms.[7] Rather, French companies cite the need for

[7] A possible explanation for this might be that the low propensity of consumers to use the web matters only for B2C applications, while the survey points out that French firms focus on B2B applications. Moreover, since many online B2C merchants target "niche" markets, the low diffusion of the Internet might be considered a second-rank barrier. Put another way, the explanation can lie in the specific path of development of e-commerce in France. However, there is a different (and complementary) line of explanation. The low propensity of customers to use the web really matters when a business seeking to develop B2C has decided to

face-to-face interactions and inadequate protection for Internet purchases as the top two barriers ahead of the global sample.

The need for face-to-face interaction is recognized as a key barrier to e-commerce by firms in all sectors, and in both large and small companies. This French specificity is also confirmed by the fact that French companies do not consider costs, security, and shortage of skills as essential barriers to the development of the Internet-based commerce, while these are important in the global sample (Table 3.11).

In contrast, the French sensitivity to inadequate protection for Internet purchases is essentially due to the opinion of SMEs (especially in the distribution and finance industries; Table 3.11). This may be due to the greater ability of large firms to implement technological and organizational solutions to secure their transactions. It can also be linked to the fact that large firms consider the Internet as a support for B2B coordination applications, rather than as a means for selling online to final consumers. In contrast, small firms consider the Internet primarily as a support for B2C commerce.

In a related comparative analysis of barriers and maturity of e-commerce use, we found that French firms are distributed across four groups differentiated by level of maturity, whereas German and Danish firms tend to fall mainly into one, usually higher, group (Brousseau & Chaves, 2004).[8] This analysis reinforces the descriptive analysis above and suggests that perceived barriers provide insight into the overall low level of use among French firms. More French firms see more barriers to e-commerce than their European counterparts and therefore engage in less use.

actually go online. If, for various reasons, firms consider that there are essential barriers that prevent them from selling online, they will not consider the low rate of adoption of the Internet as an essential barrier. Since France is characterized by a high rate of firms with a low level of maturity in terms of e-commerce, this might explain why the respondents do not consider this factor an essential barrier although it is the third highest barrier.

[8] The four groups are defined by certain key barriers which are associated with various levels of maturity in the use of e-commerce. For the lowest level of maturity, "institutional barriers" are a primary concern and use is very limited. For the second level, "adaptation costs" are a key concern although use is greater. The third level is composed of firms that are not reluctant to use the technology, but whose downstream market is not adapted to digital transactions; they therefore buy online without selling online. The fourth and highest level of maturity is represented by firms that have overcome most of the barriers to e-commerce; they buy and sell online quite intensively (Brousseau & Chaves, 2004).

Table 3.12 *Uses of the Internet, 2002*

Percent using the Internet for . . .	*Establishment size*		*Sector*			*Total*	
	SME	*Large*	*Mfg.*	*Distrib.*	*Finance*	*France*	*Global*
Advertising and marketing purposes	26	48	28	23	46	26	58
Making sales online	12	23	13	11	17	12	30
After-sales customer service and support	16	29	16	15	28	16	44
Making purchases online	24	34	19	25	27	24	47
Exchanging operational data with suppliers	35	62	50	30	44	36	48
Exchanging operational data with business customers	39	50	62	33	40	40	51
Formally integrating the same business processes with suppliers or other business partners	24	27	32	20	35	24	34

Source: CRITO GEC Survey, 2002

Diffusion of e-commerce

Like the global sample, French use of the Internet for online sales is low. Moreover, French firms lag significantly behind the global sample in use for online sales. Only 12% of French firms engage in online sales versus 30% for the global sample (Table 3.12). Other uses related to online sales, such as advertising and marketing, and after-sales service and support, also are much lower in French firms than in the global sample. Among sectors, finance is more likely to engage in such uses than either manufacturing or distribution. So are large firms rather than small firms.

Consistent with this pattern of low participation in online sales, few French firms participate in Internet marketplaces (Table 3.13).

These patterns of use reflect the earlier findings that few French households or firms are connected to the Internet (Table 3.5), and that the key barriers to Internet use perceived by firms are the need for face-to-face customer interaction, inadequate legal protection for Internet

Table 3.13 *Participation in an Internet-based trading community, 2002*

	Establishment size		*Sector*			*Total*	
	SME	*Large*	*Mfg.*	*Distrib.*	*Finance*	*France*	*Global*
Percent who have heard of the concept of an Internet marketplace	62	70	71	60	58	62	80
Percent participating as a buyer only	5	5	1	6	5	5	7
Percent participating as a seller only	8	6	15	6	0	8	12
Percent participating as both buyer and seller	6	5	6	6	5	6	17

Source: CRITO GEC Survey, 2002

purchases, and customers do not use the technology (in that order; Table 3.11). Also related to the low pattern of online sales is the earlier finding that relatively fewer French firms than the global sample use e-commerce technologies such as websites and extranets, which would enable them to engage in online sales with consumers or other businesses (Table 3.6). The greater use of online sales in the finance sector and in large firms generally is also consistent with the earlier description of industry structure for the different sectors. Finance and banking in particular has come under more pressure for economic restructuring required for EU members. Larger firms with greater resources and expertise are more able to engage in both restructuring and computerization efforts.

The greatest use of the Internet for e-commerce among French firms is for coordination with customers, suppliers, and other business partners (Table 3.12). This includes exchanging operational data with suppliers (36%), exchanging data with business customers (40%), and formally integrating business processes with suppliers or other business partners (24%).

The emphasis on coordination reflects the earlier discussion about the strong tendency of French firms to use e-commerce technologies for deepening relationships with established business partners rather than creating new channels. It is consistent also with the fact that the key motivation for Internet use is improving coordination with customers and suppliers (Table 3.10). Use for coordination is greatest in distribution, followed by manufacturing and then finance.

Table 3.14 *Use of online technologies for operational tasks*

Percent of firms that use online technologies with their business partners to . . .	
Design new products	16
Forecast product demand	16
Manage capacity or inventories	12
Exchange documents electronically with suppliers, e.g., orders	44
Exchange documents electronically with customers	45
Negotiate contracts	15

Source: e-Business Watch survey (European Commission, 2003)

Some empirical indication of the deep relationships is provided in Table 3.14, which shows the proportion of French firms using online technologies with their business partners for specific operational tasks. As in Table 3.12, the greatest use is for exchanging information with suppliers and customers, as around 45% of the firms report doing so. However, about one-sixth also use it for designing new products, forecasting demand, managing inventories, and negotiating contracts.

In summary, a smaller proportion of French firms is involved in various uses of e-commerce than the global sample. In particular, fewer French firms use the Internet to buy or to sell than the global sample. Although coordination is the highest use among French firms, it also is below the global sample. Yet, where it is used, the relationships appear to be broad and deep.

Impacts of e-commerce

Increased efficiency, rather than increasing sales

France has followed a different path of development in e-commerce and therefore the impact of e-commerce is also different, compared with the global sample. Since French firms use e-commerce technologies (intranets) that are strongly integrated within their internal operations (Table 3.9) and have not developed online sales (Table 3.12), the major impact of e-commerce has been on the efficiency of internal

Table 3.15 *Impacts of doing business online, 2002*

	Establishment size		*Sector*			*Total*	
Percent indicating high impact	*SME*	*Large*	*Mfg.*	*Distrib.*	*Finance*	*France*	*Global*
Sales impacts							
Sales increased	9	8	2	12	4	9	21
Sales area widened	19	25	11	22	22	19	31
International sales increased	13	12	5	17	9	13	20
Efficiency impacts							
Internal processes more efficient	38	34	27	44	23	38	34
Staff productivity increased	26	18	17	31	14	26	27
Customer service improved	24	29	28	23	22	24	35
Procurement costs decreased	7	3	12	5	5	7	18
Inventory costs decreased	4	3	13	0	7	4	14
Coordination impacts							
Coordination with suppliers improved	24	28	31	22	24	24	30
Competitive impacts							
Competitive position improved	12	23	7	15	11	12	30

Source: CRITO GEC Survey, 2002

operations and on staff productivity. Around 38% of firms report greater operational efficiency and 26% report greater staff productivity (Table 3.15). The proportion of firms reporting greater operational efficiency is greater than that of the global sample (34%). These impacts occur across industry sectors and firm size, but especially in the distribution industry and in smaller firms. Firms in all industries also report enhanced services to customers, but this effect is less intensive in France than it is abroad. It is somewhat greater in the manufacturing sector than the others.

Consistent with their low use of the Internet for online sales, few firms report an impact of e-commerce on overall sales (9%), but more do report that their sales area has widened (19%) and international sales have increased (13%). However, these proportions are again considerably below the global sample.

Table 3.16 *Impacts of doing business online, 2002*

Percent indicating . . .	*Establishment size*		*Sector*			*Total*	
	SME	*Large*	*Mfg.*	*Distrib.*	*Finance*	*France*	*Global*
Number of distribution channels							
Increased	20	24	14	22	26	20	40
No change	73	75	86	67	74	73	56
Decreased	7	1	0	11	0	7	4
Number of suppliers							
Increased	16	10	22	13	17	16	30
No change	76	83	72	78	75	76	64
Decreased	8	7	5	9	8	8	6
Number of competitors							
Increased	11	9	3	13	17	11	28
No change	78	81	90	73	76	78	67
Decreased	11	10	7	14	7	11	5
Intensity of competition							
Increased	34	21	37	33	35	34	42
No change	57	79	63	53	65	57	54
Decreased	9	0	0	14	0	9	4

Source: CRITO GEC Survey, 2002

Improved coordination in value networks

As pointed out earlier, e-business in France is mainly seen as a way to re-engineer inter-firm relationships in order to benefit from more efficient cooperative operations along firm value chains. Consequently, B2C is considered less strategic than B2B, and the development of B2B is based on the implementation of inter-firm coordination systems rather than electronic marketplaces. This explains why French firms report that the use of e-commerce has improved coordination with suppliers. Given the low use of extranets, it is likely that this impact comes from firm use of traditional EDI that is well adapted to inter-firm cooperation.

Given the emphasis on inter-firm coordination, it is not surprising that French firms do not perceive the Internet as a means to increase the number of their suppliers or distribution channels (Table 3.16).

Moreover, since online markets did not develop, and since the Internet is not used as a new distribution channel, the development of e-commerce has no significant impact on the number of competitors.

Greater intensity of competition, without improved competitive position

An important impact of e-commerce appears to be greater intensity of competition without improved competitive position for French firms. Table 3.16 shows that French firms report the intensity of competition has increased significantly with the development of e-commerce (although fewer firms do so than in the global sample). However, Table 3.15 showed that few firms report that their competitive position has been improved.

One explanation for this is that while French firms have achieved improved coordination, it has been a *response* to the more intensive competitive pressure in the European and international environment. Thus, it is possible that the flexibility of digital technologies allows firms to question at any point in time the relevance of existing cooperative links, since the technology purportedly decreases the costs of switching to other partners. The technology increases the "contestability" of partnerships, and therefore it increases competition without leading to the rise of new markets.

This contestability explanation may appear to be inconsistent with the low propensity of French firms to increase the number of channels or suppliers (Table 3.16). Although French firms report that e-commerce has increased the number of distribution channels, suppliers, and competitors, the proportion is only one-half that of the global sample in each case. However, our analysis is that information technology facilitates switching from one (exclusive) business partner to another. Therefore the number of partners should not increase.

Additional support for this interpretation is provided in Table 3.17, which shows results from a European Commission survey conducted in 2003. Here 27% of French firms reported that online procurement had increased the number of suppliers; only 3% reported a decrease in the number of suppliers, although 70% reported that the number of suppliers had stayed the same. In addition, more than half of the firms reported that their relationships with suppliers and customers

Table 3.17 *Impacts of doing business online, 2003*

Effect of e-commerce on . . .	*Increased*	*Decreased*	*Remained about the same*
Number of suppliers	27	3	70
	Changed significantly	Changed somewhat	Has not changed
Relationship with suppliers	9	43	48
Relationship with customers	18	47	35

Source: e-Business Watch survey (European Commission, 2003). N = 143 out of 400 French firms sampled

had changed as a result of e-commerce.[9] Thus, it appears that French firms change suppliers but do not necessarily increase or decrease the number they use.

Conclusion

This chapter has drawn on several lines of analysis in earlier papers on the path of development of e-commerce in France (Brousseau, 2001; Brousseau & Kraemer, 2003; Brousseau & Chaves 2004, 2005) and integrated them with this comprehensive analysis of GEC and secondary data on the Internet and e-commerce in France. Due to the early adoption of e-commerce practices based on the earlier generation of online and digital technologies (EDI and Minitel), French companies missed the opportunity to become early adopters of the Internet and related practices. The GEC Survey, conducted with 200 companies in France, has confirmed the lower level of development of Internet-based e-commerce there, compared with other countries with similar levels of economic development. Traditional technologies seem to provide French firms with satisfying solutions to support their operations.

It is important to point out that the survey data analyzed in this chapter enabled an interesting and nuanced understanding of the complex

[9] To provide an additional reference point for these percentages, it is useful to note that more firms in France consistently report an increase in the number of suppliers and a change in relationship with suppliers and customers than either Germany or Denmark (data not shown).

impact that adoption of earlier technologies can have on the adoption of later superior technologies by creating path dependencies that are hard to break out of. Indeed, early adopters of information technologies and the early developers of online services should have been the early adopters of the Internet and related technologies since they benefited both from their digital literacy and investments in re-engineering of their operations. However, earlier investments prevented them from switching to the new technological base and related practices. The French story clearly suggests that the effect of path dependency is more important than the effects of being first adopter – especially when there is a major shift in technology platforms.

Presently, several factors combine to produce a slow rate of Internet and e-commerce adoption in France. Industry remains characterized by differences among firms related in particular to their industry sector and size. As many tables in this chapter show and as is illustrated by the cluster analysis of the drivers and barriers to e-commerce (Brousseau & Chaves, 2004, 2005), France is characterized by a level of adoption which remains low and which involves a huge number of digital bottlenecks. Digital France is characterized by digital archipelagos – within which firms are cooperatively using digital networks to coordinate their activities – in the middle of a non-digital ocean. This structure does not favor diffusion since these archipelagos correspond to clusters of firms relatively independent from the rest of the economy, and since the increasing returns of adoption are weaker than economies without such bottlenecks among archipelagos. In addition, there are fewer motivations for adoption. French business and consumer culture prefers face-to-face interaction and French distribution systems do not induce consumers or businesses to shop online; indeed, for the most part they do not provide the opportunity to do so. This situation is a self-reinforcing vicious cycle: the low level of Internet users in the population does not incite businesses to move their operations or sales to the Internet, and the low availability of Internet offerings by businesses does not incite more users to adopt either.

These features of its early adoption strongly influence the French way of considering e-business and e-commerce. The French are original in the sense that they do not see digital networks primarily as places to buy or sell online – digital marketplaces or places of trading exchange. They do see the networks as enabling more efficient coordination and integration, both within firms and within cooperative networks, while believing that most market transactions require face-to-face interaction. They therefore deeply integrate their online applications with their internal information systems, and in some cases with their business partners. This is linked to the vision that e-commerce is above all the deepening of a rationalization process in industry. Both visions lead most firms involved in e-business to implement coordination systems rather than marketplaces, and to target B2B rather than B2C. These have obviously had an impact on the pace of adoption and on the nature of e-commerce.

Therefore, French e-commerce is quite specific. It is rather weak in B2C as shown from comparisons abroad. It is stronger in B2B than in B2C, but lags the global sample in even its strongest use of the Internet for coordination. French e-commerce is very low in online sales. Consequently, the impact of French e-commerce is essentially on internal costs and external coordination, while it does not really generate sales or have much impact on competition.

However, there are contrasts among industries. Manufacturing is clearly the industry that leads the development of B2B. Distribution seeks to develop online procurement to rationalize its operations, but is reluctant to develop B2C since it could cannibalize its traditional marketing channels. The French banks and finance companies benefit from their strong competitive position in the domestic market and from the concentration of the industry. Competition does not drive them to aggressively develop online and they already operate an efficient payment and distribution system. Their incentives to develop B2C (consumer banking and others services) and B2B (merchant banking and services) e-commerce are weak.

Overall, the French-specific path for e-commerce has been shaped by the characteristics of the country's economy and innovation system. The French national system of innovation is led by large established firms that are not well adapted to the decentralized process of innovation at the heart of the Internet revolution. Moreover, few start-ups were able to develop in the Internet sector. This has hindered the development of e-commerce as innovation has occurred only in industries where dominant firms were driven to go online in response to international competition.

This influenced as well the nature of e-commerce development. First, B2C e-commerce has been dominated by major retailers which deliver goods via their existing distribution channels rather than cannibalize sales via competing channels. Likewise banks have been slow to develop online services that could compete with existing branches and ATMs. Second, French firms have implemented technologies that support coordination rather than online transactions, as they still prefer to conduct transactions via personal interaction. Third, while the country has been slow to adopt e-commerce, French adopters have tended to integrate their web applications more tightly into existing information systems than firms in other countries. Thus, the French economy and its innovation system have led to a unique pattern of e-commerce adoption, which has in turn shaped its impacts. Although French e-commerce will move to the common Internet platform in the future, there will continue to be considerable diversity in the way that consumers, firms, and industries adapt the technology to their particular needs and interests. Thus, the French development path to Internet-based e-commerce is a powerful case of the triumph of national diversity over globalization, reinforcing a central theme of this book.

References

Autorité de Régulation des Télécommunications (ART) (The French Telecommunications Regulator). *Observatoire des Mobiles*. Retrieved May 21, 2005, from http://www.art-telecom.fr/observatoire/index-d.htm

Bertrand, M. M., Schoar, A. S., & Thesmar, D. (2004). *Banking Deregulation and Industry Structure: Evidence from the French Banking Reforms of 1985, Center for Economic Policy Research*. Retrieved May 2005, from www.cepr.org/pubs/dps/DP4488.asp

Boutillier, M., Gaudin, J., & Grandperrin, S. (2004). La Situation Concurrentielle des Principaux Secteurs Bancaires Européens Entre 1993 et 2000: Quels Enseignements Pour la Future Structure des Marches Financiers Issue de l'UEM? Working paper. MODEM, University of Paris X, February.

Boyer, R. & Freyssenet, M. (2002). *The Productive Models, The Conditions of Profitability*. London, New York: Palgrave Macmillan.

Brousseau, E. (2001). Globalization of E-Commerce: Growth and Impacts in France. Report for the Center for Research on Information Technology and Organizations (CRITO). University of California at Irvine, and the US National Science Foundation (CISE/IIS/CSS), Globalization and E-commerce Project; www.crito.uci.edu/git/gec/

Brousseau, E. (2002). The Governance of Transaction by Commercial Intermediaries: An Analysis of the Re-Engineering of Intermediation by Electronic Commerce. *International Journal of the Economics of Business*, 8(3), 353–374.

Brousseau, E. (2003). E-Commerce in France: Did Early Adoption Prevent the Development? *The Information Society*, 19(1), 45–57.

Brousseau, E. & Chaves, B. (2004). *Diffusion and Impact of E-Commerce: The French Specific Path*. Retrieved May 21, 2005, from the Center for Research on Information Technology and Organizations (CRITO), University of California at Irvine, http://crito.uci.edu/pubs/2004/franceGECIII.pdf

Brousseau, E. & Chaves, B. (2005). Contrasted Paths of Adoption: Is E-Commerce Really Converging Toward a Common Organizational Model? *Electronic Markets*, 15(3), 181–199.

Brousseau, E. & Kraemer, K. (2003). Globalization and E-Commerce: The French Environment and Policy. *Communications of the Association for Information Systems (CAIS)*, 10, 73–127.

De Bandt, O. & Davis, E. P. (2000). Competition, Contestability and Market Structure in European Banking Sectors on the Eve of EMU. *Journal of Banking and Finance*, 24, 1045–1066.

European Central Bank (2004). *Report on EU Banking Structure*. Frankfurt: ECP.

European Commission (1999). *E-Europe – An Information Society For All*. Communication on a Commission Initiative for the Special European Council of Lisbon, March 23 and 24, 2000, retrieved May 21, 2005, from the Information Society website: http://europa.eu.int/ISPO/basics/eeurope/i_europe_follow.html

European Commission (2003). e-Business Watch. The European e-Business Market Watch. Brussels: Enterprise Directorate General.

Frydel, Y. (2005). Un Ménage sur Deux Possé de un Micro-Ordinateur, Un sur Trois a Accès à Internet. *INSEE Première*. Retrieved May 21, 2005 from www.insee.fr/fr/ffc/docs_ffc/IP1011.pdf

GfK/SVM Sciences et Vie Micro (2003). Retrieved July 2003, from http://svm.vnunet.fr/

Heitzmann, R. & Dayan, M. (2004). *E-Commerce Scoreboard Update 6*. Retrieved May 21, 2005, from the Department of Industrial Research and Statistics (Sessi), General Directorate for Industry, Information Technologies and the Post Office – DiGITIP (French Ministry for Economic Affairs, Finance and Industry) website: www.men.minefi.gouv.fr/webmen/gb/0327-05-EN-CIB.pdf

International Data Corporation (IDC) (2003). *Internet Commerce Market Model v.8.3*. Framingham, MA.

International Planning and Research Corporation (IPR) (2003). *Eighth Annual Business Software Alliance (BSA) Global Software Piracy Study,*

Trends in Software Piracy 1994–2002. Washington, D.C.: Business Software Alliance.

International Telecommunication Union (ITU) (2004). *World Telecommunication Indicators Database* (8th Ed.). Geneva, Switzerland.

Le Journal du Net (2003). Retrieved July 2003, from www.journaldunet.com/chiffres-cles.shtml

Médiamétrie (2004). *L'Observatoire des Usages Internet*. Retrieved May 21, 2005, from www.mediametrie.fr/contenu.php?rubrique = net&rubrique_id = 259&menu_id = 257

Organization for Economic Cooperation and Development (OECD) (1996). *Information Infrastructure Convergence and Pricing: The Internet*. Paris: Committee for Information Computer and Communications Policy.

The Economist (2005). Demon Monde: The French Denounce Globalization, But Their Companies Embrace It. *The Economist*, 376 (8433), July 2–8, 47.

World Bank (2004). *WDI Online*. From http://publications.worldbank.ord/WDI/

Zhu, K, Xu, S., Kraemer, K. L., & Gurbaxani, V. (2006). Migration to Open-Standard Interorganizational Systems: Network Effects and Path Dependency. *MIS Quarterly*.

4 *Germany: a "fast follower" of e-commerce technologies and practices*

WOLFGANG KOENIG,
ROLF T. WIGAND, AND
ROMAN BECK

Introduction

Germany not only has a long history of being a leading innovator in several areas, but has also been a fast follower in adopting innovations, including information technologies. German firms generally have embraced and implemented IT solutions only after they have proved successful in other countries, but once proven, there is widespread adoption across large and small firms, and new technologies are integrated with existing technologies to obtain maximum benefits. This is somewhat analogous of many firms' adoption strategy for new information and communications technologies. These firms are unwilling to be the guinea pigs for brand-new, often cutting-edge or bleeding-edge ICT which is often unproven, "buggy," unstable, and not perfected in many ways. Instead, fast-follower firms wait until right after early adopters have started the diffusion and just before "critical mass" has been achieved.

Two important factors driving adoption of IT in Germany are the international orientation of the country's economy and the dynamism of its small and medium-sized enterprises (SMEs), the so-called *Mittelstand*. Large multinational firms use technologies such as EDI very heavily to coordinate regional and global operations and to compete in a high-wage environment. However, Germany stands out among other countries in that its SMEs use many of these technologies to an equal, and sometimes greater, extent than large firms. As suppliers to large multinationals and as international competitors in their own right, German SMEs have had to be innovative and flexible to survive.

The extensive use of established technologies such as EDI and EFT may have delayed adoption of Internet-based e-commerce due to switching costs and a reluctance to replace proven technologies. Ultimately, however, German firms embraced the Internet as a complement to earlier technologies. As a result, while Germany was slower to adopt e-commerce than the USA and some European countries, it has since caught up on most measures of use.

Results from the GEC Survey highlight the following characteristics of e-commerce evolution in Germany:

- *German firms are driven to go online mainly to expand markets*, and secondarily to improve coordination and respond to competitive pressure. They perceive fewer barriers to doing business online than do their counterparts in other countries, with much less concern over privacy and legal protections.
- *Perhaps as a result of their confidence in the legal/regulatory environment, German firms are much more likely to actually buy and sell online*. Compared with the global GEC sample, Germany has twice as many firms selling online, led by SMEs, which are much more likely to sell online than the larger firms. They also have a higher share of total sales online, especially in B2C transactions, where German firms are far ahead of the global sample. This reflects the breadth of e-commerce use by firms as well as the readiness of consumers to buy online.
- *German firms integrate the Internet with their internal IT systems and those of their trading partners more extensively than firms in other countries*. The Internet is used mainly to address existing channels, rather than to replace or compete with those channels, reinforcing the idea of the Internet as a complement and extension to established business practices and technologies.
- *German firms do not report higher levels of positive impacts since adopting the Internet than firms in other countries*. Among German firms, SMEs report greater benefits in terms of improved internal processes, increased sales, widened sales area, and increased international sales. These differences likely reflect the fact that SMEs are using the Internet more extensively to sell online, and may suggest that they are using the Internet to target international markets that were beyond their reach before. These findings may point to the fact that German firms, particularly larger ones, were already intensive users of EDI, and had less room for improvement from adopting the Internet.

Table 4.1 *Macroeconomic statistics, 1998–2002*

	1998	*1999*	*2000*	*2001*	*2002*
GDP in US$bn	2,144	2,103	1,866	1,846	1,976
GDP per capita US$	26,137	25,623	22,699	22,421	23,955
Trade (percent of GDP)	56	58	67	68	67

Source: World Bank, 2004

Country background: environment and policy

Economic environment

Germany is the largest economy in Europe, with a GDP of nearly $2 trillion in 2002, and one of the wealthiest, with a GDP per capita of $23,955 (Table 4.1). Germany's large internal market is part of the larger market of primarily German-speaking people, who number 120 million in Europe. The size, wealth, and common language of this population make it an attractive market for e-commerce. In addition, Germany's relatively flat income distribution and high education levels mean that most of the population has the means to participate in e-commerce (König et al., 2002). The highly educated and skilled population should also help reduce workforce shortages in the IT industry and in industries deploying e-commerce in the future.

During the early 1990s, while other countries were beginning to adopt the Internet for business, Germany's interest was more focused on rebuilding the East German infrastructure to bring the new local states to the levels and standards of the rest of the country. However, over the past several years challenges such as restoring economic growth and developing the infrastructure and institutional environment for e-commerce have become increasingly important to business, government, and the public.

Information and communications infrastructure

Public interest and willingness to take an active part in developing an "e-society" have increased greatly in recent years. The utility of the Internet in the office or at home, together with the maturity of services

Table 4.2 *Technology infrastructure, 1998–2002*

	1998	*1999*	*2000*	*2001*	*2002*
Telecommunications					
Main phone lines per 1,000 pop.	567	586.76	610.59	634.21	650.36
Cell phone subscribers per 1,000 pop.	169	285.36	586.05	682.31	716.71
Cable subscribers per 1,000 pop.	215	225.77	247.79	246.26	249.76
Internet					
Internet hosts per 1,000 pop.	18	20	25	29	31
Internet users per 1,000 pop.	98.74	208.12	301.53	373.64	411.62
IT					
IT as percent of GDP	2.97	3.23	3.43	3.40	3.07
PCs per 1,000 pop.	279.14	296.97	336.05	379.91	430.99

Sources: IDC, 2003b; IPR, 2003; ITU, 2004; World Bank, 2004

and products available online, have convinced users and customers of the need to use the Internet. In addition, Internet access costs have fallen along with telecommunications costs. As a result, the number of Internet users quadrupled from 1998 to 2002, nearly matching the number of PC users (Table 4.2). Given the even higher levels of cell phone penetration, it is likely that Internet use will continue to grow as more people begin to access the Internet from cell phones.

Since becoming one of the first European countries to open its local loop to competition, local access is available from competing companies. Competition, forcing the reduction of local voice tariffs, and the increasing reliance on mobile services are major inhibitors of growth in the German fixed-line arena. Carriers are looking for alternative ways to generate revenues, including broadband DSL services (EITO, 2002). Germany leads Europe in terms of the total number of broadband connections, which increased by an order of magnitude from 2001–2003. This is due in part to relatively early deployment of services, as well as an aggressive strategy pursued by the telecommunications service providers.

In the mobile area, data still represent a small amount of the overall traffic, but that is expected to change. German mobile carriers already offer some mobile applications, which include general packet radio service (GPRS) location-based services and Internet access. More advanced mobile multimedia services (MMS) are also available on

GPRS networks. These services combine text messages with sound and pictures. In March 2002, German cell phone operator E-plus was one of the first in Europe to launch location-based I-mode services that allow subscribers to search for restaurants, cinemas, ATMs, hotels, and other services on their mobile phones (Beck et al., 2003; EITO, 2002).

International orientation

Germany's economy is highly internationally oriented, especially for a large economy. Foreign trade is equal to 67% of the GDP, compared with 52% for France, 23% for the USA, and 21% for Japan (World Bank, 2004). Germany's location in the center of Europe helps attract foreign investment and facilitates the entry of German companies into other European markets, as well as making it a logistics hub for European trade. Still, while half of Germany's trade is within the EU, its largest single export market is the USA, so its international scope goes beyond being just a European trading nation (König et al., 2002).

Compared with firms in other GEC Survey countries, German firms are more likely to have foreign establishments and headquarters.[1] A higher percentage of their sales and procurement are from abroad, and they are more highly affected by foreign competition (Table 4.3). These indicators are considerably higher for large firms than for SMEs, reflecting the international reach of larger firms. They are highest for manufacturers while much lower for financial firms, highlighting Germany's internationally competitive manufacturing industry compared with its more nationally oriented banking/insurance market. The retail/wholesale sector is currently consolidating via merger and acquisition (M&A) activities. Global players such as Wal-Mart and others have increased competitive pressure in the national market and may be encouraging more foreign procurement by local retailers and distributors to reduce costs. Although Wal-Mart entered the German retail market in 1997, at the time of writing it was still not operating profitably. These developments must also be seen in the light of the already highly competitive retail market dominated by large discounters.

[1] The global average is the mean of all firms in the GEC database. We use the term "global average" throughout to indicate the "average value of all GEC firms."

Table 4.3 *Internationalization of German firms*

	Establishment size		*Sector*			*Total*	
	SME	*Large*	*Mfg.*	*Distrib.*	*Finance*	*Germany*	*Global*
Percent of companies with establishments abroad	39	69	36	42	30	40	24
Percent of companies with headquarters abroad	11	24	24	8	17	12	8
Mean percent of total sales from abroad	15	24	18	15	13	15	12
Mean percent of total procurement spending from abroad	23	20	29	24	2	23	20
Degree affected by competitors abroad (percent)							
Low	65	38	60	64	81	65	68
Moderate	15	26	15	15	13	15	16
High	20	36	25	21	6	20	15

Source: CRITO GEC Survey, 2002

The international orientation of German firms is a driver in technology adoption. German firms, particularly large manufacturers, use ICT to reach external markets and to coordinate international operations. Even smaller and more local firms need to adopt ICT to do business with German and foreign multinationals, or to respond to foreign competition in the domestic market. As a result, German firms have been aggressive in adopting technologies such as EDI and Internet-based e-commerce.

Technology adoption and innovation by large and small firms

Another important characteristic of the German economy is the role of large firms and SMEs as technology innovators and users. Large firms account for a small share of total firms in the economy (just 0.25%), yet produce over 54% of total sales. In the manufacturing sector, 0.97% of firms are large enterprises, but they account for 70.2% of all sector sales (König et al., 2002; Statistisches Bundesamt, 1999). Large firms have been aggressive in embracing IT-related innovations in many processes. These include innovations in e-procurement and customer relationship management, as well as electronic supply chain management. Often e-commerce applications are developed first by large firms whose scale enables them to achieve greater cost savings and efficiency gains. Moreover, in order to achieve competitive advantage, large firms have no choice but to overlay nearly all processes they engage in with e-commerce practices (ZEW, 2002).

While large firms may be the most visible adopters of IT and e-commerce, SMEs also face pressure to adopt these technologies. Typically a *Mittelstand* firm is a supplier to large firms which increasingly dictate how these smaller firms must structure themselves so that the larger firms can conduct e-business with them. When smaller firms are not e-commerce-ready, larger firms are not interested even in talking to them. In addition, many leading SMEs trade directly with international partners and have adopted IT and e-commerce to serve foreign markets. These pressures force the *Mittelstand* to be innovative on a persistent and ongoing basis (MIND, 2002). As the survey data will show, German SMEs match and sometimes even lead their larger counterparts on most measures of e-commerce use, and achieve similar benefits from using the technologies (Beck et al., 2005).

E-commerce policy

Germany has promoted e-commerce both indirectly and directly through various policies. Indirectly, telecommunications liberalization has been important in encouraging competition and lowering access costs for Internet use. Since 1998, telephone customers have been able to choose among different carriers for each long-distance call. As a result, prices for national long-distance connections declined more than 90% from 1998 to 2000 (Federal Commissioner for Foreign Direct Investment in Germany, 2001). More recently, the German regulatory authority has worked to break down the de facto local monopoly of Deutsche Telekom. On 10 October 2001 a German court ordered Deutsche Telekom to open the local phone networks for its competitors, which has created local competition and has led to lower local tariffs. The fall in telecommunications costs was matched by a rapid decline in Internet access costs, which fell from $58.41 for forty hours at off-peak time in 2000 to $21.12 at the beginning of 2002 (König et al., 2002).

The German government also has promoted e-commerce through specific initiatives, both on its own and as part of the European Community (Andersen et al., 2005). The Federal Ministry of Economics and Technology's "e-commerce" program started in 1996 and still exists. Most of the activities in the initiative are aimed at increasing awareness of the possibilities of e-commerce; others intended to impact international policy in certain key areas such as cryptology, security, and taxation.

In 1998 the Ministry of Economics and Technology established a network of twenty-four e-commerce competence centers in all regions of Germany. The objective was to offer regional information and consulting services for SMEs and to make them aware of the opportunities offered by e-commerce. Furthermore, the initiative "Pilot Projects Fostering Electronic Commerce Application in SMEs," funded by the ministry, supports SMEs in development of specific B2B solutions and implementation of new e-commerce business models, as well as the use of digital payment, cryptology, and digital signature technologies.

As a member of the European Community, Germany also follows e-commerce directives covering areas such as electronic signatures, country-of-origin principles, recognition of electronic contracts, copyright, and rules for applying value added tax. Perhaps most important is the Data Protection Directive, which ensures a high level of privacy protection for individuals. While this was controversial when it entered into force (1998), data from the GEC Survey show that European firms have significantly lower concerns about privacy and security of data than their counterparts in other regions, perhaps because of just these stringent protections.

E-commerce readiness

Diffusion of e-commerce technologies

The overall e-commerce readiness in German firms in the GEC Survey is high, including both large firms and SMEs (Table 4.4, Figure 4.1). Only slight differences are evident between SMEs and large firms, the greatest

Table 4.4 *Use of e-commerce technologies in German firms, 2002*

	Establishment size		*Sector*			*Total*	
Percent using . . .	*SME*	*Large*	*Mfg.*	*Distrib.*	*Finance*	*Germany*	*Global*
Email	100	100	100	100	100	100	99
Website	92	100	90	92	94	92	74
Intranet	84	84	78	86	89	84	64
Extranet	22	52	39	16	37	22	33
• accessible by suppliers/ business partners	14	33	27	8	28	14	21
• accessible by customers	11	29	23	8	14	12	18
EDI	68	68	56	71	62	68	43
• over private networks	31	38	20	34	28	31	19
• Internet based	10	8	16	8	12	10	8
• both	27	22	20	29	22	27	16
EFT	87	72	95	85	77	87	43
Call center	30	56	26	29	51	30	32

Source: CRITO GEC Survey, 2002

being in the use of extranets and call centers. This latter difference might be explained by the need to have a certain scale to justify setting up a call center operation. As for extranets, large firms may be more likely to create an extranet, while SMEs would simply have access to the extranets of their larger customers or suppliers.

IT investment and resources

At the firm level, the survey shows that German firms have more PCs per employee (Table 4.5), while IT budgets and IT employees are comparable with the global average. The highest IT investment levels are in the banking/insurance industry, followed by the retail/wholesale industry, and the manufacturing industry. Surprisingly, SMEs have significantly higher levels of investment and use on all measures, reflecting the innovative orientation of German SMEs.

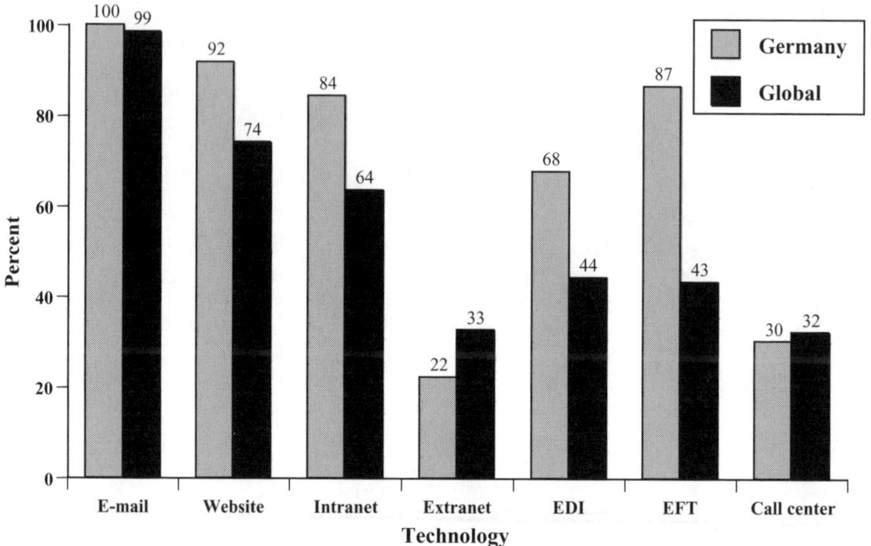

Figure 4.1 Use of e-commerce technologies
Source: CRITO GEC Survey, 2002

Considerable web-based investments were made (especially in the German banking sector) to build up a large variety of retail banking and brokerage online services. Most of these investments were followed by additional back-end integration investments to connect already existing IT infrastructures. Today, banks realize that these customer-oriented free services, while welcomed by customers, do not necessarily increase their own profitability. In the manufacturing industry, the Internet is used mainly as a cheap transmission layer to transport data between former non-EDI-capable suppliers or customers. Internet-based EDI or Web EDI solutions in different variations and even some standardized Web EDI solutions such as those in the consumer products industry are becoming more popular.

IT integration

The extent of integration of Internet applications with internal databases or information systems is about the same in Germany (27% reporting a great deal of integration) as in the global sample (24%) (Table 4.6). The electronic integration of customers and suppliers is

Table 4.5 *IT investment and resources by German firms, 2002*

	Establishment size		*Sector*			*Total*	
Percent using . . .	*SME*	*Large*	*Mfg.*	*Distrib.*	*Finance*	*Germany*	*Global*
PCs per employee	1.19	67	66	1.33	1.10	1.17	.82
IT employees as percent of total employees	10.10	4.59	4.17	11.44	11.46	9.99	9.12
IS operating budget as percent of 2001 revenue	7.23	4.75	3.79	7.23	15.38	7.19	7.75
Web-based spending as percent of IS operating budget	23.10	12.41	18.45	23.39	30.03	22.93	14.89

Source: CRITO GEC Survey 2002; weighted sample

Table 4.6 *Enterprise integration strategy*

Extent to which Internet applications are electronically integrated with . . .	*Establishment size*		*Sector*			*Total*	
	SME	*Large*	*Mfg.*	*Distrib.*	*Finance*	*Germany*	*Global*
Internal databases and information systems							
Percent little to none	56	38	67	54	46	56	53
Percent some	17	32	17	16	31	17	24
Percent a great deal	27	30	16	30	23	27	24
Those of suppliers and business customers							
Percent little to none	72	68	83	69	78	72	72
Percent some	11	20	16	9	13	11	18
Percent a great deal	17	12	1	22	9	17	10

Source: CRITO GEC Survey, 2002

still low, but higher than in other countries. Nearly double the percentage of German firms as in the global sample, i.e., 17% in comparison with 10%, respectively, have integrated their business partners electronically. There is anecdotal evidence that German firms seem to wait until they can benefit from Internet application integration, but they integrate completely if they see an advantage in doing so.

There are differences across industry sectors when firms are asked about the extent of customer and supplier integration. The retail/wholesale industry is most advanced in its external integration of Internet applications, with 22% of firms reporting a great deal of integration, compared with only 9% for finance and 1% for manufacturing. The low penetration of business partner integration in the manufacturing and financial industries is difficult to interpret. In the manufacturing sector, the automotive and mechanical engineering industries are known for their deep integration of first- and second-tier partners into the supply chain. In the banking sector, electronic data interchange with large customers, as well as electronic interbank clearing, is an established and common solution. In sum, the data suggest that the integration in these two sectors is being done through non-Internet-based EDI, rather than through Internet solutions.

Drivers of and barriers to e-commerce

Though IT and e-commerce solutions are able to support a variety of business processes, the drivers of and barriers to e-commerce adoption and use are closely connected to the structure, traditions, and characteristics of individual industry sectors.

Drivers

The most important drivers of Internet usage in Germany are the desire to expand markets for products and services online (58%) and the desire to enter new businesses and markets (46%) (Table 4.7 and Figure 4.2). At the industry level, this factor is somewhat less important for German bank and insurance institutions due to the existing multichannel distribution strategy of their services on the national market. Banks and insurance companies mainly use branches or traveling salespeople to distribute their products, but the fact that 45% of finance

Table 4.7 *Drivers of e-commerce*

Percent indicating driver is a significant factor	*Establishment size*		*Sector*			*Total*	
	SME	*Large*	*Mfg.*	*Distrib.*	*Finance*	*Germany*	*Global*
Customers demanded it	25	37	33	22	28	25	37
Major competitors were online	43	42	30	46	54	43	31
Suppliers required it	8	14	32	2	0	8	22
To reduce costs	20	18	32	16	25	20	36
To expand market for existing product or services	58	32	51	61	45	58	48
To enter new businesses or markets	46	39	39	50	28	46	42
To improve coordination with customers and suppliers	42	49	59	38	35	42	44
Required for government procurement	2	11	8	0	6	2	15
Government provided incentives	2	1	9	0	2	2	8

Source: CRITO GEC Survey, 2002

companies are using the Internet to expand markets suggests that there is room to reach new customers online.

For manufacturers (51%), and especially for retailers and wholesalers (61%), the Internet appears to have even more potential for expanding markets. This reflects the potential of B2B- and B2C-oriented investments in the retail/wholesale industry, where traditional catalog sellers have increased their online business significantly and successfully. They have been able to reach more customers at lower

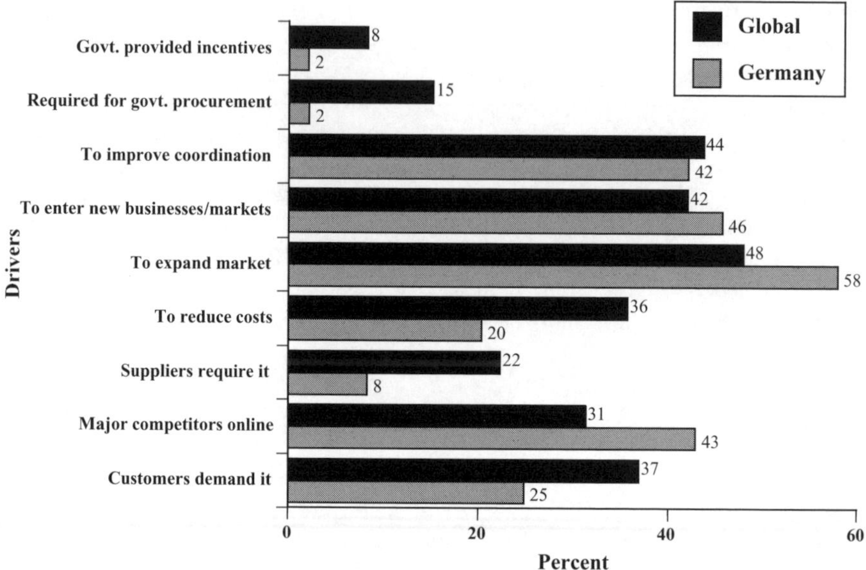

Figure 4.2 E-commerce drivers
Source: CRITO GEC Survey, 2002

cost by reducing the number of printed catalogs in favor of more web investments and web advertising.

Another leading driver is the fact that competitors are online, perhaps reflecting the fast-follower mentality of German firms. Once some firms had adopted e-commerce, others felt it was necessary to move as well. Competitive pressure was the top driver in the finance sector, where competition is local and easily visible. Unfortunately, the banking/insurance sector has to cope with declining service prices and free online services, such as online banking and brokerage services. Thus, online services may be valuable to customers and a requirement for keeping up with competitors, but the ability of banks and insurance companies to appropriate some of this value is unclear.

Surprisingly, pressure by customers (25%) or suppliers (8%) to use the Internet is rather low in Germany, compared with the global sample. One explanation may be the extensive usage of EDI to transmit business messages, lessening pressure from customers or suppliers to adopt Internet-based e-commerce. This also may explain the relatively low importance of reducing costs as a driver, as prior EDI adoption may have already driven significant cost reductions.

The last important driver for Internet usage in the three industry sectors is the opportunity to improve coordination with customers and suppliers. Fifty-nine percent of establishments in the manufacturing industry expect coordination benefits from using the Internet, while only 38% in the wholesale/retail industry and 35% in the banking/insurance industry, respectively, do so. In this case, the Internet is perceived to provide potential coordination gains, even though EDI may already be in use, perhaps because of the greater richness of information that can be transmitted via Internet applications.

Extremely unimportant are government-related factors which, consequently, cannot be regarded as drivers for the usage of Internet technologies. Neither government demand for online procurement capability (2%), nor direct governmental incentives or subsidies (2%), are mentioned as significant drivers for adoption decisions. On the contrary, the results suggest that lack of e-commerce knowledge and projects inside the government will become an impediment not only today but especially in the near future. While most B2B processes can be conducted online, firms have to prepare paper-based and therefore inefficient processes in parallel to the business-to-government (B2G) side.

Barriers

In comparison with the global average, most barriers to e-commerce adoption are less important or restrictive in Germany (Table 4.8 and Figure 4.3). For example, the need for face-to-face customer interaction (12% in Germany in comparison with 34% in the global sample) is not seen as a significant barrier. Concerns about privacy of data or even security issues are not a major obstacle in Germany (only 25% selected this issue as an important barrier) in contrast with the global sample (44%). This indicates that Germans have had good experiences with the Internet and are losing more of their resistance to using it. It also may reflect strong data privacy laws in Germany and in the European Union. However, privacy and data security concerns are a major barrier for finance companies, which deal with sensitive financial information.

German establishments cite other barriers that are important as well. Finding qualified and experienced e-commerce staff is more of a

Table 4.8 *Barriers to e-commerce*

	Establishment size		*Sector*			*Total*	
Percent indicating statement is a significant obstacle	*SME*	*Large*	*Mfg.*	*Distrib.*	*Finance*	*Germany*	*Global*
Need for face-to-face customer interaction	12	26	23	9	12	12	34
Concern about privacy of data or security issues	25	32	21	22	65	25	44
Customers do not use the technology	24	14	26	24	18	24	31
Finding staff with e-commerce expertise	42	15	28	48	14	41	27
Prevalence of credit card use in the country	22	16	17	23	20	22	20
Costs of implementing an e-commerce site	32	29	22	37	14	32	34
Making needed organizational changes	31	40	27	34	9	31	24
Level of ability to use the Internet as part of business strategy	14	14	15	14	15	14	25
Cost of Internet access	2	2	5	0	9	2	15
Business laws do not support e-commerce	5	14	17	0	22	5	24
Taxation of Internet sales	2	3	7	0	1	2	16
Inadequate legal protection for Internet purchases	21	24	13	22	26	21	34

Source: CRITO GEC Survey, 2002

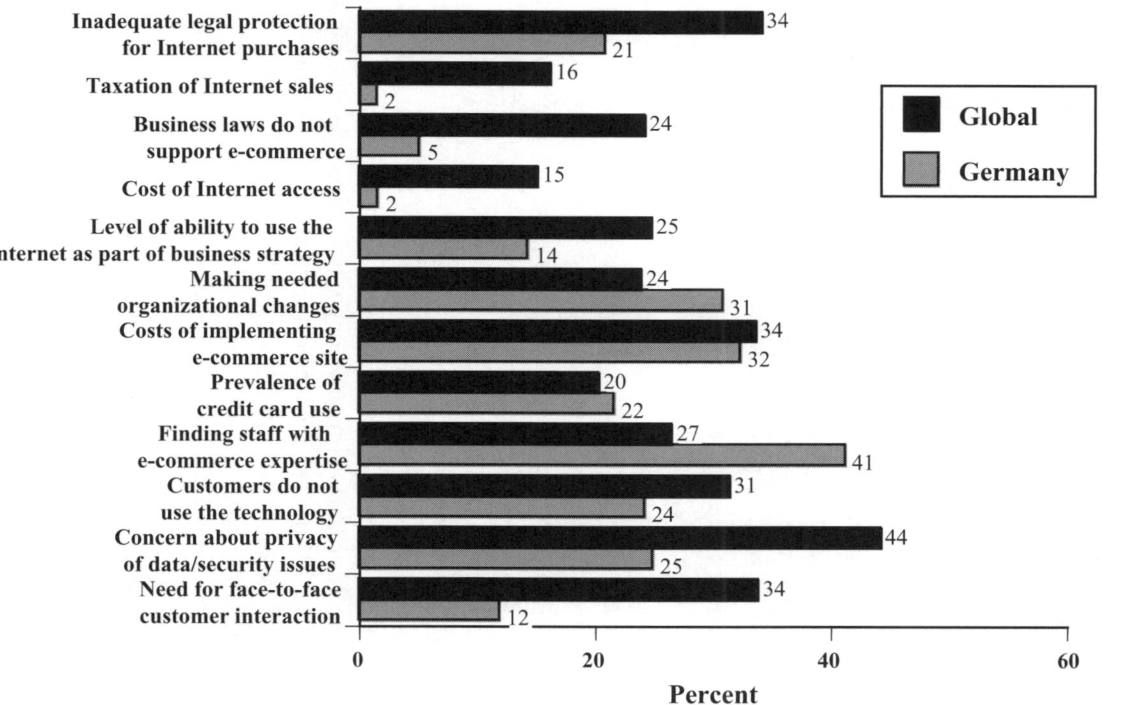

Figure 4.3 E-commerce barriers
Source: CRITO GEC Survey, 2002

problem in Germany (41%) than anywhere else (27%). The lack of IT specialists is especially critical in the retail/wholesale industry, and among SMEs, possibly because of lower wages paid in those sectors or the fact that skilled IT professionals prefer to work for larger, better-known manufacturing and financial firms.

The low diffusion of credit cards in Germany is an obstacle in the B2C area. In fact, it is more common to use debit cards than credit cards for payment at stores or gas stations. Concerns about possible abuse associated with providing credit card numbers online has reduced the number of potential users.

An additional barrier for German industry is the necessity of changing existing business processes when implementing e-commerce solutions. More than 30% of German establishments are worried or not able to implement necessary organizational changes. This issue is especially salient in the retail/wholesale industry (34%), where the necessary prerequisites such as ERP or a general IT infrastructure are less likely to be available in comparison with other sectors.

Apart from the difficulties in finding experienced staff and the expensive costs of e-commerce sites, organizational changes are the most significant impeding factors hindering the fast diffusion of e-commerce in Germany, although German establishments deal with lower barriers in comparison with the global sample. However, without skilled staff, other obstacles such as making organizational changes remain unsolved problems hampering the process of diffusion and usage. Moreover, without IT know-how, investments in more sophisticated and difficult-to-implement e-commerce solutions cannot be realized, again hampering further development. Even after the dot.com bubble burst, the limited availability of IT personnel is the most serious bottleneck today and in the near future for German industry.

Policy issues are generally not important obstacles for doing business online. Good legal protection together with clear taxation and business laws, e.g., the long-distance distribution law which covers traditional catalog sellers as well as online retailers, are viewed by the respondents as drivers rather than barriers for doing business online in Germany. Other less important barriers are Internet access costs, thanks to the open and competitive telecommunications market, the inadequate support of business laws, due to one of the earliest e-commerce and digital signature laws in the world, and the taxation of online sales,

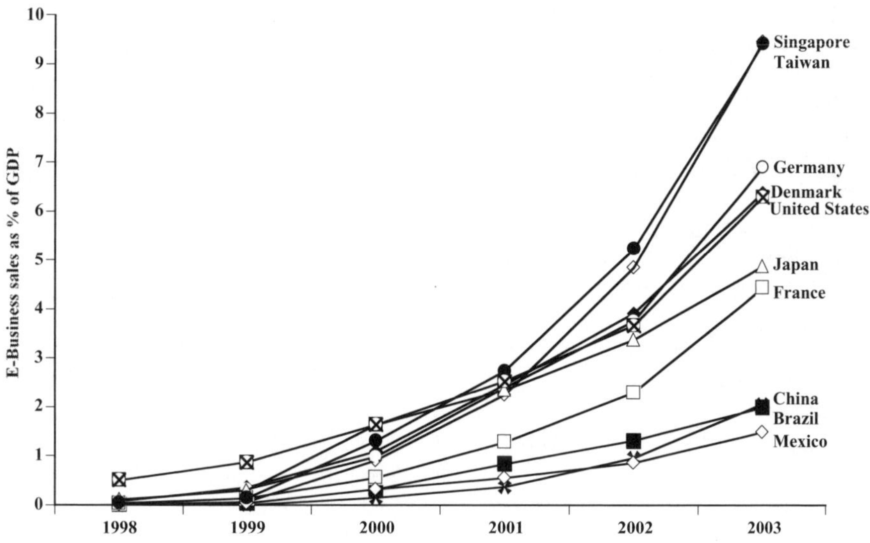

Figure 4.4 Internet-based e-business diffusion, 1998–2003
Source: IDC, 2003a

which are taxed at the same rate as traditional businesses in Germany and Europe.

Diffusion of e-commerce

Despite the economic downturn following the dot.com bust, e-commerce usage has grown rapidly. Traditional firms imitated or reinvented successful business models across much of the economy, consistent with Germany's "fast-follower" tradition. Reflecting widespread adoption, e-commerce sales as a share of GDP jumped ahead of the USA to reach nearly 7% of the German GDP in 2003 (Figure 4.4).

Firms' usage of the Internet

German firms use the Internet at a pace that is equal to or greater than the global average on every metric of the GEC Survey (Table 4.9 and Figure 4.5). This again reflects the breadth of Internet use once Germany's "fast followers" made the move online. In particular, the

Table 4.9 *Uses of the Internet*

Percent using the Internet for . . .	*Establishment size*		*Sector*			*Total*	
	SME	*Large*	*Mfg.*	*Distrib.*	*Finance*	*Germany*	*Global*
Advertising and marketing purposes	78	77	72	79	78	78	58
Making sales online	58	34	28	68	38	57	30
After-sales customer service and support	53	48	44	55	58	53	44
Making purchases online	61	54	51	65	45	61	47
Exchanging operational data with suppliers	60	53	48	65	43	60	48
Exchanging operational data with business customers	52	50	56	50	56	52	51
Formally integrating the same business processes with suppliers or other business partners	48	38	23	56	37	48	34

Source: CRITO GEC Survey, 2002

difference is substantial for advertising and marketing, making sales online, and integrating with suppliers or other business partners.

Among these, the most striking is the high level of firms actually selling online in Germany, at 57% compared with the global average of 30% (Figure 4.5). This is consistent with the high level of online sales at the national level, but its significance goes further. It means not only that e-commerce transactions are high in volume, which could be simply a result of some large firms doing very high levels of online sales and procurement, but that the use of the Internet for selling is widespread among firms. Even more interesting is that SMEs are much

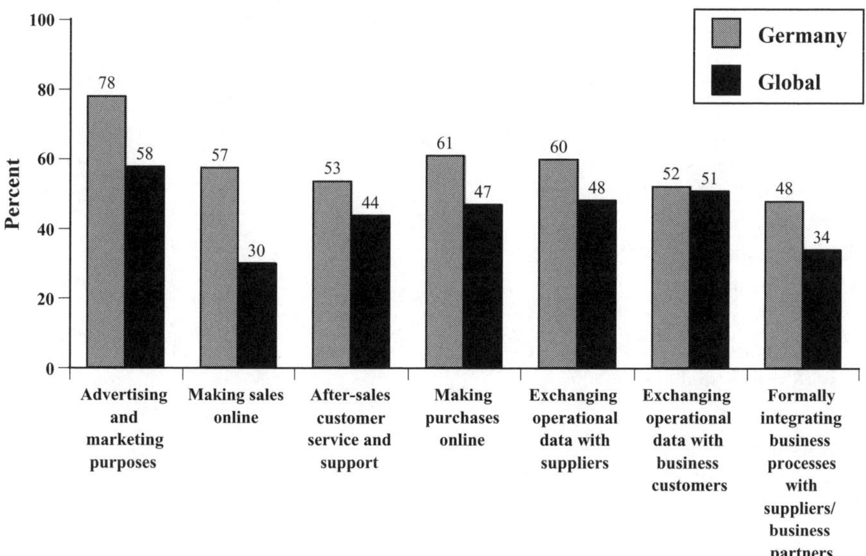

Figure 4.5 Use of the Internet
Source: CRITO GEC Survey, 2002

more likely to make sales online, which shows again the aggressiveness of technology adoption by the German *Mittelstand*, even compared with larger German firms.

Industry differences are evident as well, as significantly more retail/ wholesale firms use e-commerce for online sales and purchasing, as well as data exchange with suppliers and formal integration of the same business process, than firms in the other two sectors. The fact that the distribution sector does more buying and selling online is not so surprising given the transaction intensity of its business, but it is somewhat surprising that this sector also is the leader in using the Internet for coordination by sharing information and integrating processes. This could again reflect the fact that manufacturers are satisfied with using EDI to coordinate with external partners, but also shows how far the distribution sector has gone already in integrating the Internet into its business processes.

Channel strategies

In contrast to other countries, German firms do not use the Internet and electronic commerce as a substitute for traditional markets or

Table 4.10 *How firms use the Internet to sell products and services*

Percent indicating Internet used to . . .	*Establishment size*		*Sector*			*Total*	
	SME	*Large*	*Mfg.*	*Distrib.*	*Finance*	*Germany*	*Global*
Address new markets only	8	8	0	9	0	7	15
Address traditional distribution channels only	76	81	91	73	85	76	44
Compete directly with traditional distribution channels	17	10	9	18	15	17	27
Replace traditional distribution channels	0	1	0	0	0	0	13

Source: CRITO GEC Survey, 2002

distribution channels, but rather as a complementary tool to complete and support the already sophisticated market channels (Table 4.10). As a result, it is not that important to address only new markets because national and international channels are already well established, and only 7% of respondents stated that the Internet was used to address new markets only. In some cases it also may not be possible to eliminate existing channels even if the Internet makes it economically possible to do so. For instance, the increasing number of online services makes it less necessary for banks to have branches in each city or village. But banks are not able to close their branches out of consideration for older or low-income customers without Internet access. Consequently, 76% of German firms reported using Internet capabilities to address existing distribution channels, while none reported using the Internet to reduce or replace traditional distribution channels, and only 17% used it to compete with other distribution channels.

B2B vs. B2C e-commerce

Fifty-two percent of firms use the Internet for B2B sales (34% B2B only plus 18% doing both B2B and B2C), compared with just 28%

(13% B2B only plus 15% both) for the global sample (Table 4.11). However, the use of B2C commerce in Germany (30% – 12% B2C only plus 18% both) is much lower, although still somewhat ahead of the global sample (22% – 7% and 15%), yet, the volume of B2C sales actually is slightly higher than B2B sales (9% of total versus 8%), because among those firms which conduct B2C sales, a relatively high amount of overall sales is done online (31% versus 16% for B2B).

There is a distinct difference between large firms and SMEs in their use of B2C versus B2B sales. Fifty-three percent of SMEs conduct B2B sales (34% plus 19%), compared with just 28% of large firms, while 30% of SMEs conduct B2C sales, versus 21% of large firms. In terms of sales volume, however, SMEs do 31% of their B2C sales online compared with just 7% for large firms (among those which sell online), but for B2B the positions are reversed, with 16% of SME sales done online versus 20% for large firms. This provides further evidence of the willingness of SMEs not only to adopt but to use e-commerce extensively, surpassing large firms in many dimensions of use.

The survey shows that retail/wholesale firms have the highest share of B2C sales online, at 33% for those that participate, while finance has the highest share of B2B sales online at 26%. The distribution sector has the most firms selling online, the most which support online payment, and the highest overall share of sales online. This again may suggest that manufacturers conduct transactions via EDI systems, but also shows that the distribution sector is using the Internet heavily for transactions, in spite of the potential for channel conflict with retail outlets.

Mobile commerce

German industry has adopted a wait-and-see mentality followed by careful integration of e-commerce technologies, and has generally avoided the hype of the dot.com era. Nevertheless, in the field of mobile commerce (m-commerce), Germany has been driven to an extent by hype, thanks in part to the high levels of cell phone diffusion and enthusiastic adoption of mobile services such as the short messaging service. At the time of writing, however, the expected m-business boom has not started yet, as a lack of promising mobile business models hinders broader business deployment. In comparison with the global sample, slightly more German firms have installed m-commerce solutions (18%

Table 4.11 *Online sales*

	Establishment size		*Sector*			*Total*	
	SME	*Large*	*Mfg.*	*Distrib.*	*Finance*	*Germany*	*Global*
Type of online sales							
Percent B2B only	34	19	19	40	12	34	13
Percent B2C only	11	12	3	13	16	12	7
Percent both B2B and B2C	19	9	10	21	20	18	15
Mean percent of total consumer sales conducted online (all establishments)	9	1	1	11	7	9	4
Mean percent of total business sales conducted online (all establishments)	8	4	6	9	8	8	4
Mean percent of total consumer sales conducted online (only those doing B2C sales online)	31	7	8	33	22	31	19
Mean percent of total business sales conducted online (only those doing B2B sales online)	16	20	19	15	26	16	15
Percent of websites that support online payment (only those doing online sales)	42	38	28	44	31	42	34

Source: CRITO GEC Survey, 2002

compared with 14%), but willingness to invest in further implementation is somewhat below average (12% compared with 18%). High implementation rates were observable only in the banking/insurance sector, where mobile payment methods, as well as mobile banking and brokerage, enjoy a degree of popularity (28%). Most insurance companies do not offer any mobile access at the moment, but plan to offer customized insurance on demand, e.g., ordering special one-day accident insurance at mountain ski lifts via cell phone.

Since the next generation of mobile communication standards has already appeared on the horizon with a vast installed base of wireless access points for PCs and mobile handhelds, most Germans believe that the Universal Mobile Telecommunications System (UMTS, or third generation of mobile standards) will be leapfrogged by WiFi hot spots-based applications and business models.

The e-commerce industry

While Germany's adoption of e-commerce largely mirrors the fast-follower model on the user side, the country did not entirely escape the dot.com boom and bust. From 1993 to 2000, Germany saw the emergence of around 15,000 start-ups, peaking around 1997. Most were B2C and B2B companies which offered products and services online. Among the companies using an Internet or e-commerce business model, three segments may be identified: 15% of firms are offering products and services via the Internet in the B2B and B2C e-commerce sector; roughly 77% of all start-ups are in the Internet-related service sector (multimedia, Internet service providers (ISPs), and integrators); and only 6% are in the Internet technology sector (infrastructure and software) (Krafft, 2000).

At the beginning of 2001, roughly 100 e-commerce firms were listed on the stock exchange, most of them in the so-called "new market" (*Neuer Markt*) segment. Most of the 750 initial public offering (IPO) candidates at this time were venture capital backed, while around 14,000 small and medium-sized start-ups with up to 50 employees were financed by their own funds or bank credits (Krafft, 2000).

As in other countries, the technology collapse and economic slowdown of 2001–2002 hit the young German e-commerce industry hard. A large number of formerly well-known and promising dot.coms failed during the consolidation process. After the insolvency wave, accompanied by bad debt losses and failure of customer trust, the overall gloomy mood affected even solid firms. Germany saw 443 insolvencies and an additional 470 bankruptcies in 2001 and approximately 40–50 insolvencies per month in 2002. According to German law, insolvency is more or less equivalent to the US protection by Chapter Eleven, when a firm is finally closed after reorganization was unsuccessful. E-commerce business models in the B2C area struggled the most, but multimedia agencies and software developers encountered similar difficulties. The insolvencies of innovative university and research spin-offs must be regarded as critical hindrances for the further development of e-commerce in Germany (Krafft, 2002).

Impacts of e-commerce

Given the high levels of use over a broad range of large and small firms, one might expect German firms to have experienced significant impacts on business performance. Yet the survey data show that overall impacts are comparable with global averages (Table 4.12). The only cases where German firms have enjoyed significantly higher impacts are in internal process improvement and increased international sales. The former may reflect the emphasis on integration with existing processes and technologies, while the latter reflects the international orientation of German firms. By contrast, only 14% of German firms reported that coordination with suppliers had improved, compared with 30% of the global sample. German firms also lagged in improving productivity, reducing inventory, and improving their competitive position.

Apart from operational process improvements, e-commerce also has positive effects on the external, market-oriented side. Twenty-eight percent of German firms (compared with only 20% of the global sample), especially in the retail/wholesale sector (36%), were able to increase their international sales via the Internet. In contrast, procurement costs decreased less significantly than in the global sample. Only 1% of the manufacturing and banking/insurance industries were able to reduce their costs of procurement, in comparison with the retail/wholesale sector where 15% mentioned decreases. This may be due to already low prices within the competitive traditional market. The same holds true for inventory costs. Most establishments have an efficient system in place, so the possibilities of additional optimization benefits are rather

Table 4.12 *Impact of e-commerce on performance*

Percent indicating high impact	Establishment size		Sector			Total	
	SME	Large	Mfg.	Distrib.	Finance	Germany	Global
Internal processes more efficient	42	20	41	44	23	42	34
Staff productivity increased	19	20	11	20	24	19	27
Sales increased	19	9	12	21	21	19	21
Sales area widened	32	12	20	35	31	32	31
Customer service improved	35	37	23	37	51	36	35
International sales increased	28	11	14	36	1	28	20
Procurement costs decreased	11	17	1	15	1	11	18
Inventory costs decreased	6	9	4	7	2	6	14
Coordination with suppliers improved	14	34	32	9	19	14	30
Competitive position improved	23	29	21	22	36	23	30

Source: CRITO GEC Survey, 2002

slim. Therefore, the impact of online services is not as important and far-reaching for German firms.

More notable are differences between large and small firms, and across industries. SMEs enjoy much higher impacts in terms of improving internal processes, increased sales, widened sales area, and increased international sales. The last three likely reflect the fact that SMEs are using the Internet more extensively to sell online, and may suggest that they are using the Internet to target international markets that were beyond their reach before. Large firms do better only in terms of coordination with suppliers, which could be related to their ability to use the Internet with smaller suppliers which do not have EDI capabilities. At the sectoral level, it is distribution firms that have

Table 4.13 *Impact on competition*

	Establishment size		*Sector*			*Total*	
Percent indicating . . .	*SME*	*Large*	*Mfg.*	*Distrib.*	*Finance*	*Germany*	*Global*
Number of distribution channels							
Increased	63	44	42	69	47	63	40
No change	36	54	55	31	47	36	56
Decreased	1	2	3	0	6	1	4
Number of suppliers							
Increased	25	21	28	23	44	25	30
No change	68	72	68	70	49	68	64
Decreased	7	7	4	7	7	7	6
Number of competitors							
Increased	18	18	11	17	38	18	28
No change	74	77	85	74	50	74	67
Decreased	8	5	4	9	12	8	5
Intensity of competition							
Increased	45	30	45	43	63	45	42
No change	48	70	52	50	31	49	54
Decreased	7	0	3	7	6	6	4

Source: CRITO GEC Survey, 2002

experienced the greatest impacts, again reflecting their relatively high levels of use, particularly for online transactions.

The data on impacts may again point to the fact that German firms, particularly larger ones, are relatively intensive users of EDI, and had less room for improvement in adopting the Internet. It may also be true that smaller firms are more flexible and thus better able to incorporate the Internet into their businesses in ways that improve performance, as found by Zhu et al. (2004).

Another impact of going online is the number of trading partners and the intensity of competition firms face. The number of distribution channels increased significantly in comparison with the global sample (63% versus 40% reporting an increase), with the greatest difference being observed in the retail/wholesale sector (Table 4.13). Since most establishments use online business as a complement to rather than a substitute for existing channels, this may mean that most firms are using the Internet to support new channel partners in previously unserved markets. The figure was much higher for SMEs, which probably had more room to expand their distribution base. By contrast, the number of suppliers increased somewhat less than the global sample (25% versus 30%), with SMEs and large firms experiencing similar impacts. It may be that firms already have established an adequate supply base and are not as motivated to find additional suppliers, even though the Internet might reduce the cost of finding and adding suppliers.

In terms of competitive environment, only 18% of German firms felt that they faced more competitors since adopting the Internet, compared with 28% for the global sample. Yet, 45% of German firms felt that the intensity of competition had increased, suggesting that the Internet was escalating competition among the same group of firms rather than introducing new competitors.

Conclusion

Our analysis supports the view of Germany as a fast follower of e-commerce technologies. While German adoption of the Internet started somewhat later than that of many other European countries, Germany has now reached high levels of adoption and intensity of use across a wide range of e-commerce activities. Adoption is widespread, led as much by SMEs as by large firms.

The role of SMEs is an important part of the German e-commerce story. This is partly due to the innovative, dynamic nature of the German *Mittelstand*, which is shown by their enthusiastic adoption of the Internet. There is also a contrast with larger firms in the flexibility of SMEs and the fact that they were less locked into pre-Internet technologies.

Overall, the extensive prior adoption of EDI and other technologies may have slowed adoption of the Internet in Germany initially. Some of the efficiency and coordination gains achievable through e-commerce had already been captured, and there were potential switching costs involved in moving to the Internet. This was especially true of larger firms and manufacturers, which moved deliberately to integrate e-commerce with their existing technologies. Still, when Internet-based e-commerce began to be widely adopted, it was smaller firms and retail/wholesale distributors which were more aggressive in its use, and which realized the greatest benefits.

While Germany has adopted a number of policy initiatives to facilitate e-commerce, government is not seen as an important driver, either by offering subsidies or by actively using e-commerce technologies itself. In fact, the public sector is still far behind in EC diffusion compared with the other sectors studied in this survey (König et al., 2002). However, it should be noted that strong policies to protect privacy and the general high levels of confidence in legal protections for online commerce provide an important institutional infrastructure that matches Germany's excellent physical and communications infrastructure. The result is relatively low barriers to e-commerce, as reported in the survey.

A more important driver of e-commerce than government promotion has been the highly international orientation of the German economy. As a trading hub for Europe, and home to internationally competitive firms in many industries, Germany has a strong motivation to adopt e-commerce to coordinate international operations and to sustain its competitive advantage. This international orientation reaches from large firms down to many SMEs, and has driven e-commerce more than in most countries, and certainly more than in the other large economies in this study.

Sidebar on SME innovation

ARBURG GmbH (www.arburg.com/com/COM/en/index.jsp) was founded in 1923 to manufacture precision medical instruments. The company is located in the rural Black Forest region (in the south-west state of Baden-Württemberg) which is famous for SMEs' ingenuity. ARBURG originally delivered its products to large companies along the Rhine River or to the metropolitan area of Stuttgart – where, for example, DaimlerChrysler and Porsche and the headquarters of IBM Germany are located. ARBURG is still a family-owned business (a common characteristic of German SMEs). During its history, the innovative company has evolved from making flashlights for photographers to being a successful producer of injection molding machines.

Today, ARBURG has a workforce of 1,900 people, with sales and service offices in 21 countries all over the globe, serving customers in 48 countries. ARBURG was one of the early adopters of the Internet technology, trying to reduce communication costs and to increase serviceability of its products (e.g., by remote monitoring of systems in the field, and planning the replacement of product parts via networks).

More than 1,000 PC workplaces providing technical data processing (e.g., engineering support, bills of materials, operations sequencing) and accounting, controlling, and other business applications are in use. The ARBURG ICT network handles more than 800,000 transactions per day. ARBURG provides its foreign branches with a centrally hosted shopping cart solution for spare parts, with a 3% discount for customers using the online shop. Since 2001, ARBURG offers catalog data as Internet files (Extensible Markup Language, cXML; or Comma-Separated Values, CSV) for its customers to enable a semi-automatic order-processing capability. Furthermore, remote monitoring of the molding machines is partly possible via the Internet. But most importantly, the Internet-based services are aimed at improving the worldwide availability of product information to provide customers around the globe with fast access to the necessary information for ordering.

References

Andersen, K. V., Beck, R., Wigand, R. T., Brousseau, E., & Andersen, N. B. (2005). European E-Commerce Policies in the Pioneering Days, the Gold Rush and the Post-Hype Era. *Information Polity*, 9, 3/4.

Beck, R., König, W., & Wigand, R. T. (2003). Creating Value in E-Banking: Efficient Usage of EC Applications and Technologies. *Proceedings of the 7th Pacific-Asia Conference on Information Systems (PACIS)*. Adelaide, Australia: PACIS. From www.pacis-net.org/m4.htm

Beck, R., Wigand, R. T., & König, W. (2005). The Diffusion and Efficient Use of Electronic Commerce in Small and Medium-Sized Enterprises: An International Three-Industry Survey. *Electronic Markets,* 15(1), 1–16.

European Information Technology Observatory (EITO) (2002). *European Information Technology Observatory 2002*, update October 2002. Frankfurt.

Federal Commissioner for Foreign Direct Investment in Germany (2001). *Germany: Gateway to Europe.* From www.foreign-direct-investment.de/gateway112002.pdf

International Data Corporation (IDC) (2003a). *EIM-Country View*. Framingham, MA.

International Data Corporation (IDC) (2003b). *Internet Commerce Market Model v.8.3*. Framingham, MA.

International Planning and Research Corporation (IPR) (2003). *Eighth Annual Business Software Alliance (BSA) Global Software Piracy Study, Trends in Software Piracy 1994–2002*. Washington, D.C.: Business Software Alliance.

International Telecommunication Union (ITU) (2004). *World Telecommunication Indicators Database* (8th Ed.). Geneva, Switzerland.

König, W., Wigand, R. T., & Beck, R. (2002). *Globalization of E-Commerce: Environment and Policy in Germany.* From the CRITO website: www.crito.uci.edu/publications/pdf/GEC2_Germany.pdf

Krafft, L. (2000). *Current Status and Perspectives for the Internet/E-Commerce Startup Landscape in Germany.* Retrieved October 28, 2002, from www.e-startup.org/downld_e/landsca.ppt

Krafft, L. (2002). *Aktuelle Ausfallraten bei Internet/EC-Gründungen in Deutschland.* Retrieved October 28, 2002, from www.e-startup.org/download/kon_6_02.ppt

MIND (2002). *MIND, Mittelstand in Deutschland.* Cologne, Gruner Jahr. Retrieved February 2, 2002, from www.mind-mittelstand.de/studie/pdf/gesamt.pdf

Statistisches Bundesamt (1999). From www.destatis.de/download/fist/abs_99.xls

World Bank (2004). *WDI Online.* From http://publications.worldbank.ord/WDI/

Zentrum für Europäische Wirtschaftsforschung GmbH (ZEW) (2002). *The Adoption of Business-to-Business E-Commerce: Empirical Evidence for German Companies.* Retrieved October 4, 2002, from ftp://ftp.zew.de/pub/zew-docs/dp/dp0205.pdf

Zhu, K., Kraemer, K. L., Xu, S., & Dedrick, J. (2004). Information Technology Payoff in E-business Environments: An International Perspective on Impacts of E-Business in the Financial Services Industry. *Journal of Management Information Systems*, 21(1), 17–54.

5 Japan: local innovation and diversity in e-commerce

DENNIS S. TACHIKI,
SATOSHI HAMAYA, AND
KOU YUKAWA

Introduction

Japan is characterized by a unique industrial landscape, including interlocking networks of firms (*keiretsu*), a highly interwoven political economy (iron triangle), and a distinctive business culture. The combination of these factors leads to a somewhat insular business environment, as indicated by globalization measures uniformly below the global average of firms in the GEC database. Despite the importance of globalization to innovation, Japan is comparable with other economies along the various e-commerce usage measures contained in the global sample. However, Japan lags far behind in achieving some of the key benefits associated with Internet adoption, such as increased sales and reduced procurement costs. Japan thus illustrates the salience of local factors in the adaptation of new technologies such as e-commerce within national environments. In contrast to the notion of the Internet and e-commerce driving a borderless global economy, Japan illustrates that characteristics of the national economy may be reinforced by the use of the Internet and e-commerce, and not be muted by the global melting pot.

Japanese firms have made great strides in adopting a wide variety of e-commerce technologies. Together with adaptation of proven models such as the Silicon Valley model in Tokyo's Bit Valley, e-commerce emerges as an important, though not necessarily transformational, technology enabling operational efficiencies along industry supply chains. However, the level of information systems spending is modest compared with the average firm in the global sample. This has led to the idea that Japanese companies lag in getting online. Moreover, it is not always clear to Japanese managers that e-commerce represents a better business model than their existing style of management. Thus, we found Internet-based information systems often coexist with EDI systems, suggesting a hybrid approach to e-commerce in Japan.

Results indicate that the Japanese e-commerce experience has been mixed. Specific results of our study are summarized as follows:

- *Overall e-commerce experience.* Results from our study using GEC Survey data indicate that the Japanese e-commerce experience has been mixed. Overall diffusion is comparable to global averages. E-commerce appears to enable a reshaping of distribution channels in the wholesale and retail sector, aided in part by government deregulation. In terms of impacts, Japanese firms are much lower than their global counterparts on a number of indicators, possibly due to frictional factors such as *keiretsu*.
- *Low IS spending.* We observed great strides in adopting a wide variety of e-commerce technologies, but the level of spending for information systems (IS) is modest compared with the global sample.
- *Liberalization and deregulation.* A key finding in our study is that liberalization and deregulation policies matter the most, opening economic space for unaffiliated *keiretsu* companies to develop new business models. Contrary to the convergence hypothesis, we found that the state has some role in setting the rules of the game in order to promote e-commerce.
- *Industry differences.* Each industry plays a different role in the economy and has different ties to the global economy. The manufacturing sector is more involved in upstream business functions, the wholesale and retail sector in distribution business functions, and the banking and finance sector in capital intermediation functions. These functions are the most international in the manufacturing sector and most domestically oriented in the wholesale and retail sector. In short, industry sectors or sub-sectors with the deepest global reach are more likely to be in a position to take advantage of emerging opportunities. In the Japanese case, the *keiretsu* play an important role. Though some believe that the days of the *keiretsu* are in their twilight, an important finding of this study is that they are reconstituting themselves – their survival may well depend on how well they identify and implement their e-commerce initiatives.

Table 5.1 *Information and communications technologies, 1998–2002*

	1998	*1999*	*2000*	*2001*	*2002*
Telecommunications					
Main phone lines per 1,000 pop.	534.01	556.89	585.75	576.04	557.90
Cell phone subscribers per 1,000 pop.	374.33	448.84	526.19	587.78	636.07
Cable subscribers per 1,000 pop.	125.16	139.34	147.38	166.97	182.95
Internet					
Internet hosts per 1,000 pop.	13.35	20.82	36.57	55.92	72.61
Internet users per 1,000 pop.	134.04	213.66	299.40	384.16	448.52
IT					
IT as percent of GDP	2.37	2.42	2.45	29	2.69
PCs per 1,000 pop.	237.38	286.62	315.16	358.23	381.87
Software piracy rate (percent)	0.31	0.31	0.37	0.37	0.35

Sources: IDC, 2000; IPR, 2003; ITU, 2004; World Bank, 2004

Country background

Japan in context

Macroeconomy

With a GDP of approximately $4 trillion, Japan is the second largest economy in the world and represents over half of the combined economic activity in East Asia (METI, 2004). It is a relatively wealthy economy, with a per capita income of roughly $31,000, placing it among the world's leading developed economies. This statistical snapshot of Japan belies the prolonged stagnation in its economy, however, resulting from the bursting of the asset bubble economy in the 1990s. The major challenge facing the government and companies is reviving the Japanese economy over the first decade of the new century.

Environment and policy

The debate surrounding the *IT Kakumei* (information technology revolution) since the turn of the century suggests Japan is moving belatedly towards utilizing e-commerce to revive its economy. Roughly 64% of the population uses cell phones, eclipsing wireline installations at 56% (Table 5.1). The large wireless infrastructure is a result of innovative m-commerce applications spearheaded by NTT DoCoMo and its competitors. Internet hosts have risen dramatically, from 13 per 1,000 in 1998 to 73 per 1,000 in 2002. In this same time period, Internet use more than tripled, from 134 per 1,000 to 449 per 1,000. Yet, IT as a percentage of GDP remains low (2.7%), while the number of PCs is 382 per 1,000. This latter number is small compared with other leading developed nations such as the USA and is one indicator of the slow adoption of IT in Japan, with the exception of its innovative and leading mobile e-commerce applications.

The mismatch between the IT infrastructure and demand for e-commerce services has stimulated a policy debate in Japan to close this gap. Since 2000, Japan has been pursuing an e-Japan Strategy based on four pillars. First, building a high-speed fiber-optic network reaching 30 million families within five years with open access at a competitive price, and ensuring the protection of privacy and security. Second, promoting e-commerce by encouraging companies to shift from brick-and-mortar business models to the use of virtual space, thereby increasing the B2B market by 10 times and the B2C market by 50 times. Third, creating an e-government that allows citizens to conduct public administration business online. And fourth, implementing e-learning programs within the formal education system and across society. The e-Japan strategy suggests this country is now moving online in order to increase the competitiveness of its companies and become a civil society.

Prior research asserts that the Internet and e-commerce diffuse rapidly across countries, reducing the role of the state in people's lives and bringing equal opportunities for large and small firms across all industries. We use the CRITO analytical framework as a baseline model to assess these assertions. However, we add a "relational context" to highlight the role of the *keiretsu* and political economy (iron triangle) to localize our story of e-commerce in Japan (Kraemer *et al.*, 2003) (Figure 5.1). A relational context provides us with a prism for examining how endogenous factors also facilitate and hinder the spread of e-commerce.

A *keiretsu*, a group of firms organized around a lead bank, is a good example of the closely tied interlocking network relationships that shape the business landscape in Japan. Long-term relationships are maintained and stability among suppliers and customers is strengthened. Such networks are likely to be a key factor in shaping e-commerce diffusion. Overlaid on the *keiretsu* is Japan's "iron triangle" political economy of close and long-lasting relationships among key members of

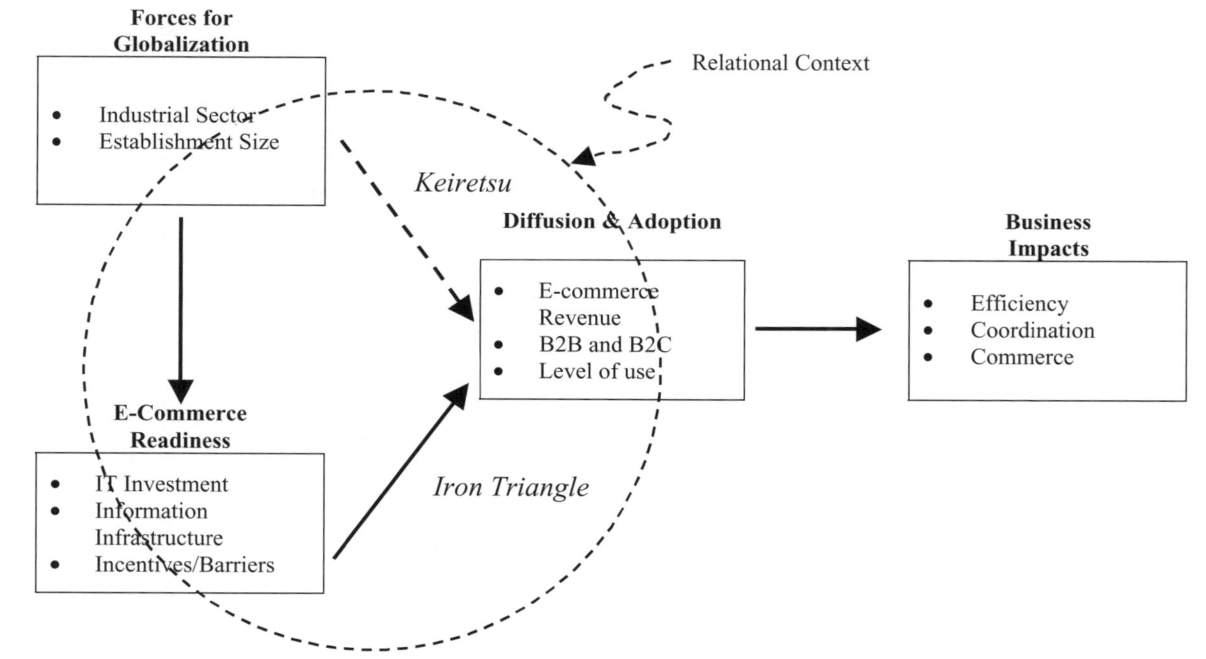

Figure 5.1 Analytical framework
Source: Adapted from Kraemer et al., 2003

three constituencies: the ruling political parties (especially the Liberal Democratic Party), the bureaucracy, and major business organizations. Together, *keiretsu* and the iron triangle represent a complex network of inter-related organizations and individuals, which no doubt plays a major role in the adoption of e-commerce.

So does the total quality management (TQM) movement. In the 1960s Japan embraced the ideas of W. Edwards Deming for increasing productivity by simply reducing the defect rate while keeping production volumes and labor costs constant (Tachiki, 1990). This simple notion became the basis for Japan's renowned TQM. Practices such as the just-in-time delivery system in the manufacturing sector and strategic information systems (SIS) used in the retail (convenience stores) and transport services (takkyubin – overnight delivery) sectors. These practices used closed EDI information systems. Since TQM emerged to become a key element of Japan's business culture, how companies resolve replacing their "closed" EDI information systems with the "open" Internet-based information systems is important for understanding the diffusion of e-commerce in Japan.

Globalization

Countries with more globally oriented economies in terms of trade and foreign investment have higher levels of information and communications technology investment (Caselli & Coleman, 2001; Shih et al., 2002). GEC data enable us to assess the degree to which companies are global, in terms of the international nature of their operations, sources of revenues, and competition (Kraemer et al., 2003). Relative to the average firm in the global sample, Japan is low on globalization indicators (Table 5.2). Impediments to doing business in Japan, including high operating costs, complex distribution networks, and "closed" business practices, are determinant factors in observed differences (Encarnation, 1999). The global sample thus suggests that the Japanese economy is not very permeable to the forces of globalization. However, we can refine understanding by providing a more granular description of the manufacturing, distribution, and finance industries as well as firm size.

Manufacturing

The manufacturing sector accounts for 26% of GDP and 21% of the labor force. Table 5.2 indicates that it is the most globally oriented

Table 5.2 *Internationalization of Japanese firms*

	Establishment size		*Sector*			*Total*	
	SME	*Large*	*Mfg.*	*Distrib.*	*Finance*	*Japan*	*Global*
Percent of companies with establishments abroad	18	49	48	10	4	19	24
Percent of companies with headquarters abroad	2	16	10	0	1	3	8
Mean percent of total sales from abroad	5	12	17	2	0	5	12
Mean percent of total procurement spending from abroad	13	11	32	8	0	13	20
Degree affected by competitors abroad (percent)							
Low	84	48	53	91	93	82	68
Moderate	8	17	11	8	5	9	16
High	8	35	36	1	2	9	15

Source: CRITO GEC Survey, 2002

sector in the Japanese economy. Nearly half of the companies have establishments overseas, a third procure from abroad, and nearly half report moderate to high foreign competitive pressures. Japanese manufacturers are less likely to have overseas headquarters (10%) or gain sales from abroad (17%). Though Japanese companies derive their revenues primarily in the domestic market (83%), exports play a major role in key sub-sectors such as electric/electronics, automobiles, and machinery. A more nuanced view of the manufacturing sector thus indicates a dichotomy between a small export-driven sub-sector and a large sub-sector oriented toward the domestic market.

The major manufacturing sub-sectors include electric/electronic equipment, precision equipment, automobiles, general machinery, and chemicals. The dominant players in these sub-sectors are large companies belonging to a horizontal and/or vertical *keiretsu*. A horizontal *keiretsu*, such as Mitsui, Sumitomo, and Mitsubishi, is an *inter*-industry/inter-firm grouping that consists of a main bank and large, leading companies. In contrast, a vertical *keiretsu* is an *intra*-industry/inter-firm grouping organized around a major lead company, such as Toyota Motor or Hitachi Ltd., and three or more distinct layers of SME suppliers (Gerlach, 1992). The *keiretsu* companies and affiliated SMEs drive Japan's export-oriented economy and employ workers across all occupational categories, with many under a lifetime employment and age-based seniority system.

Wholesale and retail distribution

The wholesale and retail sector accounts for 12% of GDP and 32% of the labor force. The sample indicates that 10% of the wholesale and retail companies have overseas establishments and 8% procure from abroad. This sector is primarily oriented toward the domestic market, as 91% feel little foreign competitive pressure. What little globally oriented activities they do engage in tend to be found in upstream business functions (procurement) but not much in downstream business functions (sales).

Among wholesalers, food and medicine are the largest sub-sectors. A key characteristic of this sector is a complex multilayered distribution system of intermediaries between producer and domestic customers. The gradual liberalization of the Japanese economy is opening up the distribution channels and forcing some wholesalers to procure goods overseas for sale in the domestic market (METI, 2004). In the sample, it is the wholesalers which are becoming globally oriented. In contrast, the retail sector consists mostly of many independent small-scale (between one and four employees) establishments with direct domestic customer contact. By number of stores, the 100-yen shops, drugstores, and casual-wear stores are the largest retail subsectors. Although a few retailers have made forays overseas, the retail sector in the sample reveals a strong orientation to the domestic market.

Banking and finance

The banking and finance sector accounts for 5% of GDP and 3% of the labor force. It is the least globally oriented sector in the GEC Japan database – 4% of the banking and finance companies have establishments abroad. Moreover, virtually none is engaged in overseas procurement or sales activities. Despite these figures, banks have historically been very active overseas in support of the foreign direct investments of *keiretsu* companies, although this business activity shows up predominately on the domestic side of the ledger (Mason, 1999). Thus, the banking and finance sector does have an international dimension in support of export-oriented Japanese companies.

A few large banks, insurance companies, and securities brokers dominate a larger number of smaller players in these sub-sectors. The banking sub-sector has recently consolidated into five major *keiretsu* main bank groups – Mizuho Holdings Inc., Sumitomo Mitsui Banking Corp., Mitsubishi Tokyo Financial Group, Inc., UFJ Holdings, Inc., and Resona Group – and a scattering of smaller regional banks and financial institutions (trust banks, credit unions, etc.). A notable characteristic of this market is the dominance of the *keiretsu* "main bank system" and the government postal savings and insurance system in intermediating 40–60% of the domestic capital flows (Gerlach, 1992). Their dominance of the capital market is reinforced by government policies favoring debt over equity financing, giving them a stranglehold over the corporate banking market and forcing other financial services players to the periphery of the retail financial market. Although market leaders Nomura Securities (securities) and Dai Ichi Insurance (insurance) are relatively independent companies, most of the remaining midsize security brokers and major insurance companies have an affiliation with one of the *keiretsu* banks.

Establishment size

The SMEs in the global sample are less globally oriented than large establishments across the globalization indicators in Table 5.2, except on the overseas procurement measure. This indicates that SMEs in the wholesale sector and a few notable cases in the retail sector are shifting procurement toward overseas sources, especially to China for low-price goods, and to Europe for luxury goods (JSBRI, 2001). In addition, if we add to this pool the SMEs indirectly involved in international trade as suppliers to the *keiretsu* companies, especially in the manufacturing sector, and the banks financing the overseas operations of *keiretsu* companies, this relational context brings into sharp relief the existence of a greater number of "globalized companies." This picture provides a sharper definition of the major fault lines between globally and domestically oriented establishments in the industrial landscape of Japan.

Table 5.3 *Investment in information technology*

	Establishment size		*Industry sector*			*Total*	
	SME	*Large*	*Mfg.*	*Distrib.*	*Finance*	*Japan*	*Global*
IS as percent of revenues							
<10 percent	47	39	43	50	23	47	40
10–20 percent	1	0	0	0	6	1	8
20–50 percent	7	3	7	8	0	7	7
>50 percent	0	0	0	0	0	0	1
Don't know/refused	45	58	50	42	71	45	44
Operating budget ($, 000)	6,387	12,898	1,499	7,712	6,027	6,519	8,968
Web as percent of IS revenues							
<10 percent	36	18	23	41	18	35	33
10–20 percent	4	10	17	0	6	5	8
20–50 percent	9	17	12	9	1	9	11
>50 percent	12	5	21	8	10	11	8
Don't know/refused	39	50	27	42	65	40	40
Operating budget ($, 000)	1,548	2,332	505	1,919	1,228	1,566	2,553

Source: CRITO GEC Survey, 2002
Notes: See Appendix I for GEC Survey details such as measures and question wording

E-commerce readiness

IT investment

The key economic indicator for capital spending in Japan has traditionally been machinery orders, especially for factory production. Corporate spending for information systems represents a new type of capital spending for Japanese companies. The extent that companies increase capital spending for IS and web-based initiatives, then, is one indicator of a shift toward adopting e-commerce and Internet-based business processes.

Given the high number of non-responses, it is difficult to draw conclusions from these data. With this caveat, however, the survey sample indicates that roughly half of the Japanese firms spend less than 10% of their revenue on IS (Table 5.3). By sector, the sample suggests that the banking sector spends more on IS as a percentage of revenues versus others. Given the high level of information processing in the finance sector, such a result is not unexpected.

We posit several reasons for low observed IS spending. First, Japan's low degree of globalization may not provide sufficient incentives to spend more on IS. Second, Japan has been mired in a prolonged economic recession. The bursting of the asset bubble in 1990 continues to weigh heavily on the domestic economy. Consequently, most *keiretsu* companies are still in the process of paying down corporate debt and addressing their overcapacity, handicapping them in diverting organizational resources for new Internet-based IS. The third potential determinant is Japanese personnel practices. Among the most global companies, there are few chief information officers in *keiretsu* companies to promote web-based initiatives (METI, 2004). Instead, the technical staff is usually in charge of introducing such initiatives, but they must report to a senior manager to gain budgetary approval. Since Japan's aged-based seniority system (*nenko joretsu*) and lifetime employment (*shin shu koyo*) mean older non-technical executives are making these budget decisions, the survey results may reflect psychological and age factors in understanding the importance of firm e-commerce readiness.

Another dimension of firm e-commerce readiness is spending on web-based initiatives as a percentage of the IS budget. These include Internet, extranet, and intranet initiatives (systems, software, IT services, consulting and internal staff). Table 5.3 shows that around one-third of the companies spend less than 10% of their IS budget on developing web-based initiatives. The manufacturing sector leads in terms of the number of firms spending more than 50% of their IS budget (21%), followed by finance (10%) and wholesale/retail (8%).

Information infrastructure

Types of e-commerce technologies

Japanese companies have adopted most types of e-commerce technologies (Table 5.4). Japan exceeds the global averages for intranet, extranet, EDI, and call center technologies, and is comparable in the use of email and websites. Only for EFT use is it lower than the global sample. EFT is quite common in Japan, but normally a company's main *keiretsu* bank handles such business transactions on its behalf (IAJ, 2001). In short, despite a late start in getting online, Japan has made up some of this temporal lag by adopting many of the prerequisite technologies necessary for e-commerce.

Table 5.4 *Use of e-commerce technologies*

	Establishment size		*Sector*			*Total*	
Percent using . . .	*SME*	*Large*	*Mfg.*	*Distrib.*	*Finance*	*Japan*	*Global*
Email	100	99	100	100	95	100	99
Intranet	81	84	74	83	81	81	64
Website	72	100	86	68	91	73	74
EDI	64	66	71	64	21	64	44
• over private networks	35	14	10	44	10	34	19
• Internet-based	8	9	29	0	4	8	8
• both	21	42	32	19	6	22	16
Extranet	50	35	33	57	20	50	33
• supplier/business partner access	26	28	11	33	6	26	21
• customer access	22	20	16	24	6	22	18
Call center	40	40	15	50	20	40	32
EFT	7	18	26	1	16	8	43

Source: CRITO GEC Survey, 2002

In Japan, the adoption of Internet-based e-commerce technologies does not correspond with a decline in existing EDI networks: the use of EDI in Japan (64%) far exceeds the global average (44%). Most EDI is over private networks or both private and Internet-based networks. Only a small percentage of companies (8%) have moved their EDI activities online to the Internet. The private EDI networks are a legacy of information systems dating back to the 1970s. Given GEC data, then, the overall picture that emerges is one in which EDI networks co-exist with other e-commerce technologies in many companies.

An examination of the differences by industry sector and establishment size gives us further understanding of this hybrid outcome. The wholesale and retail sector is the most likely to use private EDI networks (44%), whereas the manufacturing sector most often uses Internet-based EDI networks (29%) or both private and Internet-based EDI networks (32%). More specifically, the manufacturing sector uses a mixture of open and closed networks to coordinate its domestic (private EDI networks) and overseas production (EDIFACT, the international EDI standard developed under the United Nations, and Internet-based EDI networks), whereas the wholesale sector is essentially dependent on the existing domestic private EDI distribution networks (JEDIC, 2001). In the global sample, the banking and finance sector is the least likely to use EDI networks.

Email, intranet, and website e-commerce technologies form the core e-commerce technologies that most Japanese companies adopt initially. The companies diverge by industry on the remaining e-commerce technologies of extranet, call centers, and EFT. The wholesale and retail sector is more likely to use extranet (57%) and call centers (50%) than the other two sectors. JSBRI (2001) case studies suggest that it is probably the wholesalers that are using extranets in parallel with their private EDI networks, and the retailers using call centers in addition to their EDI networks. The manufacturing sector, in turn, is the biggest adopter of EFT (26%) and the second biggest user of extranets (33%), especially for customer access. However it is the least likely sector to use call centers (15%). Thus, this sector primarily adopts e-commerce technologies to complement its EDI networks in operations management functions, but less so in its downstream customer contact sales and marketing functions. Finally, the banking and finance sector nominally uses e-commerce technologies for corporate and individual customer service functions, drawing equally upon call centers (20%), extranet (20%), and EFT (16%) e-commerce technologies.

By establishment size, there is not much difference between large companies and SMEs except in two e-commerce technologies. Large companies (100%) are more likely than the SMEs (72%) to use websites. However, SMEs (50%) are more likely to use extranets than are large companies (35%). Based on a JSBRI (2001) report, these particular companies are probably SMEs in the wholesale and retail sector using the extranet to give preferred suppliers and business partners secure but limited access to their information systems. A more nuanced picture shows a widespread adoption of e-commerce technologies either to complement an existing EDI network (creating a hybrid open/closed e-commerce information infrastructure) or to enhance a specific business function.

IT and web integration

Another dimension of firm readiness is the extent to which companies are electronically integrating their business functions. This provides a clearer picture of whether the relatively high adoption of the technological building blocks for e-commerce is strategically incorporated into the daily business practices of Japanese companies.

Table 5.5 *Enterprise integration strategy*

Extent to which Internet applications are electronically integrated with . . .	*Establishment size*		*Sector*			*Total*	
	SME	*Large*	*Mfg.*	*Distrib.*	*Finance*	*Japan*	*Global*
Internal databases and information systems							
Percent little to none	57	45	45	60	73	57	53
Percent some	29	36	30	29	20	29	24
Percent a great deal	14	19	25	11	7	14	24
Those of suppliers and business customers							
Percent little to none	82	69	58	90	78	81	72
Percent some	16	20	34	10	19	17	18
Percent a great deal	2	11	8	0	2	2	10

Source: CRITO GEC Survey, 2002

Japanese companies are less likely to report that their Internet applications are electronically integrated "a great deal" (14%) with their *internal* databases and information systems, relative to the global sample (24%) (Table 5.5, Figure 5.2). Given the high adoption rate of most e-commerce technologies, this outcome suggests that there is relatively modest company-wide coordination in their use across different business units. By industry, the sample indicates that the manufacturing sector (25%) exceeds the wholesale and retail sector (11%) and the banking and finance sector (7%) in terms of internal integration. By establishment size, large companies (19%) are slightly more likely than SMEs (14%) to electronically integrate their internal databases and information systems. Consequently, it is the large companies in the manufacturing sector that have taken a modest lead in electronically reorganizing their standard operating procedures.

Japanese companies are also less likely to report that their databases and information systems are electronically integrated "a great deal" (2%) with those of their *external* suppliers and business customers than the global sample (10%). By industry, manufacturing (8%) is the most likely sector to electronically integrate with suppliers and business customers, followed by the banking and finance sector (2%). This trend follows the globalization fault lines in the Japanese industrial landscape. The wholesale and retail sector is the biggest adopter of

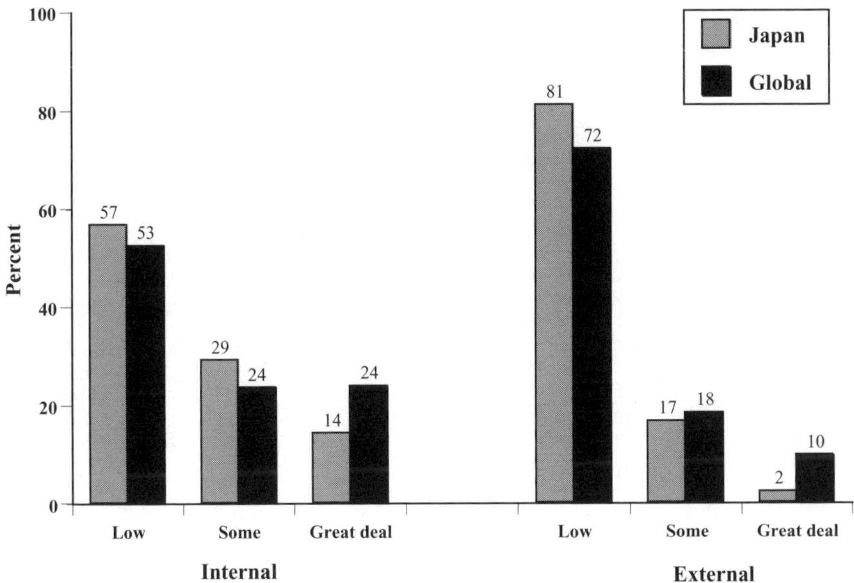

Figure 5.2 E-commerce readiness – enterprise integration
Source: CRITO GEC Survey, 2002

extranets, but it is the least likely to electronically integrate with its suppliers and business customers (0%). Given that a large percentage of this sector uses private EDI networks, these contrasting findings suggest that online transactions are concentrated within business units, but that enterprise integration across business units is conducted most often through closed networks.

The pattern of internal and external enterprise integration maps the presence of the vertical and horizontal *keiretsu* in the industrial landscape of Japan. The low level of enterprise integration, especially externally and, to a lesser extent, internally, highlights the continuing importance of secure EDI networks and interpersonal relations in the daily business activities of *keiretsu* companies. Consequently, the Internet electronically mediates some intra-firm relationships, but very little of the existing inter-firm relationships among Japanese companies. Toyota Motor, for example, places a premium on its proprietary technology (e.g., eco-friendly and luxury car product lines), and thus chooses to stay offline and conduct its business through trusted networks. Given that the e-commerce technology building blocks

Table 5.6 *Drivers for Internet use*

Percent indicating driver is a significant factor	*Establishment size*		*Sector*			*Total*	
	SME	*Large*	*Mfg.*	*Distrib.*	*Finance*	*Japan*	*Global*
Customers demanded it	36	58	48	34	19	37	37
Major competitors were online	19	39	22	18	36	19	31
Suppliers required it	26	33	32	25	11	26	22
To reduce costs	27	43	56	18	32	27	36
To expand market for existing product or services	23	52	37	17	47	24	48
To enter new businesses or markets	34	31	11	42	29	34	42
To improve coordination with customers and suppliers	33	46	54	26	37	33	44
Required for government procurement	4	15	18	0	5	5	15
Government provided incentives	2	3	8	0	0	2	8

Source: CRITO GEC Survey, 2002

and hybrid enterprise integration strategies are basically in place, e-commerce among Japanese companies should grow as the merits of online Internet-based transactions address their business challenges.

Drivers and barriers to e-commerce

The national and political environment in which business managers operate can slow or speed the forces of globalization. In the case of Japan, the political economy is embedded in an iron triangle, i.e., a three-way institutionalized interaction among political parties, the bureaucracy, and business (Tachiki et al., 2002). We expect this interwoven set of relationships to shape the trade-offs between drivers and barriers to the adoption of e-commerce and the Internet.

Drivers

The top factor driving the use of the Internet is customer demand (37%) (Table 5.6, Figure 5.3). This is consistent with the quality function

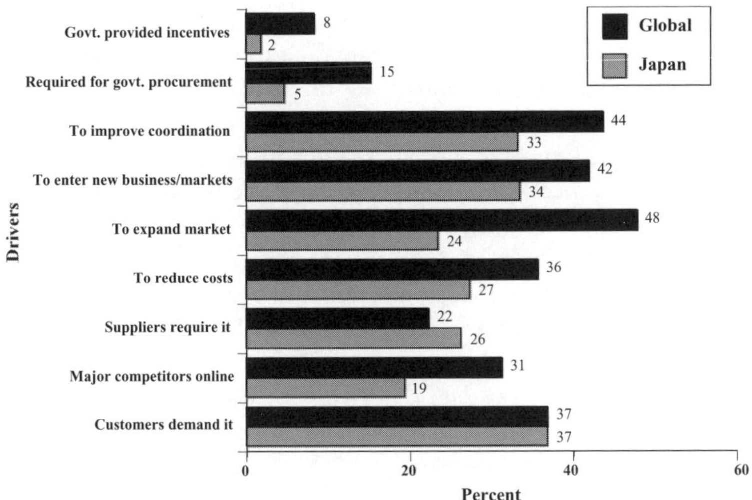

Figure 5.3 E-commerce drivers for Internet use
Source: CRITO GEC Survey, 2002

deployment (QFD) approach found in leading Japanese companies. The QFD is a series of embedded matrices translating the voice of the customer into design targets. The QFD cascades upstream to establish quality assurance checkpoints throughout the different segments of a company's value chain (Akao, 1990). The reverberation of customer demands back into the chain of QFD matrices accounts for the concurrent emphasis on the use of the Internet for entering a new business or market (34%) and improving coordination with customers and suppliers (33%), the second and third top drivers. As an example, second-generation (2G) and third-generation (3G) cell phones allow customers to express their demands to producers instantaneously (MPHPT, 2002). Among the remaining drivers in Table 5.6, major competitors being online (19%), government procurement requirements (5%), and government incentives (2%) are relatively less important factors.

The manufacturing sector is realigning its production segment of the value chain to reduce cost (56%) and improve coordination with customers and suppliers (54%) in response to price- and style-sensitive customers. In the wholesale and retail sector, the main driver for Internet use is for entering new businesses or markets (42%), shifting the spotlight to the marketing and sales segments of the value chain in response to potential customers beyond their traditional markets. This driver is marginally more important for the SMEs (34%) than for large companies (31%). Companies in the banking and finance sector, in contrast, use the Internet primarily to expand the market for existing products and services (47%) and to improve coordination with customers and suppliers (37%). This may be a defensive response to online competitors (36%) luring traditional customers. We note that these different characteristics of customer demand correspond to segments of the Japanese economy that have undergone liberalization (Tachiki et al., 2002).

In sum, aggregate GEC data on drivers for Internet use reveal that customer-related market and strategic factors are greater drivers for e-commerce than are competitors and public policy. Indeed, the Internet access rate using personal computers and mobile devices in Japan has nearly reached saturation point. Most companies cannot ignore the growing potential for online sales, leading to the realignment of their value chains in order to respond to customers in real time (Hamaya et al., 2001).

Barriers

Key factors inhibiting the use of the Internet in business (Table 5.7, Figure 5.4) are privacy and security issues (55%), followed closely by the cost of implementation (53%). Both factors are significantly higher than the global averages, reflecting a strong suspicion about Internet transactions (IAJ, 2001) as well as business concerns about its cost. Nippon Keidanren (2003), the leading business organization in Japan, reported that companies are becoming more concerned about policy issues such as online transactions replacing their existing offline business practices. Despite this, companies place government policies toward the bottom of their list of concerns. The use of credit cards (9%) is not a factor hindering companies from doing business online. The reason is that Japan has a number of alternative payment systems for online purchases using financial institutions, transport companies, and convenience stores.

The manufacturing sector (55%) and the wholesale and retail sector (54%) emphasize the cost of implementation as one of their top two significant obstacles to doing business online. This barrier is greater for

Table 5.7 *Barriers/difficulties in e-commerce*

Percent indicating statement is a significant factor	*Establishment size*		*Sector*			*Total*	
	SME	*Large*	*Mfg.*	*Distrib.*	*Finance*	*Japan*	*Global*
Business environments							
Concern about data privacy or security issues	55	64	70	50	65	55	44
Need for face-to-face customer interaction	43	45	41	42	61	43	34
Customers do not use the technology	30	26	22	33	20	30	31
Prevalence of credit card use in the country	9	13	10	8	16	9	20
Organizational resources							
Costs of implementing an e-commerce site	53	44	55	54	20	53	34
Level of ability to use the Internet as part of business strategy	31	35	46	26	40	31	25
Finding staff with e-commerce expertise	29	27	39	26	33	29	27
Making needed organizational changes	28	22	38	25	23	28	24
Cost of Internet access	24	24	26	25	15	25	15
Government policies							
Business laws do not support e-commerce	21	32	38	17	16	22	24
Inadequate legal protection for Internet purchases	20	30	32	17	22	21	34
Taxation of Internet sales	15	11	12	17	7	15	16

Source: CRITO GEC Survey, 2002

SMEs (53%) than for large companies (44%). In contrast, the banking and finance sector, having already taken a lead in IS spending, has moved on to concerns about how to use the Internet as part of its business strategies (40%) as the third factor inhibiting its ability to conduct business online.

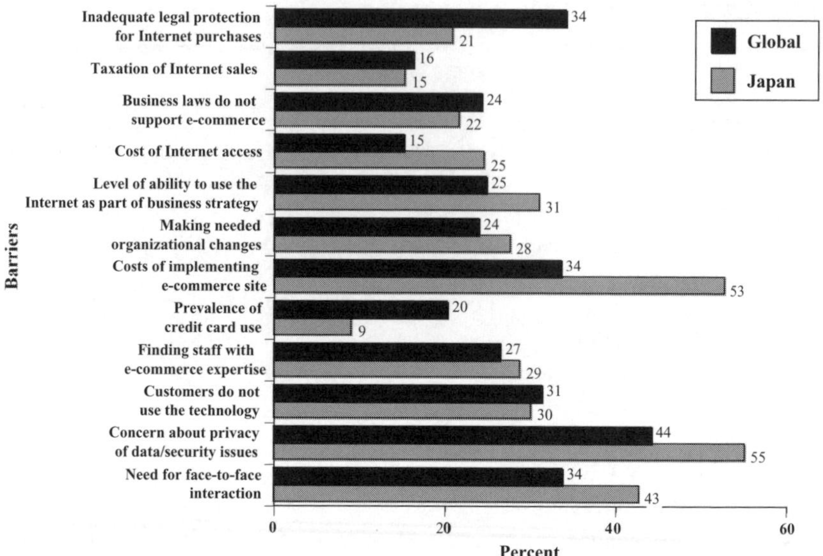

Figure 5.4 E-commerce barriers to Internet use
Source: CRITO GEC Survey, 2002

Diffusion of e-commerce

Online services

Relative to the global average, more Japanese firms use either business-to-business (30% versus 23%) or business-to-consumer (19% versus 13%) e-commerce (Table 5.8). In contrast, fewer use both B2B and B2C (15% versus 33%). A look at industry data helps with the interpretation of these economy-wide figures. The manufacturing sector uses websites more for product specifications (60%) and product configuration (57%) than for back-office functions such as service and technical support (39%), account information (10%), and order tracking (19%). The wholesale and retail distribution sector focuses on the marketing side of B2C transactions, including product reviews (39%), product catalogs (38%), and gift certificates and/or registry (24%). It focuses significantly less on using websites for sales functions such as account information (13%) and individual customization (13%). Finally, the banking and finance sector emphasizes using websites for access to account information (35%) and online services (30%), but

Table 5.8 *Online services*

	Establishment size		*Sector*			*Total*	
	SME	*Large*	*Mfg.*	*Distrib.*	*Finance*	*Japan*	*Global*
Type of online service							
Percent B2B only	29	45	54	22	18	30	23
Percent B2C only	19	21	4	23	35	19	13
Percent both B2B and B2C	14	33	24	12	27	15	33
Mean percent of total consumer services conducted online	8	11	7	8	7	8	8
Mean percent of total business services conducted online	11	15	29	7	4	12	11
Percent of manufacturing websites which support							
Product configuration	57	53	57			57	55
Order tracking	20	12	19			19	22
Service and technical support	39	38	39			39	54
Product specification	58	71	60			60	80
Account information	11	7	10			10	17
Percent of wholesale/retail distribution websites which support							
Gift certificates and/or registry	24	21		24		24	21
Product catalog	38	54		38		38	70
Product reviews	38	56		39		39	49
Individual customization	13	22		13		13	21
Account information	12	25		13		13	22
Percent of banking and insurance websites supporting							
Online services such as filing applications, filing claims, paying bills, transferring funds	27	75			30	30	54
Access to account information	32	84			35	35	57
Online tools such as research tools, planning tools, etc.	18	24			19	19	52

Source: CRITO GEC Survey, 2002

less so for marketing functions such as providing online tools (19%). The story that emerges from Table 5.8, regardless of industry sector, is that companies provide online services to meet their immediate customer demands, but they are less likely to provide online services where privacy is paramount, elaborating on our earlier findings about the defining factors dividing the drivers for and obstacles to e-commerce.

This story changes somewhat by establishment size. SMEs in the manufacturing sector clearly conduct more of their customer services online, for both procurement and back-office functions, than larger companies. For the wholesale and retail sector, SMEs are more active in conducting sales related to gift certificates, but large (wholesale) companies provide greater access to product reviews, account information, individual customization, and product catalog. In the banking and finance sector, SMEs (regional banks, trust banks, securities) are less likely than large *keiretsu* banks to conduct customer service over their websites, but they are slightly more likely to provide access to online tools. SMEs in the manufacturing sector, and to some extent in the banking and finance sector, are moving online to allow the voice of the customer to reverberate electronically further back into their value chain, whereas in the wholesale and retail sector they use their websites to reach out to new customers. Anecdotal evidence suggests these are SMEs falling outside a *keiretsu* nexus and/or falling within a segment of the economy undergoing liberalization or deregulation.

Online sales

Japanese respondents report lower online sales to both businesses and customers (13%), to businesses only (7%), or to customers only (1%) than the global sample (15%, 13%, and 7% respectively) (Table 5.9). Nevertheless, when we limit the sample to only those Japanese companies actually conducting B2C sales, they are almost twice as likely to conduct sales online than firms in the global sample (36% versus 19%). Turning to the B2B story, Japanese companies (15%) are just as likely as the global sample (15%) to conduct business sales online. This suggests a bimodal split in the use of e-commerce among Japanese companies: a large majority of companies conducting very little B2C and B2B sales online as opposed to a distinct minority of companies intensively conducting on average a third of their B2C sales online, with a strong link to their accounts receivable systems. Indeed, 94% of the

Table 5.9 *Online sales*

	Establishment size		*Sector*			*Total*	
	SME	*Large*	*Mfg.*	*Distrib.*	*Finance*	*Japan*	*Global*
Type of online sales							
Percent both B2B and B2C	13	13	2	16	16	13	15
Percent B2B only	7	14	28	1	0	7	13
Percent B2C only	1	5	2	1	13	1	7
B2C							
Mean percent of total consumer sales conducted online (all establishments)	5	1	1	7	1	5	4
Mean percent of those only doing B2C sales online	37	9	16	40	3	36	19
B2B							
Mean percent of total business sales conducted online (all establishments)	3	3	3	3	0	3	4
Mean percent of those only doing B2B sales online	15	11	8	20	1	15	15
Web payment							
Percent of websites that support online payment (only those doing online sales)	97	71	100	64	32	94	34

Source: CRITO GEC Survey, 2002

Japanese companies support online payments through their websites, compared to 34% for the global sample. The most common payment method is to charge customers on their credit card or telephone bill (e.g. DoCoMo). In addition, customers can make payments through banks, convenience stores, or directly to the delivery person (post office or delivery service company).

The industry sector and establishment size data provide additional insight into where online sales activities are most advanced. The wholesale and retail sector conducts a greater percentage of B2C (40%) and B2B (20%) than the other two sectors. The wholesale and retail sector also reports a high percent of website support for online

Table 5.10 *How establishments use the Internet to sell products and services*

Percent indicating Internet used to . . .	*Establishment size*		*Sector*			*Total*	
	SME	*Large*	*Mfg.*	*Distrib.*	*Finance*	*Japan*	*Global*
Channel conflict							
Compete with traditional distribution channels	37	38	23	48	19	37	27
Replace traditional distribution channels	30	18	3	47	17	29	13
Enhance or expand channels							
Address traditional distribution channels only	22	30	49	4	31	22	44
Address new markets only	11	14	25	1	33	12	15

Source: CRITO GEC Survey, 2002

payment (64%). In contrast, the manufacturing sector conducts only 16% of its B2C and 8% of its B2B sales online, but backs it up with an online payment system used extensively. This suggests that these two sectors are reorganizing their sales and payment activities to an online system – the wholcsale and retail sector for both sales and payment, the manufacturing sector for hybrid EDI and Internet networks and payment systems. In particular, SMEs are more likely to engage in such activities than large companies. Thus, it is the SMEs in the wholesale and retail sector that are the most active minor players using Internet-based networks for B2C online sales.

Channel strategy

Japanese companies report "competing directly with traditional distribution channels" (37%) as the primary reason for using the Internet to sell products and services (Table 5.10). The second highest reason is to replace traditional distribution channels (29%). Remaining reasons include enhancing their traditional distribution channels (22%) and addressing new markets only (12%). In other economies this is known as "channel conflict." However, in the Japanese context it is a way of getting around channel bottlenecks. The distribution system in Japan is quite hierarchical, consisting of more than three intermediaries between producer and customer. Indeed, foreign companies often cite the complex multilayered distribution system as a major structural impediment to doing business in Japan. In this segment of the value chain, then, the voice of the customer becomes a function of improving *quality*, reducing *cost*, and decreasing *delivery* time (Tachiki, 1990).

Among the three sectors, the manufacturing sector has the greatest number of distribution layers between a company and its customers. This sector primarily uses the Internet to enhance traditional distribution channels (49%), but is less likely to replace traditional distribution channels (3%). Consequently, the EDI supplier–manufacturer networks remain relatively intact, but they are moving toward the use of the Internet in the downstream segments of their value chain to distribute products and services. When we look downstream to the retail side of the story, supermarkets and department stores dominate the sector, followed by specialty stores, convenience stores, and cooperatives. The supermarkets and department stores are using the Internet to procure fresh and/or reasonably priced products directly from producers for consumers. For example, leading retailer Aeon (formerly Jusco Company) bypasses wholesalers and orders goods directly from domestic and overseas producers. Specialty stores, once a vibrant sector, find that younger consumers turn to discount stores or the Internet for computers, music, books, etc., forcing them to adopt a click-and-mortar business model.

Squeezed between manufacturers and retailers is the wholesale sector whose response to the channel conflict issue is the strongest. The biggest threat to wholesalers is "disintermediation" from the distribution process. Not only do online purchases pose a threat to their intermediary role, but the liberalization of this sector (e.g., "Large and Small Store Law") has led to the emergence of competitive challenges from direct marketing (telephone call centers, catalog orders, etc.) and large mega-stores (e.g., Carrefour, Costco, etc.). In response, wholesalers are increasing purchases of private brands by importing from China and other overseas vendors to bypass high-cost domestic producers (JETRO, 2003).

The banking and finance sector reports less channel conflict than the other two sectors. However, the "big bang" financial liberalization of the sector in the mid-1990s has opened the door to non-bank bank competitors. Japanese government policies have historically favored debt financing over equity markets and thereby restrict market entry through monetary policies. Subsequent to the liberalization of this sector and the rise of e-commerce after 1994, non-bank banks, such as

Table 5.11 *Online procurement*

	Establishment size		*Sector*			*Total*	
	SME	*Large*	*Mfg.*	*Distrib.*	*Finance*	*Japan*	*Global*
Percent doing online purchasing	32	45	54	26	26	33	51
Mean percent spent on parts for production	21	8	20	—	—	20	8
Mean percent spent on goods for resale	0	1	—	0	—	0	7
Mean percent spent on supplies and equipment for business is ordered online	0	1	0	0	2	0	8

Source: CRITO GEC Survey, 2002

IY Bank and Sony Bank, have been making headway in the area of retail banking and securities, requiring traditional banks and financial services to protect and expand their market share. Consequently, companies in this sector are more likely to use the Internet to enhance traditional branch distribution channels (31%) or expand into new markets (33%). Overall, the initial impact of the Internet and liberalization has led to a chain reaction spreading across the three sectors and gradually flattening and internationalizing the previously hierarchical domestic distribution channels in Japan.

Online procurement

When we move further up the value chain, demand for Internet-based transactions is weaker in Japan than the global sample. Only 33% of Japanese companies purchase online compared with the global sample of 51% (Table 5.11). The manufacturing sector is the most active in procuring online, nearly half of which is parts for production. At the center of a manufacturing company's procurement segment of the value chain is some derivative of Toyota Motor's just-in-time (JIT) and *kamban* delivery system (Monden, 1983). Under this system, companies decide whether to use an open or closed procurement system depending on the product architecture. For products with a modular design, i.e., products using standardized, mass-produced components, online procurement is an option. But for integrated product designs, i.e., products with high-tech core components, a closed EDI system is the most secure way to protect intellectual property (Fujimoto, 2002). Japanese companies tend to use closed EDI networks for integrated product designs, but are more flexible about modular product designs. The pattern of online procurement activity thereby results from the existence of hybrid EDI and Internet-based networks for procuring parts for production.

The wholesale and retail sector (26%) and banking and finance sector (26%) are half as likely as the manufacturing sector to purchase online. The outcome for the wholesale and retail sector is consistent with our earlier finding that it is a heavy user of EDI networks. Nevertheless, the sample shows no online purchasing for resale goods, which does not have an immediate explanation. For the banking and finance sector, nominal online orders for supplies and equipment suggest fewer intra-firm online business activities. This contrasts with its active use of the Internet to reach external customers.

Supply chain

The *keiretsu* form of business organization has been one of the key elements contributing to the success of the Japanese economy (Gerlach, 1992). Our discussion suggests the *keiretsu* is also important to the e-commerce story. Nevertheless, the diffusion of e-commerce within companies is changing the balance of power between producers and customers. In this regard we shift our analytical tack to examine the extent Internet use is changing the traditional organizational boundaries of Japanese companies.

Upstream versus downstream

Japanese companies are using the Internet for exchanging operational data with business customers (53%), advertising and marketing (53%), and exchanging operational data with suppliers (53%) (Table 5.12, Figure 5.5). These levels of Internet use compare favorably with the global sample. In contrast, Japanese companies are less likely to use the Internet for online purchases (33%), after-sales support (25%), online sales (21%), and integrating processes with suppliers (16%) than firms in the global sample. These divergent outcomes indicate that

Table 5.12 *Uses of the Internet*

	Establishment size		*Sector*			*Total*	
	SME	*Large*	*Mfg.*	*Distrib.*	*Finance*	*Japan*	*Global*
Upstream versus downstream (percentage indicating a significant factor)							
Advertising and marketing purposes	53	57	38	58	53	53	58
Making sales online	21	26	31	17	30	21	30
After-sales customer service and support	24	41	40	19	31	25	44
Making purchases online	32	44	54	26	26	33	47
Exchanging operational data with suppliers	52	55	64	51	25	53	48
Exchanging operational data with business customers	53	60	66	50	29	53	51
Formally integrating business processes with suppliers or other business partners	16	23	18	17	3	16	34
Internet marketplace (percentage)							
Heard of an Internet marketplace	72	81	88	67	80	73	80
Participating as a buyer only	0	7	1	1	0	1	7
Participating as a seller only	14	9	17	13	0	14	12
Participating as both a buyer and a seller	0	7	0	0	1	0	17
Content/services to mobile customers (percentage providing or planning to provide)							
Already available	16	22	10	17	42	16	14
Plan to add within the next year	15	9	14	16	1	15	18

Source: CRITO GEC Survey, 2002

Japanese companies are incorporating the Internet at their traditional customer–organization boundaries; however, this integration does not extend very deep into the organization.

There are some interesting variations by industry sector. The manufacturing sector emphasizes upstream business activities such as exchanging operational data with business customers (66%) and suppliers (64%), and online purchases (54%) as its most important

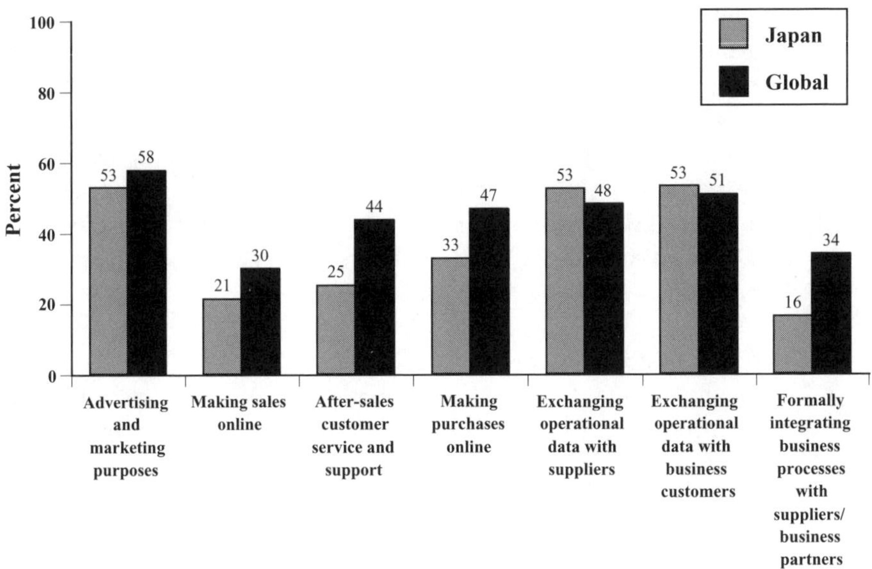

Figure 5.5 E-commerce adoption – types of use
Source: CRITO GEC Survey, 2002

reasons for using the Internet. In contrast, the banking and finance sector primarily emphasizes the importance of downstream activities such as advertising (53%), after-sales support (31%), and online sales (30%) as reasons for using the Internet. The wholesale and retail sector is split between emphasizing downstream activities such as advertising (58%), and upstream activities such as exchanging operational data with suppliers (51%) and business customers (50%). This pattern is consistent with our earlier discussion of variations in the value chain. The manufacturing sector is motivated to use the Internet to support B2B activities, but the banking and finance sector is motivated to use the Internet to support B2C activities.

Internet marketplaces

Since most inter-firm B2B transactions in Japan are conducted within EDI networks, the emergence of Internet marketplaces promises to change some aspects of existing business models. Roughly 73% of Japanese companies are familiar with the Internet marketplace concept, only slightly lower than the global average of 80%. Companies in the manufacturing sector (88%) are more likely to have heard of an Internet marketplace than in the banking and finance sector (80%) and the wholesale and retail sector (67%), but the majority of all companies neither buys nor sells in Internet marketplaces. Despite the high level of awareness, the functional merits of an Internet marketplace do not overshadow the existing organizational framework supporting EDI networks, one of the key inhibiting factors identified earlier in this chapter.

Mobile customer access

The popularity of i-Mode, a proprietary m-commerce platform, and advances in other forms of ubiquitous commerce in Japan are creating a large mobile customer base. According to a Mobile Computing Promotion Consortium (2003) study, more than 70% of the population owns a cell phone. Currently, only 16% of the companies are currently participating in m-commerce, with another 15% indicating they plan to add this service within a year. Interestingly, two-thirds of the companies have no current plan. Despite Japan's high diffusion of mobile devices, it is only slightly more likely to already provide content or services for mobile customers (16%) than the global sample (14%).

The banking and finance sector is the most advanced in allowing mobile users to access its websites (42%), with the wholesale and retail sector a distant second at 17%, and the manufacturing sector at 10%. By establishment size, the large companies (22%) are more likely than the SMEs (16%) to provide content or services for mobile customers. However, SMEs are more likely to say they plan to add such content and services within the next year. Despite the high potential consumer demand for mobile access to companies and the widespread adoption of e-commerce technologies, the privacy and organizational constraints on what a company can actually provide are salient here.

Impacts of e-commerce

Efficiency

Japanese companies are less likely to experience efficiency in internal processes (29%) and staff productivity (24%) than the global sample of 34% and 27%, respectively (Table 5.13). By industry, the

Table 5.13 *Impacts of doing business online*

Percent indicating a significant factor	*Establishment size*		*Sector*			*Total*	
	SME	*Large*	*Mfg.*	*Distrib.*	*Finance*	*Japan*	*Global*
Efficiency							
Internal processes more efficient	29	32	41	25	21	29	34
Staff productivity increased	24	23	26	25	12	24	27
Coordination							
Procurement costs decreased	4	12	16	0	1	4	18
Inventory costs decreased	5	4	20	0	5	5	14
Coordination with suppliers improved	34	28	40	33	11	34	30
Commerce							
Sales area widened	3	12	9	1	12	3	31
Sales increased	1	7	1	0	14	1	21
International sales increased	5	6	21	0	0	5	20
Competitive position improved	10	9	15	9	6	10	30
Customer service improved	11	18	42	1	7	11	35

Source: CRITO GEC Survey, 2002

manufacturing sector cites internal process efficiency (41%) more frequently than do the wholesale (25%) and banking (21%) sectors. This suggests Japanese companies have not integrated their hybrid closed-open information systems. A major issue facing companies, then, is moving their EDI online to an Internet-based system.

By firm size, large companies (32%) are more likely to achieve internal process efficiency than the SMEs (29%), but the SMEs (24%) are slightly more likely to report increases in staff productivity than large companies (23%). Since large companies are more likely to engage in e-commerce with other businesses, conducting business online is one way to reduce transaction costs with suppliers, distributors, and sales people. For SMEs, they are more likely to have direct customer contact, so doing business online is one way to increase the efficiency of its staff. Nevertheless, Japanese companies can learn from the experiences of other countries.

Coordination

On the coordination measures, Japanese companies are less likely than the global sample to report decreases in procurement costs (4% versus 18%) and decreases in inventory costs (5% versus 14%). But they do report more improvement in coordination with suppliers (34% versus 30%). This is an area where the manufacturing sector has made improvements. We attribute these results to the hybrid closed and open information systems in manufacturing companies. When manufacturing companies compare the cost-benefit of closed versus open information systems, it seems the EDI still retains some advantage over Internet-based ones in the areas of procurement and inventory. However, for coordination with suppliers, the existing EDI are beginning to move online. The wholesale and retail sector is lower than manufacturing on all measures, as is the banking and finance sector. Coordination will become a more significant issue in this latter sector, however, to meet the new competitive challenges from non-bank banks (e.g., Sony Bank, IY Bank, etc.).

The large companies are more likely to report improved coordination in the areas of procurement. SMEs are more likely to report decreases in costs for coordination with suppliers than large companies. When compared to the global sample, Japanese companies place more emphasis on using online business to improve coordination with suppliers, but still maintain a "closed" stance towards B2B transactions in the areas of procurement and inventory.

Commerce

Japanese companies have not benefited as much as the companies in the global sample on the measures of commerce: widening sales area, increased sales, increased international sales, improved competitive position, and improved customer service. Only the banking and finance sector shows improvement in widening sales area and increasing sales, a key reason companies give for adopting e-commerce. The wholesale and retail sector reports improving its competitive position and improving customer service. Since the wholesale and retail sector and banking and finance sector focus their e-commerce in downstream activities, we would have expected more improvement in these sectors. Perhaps a combination of their domestic-oriented market focus and the poor state of the Japanese economy has muted the potential positive impact of the Internet. In contrast, the manufacturing sector exceeds the global sample in improved customer service and increased international sales. As structural reforms in the Japanese economy proceed, we should expect more benefits from e-commerce in the near future.

By establishment size, large companies have benefited more than SMEs; however, none of the measures exceeds the global sample. As the diffusion of e-commerce tends to eliminate inefficiencies, a large company's full-scale entry into e-commerce is promoting market reorganization of each industry. Our case of the Bit Valley entrepreneurs suggests there are segments of the Japanese economy benefitting from e-commerce, but their impact on the economy has not yet surpassed the *keiretsu* companies.

Conclusion

According to conventional wisdom, the diffusion of e-commerce is a function of the extent to which firms are integrated into the global economy. The Internet and e-commerce diffuse rapidly across economies the more they are integrated into the global economy, reducing the role of the state and bringing equal opportunities for the largest and smallest firms in all industries, i.e., a "leveling hypothesis." In Japan, the forces of globalization are relatively low. However, the diffusion of e-commerce across Japanese companies is comparable with, and on some measures exceeds, the global sample. This provides some evidence that local factors play an important role in the diffusion of e-commerce and the Internet across economies.

In Japan, the relational context is key and provides an important lens through which to interpret GEC Survey findings and identify key local forces driving e-commerce diffusion. The Japanese business landscape is unique in that the *keiretsu* and iron triangle form a complex network of interrelated organizations and individuals. By analyzing the role of these institutions within three industry sectors, we were able to provide a nuanced view of the forces driving and impeding the diffusion of e-commerce and the Internet.

Overall, diffusion is comparable with the global sample, but each industry plays a different role in the economy and has different ties to the global economy. The manufacturing sector is more involved in upstream business functions, the wholesale and retail sector in distribution business functions, and the banking and finance sector in capital intermediation functions. These functions are the most international in the manufacturing sector and most domestically oriented in the wholesale and retail sector. In short, industry sectors or sub-sectors with the deepest global reach are more likely to be in a position to take advantage of emerging opportunities.

We observed great strides in adopting a wide variety of e-commerce technologies, but the level of spending for information systems is modest compared with the global sample. This has led to the impression that Japanese companies lag in getting online. Nevertheless, our analysis suggests that the interaction between exogenous forces for globalization and endogenous business practices has led to this uneven diffusion of e-commerce within companies. It is not always clear to Japanese managers that e-commerce represents a better business model than their existing style of management. Thus, we found Internet-based information systems often co-exist with EDI systems, suggesting a hybrid approach to e-commerce in Japan.

The diffusion of e-commerce partially equalizes opportunities for some SMEs. It has led to some reorganization of the distribution channels in the wholesale and retail sector. Moreover, it has broadened SME sales channels and extended their reach to provide customers greater access to their services. Where the government has liberalized regulations and public procurement, this trend seems to have advanced the furthest. Thus, how well companies can overcome the barriers and inefficiencies in the political economy affects the extent to which they can take advantage of new business opportunities utilizing the Internet as much as the forces of globalization.

Japanese companies are sensitive to consumer and market pressures; however, we found they pay more attention to the general business environment in setting the course for their competitive strategies. Consequently, the survey respondents rank government policy as neither an incentive nor a barrier to the adoption of e-commerce. When we turn to specific issues, the number one concern is over security/privacy, issues under the purview of the government. When we examine public policy, the government's efforts in liberalizing markets are opening up new business opportunities. In addition, SMEs are particularly sensitive to the issue of taxation. In short, policy matters. Liberalization and deregulation policies matter a great deal, opening economic space for unaffiliated *keiretsu* companies to develop new business models. Contrary to the leveling hypothesis, then, we found the state has some role in setting the rules of the game in order to promote e-commerce.

References

Akao, Y. (1990). *Quality Function Deployment: Integrating Customer Requirements into Product Design*. Portland, OR: Productivity Press. (Originally published as *Hinshitsu tenkai katsuyo no jissai* by the Japanese Standards Association in 1988.)

Caselli, F. & Coleman III, W. J. (2001). Cross-Country Technology Diffusion: The Case of Computers. *The American Economic Review*, 91(2), 328–335.

Center for Research on Information Technology and Organizations (CRITO) (2002). *Global E-Commerce 10-National Survey Database*. Irvine, CA: CRITO, University of California at Irvine.

Encarnation, D. (1999). Asia and the Global Operations of Multinational Corporations. In D. Encarnation (Ed.), *Japanese Multinationals in Asia: Regional Operations in Comparative Perspective*. Oxford: Oxford University Press, 46–86.

Fujimoto, T. (2002). Relocation and Reorganization of Japanese Industries: Automobiles. In D. Tachiki & J. Kurihara (Eds.), *Can Japan Be a Global Player? Industry and National Perspectives*. Tokyo: Fujitsu Research Institute.

Gerlach, M. L. (1992). *Alliance Capitalism: The Social Organization of Japanese Business*. Berkeley, CA: University of California Press.

Hamaya, S. et al. (2001). *Intaanetto Bijinesu Hakusho* 2001 (Internet Business White Paper 2001). Tokyo: Internet Research Association.

International Data Corporation (IDC) (2000). *The 2000 IDC/World Times: Information Society Index*. From www.idc.com:8080/Data/Global/ISI/ISIMain.htm

International Planning and Research Corporation (IPR) (2003). *Eighth Annual Business Software Alliance (BSA) Global Software Piracy Study, Trends in Software Piracy 1994–2002*. Washington, D.C.: Business Software Alliance.

International Telecommunication Union (ITU) (2004). *World Telecommunication Indicators Database* (8th Ed.). Geneva, Switzerland.

Internet Association of Japan (IAJ) (2001). *Intaanetto Hakusho* (Internet White Paper 2001). Tokyo: Author & IMPRESS.

Japan Electronic Data Interchange Council (JEDIC) (2001). *Survey on Current EDI Status in Japan*. Tokyo.

Japan External Trade Organization (JETRO) (2003). *White Paper on Trade and Investment*. Tokyo.

Japan Small Business Research Institute (JSBRI) (2001). *White Paper on Small and Medium Enterprises in Japan*. Tokyo: Small and Medium Enterprise Agency and METI.

Kraemer, K. L., Gibbs, J., & Dedrick, J. (2003). Impacts of Globalization on E-Commerce Adoption and Firm Performance: A Cross-Country Investigation. Working paper. Irvine, CA: Center for Research on Information Technology and Organizations, University of California at Irvine.

Mason, M. (1999). The Origins and Evolution of Japanese Direct Investment in East Asia. In D. Encarnation (Ed.), *Japanese Multinationals in Asia: Regional Operations in Comparative Perspective*. Oxford: Oxford University Press, 17–45.

Ministry of Economy, Trade and Industry (METI) (2004). *White Paper on International Trade 2003*. Tokyo.

Ministry of Public Management, Home Affairs, Post and Telecommunications (MPHPT) (2002). *Joho tsushin hakusho heisei 14 nendoban* (communications in Japan 2001). Tokyo.

Mobile Computing Promotion Consortium (2003). From www.mcpc-jp.org

Monden, Y. (1983). *Toyota Production System*. Norcross, GA: Institute of Industrial Engineers.

Nippon Keidanren (2003). Expectations for the World Summit on the Information Society (WSIS). From www.keidanren.or.jp

Organization for Economic Co-operation and Development (OECD) (1999). *The Economic and Social Impact of Electronic Commerce*. Paris.

Shih, C. F., Dedrick, J., & Kraemer, K. L. (2002). Determinants of IT Spending at the Country Level. CRITO unpublished paper, University of California at Irvine.

Tachiki, D. (1990). *Total Quality Control: The Japanese Approach to Continuous Improvement*. Tokyo: Sakura Institute of Research.

Tachiki, D., Hamaya, S., & Yukawa, K. (2001). *Intaanetto Bijinesu Hakusho 2001* (Internet Business White Paper 2001). Tokyo: Internet Research Association.

Tachiki, D., Hamaya, S., & Yukawa, K. (2002). E-Commerce National Environment and Policy Environment in Japan. Working paper. Irvine: Center for Research on Information Technology and Organizations, University of California at Irvine.

World Bank (2004). *WDI Online*. From http://publications.worldbank.ord/WDI/

6 China: overcoming institutional barriers to e-commerce

ZIXIANG (ALEX) TAN AND OUYANG WU

Introduction

As a large developing country with an ambition to become one of the world's economic superpowers, China sees its future closely tied to its information technology industry, as well as to the deployment and use of IT, the Internet, and e-commerce. However, currently there is a great disparity between this vision for "informatization"[1] and the reality of e-commerce diffusion and use. That disparity is rooted in aspects of China's environment and policy which shape the diffusion, use, and impacts of e-commerce.

China's economy has grown at an annual rate of more than 8% since 1995, but that growth has been accompanied by increasing inequality in income. There is also wide geographic inequality, with the eastern coastal regions around Beijing, Shanghai, and Guangdong having much higher incomes than the rest of the country. These regions, and especially their cities, have much better infrastructure and many more Internet users than the remote and economically poorer provinces elsewhere in the country. The larger enterprises, especially those located in these coastal regions, have larger IT budgets and better-trained staff than small and medium-sized enterprises, and are more capable of engaging in e-commerce, but tend to be conservative. The smaller, more entrepreneurial companies often lack the financial and human resources to engage in e-commerce.

Ironically, the growing inequality is something of a plus in terms of e-commerce adoption, as there is now a significant upper-middle class

[1] Informatization is a term used in China (and in some European economies) to refer to the shift of modern economics from industrial to information economics, as suggested by David Bell (1973) and Marc Porat (1977). In China, it also refers to government efforts to develop IT industries and to promote IT use as a means of creating local demand and modernizing the economy (Kraemer & Dedrick, 1995, 2002).

that has the income to pay for PCs, Internet access, and cell phones, and can afford to shop online. Also, since they are geographically concentrated, it is easier to serve this population with the necessary logistics, information infrastructure, and low-cost access to Internet cafés. Similarly, the most internationally oriented businesses, including many Asian and other foreign MNCs, are concentrated in these regions, which have the needed port, logistics, and other support services in addition to a large workforce. Thus, the concentration of e-commerce-ready businesses and higher-income customers can be seen as a positive force for e-commerce diffusion (Dedrick, 2004).

However, despite vigorous government promotional campaigns, both businesses and consumers face significant institutional barriers to engaging in e-commerce. This is primarily due to the lack of national package distribution networks, adequate payment systems, and government policy providing business laws that support e-commerce, legal protection (and enforcement) for Internet purchases, intellectual property, and privacy and security (Dedrick, 2004).

As might be expected, these environmental and policy factors lead to a disparity between China's vision of informatization and the reality on the ground. China is the world's second largest producer of PCs and the second biggest market. While Internet adoption has been rapid in recent years (Guo & Chen, 2005), diffusion remains low on a per capita basis. Given that e-commerce is still new to China, and remains beyond the reach of most Chinese firms and consumers, the impacts are not significant at the macro level as yet. However, among those segments of the business and consumer population that are active users, there have been impacts. In fact, Chinese firms that use the Internet for business are not very different from their global peers. Most use is aimed at sales, marketing, and customer service. The biggest impacts are widened sales area, improved competitive position and customer services, and increased international sales. However, use of the Internet for buying and selling online is very low. Accordingly, the biggest impacts are a broader reach for sales and improved customer service, but not increased sales.

Despite its mixed record, there is evidence that China may have sustainable growth in e-commerce in the years to come. The fundamental drivers are continued economic growth, increased consumer wealth, broad technology diffusion, and economic liberalization. China is becoming a more global economy, with entry into the WTO, large inflows of foreign direct investment, and flows of people and information into and out of the country. The business community is also beginning to produce some success stories. These include short messaging services, advertising, and online gaming services. However, broader-based buying and selling on the Internet will remain limited until better payment systems are in place and both consumers and businesses develop more trust in online transactions. China's biggest challenge will be to provide the needed institutional complements: payment systems, legal framework, and a culture of trust for e-commerce to flourish (Dedrick, 2004).

Against this background, we summarize some key findings from our China case study:

- *Wealth and geographic inequalities.* Certain wealthy regions, mostly in the large cities and coastal areas, have a GDP per capita that is comparable to that of newly industrialized countries (Tan & Wu, 2004). However, due to its large population, the overall GDP per capita of China is well below that of developed countries. Such inequalities are also reflected in the IT infrastructure and e-commerce diffusion.
- *Fast technology adoption, slow provision of needed complements.* Chinese firms have followed a leapfrog approach to significantly upgrade technology infrastructure for e-commerce diffusion and to establish a web presence while bypassing traditional technologies such as EDI. However, the lack of organizational and institutional complementarities necessary for successful adoption slows e-commerce diffusion and use. These include environmental barriers such as the lack of a solid historic foundation of deploying and utilizing internal information systems, and poor integration of business processes with information systems. They also include barriers due to the lack of government policy protecting Internet purchases, providing for the rule of law, and protecting privacy and security. As a result, China's online purchases are the lowest among the economies in the study and its online sales are the second lowest.
- *Significant sectoral differences.* Across the three surveyed industry sectors, e-commerce diffusion is taking different paths. The finance sector stands out as a traditionally information-intensive sector with a long history of government investments in these large, state enterprises, thereby building up the finance sector's information infrastructure and integrating its business operations with information system applications. These factors have contributed to successful

e-commerce diffusion, particularly business-to-consumer, in banking and insurance. The distribution sector, in contrast, suffers from its inferior IT infrastructure, poor credit-monitoring capacity, and backward package delivery and payment systems. B2C transactions, which are strong in other countries' distribution sector, are significantly lower in China. Finally, the manufacturing sector, which is characterized by great differences in firm size, ownership structure, and IT infrastructure, also has a mixed pattern of e-commerce use (Guo & Chen, 2005).

- *Sleeping e-commerce giant.* China has been aggressively upgrading its technology infrastructure for e-commerce diffusion in recent years. However, business, legal, and cultural barriers hinder technological progress. As a result, there is a very limited amount of actual B2B and B2C transactions in China, compared with other sample economies. This is because most Chinese websites do not offer or support online business, although there is a large percentage of web presence among Chinese firms. In some cases, such as wireless SMS services, where business, legal, and cultural barriers are resolved, technology upgrades allow China to experience e-commerce diffusion on par with or even beyond other countries. In general, though, China falls behind the average of sample countries in its e-commerce diffusion. But, the impressive annual growth rates of B2B and B2C transactions in recent years, as well as the positive forecasts, indicate that China is gradually improving business, legal, and cultural issues while upgrading its technology infrastructure. With respect to B2B, given China's large and growing manufacturing base, it is indeed a sleeping e-commerce giant. It remains to be seen how quickly these barriers can be reduced or even eliminated for China to realize its ambition for economic growth through informatization.

In reading this chapter, it is important to remember that the China case is based on qualitative and quantitative data and on multiple data sources. Also, the main quantitative source, which is the GEC Survey, was conducted in cities mainly in the coastal provinces, whereas other data are from secondary sources and cover the country as a whole. The provinces where data were collected were Beijing, Shanghai, Guangdong, and Chengdu. Thus, as mentioned earlier, the firms in the survey are more similar to their global peers than to the great majority of China's local enterprises. However, they also reflect some key features

Table 6.1 *Macroeconomic statistics, 1998–2002*

	1998	*1999*	*2000*	*2001*	*2002*
GDP in US$bn	946.30	991.36	1,080.43	1,159.03	1,237.15
GDP per capita	761.81	790.81	855.81	911.29	965.78
GDP growth (annual percent)	7.80	7.10	8.00	7.50	8.00
GFDI (percent of GDP)	5.30	4.54	4.32	4.83	4.69
Trade (percent of GDP)	39.21	41.49	49.06	48.54	54.77
Income distribution: richest 20%: poorest 20%					8.0

Source: World Bank, 2004

of China's broader environment and policy as might be expected in such a special country.

Country background: environment and policy

Economic characteristics

China is a large economy, close to that of France (Table 6.1, Chapter 3), with a gross domestic product in 2002 of $1.24 trillion (Table 6.1). However, its huge population brings its GDP per capita ($966) well below developed countries and in line with many developing economies. Some wealthy regions, including mostly coastal provinces, have a GDP per capita close to that of newly industrialized countries, but inland provinces have a much lower GDP (Tan & Wu, 2004).

Foreign trade is equal to more than half of the country's economy as China has become the world's low-cost manufacturing shop, making everything from automobiles to electronics to textiles and toys. As a result, its economy has grown at an annual rate of around 8% since 1998 (Table 6.1).

China's tremendous economic growth has moved millions of people onto income levels which enable them to afford consumer products such as TVs, VCRs, and PCs. The growth has been accompanied by increasing inequality in income, so that the top 20% of the income distribution earns about 46% of total income, or eight times more than the bottom 20%, which earns just 6% of total national income (UNDP, 2002 and Table 6.1). For those who cannot afford the technology, an alternative is the Internet bar or café, of which there are tens of thousands across China. Still, there are hundreds of millions of people who lack the income, technical skills, and Internet access to buy online.

Outside the large urban regions, key aspects of China's financial and physical infrastructure are much less well developed. Until recently, there has been no national network for ATMs or other electronic financial systems, which limits all kinds of e-commerce. Now the government is moving to create such national networks. The penetration of credit card use is just 6%, meaning only a small fraction of the wealthy, urban population has a means of paying for goods online. Even among those with credit cards, usage is quite low (Tan & Wu, 2002).

There is a similar problem in transportation and delivery infrastructure, as China lacks nationwide courier services such as UPS or FedEx to deliver goods to businesses and consumers. While the country has improved its ability to move cargo for export from the coastal regions, its internal transportation networks are poor. However, the situation is starting to change, as the government pours money into road-building projects, and allows foreign courier companies to operate more widely.

The firms in the GEC Survey reflect the large role of international trade as the Chinese firms are as internationally oriented as those in the global sample. They have a larger percent of companies with headquarters abroad, have a higher percent of sales and procurement abroad, and have a larger proportion of firms that are highly affected by competitors abroad (Table 6.2). There is no difference between large and small firms, except for procurement abroad, where small firms procure almost three times the dollar value of inputs as large firms, which reflects their assembly role in production and intermediary role in commodity networks. Finance is the most internationally oriented sector and reflects both expansion abroad by Chinese enterprises and the influx of foreign banking, insurance, and other financial firms into China.[2] Both manufacturing and distribution firms generally are more

[2] For example, by the end of 2001 there were 157 foreign bank branches authorized to conduct banking business in China. Although these banks represent only around 2% of banking assets in China, they were incredibly active and created pressure on China's banks to reform, modernize, and capture customer loyalty before the WTO opening in 2002 (He & Fan, 2004).

Table 6.2 *Internationalization of China's firms*

Internationalization characteristics	*Establishment size*		*Sector*			*Total*	
	SME	*Large*	*Mfg.*	*Distrib.*	*Finance*	*China*	*Global*
Percent of companies with establishments abroad	24	27	19	29	48	25	24
Percent of companies with headquarters abroad	12	14	12	11	21	12	8
Mean percent of total sales from abroad	15	13	8	22	3	15	12
Mean percent of total procurement spending from abroad	31	13	26	32	10	28	20
Degree affected by competitors abroad (percent)							
Low	55	52	46	62	54	54	68
Moderate	24	28	25	26	14	25	16
High	21	20	29	12	32	21	15

Source: CRITO GEC Survey, 2002

locally oriented than those in finance, but some firms are part of global production and commodity networks.

Government policy

The Chinese government has taken steps that either directly or indirectly affect the diffusion of the Internet and e-commerce. One policy with strong indirect effects has been partial liberalization of the telecommunications sector (Wu, 2002). The former monopoly, China Telecom, has been split into two separate companies, China Telecom and China Netcom, and other competitors have been allowed in the market, including China Unicom, China Mobile, and China Railcom. There is limited competition in local phone and cable TV service, but there is competition in cell phone and data services.

In the Internet access market, there are eight designated interconnecting or backbone service providers, which are the only ones allowed to connect to the global Internet. There are many more Internet access networks, which are similar to ISPs in the USA. Intense competition in this market has led to lower prices and improving service quality, especially in major cities. Foreign investors have not been allowed into the access market, but can operate as content providers. As a result of China's accession to the WTO, foreign investors will be allowed to operate in the telecommunications and Internet access markets, with varying levels of ownership depending on the service involved.

In order to create a better environment for IT and e-commerce adoption, the government has launched a variety of initiatives, beginning with the 863 plan in 1986, a technology scheme that included promotion of IT production and use. Most significant were the "Golden" projects, including the Golden Bridge national data network, which is now one of China's Internet backbone networks (Clark & Sviokla, 1996). IT is an important part of the Tenth Five-Year Plan (2001–2005), which calls for extensive use of IT and the Internet in all sectors of society (Kraemer & Dedrick, 2002). The plan specifically emphasizes the use of e-commerce and IT in sectors such as banking and finance, and in government ministries and agencies.

Steps also have been taken to promote e-commerce, including the creation of the China Financial Certification Authority to enable secure online financial transactions. The government is also sponsoring efforts to create standards and mechanisms for certificate authorization, digital signature, and other e-commerce facilitators.

Two major efforts to promote use of the Internet are the Government Online Project and the Enterprise Online Project (Tan & Wu, 2002). The first is an e-government initiative aimed at getting government agencies online, first by developing a web presence and then by offering actual services online. So far success has been limited due to lack of IT skills and infrastructure in the agencies. The Enterprise Online Project is an effort to get large, medium, and small firms online. It provides technical support, an e-commerce portal, and packaged B2B e-commerce software. However, the lack of IT skills and resources among small companies has slowed adoption.

It should be noted that China's policies to promote IT use and infrastructure development have a strong element of domestic industry promotion as well. For instance, the Ninth Five-Year Plan (1996–2000) included IT policies aimed at developing competitive domestic PC manufacturers and increasing domestic content in a variety of hardware products, as well as promoting computer use by traditional industries and households (Kraemer & Dedrick, 2002). The Tenth Five-Year

Table 6.3 *Technology penetration*

	1998	*1999*	*2000*	*2001*	*2002*
Telecommunications					
Main phone lines per 1,000 pop.	69.62	85.82	111.81	137.40	166.92
Cell phone subscribers per 1,000 pop.	19.00	34.18	65.82	110.32	160.85
Cable subscribers per 1,000 pop.	43.80	47.36	61.14	68.56	75.03
Internet					
Internet hosts per 1,000 pop.	0.01	0.06	0.05	0.07	0.12
Internet users per 1,000 pop.	1.67	7.03	17.37	25.67	46.01
IT					
IT as percent of GDP	1.00	1.16	1.49	1.73	1.67
PCs per 1,000 pop.	8.92	12.24	15.90	19.04	27.64
Software piracy rate (percent)	0.95	0.91	0.94	0.92	0.92

Sources: IDC, 2003; IPR, 2003; ITU, 2004; World Bank, 2004

Plan continues the dual focus on use and production by promoting the domestic software and semiconductor industries, along with encouraging IT and Internet use.

Despite its promotion of the Internet and e-commerce, China's broader policies regarding the rule of law and content control may be hindering e-commerce use. In the area of content control, the government restricts various content at different times, including pornography, foreign media websites, and information on sensitive issues such as Taiwan, Tibet, and Falun Gong. It also has cracked down on Internet cafés accused of catering to underage customers or allowing users to access restricted content.

Regarding the rule of law, China lacks strong business contract law, protection for Internet purchases, and intellectual property protection. For example, the Chinese government has published laws on copyright protection that cover online publications, software, and audio-video products, and has closed down factories making illegal copies of software, CDs, and DVDs. However, software piracy rates still top 92% (Table 6.3), and other violations of IPR laws are reportedly common. The problem is enforcement, which admittedly is difficult in an online environment, but which also is carried out sporadically rather than consistently. Similar enforcement problems exist with respect to business law and financial protections (Dedrick, 2004).

Industry structure

Although frequently thought of as an agricultural economy, China is primarily an industrial economy as manufacturing is the single largest economic sector and has grown to account for 44% of total GDP over the past twenty years, in comparison with agriculture which has declined from 30% to 15% of GDP (Tan & Wu, 2004). Distribution accounts for 8% of GDP and finance for 2.3%. However, as will be seen, finance historically has been the most advanced in the use of information technology, followed by distribution and then manufacturing.

China's firms are significantly different from those in other countries because of their ownership structures. Large and medium-sized firms are mainly state-owned enterprises (SOEs); these SOEs account for 70% of the number, 70% of the output value, and 85% of the employees of all large and medium enterprises. Small enterprises (SEs) are much more varied. State-owned SEs are managed by muncipal or county governments, are 0.6% of the total, and 7% of the output value. Collective SEs are managed by towns and villages, are 22% of the total, and 54% of the output value. Individual SEs are managed by owners, are 76% of the total, and 25% of the output value. Joint venture and foreign-funded enterprises are 13% of the total and 0.8% of the output value (Yu, 2002). The distribution of these firms varies by industry sector and has important implications for the use of e-commerce. For example, the SMEs tend to produce final products for local markets rather than specialized products that are inputs for larger enterprises producing for regional or global markets. Consequently, they have little need to use IT internally to manage large-scale production or externally for coordination with an extended value chain.

Finance

China's finance sector is dominated by large, state-owned enterprises. This is especially true in banking where there is a limited number of privately owned banks and some branches of foreign banks. State banks started to build their IT infrastructure in the 1980s, and today China's banking sector has one of the most advanced IT infrastructures among all industry sectors, as measured by hardware and software ownership, IT applications to support business functions, IT budgets, and employees with IT expertise.[3] This strong physical and human infrastructure is aiding the diffusion of e-commerce within China's banking/insurance sector, as well as the large-scale projects and applications, mostly deployed in the 1990s by the large state banks. In addition, a significant portion of their budgets has been allocated to the enforcement of network security systems, ERP systems, and customer relationship management (CRM) systems. All of the large state banks have set up their own websites that are able to support online transactions and payments.

Although there were only fifty-two firms in China's insurance industry at the beginning of 2002,[4] all of these have deployed sophisticated IT infrastructures to automate their core business processing systems, accounting systems, telephone dispatching systems, CRM systems, office systems, intelligence and decision-making supporting systems, and management information systems (China Monitoring Commission for Insurance Industry, 2002). Some of these firms have configured their e-commerce platforms to support online searching, online claim processing, and online commenting, as well as online sales for some products. All of the other firms have set up their websites to introduce their insurance products and services.

Given the well-established IT infrastructure in China's finance sector, significant e-commerce activities are expected to take place. Banking and insurance are traditionally regarded as highly secured businesses with strong credibility, which should alleviate business and consumer concerns about engaging in e-commerce with them.

Manufacturing

China's manufacturing sector has the largest number of firms and a great variance in terms of firm size and ownership. There are many large state-owned enterprises; many small and medium-sized state-owned, joint-stock, and privately owned establishments; some joint ventures; and some solely foreign-owned firms. The variations produce great differences among firms in terms of IT infrastructures, IT budgets,

[3] By the end of 2000, these large state banks had installed 266 large mainframe computers, 1,500 medium-sized mainframe computers, 6,000 minicomputers, 138,000 servers, 440,000 PCs, 373,000 bank teller machines, and 33,000 ATM machines across the country (Nie, 2002).

[4] These consisted of five state-owned corporations, fifteen joint-stock companies, nineteen Sino-foreign joint ventures, and thirteen foreign-owned firms.

and trained staff, but most manufacturing firms have a low level of IT infrastructure and experience. Consequently, one would expect e-commerce use to be low and to be additionally handicapped by poor legal protection, low trust among suppliers and consumers, poor internal and interorganizational information systems, and lagging delivery systems.

Distribution

Within China's distribution sector, there are various kinds of firms, which maintain very different internal IT infrastructures. Joint ventures with foreign partners and solely foreign-owned chain stores tend to have sophisticated IT facilities for internal management and coordination with their parent companies abroad. However, the percentage of joint ventures and foreign-owned stores is relatively low since China's wholesale/retail sector has only recently been opened at a very selective level to multinational corporations.

Most of China's domestic wholesale and retail establishments are state-owned SMEs and large enterprises. These firms were busy adding stand-alone computers to their stores and offices in the 1990s. The build-up of hardware and software for ERP and other decision-supporting functions occurred only recently. A very small percentage of firms has started to build up their e-commerce platforms (Wang, 2002). Therefore, significant e-commerce activity is not expected. The previously mentioned policy barriers also are expected to slow the diffusion of both B2B and B2C e-commerce within the wholesale/retail sector.

E-commerce readiness

Technology penetration

In absolute terms, China would appear to have a high state of e-commerce readiness. By the end of 2004, it was the second biggest PC market in the world, had 316 million fixed-line subscribers, 340 million cell phone users, and 94 million Internet users, and was predicted to grow to 120 million by the end of 2005 (Reuters, 2005). However, China is a large country and looks quite different in e-commerce readiness on a per capita basis (Table 6.3) and when the geographic distribution of the technology is considered. Despite its rapid growth,

China's information infrastructure is basically comparable to that of other developing countries such as Mexico and Brazil.

Telecommunications infrastructure

China has been rapidly building up its telecommunications infrastructure since the late 1980s and, on average, more than 10 million telephone lines were added to its telecom network each year in the 1990s (Mueller & Tan, 1997; Tan et al., 1997). Total telephone lines in China reached 167 per 1,000 population in 2002 (Table 6.3). While China's telephone penetration rate was only 0.3 per 100 in 1980, it exceeded 25.9 per 100 by 2002. Many big cities and economically developed areas such as Beijing, Shanghai, and Guangdong have seen telephone penetration rates of 40–50%. The remote rural areas often lag behind with single-digit penetration rates (Tan & Wu, 2004).

China's wireless phone network has experienced an even higher growth rate than its fixed phone network since the first Total Access Communication Service (TACS) cellular phone system was installed in 1987. By 2001, China was the largest mobile communications market in the world, surpassing the United States in total users. Wireless phone users in China reached 160.8 per 1,000 population in 2002, up from 19.0 in 1998. Although China is still the lowest among wireless users of the global sample on a per capita basis, wireless technology is a good fit with China's widely distributed population and its relatively low cost may make it a suitable platform for certain kinds of e-commerce such as short messaging service.

Internet infrastructure

As in the United States and many other nations, China's Internet use began in the academic community, with a connection between China's Institute of High Energy Physics and Stanford University in 1991, leading to the creation of an academic research network called the China Educational and Research Network (CERNET) (Tan et al., 1999). However, the commercialization and rapid expansion of Internet access and diffusion in China did not occur until 1996, when ChinaNet began offering commercial ISP services. Since that time, Internet use has grown at a rapid pace, going from less than 1 million users in 1998 to 60 million in 2002 and 94 million in 2004. While early users were mostly younger males, by 2002 females made up 40% of users and

Table 6.4 *Use of e-commerce technologies*

	Establishment size		*Sector*			*Total*	
Percent using . . .	*SME*	*Large*	*Mfg.*	*Distrib.*	*Finance*	*China*	*Global*
Email	95	99	92	100	99	96	99
Website	68	77	78	61	72	70	74
Intranet	58	77	67	54	72	61	64
Extranet	36	40	28	43	50	36	33
• accessible by suppliers/ business partners	28	32	16	40	32	29	21
• accessible by customers	21	26	16	26	40	22	18
EDI	26	20	23	26	39	25	44
• over private networks	10	11	10	8	28	10	19
• Internet-based	4	2	3	4	6	4	8
• both	11	6	7	14	4	10	16
EFT	26	24	27	23	46	26	43
Call center	21	22	29	12	29	21	32

Source: CRITO GEC Survey, 2002

those over 35 reached 20%, making the Internet a broadly diffused technology across different demographics.

Firm-level readiness

While China now has the second largest number of Internet users in the world, use of the web for business has been limited. China is generally below the global sample in use of e-commerce technologies (Table 6.4, Figure 6.1). Yet the gap is not significant, especially for newly deployed e-commerce technologies. This is consistent with the fact that e-commerce technologies are mostly a recent deployment both in China and in the world, which has offered China an opportunity to grow together with other nations.

For the newly deployed technologies, including email, websites, intranets, and extranets, China is close to the global average. However, it lags behind in using 'traditional' e-commerce technologies such as EDI, EFT, and call centers. Only 25% of the surveyed Chinese firms use EDI, compared with the global average of 44%. EFT is used by

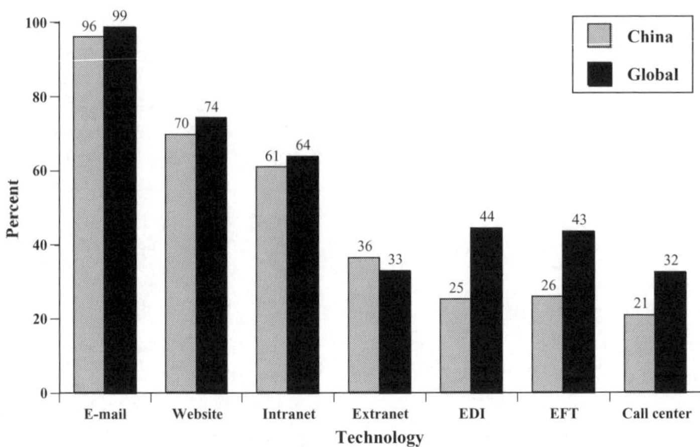

Figure 6.1 Use of e-commerce technologies
Source: CRITO GEC Survey, 2002

26% of Chinese firms, while 43% of global firms have adopted it. Call centers have been deployed in only 21% of Chinese firms, while the global average is 32%. These traditional e-commerce technologies point to a significant gap between Chinese firms and their counterparts abroad. These results are consistent with the fact that IT infrastructure has only recently been deployed in Chinese firms, thus bypassing the 'traditional' e-commerce technologies.

There is a debate over the efficacy of this bypass or "leapfrog" strategy. From the technology perspective, the constant upgrading of information and communication technology creates many advantages to later adopters in terms of lower investment and better technology. With e-commerce, later adopters could gain comparative advantages by jumping into the Internet-based technology directly and ignoring the EDI type of technology. However, the lack of experience in using traditional EDI and EFT technology means no experience in internal system integration, no business coordination in marketing and customer services, and poor familiarity with legal and policy issues. Later adopters need extra time to acquire this knowledge and these skills, which may slow down their progress. As we will see later, this is a key issue for China because, while its firms have begun to adopt the new technology, they have done so without the necessary national policy environment and without adopting the needed organizational complements.

Table 6.5 *Investment in IT by Chinese firms, 2002*

	Establishment size		*Sector*			*Total*	
Percent using . . .	*SME*	*Large*	*Mfg.*	*Distrib.*	*Finance*	*China*	*Global*
PCs per employee	.74	.30	.41	.88	1.03	.66	.82
IT employees as percent of total employees	13.92	3.99	6.85	17.78	7.44	12.24	9.12
IS operating budget as percent of 2001 revenue	9.02	5.82	4.69	11.52	11.11	8.54	7.75
Web-based spending as percent of IS operating budget	9.25	8.67	9.05	9.21	10.69	9.17	14.89

Source: CRITO GEC Survey, 2002; weighted sample

More large Chinese enterprises use newly developed e-commerce than do small and medium-sized ones. However, more SMEs have adopted EDI and EFT. This occurred even before the Internet became a viable e-commerce tool. One explanation for this pattern may be the more intensive involvement of entrepreneurial SMEs in international trade than the large state-owned enterprises.

China's banking and insurance sector generally leads the use of both the 'traditional' and new e-commerce technologies (Table 6.4), which is understandable given that the finance sector was the first to automate and was given the highest priority among the government's "Golden" projects. This sector is well supported by the government, has developed IT expertise, and is strongly motivated to serve business customers with e-commerce technologies.

IT investment

The distribution of end-user technology in Chinese firms is low compared with the global sample, but the proportion of IT employees to total employees is large, which probably accounts for the somewhat higher proportion of overall IS spending as a percent of revenues compared with the global sample (Table 6.5). The resources devoted to developing web applications, however, are low compared with the global sample. The pattern of investment across sectors reflects the importance given to the finance sector in contrast to manufacturing.

Table 6.6 *Enterprise integration strategy*

Extent to which Internet applications are electronically integrated with . . .	*Establishment size*		*Sector*			*Total*	
	SME	*Large*	*Mfg.*	*Distrib.*	*Finance*	*China*	*Global*
Internal databases and information systems							
Percent little to none	47	48	61	34	27	47	53
Percent some	37	31	33	40	32	36	24
Percent a great deal	16	21	6	26	41	17	24
Those of suppliers and business customers							
Percent little to none	65	55	69	58	45	63	72
Percent some	27	40	25	34	29	29	18
Percent a great deal	8	5	6	8	26	8	10

Source: CRITO GEC Survey, 2002

The overall pattern of investment suggests that the actual use of e-commerce will be relatively modest and will follow the sector pattern of investment. This conclusion is confirmed by Guo and Chen (2005).

Enterprise integration

Overall, the level of upstream and downstream integration of the Internet with internal databases and information systems of firms in China is similar to the global sample, but there are large differences between the industry sectors (Table 6.6, Figure 6.2). For example, firms in banking and insurance are two to six times as likely to have Internet applications integrated with their internal information systems as wholesale/retail and manufacturing, respectively. Similarly, they are three to four times as likely to be integrated via Internet applications with their suppliers and business customers as either of these two sectors. Again, this reflects the historical lead and priority given to banking in particular. It also reflects the efforts of state banks to modernize in order to compete with large foreign banks beginning to enter the country.

Mobiles and the Internet

One area in which China is comparable to the leading countries is in mobile technologies. Mobile subscribers have nearly doubled annually

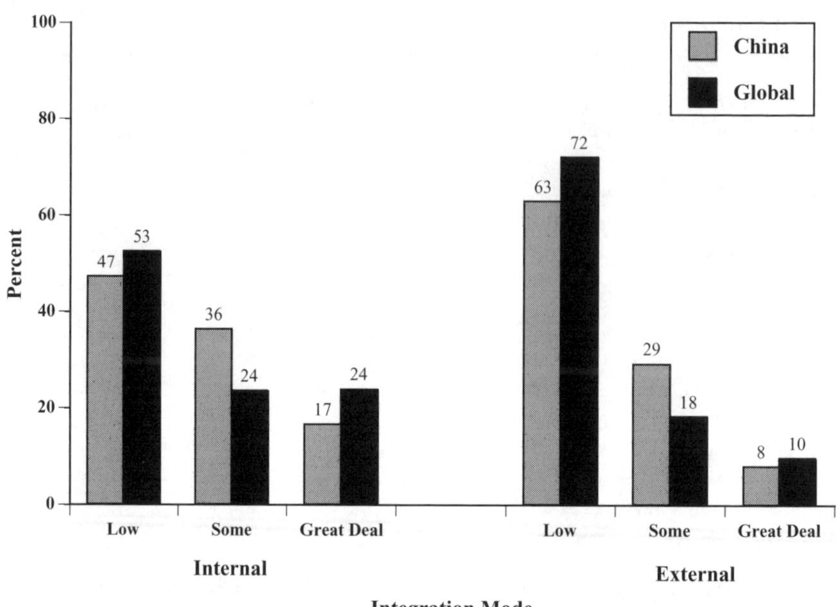

Figure 6.2 Integration mode
Source: CRITO GEC Survey, 2002

in China in recent years (Table 6.3). Among the firms in the GEC Survey, 31% offered mobile web services or planned to in the next year, compared to 32% of the global sample. This trend toward a significant mobile user increase has caught industry's attention, as 36% of China's banking and insurance firms already have mobile content or services available, which is much higher than the global average of 21% (Table 6.7). China's manufacturing sector also reports a high

Table 6.7 ***Content/services to mobile customers (percent)***

	Manufacturing		*Distrib.*		*Finance*		*Total*	
	China	*Global*	*China*	*Global*	*China*	*Global*	*China*	*Global*
Already available	22	14	7	12	36	21	15	14
Plan to add within the next year	18	18	14	18	15	19	16	18

Source: CRITO GEC Survey, 2002

mobile content availability of 22% versus the global average of 14%. This again illustrates that China is able to leapfrog earlier technologies and achieve adoption levels equivalent to other countries with newer technologies.

One highly popular offering is short messaging service, which is offered over cell phones either directly or via the Internet. In 2002, Chinese consumers sent 90–100 billion messages, generating around $1.2 billion in revenues. Internet service providers and content providers offer SMS-based services such as news, chat rooms, ring-tone downloads, and games, creating a profitable revenue stream for them. By 2003, SMS accounted for 24–40% of the total revenues of the top three portals in China – sina.com, sohu.com, and neteasy.com (Tan & Wu, 2004). Given the much higher penetration of cell phones compared with PCs in China, it might be expected that businesses will look to develop more services suitable for mobile users.

In summary, national statistics indicate that China's information infrastructure is large and growing rapidly, although still far behind developed countries on a per capita basis. The GEC Survey data suggest that Chinese firms are leapfrogging over earlier technologies to invest in lower-cost, open-standard technologies. This could be an advantage as firms avoid switching costs or the need to integrate web-based technologies with legacy applications. However, Chinese firms do not have the benefit of experience in internal system integration and adapting business processes, or familiarity with legal and policy issues. This may reduce their ability to apply the new technologies effectively (Tan & Wu, 2004). In addition, as will be seen, there are significant legal and institutional barriers to e-commerce use in China.

Drivers and barriers to e-commerce

Drivers

Chinese firms are driven to adopt the Internet mostly to expand their market reach and to satisfy customer demand (Table 6.8, Figure 6.3). This is similar to the broader global sample, although a bit more pronounced. Also, Chinese firms are more likely to be influenced by their suppliers to go online. This is not surprising, given that many Chinese manufacturing and distribution firms procure their inputs from abroad,

Table 6.8 *Drivers for Internet use*

Percent indicating a significant driver	*Establishment size*		*Sector*			*Total*	
	SME	*Large*	*Mfg.*	*Distrib.*	*Finance*	*China*	*Global*
Customer demand	47	36	34	56	40	45	37
Major competitors were online	33	31	37	28	36	33	31
Suppliers required it	28	31	32	26	13	28	22
To reduce costs	38	45	42	38	32	40	36
To expand market for existing product or services	56	51	59	52	48	55	48
To enter new businesses/markets	42	46	44	42	46	43	42
To improve coordination with customers and suppliers	36	49	46	31	35	38	44
Required for government procurement	22	23	25	20	26	22	15
Government provided incentives	12	17	14	10	16	12	8

Source: CRITO GEC Survey, 2002

especially high-tech inputs from other parts of Asia, as discussed earlier and seen in Table 6.2. As might be expected given this dependence, improving coordination with customers and suppliers is a major driver in manufacturing.

Despite vigorous government promotion of e-commerce, the role of government policy is generally limited. Only 22% of firms mentioned government procurement requirements as a driver, and 12% mentioned government incentives, the lowest ranking of all the drivers (Table 6.8). Yet, while direct government promotion plays a secondary role as a driver of e-commerce, its influence was higher than any other country except Singapore, and was well ahead of the global average (Figure 6.3). In particular, the government's effort to use the Internet to increase transparency in procurement seems to be having some effect. Field interviews with government officials and enterprise executives

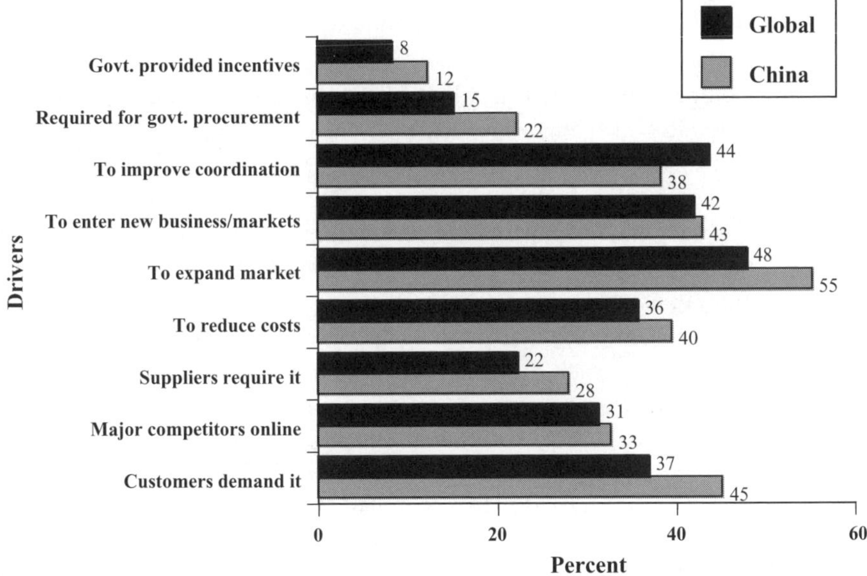

Figure 6.3 E-commerce drivers
Source: CRITO GEC Survey, 2002

indicate that the desire for transparency is shaped in part by national efforts to reduce corruption and local efforts to collect taxes, such as import and export duties. Box 6.1 provides an example of government use of the Internet to reduce corruption and costs.

Barriers

While government promotion has had a limited impact as a driver of e-commerce in China, the lack of adequate legal protections is clearly a barrier to more extensive adoption. The three biggest barriers to doing business online in the sample were lack of legal protection, lack of business laws that support e-commerce and privacy, and security concerns (Table 6.9, Figure 6.4). Concern over privacy and security issues was similar to the global sample. However, concern that business laws do not support e-commerce was reported as a barrier by 41% of the firms in China in comparison with 24% of the global sample. Similarly, inadequate protection for Internet purchases was reported by 54% versus 34% in the global sample. The "prevalence of credit

Box 6.1. Online student admissions services for colleges

Competition for college admission is still great among high school graduates in China. Universities send their admissions people to every province's center to select the right students, mostly based on students' scores in the national entrance exam held every year in July. The two major concerns are corruption and expenditure. Corruption occurs when university admissions staff misuse their authority and admit students based not on their scores but on their connections. Expenditure involves the cost of transportation, lodging, and staff time for each university to send out teams to each province.

E-commerce service was implemented to address these two concerns. Since 1999, all student profiles are put online after the national entrance exam. Each university conducts its admissions remotely through the Internet. The process is more open and few human transactions are involved. Each action is recorded for audit. In addition, expenditure is reduced. From this perspective, e-commerce serves as a tool to lower costs and fight corruption. However, those whose power is threatened oppose its implementation.

Source: Tan & Wu, 2002, CAIS

card use" is also perceived as a barrier by more Chinese firms than in other countries (30% versus 20%). The vignette in Box 6.2 shows one local adaptation to such barriers.

The next group of barriers falls into the category of consumer preferences and lack of business resources, which includes customers preferring face-to-face interaction or not using the technology, to firms' inability to incorporate the Internet into their businesses or even to afford an e-commerce site. These challenges will probably be met for the most part with greater experience, and appears to be happening even in the time since the survey. The legal/regulatory issues can be dealt with only through a combination of government initiative and perhaps the efforts of industry associations and other bodies that can set voluntary standards for online commerce.

At the industry level, privacy/security concerns were most striking in the financial sector, where they were cited as a barrier by 73% of the firms. As might be expected, this reflects both internal concerns and

Table 6.9 *Barriers/difficulties to e-commerce diffusion*

Percent indicating a significant obstacle	*Establishment size*		*Sector*			*Total*	
	SME	*Large*	*Mfg.*	*Distrib.*	*Finance*	*China*	*Global*
Need for face-to-face customer interaction	31	28	27	34	29	31	34
Concern about privacy of data or security issues	45	45	52	37	73	45	44
Customers do not use the technology	34	28	35	30	34	33	31
Finding staff with e-commerce expertise	22	9	22	18	14	20	27
Prevalence of credit card use	32	21	29	32	27	30	20
Costs of implementing an e-commerce site	27	35	34	23	28	29	34
Making needed organizational changes	22	23	21	23	34	22	24
Ability to use the Internet as part of business strategy	32	28	35	28	21	31	25
Cost of Internet access	23	19	17	27	16	22	15
Business laws do not support e-commerce	41	40	37	44	57	41	24
Taxation of Internet sales	20	16	19	19	22	19	16
Inadequate legal protection for Internet purchases	56	49	52	57	54	55	34

Source: CRITO GEC Survey, 2002

those of customers, both enterprises and consumers. Clearly, the future of online financial transactions in China will depend on providing better data security and privacy protection, and a better legal/regulatory environment for both consumers and firms.

Small and large firms share similar perceptions on the barriers to e-commerce use, except for staff recruitment and credit card use. More than twice as many small firms as large firms (22% versus 9%) report that it is difficult to recruit staff with e-commerce expertise. More small firms also consider the prevalence of credit card use as more of a barrier than large firms (32% versus 21%).

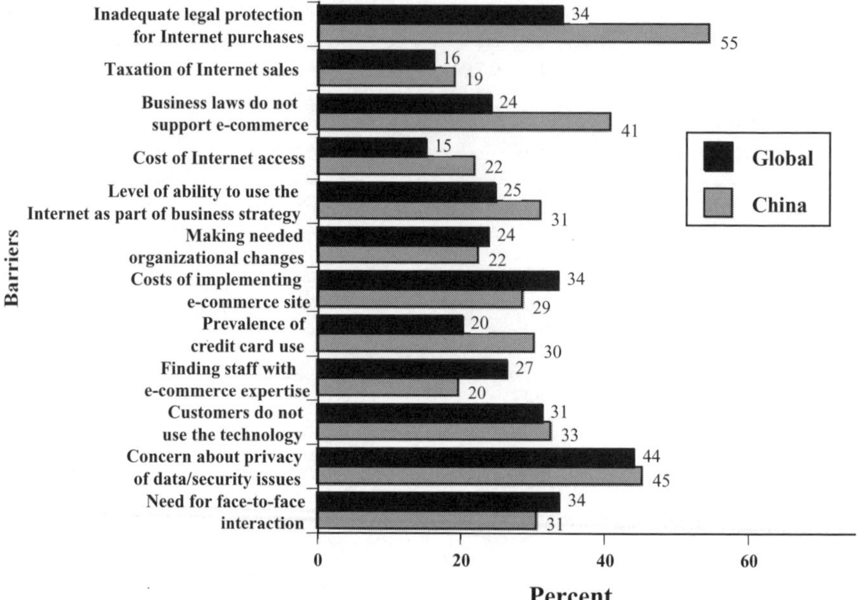

Figure 6.4 E-commerce barriers
Source: CRITO GEC Survey, 2002

In summary, market forces appear to be more of a driver of e-commerce than government policy or incentives in China, but the lack of an adequate legal framework (business laws, protection for Internet purchases, privacy, security) is a major barrier to e-commerce diffusion and use. While these barriers occur in all countries (Shih et al., 2004), they appear to be substantially greater in China where basic business law is immature, enforcement of laws is weak, and trust is low among both businesses and consumers. Thus, it appears that overcoming the disparity between China's ambition to become an information society and its current reality depends on institutional complements to the considerable diffusion of technology that has occurred.

Diffusion of e-commerce

Country-level pattern

At the macroeconomic level, we find a pattern of low levels of online transactions in China. B2C e-commerce is equal to just 0.36% of GDP,

Box 6.2. Online department store for a local community

The first example involves a typical living complex with several thirty-floor apartment buildings in Beijing (Wang, 2001). The property management operates an e-store to serve its residents. Residents type in what they want to purchase from the e-store's website (they have the option to call the operator to place the order) before 11 a.m. every day. The goods are ready for residents to pick up at 3 p.m. The e-store staff buy and sort out the goods during the four-hour window. The payment is deducted from the deposit put down by registered residents. Delivery by the e-store's staff to residents' homes is an optional service with extra charges.

This e-store has proved to be a successful case that combines online service with offline services and bypasses potential barriers such as credibility and payment method. However, it is unlikely to be extended to a citywide or nationwide service (Tan & Wu, 2002).

Source: Tan & Wu, 2002, CAIS

while B2B equals 1.7%, for a total of 2.06% (Table 6.10). These figures are much lower than those of other economies in the region, particularly Taiwan and Singapore. Nevertheless, China is slightly ahead of the other developing countries in the study – Brazil and Mexico – despite having a lower level of GDP per capita.

One interpretation of the data is that e-commerce follows the patterns seen in other types of IT adoption, with levels of use closely related to income levels. Hence, China's low levels of e-commerce transactions are typical of a developing country. Another interpretation is that e-commerce is still relatively new (at least on the Internet), and that China is likely to end up with a much higher level of online transactions as both businesses and consumers gain familiarity and experience with the benefits of e-commerce and learn how to capture those benefits.

Looking at the trend over just five years (Figure 1.4 in Chapter 1) shows how rapidly this is occurring in China and elsewhere. It also shows an increasing disparity between leaders and followers. The question is whether this is indicative of an increasing "digital divide" among nations that will leave China behind and increase the disparity between its ambition and the reality, or whether this is further evidence of an

Table 6.10 *E-commerce sales as a percent of GDP, 2003*

	B2C	*B2B*	*Total e-commerce*
Taiwan	.96	8.50	9.46
Singapore	1.18	8.24	9.42
Germany	.80	6.09	6.89
Denmark	.66	5.72	6.38
United States	.90	5.39	6.29
Japan	.40	4.47	4.87
France	.58	3.85	4.43
China	.36	1.70	2.06
Brazil	.25	1.71	1.96
Mexico	.04	1.44	1.48

Source: IDC, 2003

evolutionary pattern, with some economies having hit an inflection point in e-commerce (e.g., Singapore), while others such as China have yet to reach that point but might do so with greater investment in the organizational and institutional complements to the technology (Dedrick, 2004).

Firms' uses of the Internet

Consistent with the top driver being to expand markets, Chinese firms are most likely to use the Internet for customer-oriented processes, including service/support, advertising/marketing, and exchanging data with customers (Table 6.11, Figure 6.5). However, they are much less likely to conduct transactions, either purchasing or sales online. In comparison with other economies in the study, China has the smallest proportion of firms engaged in online purchases and the second smallest in online sales after Mexico [data not shown]. This reluctance to engage in online transactions likely goes back to the concerns over the adequacy of protection for online transactions for both consumers and businesses, as well as the higher level of website functionality and back-end process integration required for transactional activity. This does not actually explain the low levels of online procurement, since buying online can be a relatively simple process for many standardized

Table 6.11 ***Uses of the Internet***

Percent using the Internet for . . .	*Establishment size*		*Sector*			*Total*	
	SME	*Large*	*Mfg.*	*Distrib.*	*Finance*	*China*	*Global*
Advertising and marketing purposes	51	58	53	52	46	52	58
Making sales online	23	24	28	18	30	23	30
After-sales customer service and support	56	50	58	54	39	55	44
Making purchases online	35	14	31	33	20	31	47
Exchanging operational data with suppliers	46	52	47	48	38	47	48
Exchanging operational data with business customers	52	54	43	61	42	52	51
Formally integrating business processes with suppliers or other business partners	29	37	21	39	33	30	34

Source: CRITO GEC Survey, 2002

business supplies. However, the problem may be on the supply side – if suppliers are not selling online, then business customers cannot buy online.

While there are some important barriers to online transactions in China, the pattern of use found in the survey may also represent a stage in the evolution of e-commerce, as much of it reveals enduring characteristics of the Chinese environment. If one were to look at Internet usage by US businesses in the mid-to-late 1990s, a similar pattern might have been seen. It is likely that Chinese firms will engage in more online sales and procurement as both they and their customers and suppliers gain experience with the Internet, and as the country's physical and institutional infrastructure improves.

The manufacturing, wholesale/retail, and banking/insurance sectors use the Internet for different business purposes while sharing some commonalities. The primary use in manufacturing is for after-sales customer service and support (58%), whereas in distribution it is exchanging operational data with business customers (61%), and in finance it is advertising and marketing (46%).

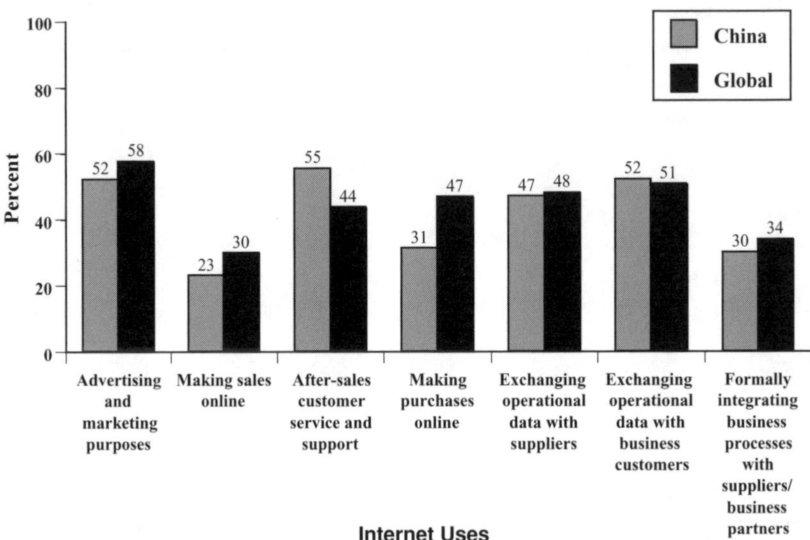

Figure 6.5 E-commerce diffusion
Source: CRITO GEC Survey, 2002

SMEs and large firms use the Internet for similar business purposes except for one major difference. More than twice as many SMEs (35%) make online purchases than large firms (14%). This is consistent with our earlier observation that many SMEs produce final products for local markets and rely on inputs for production from the outside. Thus, they would do more purchasing online. In contrast, large enterprises have more inertia and are relatively slower to conduct business transactions after they go online (Zhu & Kraemer, 2005).

Online transactions

Online sales

The results of the survey show that even among those firms using the Internet for business in China, a relatively small share is conducting either sales or purchasing online (Tables 6.12 and 6.13). This suggests that overall e-commerce volumes will be small among those firms and in the country as a whole, and the data at both levels confirm this expectation.

Table 6.12 *Online sales*

	Establishment size		*Sector*			*Total*	
	SME	*Large*	*Mfg.*	*Distrib.*	*Finance*	*China*	*Global*
Type of online sales							
Percent B2B	24	16	26	20	24	23	28
Percent B2C	16	19	20	13	23	17	22
Mean percent of total consumer sales conducted online (all establishments)	1	3	2	1	3	1	4
Mean percent of total business sales conducted online (all establishments)	2	4	2	3	2	2	4
Mean percent of total consumer sales conducted online (only those doing B2C sales online)	7	17	9	8	14	9	19
Mean percent of total business sales conducted online (only those doing B2B sales online)	8	34	6	17	14	10	15
Percent of websites that support online payment (only those doing online sales)	9	12	13	2	31	13	34

Source: CRITO GEC Survey, 2002

At the firm level, the survey shows that online sales account for just 1% of total sales to consumers and 2% of sales to businesses. Even among firms which offer either B2B or B2C e-commerce, the percent of total sales conducted online is just 9% for B2C and 10% for B2B, both of which are much lower than the global sample (Table 6.12). Finally, among small firms doing online sales, only 9% have websites that support online payment, compared wih 34% for the global sample. This reinforces the view that Chinese firms and consumers are not yet comfortable completing an entire transaction online, and that the infrastructure for secure online payment is not yet in place. Yet, it also shows that firms are finding other (offline) ways to handle payment for

Table 6.13 *Online procurement*

	Establishment size		*Sector*			*Total*	
	SME	*Large*	*Mfg.*	*Distrib.*	*Finance*	*China*	*Global*
Percent of establishments doing online purchasing	44	21	36	45	27	40	51
Mean percent of money spent for direct goods for production ordered online (all establishments)	5	0	4			4	8
Mean percent of money spent on goods for resale ordered online (all establishments)	5	5		5		5	7
Mean percent of money spent on supplies and equipment ordered online (all establishments)	4	0	1	5	1	3	8

Source: CRITO GEC Survey, 2002

goods ordered online. Examples include cash-on-delivery or money transfers through the post office for B2C, or traditional paper invoices for B2B.

Online procurement

The other half of the online transaction is purchasing, and this follows the same pattern. Under half of all firms in the survey do any online purchasing, and the actual volumes are a very small share of total goods purchased (Table 6.13).

As would be expected, China's distribution and manufacturing sectors are more active in online purchasing (45% and 36%) than the finance sector, and also spend a higher mean percentage of money on online procurement. SMEs have a higher participating percentage

(44% versus 21%) and spend more money for online purchasing, compared with large firms. This is consistent with earlier data which showed that SMEs engage more in online transactions than large firms, which might only create an online presence rather than actually conduct online business.

Taken together, these findings about online transactions indicate that Chinese firms have taken the first step toward participating in e-commerce, but that e-commerce has not yet reached the take-off point. While this might be part of an evolutionary pattern, it is also likely that China's firms lack the resources, capabilities, and both organizational and institutional complements to engage in a greater extent of e-commerce. It is likely, therefore, that the impacts of e-commerce might be less than expected and less than those achieved elsewhere.

Impacts of e-commerce

National impacts

The impacts of the Internet and e-commerce on China's economy as a whole are undoubtedly very limited, given that e-commerce is equivalent to just 2% of GDP, and Internet adoption is still confined mostly to affluent consumers, foreign businesses, and technically savvy local firms. This is not surprising because other work indicates that developing countries as a group have not yet reached a critical mass of IT capabilities to achieve productivity and growth payoffs (Dewan & Kraemer, 2000). Also, much of China's economic production and employment is in traditional industries such as agriculture, mining, construction, and services, where IT use is very low. As such, Internet-based e-commerce is not likely to have measurable effects on economic growth, productivity, or industry structure at the national level for years to come.

Firm-level impacts

When we narrow our focus to firms that are already using the Internet for business in China, however, we do find significant impacts. In fact, Chinese respondents to the GEC Survey were somewhat more optimistic than the global sample about the benefits they had reaped

Table 6.14 *Impacts of doing business online on sales, efficiency, and competitiveness*

Percent indicating impact is a great deal	Establishment size		Sector			Total	
	SME	Large	Mfg.	Distrib.	Finance	China	Global
Sales impacts							
Sales area widened	48	52	51	47	40	48	31
Customer service improved	36	42	42	32	45	37	35
International sales increased	31	41	32	34	24	33	20
Sales increased	24	32	23	28	31	26	21
Efficiency impacts							
Internal processes more efficient	28	46	38	24	44	31	34
Coordination with suppliers improved	27	41	27	32	18	29	30
Staff productivity increased	23	30	24	23	30	24	27
Procurement costs decreased	30	31	29	31	16	30	18
Inventory costs decreased	20	26	18	24	19	21	14
Competitive impacts							
Competitive position improved	40	47	44	38	49	41	30

Source: CRITO GEC Survey, 2002

from going online (Table 6.14), although tangible improvements such as increased sales or productivity or cost reduction were less obvious.

Sales impacts

Chinese firms report that the Internet has helped them to increase their reach, both in terms of widened sales area (48%) and greater international sales (33%), as well as to improve their customer service (37%) (Table 6.14). This is consistent with the fact that the biggest drivers of adoption were market expansion and customer demand. However, fewer firms report that their sales have increased as a result of doing business online. This is consistent with the earlier results regarding low use of the Internet for online sales and the low amount of actual online sales. There are not significant differences across industry sectors, but more large firms report positive sales impacts than smaller firms.

Table 6.15 *Impacts of doing business online on distribution channels and players*

	Establishment size		*Sector*			*Total*	
Percent indicating . . .	*SME*	*Large*	*Mfg.*	*Distrib.*	*Finance*	*China*	*Global*
Number of competitors							
Increased	44	39	41	46	32	43	28
No change	56	55	58	53	62	56	67
Decreased	0	6	1	1	6	1	5
Intensity of competition							
Increased	50	43	48	50	41	49	42
No change	48	48	50	46	53	48	54
Decreased	2	9	2	4	6	3	4

Source: CRITO GEC Survey, 2002

Efficiency impacts

Overall, fewer firms report efficiency impacts, whether internal process efficiency (31%), decreased procurement costs (30%), staff productivity (24%), or inventory costs (21%) (Table 6.14). More firms in the finance sector reported internal efficiencies whereas more firms in manufacturing and distribution reported improved coordination with suppliers.

Competition and firm competitiveness

The Chinese firms were also more likely to report that their competitive position had improved (41%), especially larger firms (47%) and those in the finance sector (49%), followed by manufacturing and distribution (Table 6.14). However, they were more likely than the global sample to report that the number of competitors had increased (43% versus 28%), and to a lesser extent that the intensity of competition had increased (Table 6.15). Also, smaller firms, and firms in manufacturing and distribution, were more likely to report increased competition.

Conclusion

While China's continued economic growth, consumer wealth, technology diffusion, and economic liberalization provide reason for optimism about the future of the Internet and e-commerce, there are still obstacles that will hinder widespread adoption and limit the economic impacts of these technologies in China. One is the increasingly uneven income distribution, which has helped create a large group of consumers with the income and education to use the Internet and shop online, but which has left hundreds of millions of Chinese unlikely to participate in the "new economy" for many years to come. Another is the poor financial and transportation infrastructures, although these are being addressed aggressively by the government.

Despite these obstacles, adoption of information and communications technologies in China has been rapid in recent years. While diffusion levels on a per capita basis remain low, China now leads the world in phone lines, cell phones, and TV sets, and is second or third in PCs and Internet subscribers. China also is the second largest producer of computer hardware in the world. As a result, China is vital to the global IT industry, and the production and use of IT is a key to China's economic future. This upgrading of its national level of information infrastructure has advanced China's overall level of technology readiness for e-commerce.

China's efforts are reflected in firms' rush to establish a web presence as in recent years they have recognized the potential of the Internet and e-commerce. They have taken the first step by connecting to the Internet and setting up websites to introduce and advertise their products and services. Chinese firms have leaped over "traditional" e-commerce technologies such as EDI and EFT by going directly to the Internet. However, only a very small number of firms has actually moved to the next step to conduct transactions via their websites. Chinese firms are also behind in integrating their internal databases and information systems via the Internet with upstream suppliers and downstream business partners as required for some global production and commodity networks.

Although Chinese firms use the Internet for business purposes similar to their counterparts in the global sample, there is a striking difference between Chinese enterprises and these firms when it comes to the use of the Internet for selling and purchasing products and services. The actual level of e-commerce use in China is very low, especially as measured by online sales and purchases. Thus, Chinese firms have a high web presence but low online transactions, a finding also supported by other research.[5] Consistent with this pattern of use, Chinese firms report sales-related impacts such as widened sales area, improved competitive position, and improved customer service, but very few report an increase in local or international sales as a result of e-commerce.

A critical reason for the low use of e-commerce for online transactions is that China is seriously lacking the organizational and institutional complements for e-commerce. China's enterprises lack a solid foundation of internal information systems, have poor integration of business processes with information systems, and lack the human and organizational skills to make needed business transformations. The institutional environment, consisting of both official laws and regulations and unofficial business norms and practices, also needs to be improved. Here, progress has been mixed. For instance, some provincial and local governments have established their own e-commerce rules, and the national government has passed laws on intellectual property and other issues, but there are problems with inadequate regulations and enforcement in many areas. In addition, there is no tradition of privacy protection in either law or custom, and the government's ongoing efforts to restrict information content have had a dampening effect on Internet use (Dedrick, 2004).

Despite its mixed record with the Internet, there is evidence that China is moving into a stage of sustainable growth in e-commerce. The fundamental drivers are continued economic growth, increased consumer wealth, broad technology diffusion, and economic liberalization. China is becoming a more global economy with entry into the WTO, large inflows of foreign direct investment, and flows of people and information into and out of the country.

The business community is also beginning to produce some success stories. The top portals (NetEase, Sina.com, Sohu.com), once derided as "dot.bombs," survived and have become profitable by developing new strategies and profitable business lines (Dedrick, 2004). These include SMS-based services, advertising, and, most recently, online gaming services (Fowler, 2004). Leading manufacturers such as Haier,

[5] For example, a 2001 survey of 638 large and medium-sized enterprises reported that 87% had connected to the Internet and 69% of them had created websites. However, only 4% of the firms reportedly had conducted online purchases, and less than 4% of them had offered online sales for their products (Network Economy Research Center at Beijing University, 2001).

Lenovo, and Huawei have developed successful e-business strategies. Our survey results confirm that Chinese firms are optimistic about the impacts of the Internet on their businesses.

Overall, we conclude that while China has been aggressively upgrading its technology infrastructure for e-commerce in recent years, the diffusion and use of e-commerce have been slowed by inadequate complementary factors along business, legal, and cultural dimensions. Nevertheless, the impressive annual growth rates of B2B and B2C transactions in recent years, as well as positive forecasts, suggest that China may be making progress in working on the barriers while continuing to upgrade its technology infrastructure. It remains to be seen how fast these barriers can be alleviated or even removed. Doing so will be key to China achieving its ambition for informatization and economic growth.

References

Bell, D. (1973). *The Coming of Post-industrial Society*. New York: Basic Books.

China Monitoring Commission for Insurance Industry (2002). *2001–2002 Annual Review of IT Infrastructure in China's Insurance Sector*. 2002 China Information Almanac.

Clark, T. H. & Sviokla, J. J. (1996). China Internet Corporation (www.China.com), Harvard Business School case #9-396-299. Boston, MA.

Dedrick, J. (2004). China's Economy and the Internet. Working paper. Irvine, CA: Center for Research on Information Technology and Organizations, University of California, Irvine.

Dewan, S. & Kraemer, K. L. (2000). Information Technology and Productivity: Preliminary Evidence from Country-Level Data. *Management Science*, 46(4), 548–562.

Fowler, G. A. (2004). Chinese Internet Firms Propel Growth with Online Games. *The Asian Wall Street Journal*, April 16.

Guo, X. & Chen, G. (2005). Internet Diffusion in Chinese Companies. *Communications of the ACM*, 48(4), 54–58.

He, L. & Fan, X. (2004). Foreign Banks in Post-WTO China: An Intermediate Assessment. *China and World Economy*, 12(5), 3–16.

International Data Corporation (IDC) (2004). *Internet Commerce Market Model*, Framingham, MA.

International Planning and Research Corporation (IPR) (2003). *Eighth Annual Business Software Alliance (BSA) Global Software Piracy Study, Trends in Software Piracy 1994–2002*. Washington, D.C.: Business Software Alliance.

International Telecommunication Union (ITU) (2004). *World Telecommunication Indicators Database* (8th Ed.). Geneva, Switzerland.

Kraemer, K. L. & Dedrick, J. (1995). From Nationalism to Pragmatism: IT Policy in China. *IEEE Computer*, 28(8), 64–73.

Kraemer, K. L. & Dedrick, J. (2002). Enter the Dragon: China's Computer Industry. *IEEE Computer*, 35(2), 28–36.

Mueller, M. & Tan, Z. (1997). *China in the Information Age: Telecommunications and the Dilemmas of Reform*. Washington, D.C./Westport, CT: The Center of Strategic and International Studies (CSIS)/Praeger Publishers.

Network Economy Research Center at Beijing University (2001). *White Book of the Internet and E-Commerce within China's Enterprises*, December.

Nie, X. (2002). *2001–2002 Annual Review of IT Infrastructure in China's Banking Sector*. 2002 China Information Almanac.

Porat, M. (1977). *The Information Economy: Definition and Measurement*. Washington, D.C.: US Department of Commerce.

Reuters (2005). *China Predicts 120 Million Net Users by Year-End*. CNet.com. http://news.com.com/China+predicts+120+million+Net+users+by+year-end/2100-1034_3-5594063.html?tag=mainstry

Shih, C., Kraemer, K. L., & Dedrick, J. (2004). Determinants of Country-Level Investment in Information Technology. Working paper. Irvine, CA: Center for Research on Information Technology and Organizations, University of California Irvine.

Tan, Z. A., Foster, W., & Goodman, S. (1999). China's State Coordinated Internet Infrastructure. *Communications of the ACM*, 42(6), 44–52.

Tan, Z. A., Mueller, M., & Foster, W. (1997). China's New Internet Regulations: Two Steps Forward and One Step Back. *Communications of the ACM*, 40(12), 11–16.

Tan, Z. A. & Wu, O. (2002). Globalization and E-Commerce I: Factors Affecting E-Commerce Diffusion in China. *Communications of the Association for Information Systems*, 10, 4–32.

Tan, Z. A. & Wu, O. (2004). *Diffusion and Impacts of the Internet and E-commerce in China*. From http://crito.uci.edu/pubs/2004/ChinaGECIII.pdf

United Nations Development Program (UNDP) (2002). *Human Development Report*. New York: Oxford University Press.

Wang, T. (2001). *The 2001 Blue Book of E-Commerce in China*. Beijing: China Finance Press.

Wang, Y. (2002). *2001–2002 Review of IT Infrastructure Building-Up in Wholesale/Retail Sector.* 2002 China Information Almanac.

World Bank (2004). *WDI Online*. From http://publications.worldbank.ord/WDI/

Wu, B. (2002). *SMS Services in China*. From www.blogchina.com

Yu, J. (2002). A Survey of Small and Medium Enterprises in China, Appendix B, Papers on Equity Financing, *Final Report*, Vol. 2. *Asian Development Bank, TA3534-PRC, Development of SME Financing Support System:* Vols. 1–3. Tokyo: Asian Development Bank.

Zhu, K. & Kraemer, K. L. (2005). Post-Adoption Variations in Usage and Value of E-business by Organizations: Cross-Country Evidence from the Retail Industry. *Information Systems Research*, 16(1), 61–84.

7 *Taiwan: diffusion and impacts of the Internet and e-commerce in a hybrid economy*

TAIN-JY CHEN

Introduction

Taiwan has a hybrid economy that exhibits characteristics of both developed and developing economies. It has a highly developed and modern manufacturing sector, with linkages to customers throughout the world, and its companies are world leaders in the production of computers and other electronic products. Taiwan's literacy rate is comparable to mature economies, and it has a large base of technically skilled workers. Yet, the legal framework for e-commerce is developing only slowly and the rate of IT spending is relatively low, given the level of development. The result is that the Internet and e-commerce have progressed on two distinct trajectories: one for globally oriented manufacturing firms, and the other for firms selling to local consumers. The former utilize business-to-business e-commerce technologies to coordinate with global trading partners, while the latter have developed business-to-consumer strategies tailored to the preferences and buying habits of Taiwanese consumers.

The most important drivers of e-commerce use for manufacturers in Taiwan appear to be international competitive pressure and the requirements of global customers. In contrast, the retail/wholesale sector has a high density of physical retailers, is not subject to a great deal of pressure from foreign competition, and thus lags behind manufacturing in its use of the Internet and e-commerce. For Taiwanese firms, e-commerce adoption is typically undertaken either to broaden their customer base by exploring new marketing channels or to create competition for traditional channels. This stands in sharp contrast to the adoption of e-commerce by firms in the global sample, which tend to use it mainly to improve traditional marketing channels. This suggests that greater destructive effects from e-commerce will be felt within Taiwan relative to the global sample.

As in other economies, concerns over security and privacy in online trading represent the most significant barrier to e-commerce diffusion. Nevertheless, the issues of security and privacy appear to be much more entrenched in Taiwan. Respect for privacy is not a traditional value and there is a severe lack of legal protections for online transactions. As a result, the most important policy issue is the establishment of an effective legal framework under which the security of transactions and privacy of traders can be safeguarded.

In contrast to B2B e-commerce, B2C e-commerce appears to be a relatively local phenomenon, with local factors shaping the path of development. As an example, B2C is constrained by inadequate logistics services. However, by combining bricks and clicks, Taiwanese firms can use strategic alliances as a means of accessing various resources not available on the Internet, such as physical locations for payment and delivery.

A summary of the findings of this chapter is as follows:

- *International pressure drives diffusion.* International competitive pressure is the most influential factor driving diffusion of e-commerce in Taiwan, as observed in its manufacturing industry which has the most international exposure and highest levels of e-commerce diffusion. In contrast, domestically oriented firms in the retailing and finance sectors lag their counterparts in the global sample with respect to e-commerce diffusion.
- *Key barriers are security and privacy.* The most significant factor impeding the diffusion of e-commerce is the perceived lack of security and privacy associated with online trading. The costs of Internet access and website maintenance are also significant factors slowing the speed of e-commerce diffusion. In addition, the finance sector considers consumer attitudes important, as e-banking involves changes in trading habits.
- *Impacts vary.* Adoption of e-commerce enables manufacturing firms to better serve their customers, to improve the efficiency of internal processing, and to reduce inventory costs. The emphasis in the service sector is on customer service.
- *Supply chain favors forward linkages.* Relative to the global sample of firms, Taiwanese manufacturing firms are more concerned with improving forward linkages with their customers rather than improving backward linkages with suppliers.

Table 7.1 *Macroeconomic statistics, 1998–2002*

	1998	*1999*	*2000*	*2001*	*2002*
GDP in US$bn	277.61	295.86	307.85	281.26	280.86
GDP per capita US$	12,659.62	13,391.84	13,819.37	12,553.18	12,506.77
GDP growth (annual percent)	4.57	5.48	5.90	−2.20	3.60
Trade (percent of GDP)	107.90	93.70	104.40	95.42	99.98

Sources: OECD, 1996; World Bank, 2004

- *B2B very different from B2C.* The diffusion of B2C e-commerce differs completely from that of B2B e-commerce. The former appears to be a purely local phenomenon while the latter is global. Local conditions, including social, business, and cultural factors, are shaping the development of B2C e-commerce. Due to the underdevelopment of e-logistics, the volume of B2C e-commerce remains at a negligible level, limited mostly to trading in intangibles. In contrast, international forces drive the diffusion of B2B e-commerce. Market competition prompts Taiwanese firms to adopt new technologies that enable new types of trading, particularly in the manufacturing industry, where Taiwanese firms serve mainly as international subcontractors.

Economic background: environment and policy

The GDP of Taiwan in 2002 was $281 billion, representing nearly $13,000 per capita (Table 7.1). GDP experienced steady growth from 1998 through 2000, and then declined slightly in 2001 and 2002, the latest year for which data are available. This annual trend is also present in GDP per-capita figures. Taiwan is a highly open economy, with trade flows equal to about 100% of GDP. This openness to trade means that the country is heavily affected by international competition and by trends in external markets. For instance, the US recession of 2001 was reflected in Taiwan's 2.2% decline in GDP that year.

ICT infrastructure and policies

Taiwan's traditional export manufacturing industries in recent years have suffered from rising wages, thereby undermining the country's international competitiveness. In the wake of its diminished cost advantage, improvements in logistics are considered to be critical to the salvation of its manufacturing industry. One response is that the Taiwanese government and firms operating in Taiwan are looking to information technology as a useful means of regaining international competitiveness. The government launched the Regional Operations Center (ROC) program in 1995, an effort to modernize Taiwan's service sector, particularly in the areas of telecommunications, shipping, and finance.

The efforts of the government coincided with the massive relocation of manufacturers into China and Southeast Asia from the mid-1980s onward. Business firms learned that combining their regional production facilities with Taiwan's logistics capabilities via a digital network was a useful means of protecting their position in international subcontracting (Chen, 2003a). A digital network that enables instantaneous and accurate management of production and product-related services enhances the value of a subcontractor, making it difficult for the subcontractor to be supplanted within the industry. The interconnection of the digital network with the information hubs of major players in world markets also allows Taiwanese manufacturers to engage in product innovations, a path which they were previously unable to tread.

The Taiwanese government's main information and communications technologies policy tools have been tax incentives and subsidies for computer and telecommunications hardware, software, and personnel. Steady increases in IT as a percentage of GDP and both PCs and Internet users per capita partially reflect such policies (Table 7.2). The most dramatic gain has been in cell phone subscribers, who now actually outnumber the total population (due to some people having multiple subscriptions). This trend is more related to a competitive market and to consumer preferences than to specific government promotion, but creates a potential market for mobile e-commerce services.

The government's efforts to promote the diffusion of B2B e-commerce have had some success in establishing an interface between Taiwanese and international firms, but less success in establishing a corresponding interface among Taiwanese firms. The efforts to bring the financial, shipping, and service industries on to digital networks to coordinate production may prove fruitful, because this adds important value to the network, which in turn should encourage smaller firms to join.

Table 7.2 *Technology infrastructure, 1998–2002*

	1998	*1999*	*2000*	*2001*	*2002*
Telecommunications					
Main phone lines per 1,000 pop.	524.44	545.16	567.51	573.38	583.31
Cell phone subscribers per 1,000 pop.	215.56	522.41	802.36	965.52	1,064.50
Cable subscribers per 1,000 pop.	197.82	201.02	200.93	204.06	206.71
Internet					
Internet hosts per 1,000 pop.	14.08	27.02	49.19	76.43	96.64
Internet users per 1,000 pop.	137.26	217.27	281.01	349.02	382.51
IT					
IT as percent of GDP	1.11	1.36	1.47	1.72	1.75
PCs per 1,000 pop.	158.60	301.51	317.07	364.24	395.74
Software piracy rate (percent)	0.59	0.54	0.53	0.53	0.43

Sources: IDC, 2004; IPR, 2003; ITU, 2004; World Bank, 2004

The area of B2C e-commerce is a completely different story. Internet diffusion is a precondition to B2C e-commerce since online shopping is critically dependent upon the penetration of the Internet. However, it will take more than just online trading to promote Internet access. Indeed, it is likely that other non-trading activities will have the greatest effect. In the case of Taiwan, it is generally chatting and electronic communications that first bring the younger generation onto the Internet, and thereafter online gaming that prompts the penetration of broadband. It is clear that once the Internet population is large enough to create potential economies of scale, B2C e-commerce will start to emerge.

Since the aim of B2C e-commerce is to either replace or supplement traditional shopping, it offers some advantages that conventional stores cannot offer, or at least, neutralizes some of their advantages. For example, bricks-and-mortar stores are able to present the actual commodities for evaluation by viewing and touching, an overwhelmingly important advantage over the B2C alternative whereby the quality of the products can only be appreciated visually. It is therefore natural for B2C e-commerce to begin from a position of trading in intangibles, such as travel arrangements and ticket reservations. It is almost universally the case that in the initial phase of B2C trade, travel services tend to dominate (III, 2002a).

A necessary payment mechanism stands out as the most difficult hurdle to overcome in the diffusion of B2C e-commerce. Although credit cards are widely used in Taiwan, the security of online credit card usage remains shaky, and thus effectively discourages this mode of payment in electronic trading. As a result, separate payment mechanisms have to be created to supplement electronic trade; however, post offices, banks, and convenience stores have served this purpose well.

It seems that a legal and financial environment which offers secure and convenient mechanisms for payment for online trading is the most important factor influencing the diffusion of B2C e-commerce; however, both legal protections and electronic banking are currently lacking in Taiwan. Although an electronic signature law has been promulgated, the detailed provisions defining the rights and obligations of sellers, buyers, and intermediaries have not yet been made available, and it is clear that B2C e-commerce will not take off until this environment is firmly established.

International competitive environment

The international environment appears to be the most important factor influencing B2B e-commerce in Taiwan. Taiwan is an open economy with significant exposure to international competition. GEC data indicate that it exceeds the average firm in the global sample on all measures of globalization (Table 7.3). Taiwanese firms adopt online trading, data exchange, and work coordination as the means of supporting their work with international business partners. This is particularly evident in the case of the PC industry, where global logistics has become the norm for industry operation, and Taiwanese firms are forced to adapt to this new style of trading just to remain in the game. The new trading style then trickles down to working relations between Taiwanese subcontractors and their suppliers, triggering the reconstruction of supply chain networks and changes to the way they work.

However, within supply chain management, there is a considerable lag in advancements in Internet application compared with the progress made in forward linkages to international buyers. This is why the Taiwanese government designed the island's subsidized A and B projects in order to facilitate the process of transformation. The A project encourages the construction of electronic trading systems between international buyers and major Taiwanese subcontractors, while the B project

Table 7.3 *Globalization indicators*

	Establishment size		*Sector*			*Total*	
	SME	*Large*	*Mfg.*	*Distrib.*	*Finance*	*Taiwan*	*Global*
Percent of companies with establishments abroad	41	73	45	35	66	42	24
Percent of companies with headquarters abroad	21	16	13	19	48	21	8
Mean percent of total sales from abroad	51	51	48	59	6	51	12
Mean percent of total procurement spending from abroad	30	26	28	34	11	30	20
Degree affected by competitors abroad (percent)							
Low	35	38	40	25	69	35	68
Moderate	40	23	31	50	11	39	16
High	25	39	29	25	20	26	15

Source: CRITO GEC Survey, 2002

encourages the construction of such systems between the major subcontractors and their local suppliers (Chen, 2003a).

Macro view of e-commerce

Internet usage

Having achieved a 36% penetration rate by the end of 2001, Taiwan's Internet usage level is one of the highest in Asia, with broadband accounting for 14.5% of all Internet connections on the island (III, 2002b). The most important factor contributing to the rapid diffusion of the Internet appears to be the high literacy rate amongst Taiwan's population.

Business to consumer

As a proportion of consumer expenditure, B2C e-commerce in Taiwan remains at a negligible level. Two major factors apparently inhibit the diffusion of B2C e-commerce: online security and the wide range of readily available retail stores in Taiwan.

Business to business

B2B e-commerce is still at a low level in Taiwan. It was first applied to the transmission of product information, and then to price inquiries and quotations. These are functions that in most cases are adequately performed by email. Having then progressed to order placement and order tracking, some investment in hardware and software became necessary, and users could choose between the Internet and exclusive lines as their transmission channel, with the Internet being apparently more popular because of the cost advantage. The government subsidizes investment in hardware and software, but the greatest investment is in the area of internal adjustment to work routines in order to accommodate these electronic transactions. Prompted by the financial incentives offered by the government, Taiwanese firms generally adopt a group approach to such adjustment. The government took advantage of two existing institutions to promote the group approach to B2B trade, namely, the network of subcontractors surrounding the major foreign buyers, and the core-satellite system formed around domestic manufacturers. Existing network relationships are the major facilitators of this group approach (Chen, 2003a).

E-commerce readiness

Information infrastructure

Types of e-commerce

All firms in the sample use email, comparable to firms in the global sample (Table 7.4, Figure 7.1). However, in terms of Internet applications, Taiwanese firms lag the rest of the world. Only 57% of Taiwanese firms have established a website, well below the global average of 74%. Moreover, only 51% of Taiwanese firms have established an intranet, also well below the global average of 64%. Regarding extranets, Taiwanese firms (30%) are similar to the global average (33%). Traditional technologies such as EDI, EFT, and call centers are also used less widely than firms in the global sample. Overall, the picture is one of lagging use of e-commerce technologies relative to firms in the global sample.

E-commerce use by sector

The fact that Taiwan lags in the use of e-commerce technologies can be attributed largely to the underdevelopment of the retail/wholesale

Table 7.4 *Use of e-commerce technologies*

	Establishment size		*Sector*			*Total*	
Percent using . . .	*SME*	*Large*	*Mfg.*	*Distrib.*	*Finance*	*Taiwan*	*Global*
Email	100	100	100	100	100	100	99
Website	56	77	74	47	62	57	74
Intranet	50	73	62	43	62	51	64
Extranet	29	54	54	17	29	30	33
• accessible by suppliers/business partners	18	46	42	5	28	19	21
• accessible by customers	22	36	46	9	28	23	18
EDI	22	34	24	16	43	23	44
• over private networks only	10	12	8	8	24	10	19
• Internet-based only	7	10	8	4	16	7	8
• Both	5	12	8	4	2	5	16
EFT	19	40	22	16	34	20	43
Call center	19	28	28	12	28	19	32

Source: CRITO GEC Survey, 2002

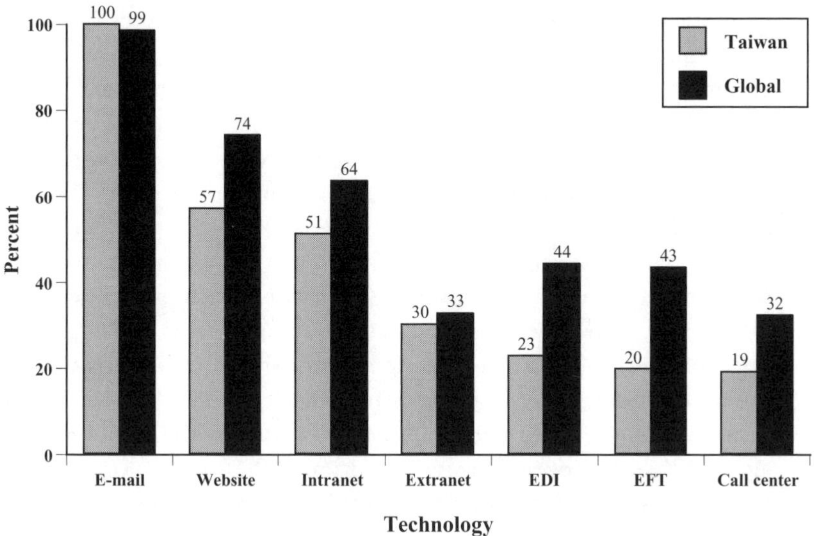

Figure 7.1 Use of e-commerce technologies
Source: CRITO GEC Survey, 2002

sector. Indeed, manufacturing firms in Taiwan are on par with the global sample in terms of website establishment and intranet applications, and ahead of the rest of the world in terms of extranet applications. This suggests that it is the retail/wholesale sector that tends to drag down the overall average. Only 43% of Taiwan's retail/wholesale firms have established an intranet, compared with the global average of 64%, and only 17% have established an extranet, compared with the global average of 33%. This provides some support for our previous argument that international competitive pressure is an important driving force for Internet penetration and e-commerce. The manufacturing sector is export oriented and is forced to adopt e-commerce to conform to the global environment, whereas the retail and finance sectors are domestically oriented. As compared with the other two sectors, the retail/wholesale sector is the one that is least affected by international pressure. In contrast, the manufacturing sector is the most internationalized amongst the three sectors, and is therefore the most affected by international competition, and consequently is also the closest to the global sample.

The finance sector is ahead of both the manufacturing and retail/wholesale sectors in terms of EDI usage. At 43%, the EDI adoption rate in the finance sector is comparable to the global sample of 44%. This is likely a manifestation of the fact that Taiwanese manufacturers are more recent adopters of e-commerce and therefore are bypassing EDI to use the Internet. In contrast, financial institutions adopted e-commerce earlier, in the age of EDI, and are more locked into the old technology. Moreover, the majority of EDI usage in the finance sector is established within private networks, as opposed to the Internet. In contrast, EDI usage in the manufacturing sector is almost equally divided between private networks and the Internet. One possibility is that there are deeper concerns in the finance industry than in the manufacturing industry over the security problems associated with information exchange. Despite the wide acceptance of EDI, Taiwan's finance industry remains behind the rest of the world in terms of the adoption of electronic funds transfer, with only 34% of the sample firms making use of this technology, as compared with the global average of 43%. The somewhat slow adoption of these technologies by the financial sector may be because Taiwan's finance industry was opened up to global competition only in recent years and remains highly regulated.

Taiwan's retail/wholesale sector is also well behind the rest of the world in terms of customer servicing through call centers, since only 12% of the sample firms have established such facilities, as compared with the global sample of 32%. Although the manufacturing and finance sectors are also behind the rest of the world in this regard, the distance separating them from their global counterparts is not as great as in the retail/wholesale sector.

IT investment

Although Taiwan is a major producer of IT hardware, the island as a whole spends a trivial amount of its income on IT equipment and software. In 2000, Taiwan spent only 1.47% of its GDP on IT products, well below the average of 3.6% in the OECD countries (Chen, 2003b). The GEC Survey indicated that the average Taiwanese firm spent around 9% of its 2001 operating budget on IT equipment and software. Of the three sectors analyzed, the highest proportion of IT expenditure was allocated by the manufacturing sector, at 12%, followed by the retail/wholesale sector, at 8%, and the finance sector, at 7%. Within their overall IT budgets, only a small proportion was devoted to web-based applications that included software, consulting, Internet staff, and the like. On average, only 10% of the budgets were devoted to web-based applications and amongst the three sectors, the finance sector topped the list, devoting 17% of its IT budget to this area.

Integration

Taiwan is comparable to the global sample in terms of internal and external integration, with Taiwanese firms equal or slightly ahead on these dimensions (Table 7.5, Figure 7.2).

As the GEC Survey indicated, most Taiwanese firms are not yet ready for e-commerce. Although the manufacturing sector has come close to the global sample in Internet usage, and is even ahead of the global sample in terms of establishing extranets, the retail/wholesale and finance sectors still lag far behind. The degree of openness in the manufacturing sector may well explain its adoption of standard technologies and practices of the global community, whereas the underdevelopment of the other two sectors, particularly the retail/wholesale sector, may

Table 7.5 *Enterprise integration, 2002*

Extent to which Internet applications are electronically integrated with . . .	*Establishment size*		*Sector*			*Total*	
	SME	*Large*	*Mfg.*	*Distrib.*	*Finance*	*Taiwan*	*Global*
Internal databases and information systems							
Percent little to none	43	42	47	50	3	43	53
Percent some	25	25	31	17	29	25	24
Percent a great deal	32	33	22	33	68	33	24
Those of suppliers and business customers							
Percent little to none	62	57	69	66	21	62	72
Percent some	27	22	15	34	41	26	18
Percent a great deal	11	21	16	0	38	12	10

Source: CRITO GEC Survey, 2002

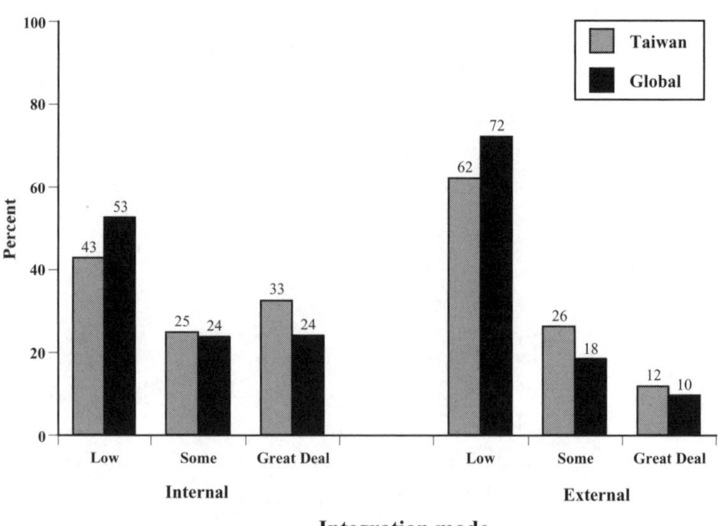

Figure 7.2 Integration mode
Source: CRITO GEC Survey, 2002

Table 7.6 ***Internet drivers in Taiwan and the rest of the world***

Percent indicating driver is a significant factor	*Establishment size*		*Sector*			*Total*	
	SME	*Large*	*Mfg.*	*Distrib.*	*Finance*	*Taiwan*	*Global*
Customers demanded it	48	50	38	50	65	48	37
Major competitors were online	40	35	36	38	59	40	31
Suppliers required it	33	30	28	36	28	33	22
To reduce costs	41	49	46	40	34	41	36
To expand market for existing product or services	47	47	43	50	42	47	48
To enter new businesses or markets	55	48	49	60	42	54	42
To improve coordination with customers and suppliers	50	55	52	52	34	50	44
Required for government procurement	23	14	30	20	18	23	15
Government provided incentives	29	23	26	28	39	29	8

Source: CRITO GEC Survey, 2002

be explained by the degree of insulation which these sectors have from global competition and the prevalence of small, traditional retail stores.

Drivers and barriers to e-commerce

Drivers

There are several important factors driving firms to adopt the Internet and e-commerce in Taiwan. Both the manufacturing and distribution sectors consider "to improve coordination with customers and suppliers" to be first and second most important, at 52% each (Table 7.6, Figure 7.3). These figures are comparable to those of firms in the rest of the sample. However, in the finance sector, customer demand (65%) and competition (59%) are considered the most important drivers. This

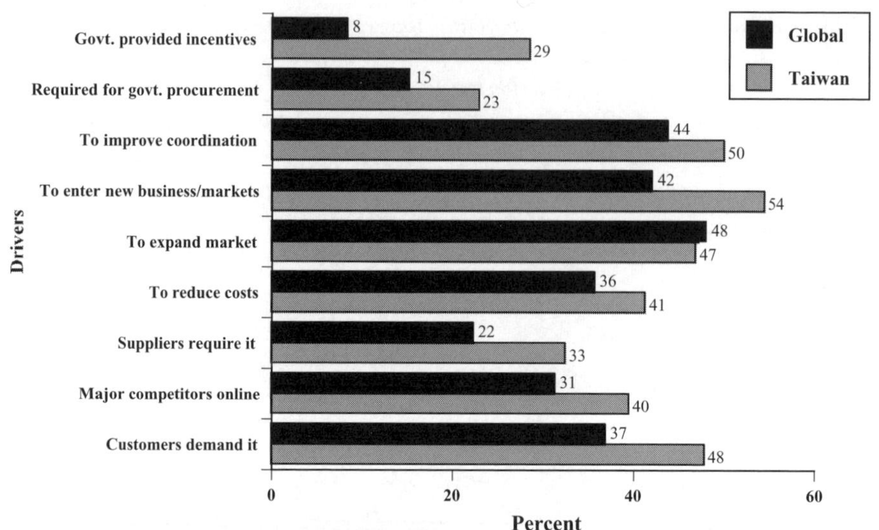

Figure 7.3 E-commerce drivers
Source: CRITO GEC Survey, 2002

is probably explained by the intense competition in Taiwan's banking sector which is overcrowded with small-sized, inward-looking banks.

Significant e-commerce drivers for the manufacturing sector are similar to those in the rest of the world. In contrast, e-commerce drivers for the retail/wholesale sector are slightly different. Specifically, both customer demand (50%) and the desire to enter new businesses or markets (60%) appear to be more important drivers in Taiwan's retail/wholesale sector compared with the global sample. This again probably reflects the local focus of Taiwan's retailers and wholesalers, which seek to expand their market reach through the Internet. All Taiwan respondents also give more weight to government incentives as drivers for Internet adoption, indicating a stronger role of government in business decisions and possibly the impact of some of the government initiatives discussed earlier.

Barriers

The GEC Survey revealed two very significant factors considered by Taiwanese firms to be fundamental barriers to e-commerce: 1) the issue of security and privacy, and 2) the level of legal protections for traders (Table 7.7, Figure 7.4). Although the problem of security and privacy

Table 7.7 ***Barriers to e-commerce in Taiwan and the rest of the world, by sector***

Percent indicating statement is a significant obstacle	*Establishment size*		*Sector*			*Total*	
	SME	*Large*	*Mfg.*	*Distrib.*	*Finance*	*Taiwan*	*Global*
Need for face-to-face customer interaction	37	38	31	44	18	37	34
Concern about privacy of data or security issues	67	50	65	65	74	66	44
Customers do not use the technology	31	35	21	34	41	31	31
Finding staff with e-commerce expertise	27	23	25	32	9	27	27
Prevalence of credit card use	18	14	23	16	17	18	20
Costs of implementing an e-commerce site	40	33	34	50	10	40	34
Making needed organizational changes	17	31	17	19	11	18	24
Level of ability to use the Internet as part of business strategy	24	26	14	28	33	24	25
Cost of Internet access	24	29	30	23	16	24	15
Business laws do not support e-commerce	28	31	26	25	48	28	24
Taxation of Internet sales	18	12	22	12	31	18	16
Inadequate legal protection for Internet purchases	49	37	44	54	34	49	34

Source: CRITO GEC Survey, 2002

is also the chief concern for the rest of the world, amongst Taiwanese firms this concern is even greater.

Security and privacy

Amid all of the companies surveyed, 66% pointed to the issue of security and privacy as being significant to their acceptance of e-commerce,

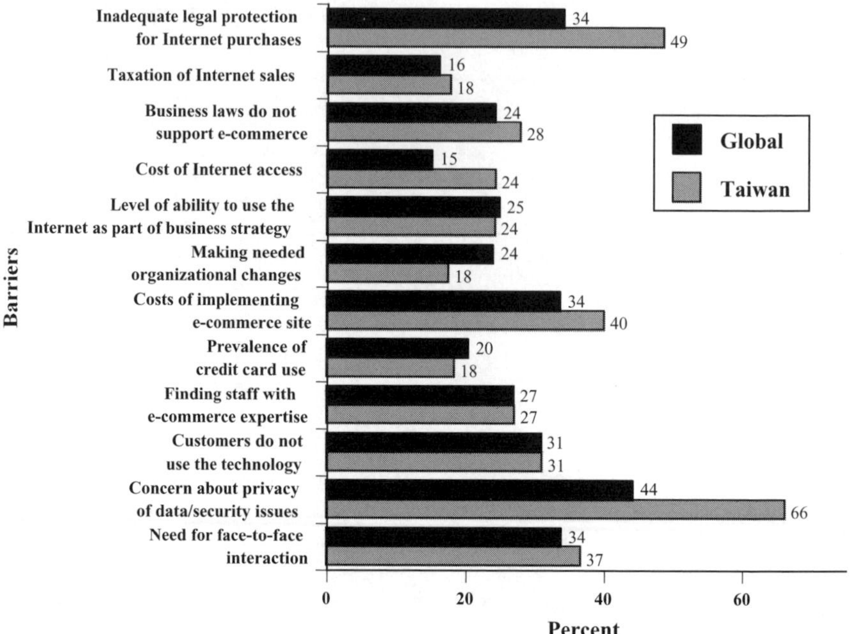

Figure 7.4 E-commerce barriers
Source: CRITO GEC Survey

well above the global sample of 44%. Of the three sectors, the finance sector is most wary of the problems associated with security and privacy. Such concerns can be attributed partly to the social environment within the country, where privacy is not universally respected, and as such electronic exchange may render privacy even more vulnerable.

Legal protections for traders

Another concern is the lack of legal protections in Taiwan. Amongst all the firms surveyed, 49% indicated that inadequate legal protection was a significant barrier to e-commerce, as compared with the global sample of 34%. While concern about the issue of security and privacy is higher in the finance sector (74%) than in the manufacturing (65%) or retail sectors (65%), firms in the retail/wholesale sector are most concerned about the problem of inadequate legal protections for electronic trade (54%). It is understandable that the issue of security and privacy takes precedence in financial transactions since concerns over such issues can impede consumers' acceptance of electronic banking.

Yet, legal protections for traders are also critical for B2C e-commerce. The prevalence of counterfeit credit cards is a major headache for B2C traders at the present time. Another issue is the difficulties involved with sellers pursuing claims against delinquent consumers.

Other barriers

In addition to these two factors, there are three others that are regarded as being significant by more than 30% of the sample firms. First, although in the rest of the world the need for face-to-face contact is considered important for trading relationships, in Taiwan such contact seems to have greater importance in the retail/wholesale trade, but less importance in financial activities. This may have something to do with the nature of the industry, since small neighborhood stores dominate the retail industry in Taiwan. In contrast, the financial sector is dominated by national institutions.

Second, there are two cost factors which are also considered significant: 1) the cost of Internet access, and 2) the cost involved in website maintenance. The latter is of particular concern to retailers and wholesalers because this sector is dominated by small firms which lack the capacity to hire IT professionals. It is nevertheless surprising that, although the cost of Internet access in Taiwan is comparable to the cost in the rest of the world, it was considered significant by 30% of the surveyed firms in the manufacturing sector, as compared with the global average of 15%. Clearly, Taiwan's manufacturing firms are highly cost conscious because they are operating on razor-thin profit margins.

It is also noteworthy that the readiness of customers was considered to be an important barrier to e-commerce within the finance sector (41%), but less so within the manufacturing sector (21%). This is because the former deals with domestic customers, while the latter relies more upon international customers. The fact that domestic consumers are not ready to accept electronic financial transactions is therefore considered by 41% of the surveyed banks and other financial institutions to be a 'significant' or 'very significant' barrier to e-commerce, well above the global average of 31%. This implies that in preparing for e-commerce, consumer education is just as important as the build-up of IT infrastructure. In contrast, the finance sector has few concerns with regard to securing appropriate IT staff for conducting e-commerce, reflecting its IT readiness as noted earlier.

Taiwanese firms are somewhat less concerned with making necessary organizational changes to accommodate e-commerce operations (18%) versus the global average (24%). This may be attributable to the flexibility of Taiwanese firms, a trait considered to be their major strength in international competition. The ability to develop appropriate business strategies to make their e-commerce operations a success is of equal concern to Taiwanese and global firms, but is a bigger issue for the finance and retail/wholesale sectors than for manufacturers.

In the area of policy, taxation is considered to be very important by the financial industry (31%), whereas, similar to the rest of the world, the other two sectors consider it to be of minor significance. Although the banking sector has been temporarily exempted from business tax in Taiwan, there are now calls for the restoration of this tax. Furthermore, securities transactions have also been temporarily exempted from capital gains tax, but this tax still has a basis in law and is likely to be restored soon; this may explain why the financial industry is more sensitive to the issue of Internet tax than the others.

The same explanation can be extended to business laws, since the financial industry in Taiwan is in a state of flux, with the government currently breaking down the walls between banks and other financial institutions. A universal banking service industry is emerging in Taiwan, paving the way for electronic banking, with some of the leading private banks, particularly those offering personalized financial services to consumers, using electronic banking to facilitate their services. The legal framework and relevant regulations will undoubtedly shape the future development of the industry.

In sum, Taiwanese firms consider the business environment and the laws which aim to protect the security and privacy of traders the most important conditions for e-commerce, with the lowering of Internet access and website maintenance costs also regarded as useful facilitators for e-commerce.

Diffusion of e-commerce

Total e-commerce

The development of e-commerce has been slow in Taiwan. In 2002, the IDC estimated that B2B trade stood at around $12.036 billion, with B2C trade being estimated at just $1.586 billion; indeed, the total amount of e-commerce was equivalent to only 4.8% of Taiwan's GDP (IDC, 2004). Nevertheless, the prospects for further development of e-commerce seem to be good. According to estimates by the Institute of Information Industry (III, 2005), 7.6% of Taiwan's enterprises had introduced online sales in 2004. Meanwhile, the proportion of enterprises that had introduced online procurement was around 12.2% in 2004 (III, 2005).

There are also developments in e-marketplaces. In 2002, nineteen e-marketplaces were registered under the umbrella of the government-run Taiwan Industry Marketplace (TIM). Although all nineteen are organized by domestic firms, they are oriented toward export trade, with an estimated annual trading volume of NT$120 billion (about US$3.4 billion).[1]

Diffusion by sector

The functions of the Internet applications of Taiwanese firms are similar to those of the rest of the world, but there are significant differences by industry. As in the rest of the world, the Internet is used for advertising and marketing purposes; however, these are the dominant Internet applications only in the retail/wholesale sector in Taiwan. Indeed, in the manufacturing and finance sectors, after-sales services are predominant. In other words, the Internet is used by Taiwanese firms for customer service more often than for product promotion. Manufacturing service is in fact a catchphrase used by Taiwan's manufacturers to highlight their intention to add value to their products through enhancements to their quality of service, for which the Internet is a useful tool. The keenness of manufacturers on after-sales service is indicated by the fact that 75% of manufacturers use the Internet for such services, well above the global average of 44% (Table 7.8, Figure 7.5). In contrast, only 20% of the retail/wholesale firms use the Internet for after-sales services. This suggests that after-sales services are not a key factor in competition, as Taiwan's densely spread retail stores compete on proximity to consumers. Apart from advertising and after-sales service, the Internet is frequently used for the purpose of exchanging operational data with suppliers (43%) and customers (46%). The difference between sectors in this regard is small, with an

[1] See *Commercial Times*, 12 November 2002.

Table 7.8 *Internet diffusion*

Percent using the Internet for . . .	*Establishment size*		*Sector*			*Total*	
	SME	*Large*	*Mfg.*	*Distrib.*	*Finance*	*Taiwan*	*Global*
Advertising and marketing purposes	48	56	66	42	29	48	58
Making sales online	33	23	40	23	58	33	30
After-sales customer service and support	41	42	75	20	60	41	44
Making purchases online	27	21	24	27	34	27	47
Exchanging operational data with suppliers	43	40	51	36	49	43	48
Exchanging operational data with business customers	46	54	45	46	51	46	51
Formally integrating the same business processes with suppliers or other business partners	24	25	25	23	25	24	34

Source: CRITO GEC Survey, 2002

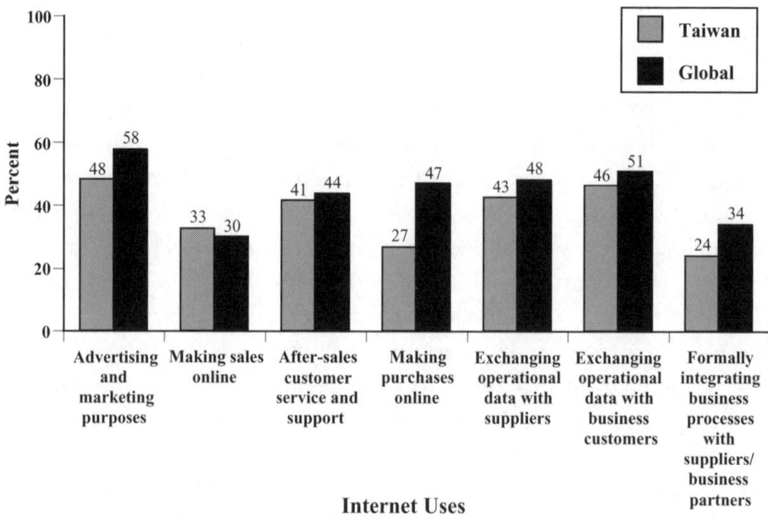

Figure 7.5 E-commerce diffusion
Source: CRITO GEC Survey, 2002

Table 7.9 *Internet usage for product sales by sector*

Percent indicating Internet used to . . .	*Establishment size*		*Sector*			*Total*	
	SME	*Large*	*Mfg.*	*Distrib.*	*Finance*	*Taiwan*	*Global*
Address new markets only	25	13	30	33	1	25	15
Address traditional distribution channels only	35	4	8	50	52	34	44
Compete directly with traditional distribution channels	19	49	23	17	18	20	27
Replace traditional distribution channels	21	34	39	0	29	21	13

Source: CRITO GEC Survey, 2002

exception in that the retail/wholesale sector uses the Internet to interact with suppliers sparingly, at 36%. This suggests that supply chain management has not taken hold in the retail/wholesale trade sector in Taiwan.

Exchanging operational data with suppliers was regarded as most important in the manufacturing sector, where 51% of the sample firms use the Internet for this purpose. This is a manifestation of the manufacturers' urge to coordinate their operations with suppliers to cut production costs and reduce time to market.

Channel strategies

The Internet channel strategies of Taiwanese firms are quite different from their global counterparts (Table 7.9). In general, Taiwanese firms use the Internet more for accessing new markets (25%) or replacing traditional channels (21%), compared with the global averages of 15% and 13%, respectively. The contrast is especially sharp in the manufacturing sector, where 69% of manufacturing firms use online sales either to address new markets or to replace traditional marketing channels. A further 23% conduct online sales in order to compete with traditional channels, leaving only 8% of these firms using the Internet to address traditional channels, for example, using the Internet to enhance services

Table 7.10 *Impacts of the Internet*

Percent indicating high impact	Establishment size		Sector			Total	
	SME	*Large*	*Mfg.*	*Distrib.*	*Finance*	*Taiwan*	*Global*
Internal processes more efficient	42	49	48	42	27	42	34
Staff productivity increased	28	30	23	31	25	28	27
Sales increased	26	22	28	27	17	26	21
Sales area widened	33	39	44	27	33	33	31
Customer service improved	43	57	34	50	41	44	35
International sales increased	33	41	36	36	16	33	20
Procurement costs decreased	25	28	27	24	24	25	18
Inventory costs decreased	24	32	37	20	9	24	14
Coordination with suppliers improved	25	44	18	34	2	26	30
Competitive position improved	38	44	34	42	27	38	30

Source: CRITO GEC Survey, 2002

to their existing downstream distributors. This suggests that broadening the marketing base is the primary purpose of the online sales offered by Taiwanese manufacturers, and that manufacturers are willing to use the Internet in competition with their traditional channels.

In the retail/wholesale sector, half of the Taiwanese firms address traditional channels only, while a third address new markets only. Here there is little channel conflict, as only 17% compete with their traditional channels, and no firm replaced those channels. In the finance sector, 52% of Taiwanese firms use the Internet to address traditional channels, while the rest compete with or replace traditional channels.

Impacts of e-commerce

As shown in Table 7.10, the most important impacts of the Internet among Taiwanese firms include improvement in customer services

(44%), enhanced internal processing efficiency (42%), and improved competitive position (38%). Taiwanese firms were significantly more likely than the global sample to report increased international sales (33% versus 20%), reflecting the openness of Taiwan's economy and the global orientation of many of its firms. This impact was great among manufacturers, as would be expected (36%), but equally strong for the retail/wholesale distribution sector, which is surprising given the more local orientation of retailers in particular.

Of the three sectors, the retail/wholesale sector experienced the greatest improvements in customer services (50%), followed by the finance sector (41%), and then the manufacturing sector (34%). In addition, it is evident that improvements in internal process efficiency were also considered important, particularly in the manufacturing sector, where 48% of correspondents felt the impact to be significant or very significant, followed by the retail/wholesale sector (42%), and then the finance sector (27%). The manufacturing sector is also most impacted by the widening of sales area, as 44% of respondents felt the impact to be significant or very significant.

Reduction of inventory costs was highest in the manufacturing sector (37%). In contrast, manufacturing rated low in the enhancement of staff productivity (23%) and improvements in coordinating activities with suppliers (18%). In short, Taiwanese manufacturers indicated that the impacts of the Internet were felt mainly in processing efficiency, improvements in customer services, and inventory control. This reflects their role as subcontractors for international buyers and the fact that their role in the supply chain encourages them to focus on forward linkages more than backward linkages, as stated above. These manufacturers have not yet advanced to those areas in which the Internet can be used as a means of improving staff productivity or coordinating activities with suppliers.

Clearly, the perceived impacts of the Internet are uneven across the different sectors. Manufacturers use the Internet mainly to keep abreast of customer demand, coordinating their internal processes so as to react to customer needs in a much more prompt and flexible manner. Retailers use the Internet both to reach new customers and to better serve existing customers with product information and after-sales services. In the manufacturing sector, it appears that savings on production and inventory costs are mainly achieved by international buyers, whereas in the retail and banking industries the major beneficiaries appear to be consumers.

In most cases, it is the large firms rather than the small firms which feel the greater impacts of the Internet. This can be seen from Table 7.10, where large firms indicate that they felt more impact than small firms, except in sales increase. As the benefits of the Internet are mainly derived from rapid information processing, large firms can take advantage of new technologies to increase the speed of their information processing. In contrast, small firms usually process information manually, with informal routines and reliance upon human judgment in decision making, leaving little room for systematic gathering and processing of information. The large discrepancy between a large and small establishment is observed in the area of coordination, with suppliers and customers suggesting the large establishment's superior capability in information management.

Discussion

It seems that the Internet is driving many industries toward vertical disintegration. In the case of the PC industry, brand marketers are increasingly concentrating on product design and marketing, while subcontractors take care of production, warehousing, and after-sales service, sourcing the necessary major parts and components from specialized producers. Working with their main subcontractors on a global basis, the brand marketers are vertically disintegrated, yet globally integrated, and the Internet is clearly the backbone to such global integration. With the coordination of digital information networks, these brand marketers and their main subcontractors can coordinate their activities on a global scale.

The market power of the brand marketers in the PC industry has declined, whereas that of consumers has grown. Thus, better customer service is the key to competing successfully, while low-cost production processes are a prerequisite. The use of foreign direct investment (FDI) by multinational firms in an effort to build up their production capacity so as to control the market is no longer feasible. Instead, firms have to respond to consumer demand by marshaling external resources, including outsourcing. Subcontractors, meanwhile, assume the role of producers and have to build up the capacity for utilizing global resources and servicing the global market.

A similar observation can be made concerning the semiconductor industry, in which design houses are increasingly disintegrated from the foundry operations, which in turn are increasingly concentrated in a few firms with geographically dispersed production sites. Integrated device manufacturers (IDM) are increasing the proportions of outsourced components, while focusing on the key functions of design and marketing. Digital information networks enable the foundry operators to participate in the "design-in" process, creating a technology synergy between designers and manufacturers.

In the case of the retail sector, the Internet has prompted strategic alliances across different industries. Retailers, in particular, have a strong incentive to partner with producers, distributors, and shippers in order to compete for the new e-commerce business. Although it is retailers that assume the driver's seat in the development of e-commerce, they will not succeed without the resources of the supply and distribution chains. In this regard, B2C e-commerce enables the virtual integration of services. There is also a strong tendency for retailers to diversify, because once a trading platform is established, the marginal cost of diversification is small.

E-commerce is apparently inducing the separation of retailing activity into three distinctive parts: sales, commodity flow, and money flow. Sales can be conducted successfully on the Internet if sufficient information can be gathered and trust can be established. Commodity flow and money flow have developed into separate industries that support online sales. Economies of scale are apparent in the industry that handles commodity flow; therefore, there is an increasing degree of concentration in the shipping industry. Meanwhile, integrated services have become the norm in money flows. Banks, which handle money flow, are actively involved in transactions instead of passively financing transactions at the request of traders.

In Taiwan, the most interesting example of a third party providing both commodity and money flow services is the case of 7-Eleven (see Box 7.1). This case illustrates an innovative approach to surmounting barriers to B2C e-commerce noted above (especially concerns regarding privacy, security, and legal protections for online shopping) and providing a unique mix of services based on the needs of online retailers and the preferences of local consumers.

Conclusion

The most important driver behind e-commerce in Taiwan appears to be international competitive pressure, which is especially evident in the manufacturing sector. Taiwanese manufacturing firms are prompted

Box 7.1. 7-Eleven

The following extract is from the author's interview with a senior executive of 7-Eleven Taiwan, which took place on 31 May 2002.

7-Eleven has over 3,000 stores throughout the country, and consumers can designate any store for product delivery from an electronic map that we provide online. To make online trading successful, we need to take care of the front-end as well as the back-end logistics. The front end refers to the service to consumers, including confirmation of the order, providing information about the progress of the order, notification about the arrival of the products, and urging the customer to pick up the products if they are left sitting in the stores for more than a certain period of time. The back-end logistics refers to product delivery and payment collection. We had no problem with the back-end logistics because of our established system in serving the island-wide convenience stores. We had more problems with the front-end logistics because this required intimate coordination with our partners.

We started our online shopping business in February 2000. We first worked together with Music Global Village, an online shop selling music products, mainly CDs. After gaining some experience, we started working with our second partner, Pokelai Bookstore. This store is more established in e-commerce, so the volume of transactions was already 2,000 cases in the first month of our cooperative venture.

We then gradually increased our partners, and the total number of shops we service today exceeds sixty. They are separated into seven categories: music and books, technology, beauty and health, travel, tickets, life, and local specialties. Initially, we provide a portal to link them together. Of course, this requires tremendous effort on the digital system, because each online shop has its own system. We also need to bring our partners online quickly even if they have very limited capacity for e-commerce. What we are looking for in an alliance is good products, not e-commerce capability. To help those shop owners with inadequate e-commerce capabilities, we formed strategic alliances with several IT services specialists to provide the necessary technical services.

Our business grew quickly as more and more partner shops were brought online. A big boost came from the development of our Biztalk system, developed with Microsoft, which enables customers to check on the status of orders, and also allows for easy hook-up with the collaborative shops. Last month, the number of transactions on our website totaled about 330,000. This represents rapid growth from the 2,000 cases when we first started out. Of course, we also encountered difficulties in the process, but most often the problems arose from human error. We have 3,000 stores which run twenty-four hours a day, and the turnover rate of storekeepers is very high.

With Biztalk, we also were able to launch some "event" products that are sold on a single occasion; for example, flowers for Mother's Day, or Chinese dumplings for the dragon boat festival. Our advantages are the ability to reach a vast range of consumers and the fact that products ordered can be picked up at our stores within a specific period of time, for example, two days prior to Mother's Day. In this case, suppliers of the products can perform something like "direct sales" without owning a store or salespeople, since there is no point in owning a store or hiring salespeople for products which are sold only once in a while.

What services do we offer our collaborative stores? The most valuable is the payment mechanism. Fake credit cards created from stolen information are so prevalent that it is hard to convince consumers that online payment is secure. Consumers feel comfortable paying at the neighborhood 7-Eleven stores at the time of picking up their products. The second thing that we offer our collaborative stores is shipping services, which are cheap and fast because of economies of scale. Our collaborative stores only have to ship their products to our distribution center in Shulin in the suburbs of Taipei. Once the products reach our distribution center, we notify the customer of the expected arrival time of the product. The third service we offer our collaborative stores is a "branding" service; being a collaborative member of 7-Eleven upgrades the image of the vendor's products because we ensure that only quality products are sold on our website.

As to the consumers, we also offer several valuable services. First of all, we provide them with a tracking service for the products they have ordered online. Through our e-checking facility, consumers can check on the status of the product at any time. The second service we offer consumers is the ability to pick up their products at any time. Unlike regular delivery services, by courier or post office, consumers do not have to wait at home for delivery. With our service, consumers can come to our store at any time to pick up their products, and they can designate any store for such a service, either a store close to their home or one close to their workplace. The third service we offer consumers is confidence in the products. Consumers can see the package before they pay. Although we cannot allow consumers to unpack the products (to avoid confusion as regards responsibilities), they can at least see the physical existence of the products before paying.

What impact does our online business have on real-time stores? We feel that the online operations are complements to the actual stores. For example, we sell books at our real-time stores, but the choice is limited because of space constraints. With Pokelai, consumers have access to tens of thousands of books. The same is true for music CDs. We carry a few hot items in the stores and the rest can be purchased through the Internet. The actual stores offer local convenience while the virtual stores offer variety for shoppers.

to make use of Internet-related technologies and applications because they realize that they need to adopt e-commerce in order to serve global markets. In Taiwan, e-commerce is more widely diffused in the manufacturing sector compared with the retail/wholesale and banking sectors, which are more domestic-market oriented. The greatest lag in the diffusion of e-commerce is in the retail/wholesale sector because B2C e-commerce is conditioned by local factors, and the high density of real-time retailers in Taiwan limits the scope of e-commerce development.

The primary motivating factor behind e-commerce adoption is to better serve customers. Taiwan's manufacturing firms also use the Internet as a means of reducing their inventory costs. In comparison with manufacturing firms in other economies, Taiwanese firms are more concerned with improving forward linkages to their customers than improving backward linkages to their suppliers. Internet applications aimed at enhancing supply chain management are still limited in Taiwan.

The purpose of e-commerce adoption for many Taiwanese firms is predominantly either to broaden their customer base by exploring new marketing channels, or to create competition for traditional channels. This stands in sharp contrast to the adoption of e-commerce by global firms, which tend to use it mainly to improve the traditional marketing channels. This implies that greater destructive effects from e-commerce will be felt within Taiwan relative to other economies and that this will possibly be accompanied by increasing market concentration. In recent years there has been some evidence of an increase in market concentration in the PC industry, in which Taiwanese firms generally serve as original equipment manufacturer (OEM) contractors.

Concerns over security and privacy in online trading represent the most significant barrier to e-commerce diffusion, similar to other economies in the GEC Survey. Nevertheless, the issues of security and privacy appear to be more entrenched in Taiwan. Reasons include cultural characteristics, since respect for privacy is not a traditional value, and a severe lack of legal protections for online transactions. The costs of Internet access and website maintenance are also considered to be significant barriers, while consumer attitudes are revealed to be an important impediment to the diffusion of e-commerce, particularly within the banking sector.

E-commerce diffusion appears to have the effect of driving the manufacturing industry toward vertical disintegration, yet with global connectivity. Multinational firms are outsourcing an increasing proportion of their functions, but this outsourcing is being managed by just a few subcontractors offering comprehensive global services. These subcontractors are, in turn, linked to a large number of specialized suppliers.

In sharp contrast to B2B e-commerce, B2C e-commerce appears to be a purely local phenomenon, with local factors shaping the path of development. The experience of Taiwan shows that innovation in payment and delivery services is a key driver behind B2C e-commerce. Without such innovation, e-commerce will be limited to the trading of intangibles. Conventional trade methods have an advantage over e-commerce in trading tangibles because they offer the opportunity for inspection. The development of B2C e-commerce is severely hampered by inadequate logistics services. Nevertheless, with regard to overcoming the logistics bottlenecks for online trading in Taiwan, the combination of convenience stores and online shops has proven to be a winning formula, as the 7-Eleven case illustrates. In general, therefore, the use of strategic alliances as a means of accessing various resources not available on the Internet seems an effective way of e-marketing.

Several policy implications can be drawn from this study. First of all, the most important policy issue that needs to be addressed in e-commerce development is the establishment of an effective legal framework under which the security of transactions and privacy of traders can be safeguarded. Second, market liberalization, which will inevitably lead to competitive pricing with regard to both Internet access and website maintenance, will also prove useful in Taiwan's efforts to promote e-commerce. Third, there are different forces driving B2B and B2C e-commerce, and therefore separate policies must be formulated to effectively facilitate these different types of trade. An economy that lags in one area may well move ahead in another area, given the right environment and policies. In particular, B2C e-commerce has little to do with international competitiveness and the degree of industrialization, and therefore presents an opportunity for industrially lagging countries to leapfrog to a higher level of economic development through local innovation.

References

Chen, T. J. (2003a). E-Commerce to Protect the Network Relationships: The Case of Taiwan's PC Industry. *The Information Society*, 19(1), 59–68.

Chen, T. J. (2003b). Globalization of E-Commerce VIII: Environment and Policy in Taiwan. *Communications of the Association for Information Systems*, 12, 326–353.

Institute of Information Industry (III) (2002a). *Digitization, E-Commerce and E-Security*. Taipei: III.

Institute for Information Industry (III) (2002b). Internet Infrastructure in Taiwan, October 2. www.find.org.tw

Institute for Information Industry (III) (2005). Business Online in Taiwan 2004. www.find.org.tw

International Data Corporation (IDC) (2004). *Internet Commerce Market Model*. Framingham, MA.

International Planning and Research Corporation (IPR) (2003). *Eighth Annual Business Software Alliance (BSA) Global Software Piracy Study, Trends in Software Piracy 1994–2002*. Washington, D.C.: Business Software Alliance.

International Telecommunication Union (ITU) (2004). *World Telecommunication Indicators Database* (8th Ed.). Geneva, Switzerland.

Organization for Economic Cooperation and Development (OECD) (1996). *Information Infrastructure Convergence and Pricing: The Internet.* Paris: Committee for Information Computer and Communications Policy.

World Bank (2004). *WDI Online*. From http://publications.worldbank.ord/WDI/

8 Brazil: e-commerce shaped by local forces

PAULO BASTOS TIGRE

Introduction

Brazil presents an interesting case study of local factors influencing the adoption and impacts of e-commerce. Globalization is typically associated with the adoption of innovative technologies such as e-commerce that facilitate expansion into international markets and management of cross-border transactions. In the case of Brazil, however, its large size and considerable geographic distance from global production networks create a relatively inward-oriented economy. Other factors besides globalization have thus driven e-commerce. These include the need for financial efficiency driven by historically rampant inflation, as well as low GDP per capita typical of developing economies. Moreover, severely disproportionate wealth distribution impedes widespread adoption of certain forms of e-commerce. The overall result is the importance of local forces relative to global forces in driving e-commerce, the leadership of the financial sector in e-commerce adoption, and the innovation of large firms relative to small firms in the use of the technology.

- *Less international orientation.* On average, firms in Brazil are less internationally oriented than those in other economies. Only 4% of firms in the sample have establishments abroad, versus 24% in the global sample. Sales from abroad are less than a third of firms in other economies (4% versus 12%), and procurement from foreign firms is less than one half (10% versus 20%).
- *Local forces key.* Local forces are more important than global forces in driving e-commerce diffusion. Reasons include Brazil's inward orientation, its large domestic economy, and its unique economic history and government policies. E-commerce in Brazil is strongly anchored in information-intensive sectors, which are affected slightly by foreign transactions.

- *Finance leads.* The finance sector is a leader in e-commerce, driven by strong IT capabilities and an historical orientation toward automation. Finance leads other sectors in terms of firms using websites, intranets, and extranets, and in the percentage of firms using the Internet for most business functions.
- *Large firms lead.* Large firms lead small firms in terms of adopting e-commerce, driven by economies of scale and scope that enhance the perceived benefits of adoption. Results indicate that large firms are more active adopters and enjoy greater benefits from e-commerce. As an example, large firms lead SMEs in almost every category of e-commerce adoption and in eight of ten impact categories.

Country background: environment and policy

Background

Economies face different opportunities and challenges as they adopt new technologies and business practices such as e-commerce. The pace and direction of diffusion are influenced by economic structure, role in the global economy, policy choices, and prior adoption of related technologies. They are also influenced by the character of the individuals and firms which deploy and use the technology. These factors also influence the impacts that a new technology has at the national, firm, and individual levels.

Brazil presents an interesting case study of local factors influencing the adoption and impacts of e-commerce. It is a large developing country in which some segments of the economy are technologically sophisticated while others are quite backward. Even after a major liberalization initiative in the early 1990s, it remains relatively inwardly oriented economically, yet it has strong linkages to international technology sources. As such, we might expect to find a mixture of global and local factors affecting e-commerce diffusion and also to find variation among industry sectors and among firms of different sizes and degrees of international orientation.

Based on existing knowledge of Brazil's economic and policy environment and its experience with other information technologies, we develop three themes that encompass a priori expectations about the diffusion and impacts of e-commerce: 1) leadership of the financial sector in adopting and reaping the benefits of e-commerce, driven by strong IT capabilities and a clear orientation toward automation; 2) leadership of large firms in adopting e-commerce; 3) greater importance of local versus global forces in driving e-commerce diffusion. We now provide an overview of the Brazilian context for e-commerce and discuss each of the major themes outlined above.

Brazil's e-commerce context

Brazil is the fifth most populated country in the world, with 170 million inhabitants. Per capita income in US dollars fluctuates with exchange rates and after the 1999 devaluation Brazilian per capita income fell from $5,000 to $3,500 a year. Income distribution is highly unequal, as the share of income of the richest 20% of the population is about 64%, while the poorest 20% earns only 2% of national income, a ratio of about 30:1. By comparison, the ratio in Mexico is 16:1 and in China is just 8:1. This concentration of income in a small share of the population means that there is a sizable group of consumers with the wealth to participate in e-commerce, but the potential market is limited to a small part of the income distribution.

From the early 1990s, inflation control was the highest priority in economic policy, as the government responded to two decades of chronic high inflation. These policies bore fruit as far as inflation control was concerned, but were detrimental to economic growth. From 1995 to 2000 average GDP growth was 2% a year, a level that was insufficient to promote employment growth.

Brazil has gone through an extensive liberalization process since the early 1990s, including lowering of trade barriers and deregulation of many sectors of the economy. As a result, trade and foreign investment have grown significantly. Foreign direct investment reached 4.4% of GDP in 2002, compared with just 2.5% for Mexico. However, Brazil remains a relatively inward-oriented economy, with trade equal to about 29% of GDP, compared with 56% for Mexico and 55% for China for instance (World Bank, 2002).

The rapid evolution of IT infrastructure in Brazil shows that there are already grounds for e-commerce development in most regions and business sectors, thanks to rapid diffusion of telephone lines, cell phones, PCs, and Internet use (Table 8.1). Brazil was a latecomer in privatizing and opening its telecommunications network to new competition and did it at the opportune time of the 'dot.com bubble.' Encouraged by very positive worldwide market signals and unsatisfied local demand,

Table 8.1 *Technology indicators, 1998–2002*

	1998	*1999*	*2000*	*2001*	*2002*
Telecommunications					
Main phone lines per 1,000 pop.	120.51	148.73	182.13	217.84	223.20
Cell phone subscribers per 1,000 pop.	44.43	89.49	136.56	167.29	200.61
Cable subscribers per 1,000 pop.	11.96	11.50	13.73	13.78	n.a.
Internet					
Internet hosts per 1,000 pop.	1.30	2.66	5.16	9.57	12.87
Internet users per 1,000 pop.	15.07	20.83	29.45	46.56	82.24
IT					
IT as percent of GDP	1.54	2.16	2.32	2.47	2.49
PCs per 1,000 pop.	30.15	36.31	50.06	62.85	74.76
Software piracy rate (percent)	0.61	0.58	0.58	0.56	0.55

Sources: IDC, 2004; IPR, 2003; ITU, 2004; World Bank, 2002

new entrants invested heavily in new capacity. From 1998, when the telecom system was privatized, to 2000, telecom investments reached an average of 1.36% of GNP a year, a percentage well above historical levels. In 2001, 58.9% of Brazilian households had telephone service (8% with cellular phones only), against 37.6% in 1999 (IBGE, 2001). Expansion of services has stalled since then, as the number of potential customers with the means to pay for phone service has been saturated. Internet infrastructure is still growing fast but may also soon reach a ceiling, as the high end of Brazil's uneven income distribution is already mostly online.

A recent survey (FGVSP, 2002) of 1,260 medium-sized and large Brazilian firms shows that 70% of staff have access to microcomputers and 46% to the Internet. Firms in the survey spent on average 4.5% of total sales in IT, compared with an estimated investment of 8% in the USA, 5% in Europe, and 3% in Latin America. In Brazil, the service sector leads with 7%, followed by manufacturing (3%) and distribution (2%).

E-commerce in Brazil: three themes

Theme 1. Financial sector leadership and path dependency

Brazil's financial sector has been the clear leader in adopting information technologies, and is widely considered a pioneering user of the

Internet for marketing, selling online, and service and support. Brazilian banks act as commercial and investment banks, building societies, securities houses, insurance companies, and stock exchange brokers. Moreover, the government in Brazil relies extensively on banks as intermediaries for its taxation and transfer activities. For this highly diversified range of activities, large banks can be described today as online "services supermarkets."

The leadership of Brazil's financial institutions in adopting IT can be explained in part by the nature of the financial services business. Financial services firms process large volumes of transactions, creating economies of scale for adopting IT in general, and e-commerce in particular. In addition, nearly all financial products and services can be digitized, making them more amenable to electronic automation than physical products and services (Mulligan & Gordon, 2002). As a result, financial services are the leading IT adopters in most economies. For instance, in the USA, financial firms on average spend 8% of their revenues on IT, compared with 2% in retail and 3% in manufacturing (Information Week, 2002).

The leadership of the financial sector in Brazil also illustrates the importance of path dependency, which states that history plays an important role in how technologies diffuse within a country (Ruttan, 1997). High inflation prevailed in Brazil for decades up to the mid-1990s, providing a strong incentive for banking automation. Banks perceived that an efficient information flow permitted them to capture extra revenue through online money transfer and overnight interest rates. Thus Brazil's banks were early leaders in adopting electronic automation, making investments in IT that now provide a strong infrastructure for online banking and other e-commerce services. Given the information intensity of its business, as well as its historical leadership in IT, we would expect the financial sector to be the leader in e-commerce adoption.

Theme 2. Large vs. small firms: economies of scale and scope

The principle of scale economies is that there will be a decrease in the marginal cost of production as a firm's output increases. Scope economies occur when enterprises spread their costs over a larger range of products and services. The Internet supports scale economies because it has allowed activities with decreasing returns of scale to be replaced by activities that have constant or increasing returns to scale.

Since information is costly to produce but very cheap to reproduce, the cost of information is dominated by the costs of the first copy. For instance, an e-business transactional homepage may require a considerable investment in design, organizational links, and data security to start with, but the costs of adding new customers can be very low. As a result, larger firms that can take advantage of scale economies and have resources to facilitate implementation may be expected to be more aggressive in adopting technologies such as e-commerce (Tornatzky & Fleischer, 1990). Yet, large firms may be less agile and flexible, and may also have existing investments in pre-Internet technologies (such as electronic data interchange), and therefore be less willing to adopt Internet-based e-commerce (Nord & Tucker, 1987).

Scope economies occur when the enterprise dilutes costs by increasing the range of products and services produced. Synergy effects between the nature of the required investment and the capabilities to produce and distribute different products with common inputs allow for scope economies. E-commerce offers opportunities to obtain scope economies because it can share infrastructure, files, equipment, technological know-how, and distribution channels. As an enterprise develops e-commerce, it can identify new opportunities to use its infrastructure and obtain scope economies. Zhu et al. (2002) argue that firms with greater scope are more likely to adopt e-business.

While smaller firms may have some advantages in adopting new technologies, and may see the Internet as a tool for competing with larger firms, we expect that on balance, the scale and scope of larger firms' activities will make them the likely leaders in adopting e-commerce. This is particularly true in a developing country such as Brazil, where larger firms are more likely to have both the financial and human resources to implement such a technology.

Theme 3. Global and local forces

International trade and business alliances are important forces driving the global diffusion of e-commerce. Both theory and empirical evidence suggest that globalization is closely linked to the diffusion of information and communications technologies (Pohjola, 2002; Caselli & Coleman, 2001; Globerman et al., 2001). In fact, the relationship is likely to be mutually reinforcing. Adoption of ICTs such as e-commerce is not only driven by globalization but also contributes to the integration of internationally dispersed activities by enabling innovative global organizational forms such as global production networks (Sturgeon, 2002; Boudreau et al., 1998). Thus, globalization is likely to be associated with the adoption of technologies such as e-commerce that make it cheaper and easier for firms to expand into international markets and manage their operations across borders (Steinfield & Klein, 1999; Cavusgil, 2002).

In the case of Brazil, however, we do not expect globalization to play a key role as an e-commerce driver comparable to other economies where trade accounts for a higher share of GDP. Few local firms are exporters, and even subsidiaries of multinational corporations rely less on international trade than their other branches worldwide.

Part of the reason for Brazil's inward orientation is its size and its distance from major markets and global production networks. Also, historical development strategies based on import substitution resulted in a relatively closed economy. Since the early 1990s, the Brazilian economy has shifted its development strategy from import substitution to export-oriented industrialization. These policies have opened up the Brazilian market for imports but so far have not produced a boom in exports. So while Brazil has become a somewhat more globally oriented economy, we would still expect local rather than global forces to drive e-commerce adoption, and the impacts to be on domestic more than international business.

Globalization

The GEC Survey confirms the inward orientation of the Brazilian economy. Only 4% of companies surveyed have establishments abroad, against 24% of the global sample of 2,100 firms (Table 8.2). Overseas sales represent a mean of only 4% in the Brazilian sample, against 12% in the inter-country sample, while for procurement abroad the mean is 10% versus 20%. Also, Brazilian firms perceive themselves to be less affected by competitors abroad.

Large firms in Brazil are more internationally oriented than SMEs, rating much higher on all measures. This suggests a significant divergence in the nature of the two groups that might have impacts on their adoption of e-commerce. The survey shows that manufacturing is the most globally integrated sector concerning both sales (9%) and procurement (10%) abroad. While financial firms are most likely to have establishments or headquarters abroad, they are the least involved in

Table 8.2 *Globalization indicators, 2002*

	Establishment size		*Sector*			*Total*	
	SME	*Large*	*Mfg.*	*Distrib.*	*Finance*	*Brazil*	*Global*
Percent of companies with establishments abroad	4	23	2	4	11	4	24
Percent of companies with headquarters abroad	3	11	1	4	6	3	8
Mean percent of total sales from abroad	3	18	9	2	4	4	12
Mean percent of total procurement spending from abroad	10	15	10	10	5	10	20
Degree affected by competitors abroad (percent)							
Low	89	62	76	95	74	89	68
Moderate	4	13	12	0	12	4	16
High	7	25	13	5	14	7	15

Source: CRITO GEC Survey, 2002

foreign sales or procurement. The implication is that there is more foreign investment in Brazil's financial sector than in other sectors, but most foreign firms in the sector are operating on a local basis.

The low overall level of globalization among Brazilian firms suggests that local factors will be more important than global forces in determining e-commerce adoption and impacts. However, for large firms, the impact of global forces is more likely to be significant.

E-commerce readiness

Adoption of e-commerce technologies

The survey shows Brazilian firms have a surprisingly high usage of technologies related to e-commerce, given the number of more developed economies in the global sample (Table 8.3 and Figure 8.1). Brazilian firms rank near or above the global average in the use of email, extranets, EFT, call centers, and websites, but are below the average for intranets and EDI. Among Brazilian firms, large establishments

Table 8.3 *Use of e-commerce technologies*

	Establishment size		*Sector*			*Total*	
Percent using . . .	*SME*	*Large*	*Mfg.*	*Distrib.*	*Finance*	*Brazil*	*Global*
Email	100	100	100	100	100	100	99
Website	70	81	78	67	84	71	74
Intranet	37	72	45	34	50	38	64
Extranet	33	45	41	29	46	33	33
• accessible by suppliers/business partners	10	34	22	5	36	11	21
• accessible by customers	16	29	22	12	35	16	18
EDI	36	72	39	36	35	37	44
• over private networks only	7	26	4	9	3	8	19
• Internet-based only	7	10	12	5	16	7	8
• both	22	36	23	22	17	22	16
EFT	52	66	46	55	52	52	43
Call center	46	62	47	46	35	46	32

Source: CRITO GEC Survey, 2002

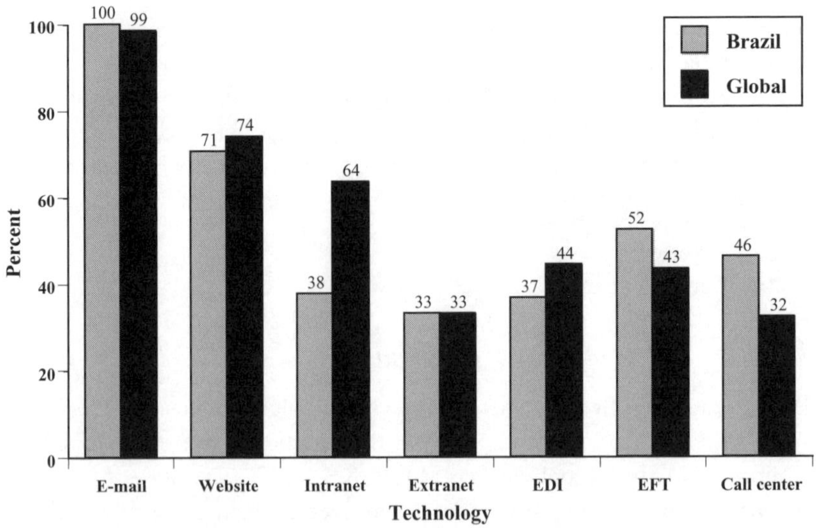

Figure 8.1 Use of e-commerce technologies
Source: CRITO GEC Survey, 2002

Table 8.4 *Enterprise integration strategy*

Extent to which Internet applications are electronically integrated with . . .	*Establishment size*		*Sector*			*Total*	
	SME	*Large*	*Mfg.*	*Distrib.*	*Finance*	*Brazil*	*Global*
Internal databases and information systems							
Percent little to none	59	42	84	47	31	58	53
Percent some	12	10	1	17	19	12	24
Percent a great deal	29	48	16	36	50	30	24
Those of suppliers and business customers							
Percent little to none	90	70	96	87	70	89	72
Percent some	8	16	2	12	11	9	18
Percent a great deal	2	14	2	1	18	2	10

Source: CRITO GEC Survey, 2002

have a higher level of use of all technologies, sometimes twice the level of small establishments. The finance sector leads in website, intranet, and extranet deployment, but trails in EDI, EFT, and call center use. The fact that the financial sector is a less intense user of EFT may be a technology choice matter. Secure extranet services may be a substitute for money transfer among different bank accounts. Overall, our analysis suggests that firm size is a more important indicator of adoption than sector, and is consistent with the economy of scale and scope argument.

Enterprise integration strategy

E-commerce readiness also can be measured by the degree to which Internet applications are integrated with internal information systems and with those of suppliers and customers. Table 8.4 and Figure 8.2 indicate that a larger percentage of Brazilian firms has integrated web applications with internal databases and information systems (30%) than the global average (24%). Integration with suppliers and business customers is below the global average.

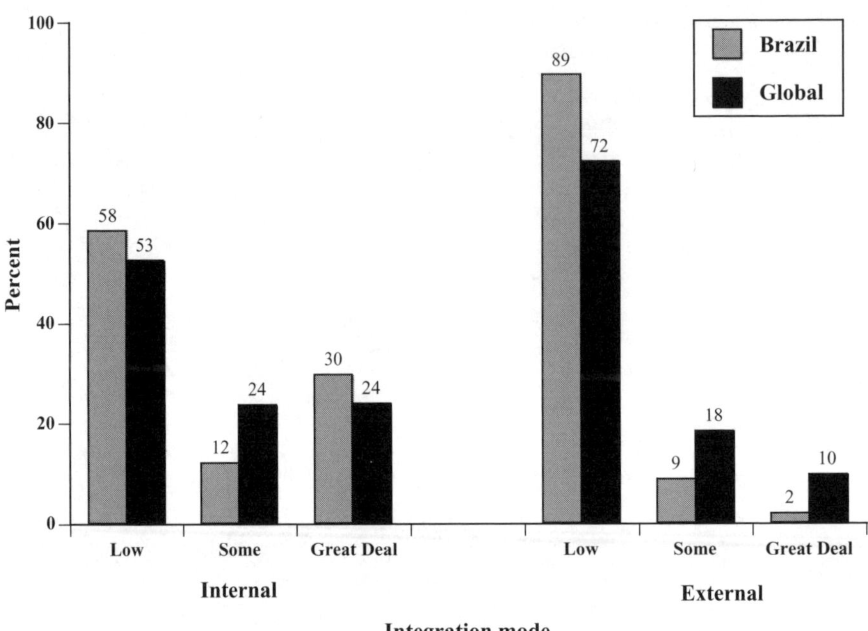

Figure 8.2 E-commerce readiness – enterprise integration
Source: CRITO GEC Survey, 2002

Table 8.4 also shows that large firms are well ahead of small ones in both internal and external integration. At the sectoral level, financial firms are clear leaders in integration. This may reflect path dependency, as financial firms have longer experience with IT and probably have greater ability to integrate Internet and other applications, which is more complex than simply developing Internet-based applications. There is very little integration with suppliers or customers except in the financial sector. This reflects the greater difficulty of external integration (also seen in the global sample).

To summarize, the Brazilian firms surveyed showed a level of e-commerce readiness that was comparable overall to the broader global sample. These firms represent only more technically advanced firms which are already using the Internet for business, but the findings show that even in a developing country, the local leaders are similar to their international counterparts technologically.

Table 8.5 *Drivers of Internet use*

Percent indicating driver is a significant factor	*Establishment size*		*Sector*			*Total*	
	SME	*Large*	*Mfg.*	*Distrib.*	*Finance*	*Brazil*	*Global*
Customers demanded it	44	56	28	50	68	45	37
Major competitors were online	26	49	8	35	38	27	31
Suppliers required it	24	45	7	31	42	24	22
To reduce costs	61	72	66	58	64	61	36
To expand market for existing product or services	59	68	48	63	91	59	48
To enter new businesses or markets	54	64	36	62	67	54	42
To improve coordination with customers and suppliers	61	67	56	63	68	61	44
Required for government procurement	26	18	3	36	20	25	15
Government provided incentives	14	22	4	18	31	15	8

Source: CRITO GEC Survey, 2002

Drivers and barriers to e-commerce

Drivers

The survey shows that large firms more than SMEs perceive greater external pressure to adopt e-commerce, both from competitors being online and from the requirements of suppliers and customers to do business online (Table 8.5, Figure 8.3). They also are somewhat more likely to perceive the opportunity to reduce cost or expand markets. The data support our expectations about the influence of size in e-business adoption. The only factor to which smaller firms attribute a higher importance than larger firms is that of e-commerce being required for government procurement. This may be because the online federal government purchasing site Comprasnet gives preference to small and medium-sized firms.

The industry analysis reveals different drivers across sectors. Financial firms are most often driven by the desire to expand existing markets

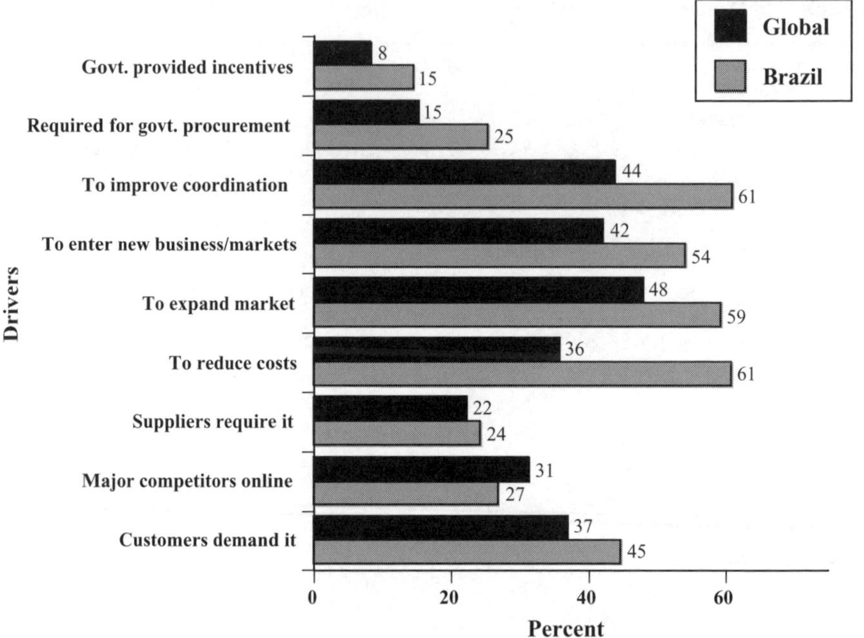

Figure 8.3 E-commerce drivers of Internet use
Source: CRITO GEC Survey, 2002

(91%), followed by the need to improve coordination with customers and suppliers (68%), and customer demand (68%). Internet banking is already a widespread business practice in Brazil and a major tool for reaching new customers. The Internet is rapidly forcing change on this business sector through 24×7 self-service systems in which customers search for information, transfer funds, and make investments.

Retail and wholesale firms, which act as intermediaries between producers and consumers, attribute the highest importance to expanding markets for existing products (63%), improving coordination with customers and suppliers (63%), and entering new markets (62%). Also, they are more sensitive to government online procurement requirements than other industry sectors.

E-commerce in the manufacturing industry is driven, more than in other sectors, by cost-reduction objectives (66%). Supply chain management is becoming a competitive weapon for inventory reduction and accelerating business cycles. As a result, the manufacturing sector in Brazil is sensitive to the need to improve coordination with suppliers and customers, especially large wholesale and retail distributors which command an increasingly demand-driven supply chain.

Finally, Brazilian firms seem to perceive more opportunities overall than their global counterparts. With only one exception (major competitors were online), they give more importance to suggested drivers than the global average (Figure 8.3). This is consistent with the finding of Zhu et al. (2002) that firms in developed economies are more cautious in their views of the benefits of electronic business than those in developing countries such as Brazil.

Barriers

E-commerce adoption can involve profound changes in business organization, government regulation, and human interactions. Since these changes can affect entire organizations, they can be more difficult and time consuming to implement than those involving more narrowly focused technologies and practices. Table 8.6 and Figure 8.4 illustrate that in Brazil, several major barriers are related to government regulations, including concern about privacy of data or security issues (49%), lack of business laws for e-commerce (32%), and inadequate legal protection for Internet purchases (41%). Concern over Internet taxation was also cited by 27% of Brazilian firms, compared with just 16% of the global sample.

These results do not support Tigre and Dedrick's (2002) proposition that governments play a more important role as users and promoters of e-commerce than as regulators. As Table 8.5 shows, 25% of the Brazilian firms consider online government procurement to be a driver for Internet use against only 15% for the global sample. Also, incentives such as tax rebates in IT purchasing play a positive role for large firms and those from the finance sector. However, the survey data in Table 8.6 reveal that the absence of legal protections is considered a more important problem than expected, suggesting the need for a stronger regulatory role for government.

Another finding is that small firms face more barriers than large ones. This result gives additional support to Theme 2 propositions about size as an advantage in overcoming barriers to adoption. An exception is the prevalence of credit card use, which is considered to be more an obstacle for large firms.

Table 8.6 *Barriers and obstacles to e-commerce adoption*

Percent indicating statement is a significant obstacle	*Establishment size*		*Sector*			*Total*	
	SME	*Large*	*Mfg.*	*Distrib.*	*Finance*	*Brazil*	*Global*
Need for face-to-face customer interaction	33	30	26	35	40	33	34
Concern about privacy of data or security issues	48	55	17	61	46	49	44
Customers do not use the technology	48	20	38	52	31	48	31
Finding staff with e-commerce expertise	34	32	17	41	30	34	27
Prevalence of credit card use in the country	23	34	26	22	22	23	20
Costs of implementing an e-commerce site	33	39	18	39	36	34	34
Making needed organizational changes	33	41	16	39	41	33	24
Level of ability to use the Internet as part of business strategy	22	25	4	29	26	22	25
Cost of Internet access	21	9	1	29	11	20	15
Business laws do not support e-commerce	32	22	26	34	22	32	24
Taxation of Internet sales	27	18	3	36	36	27	16
Inadequate legal protection for Internet purchases	42	34	36	43	47	41	34

Source: CRITO GEC Survey, 2002

As for industry sectors, it can be noted that retail and wholesale distribution faces somewhat greater obstacles than other sectors, except in credit card use. The use of credit cards for e-commerce is the lowest reported obstacle overall. Brazilian consumers are the largest users of credit cards in Latin America and the country ranks eighth worldwide, with around 30 million cards issued and more than 1 billion transactions a year. In 2000, overall purchases using credit cards reached \$26.5 billion, equivalent to 7% of total private domestic consumption in Brazil (Gazeta Mercantil Latino-Americana, 2001).

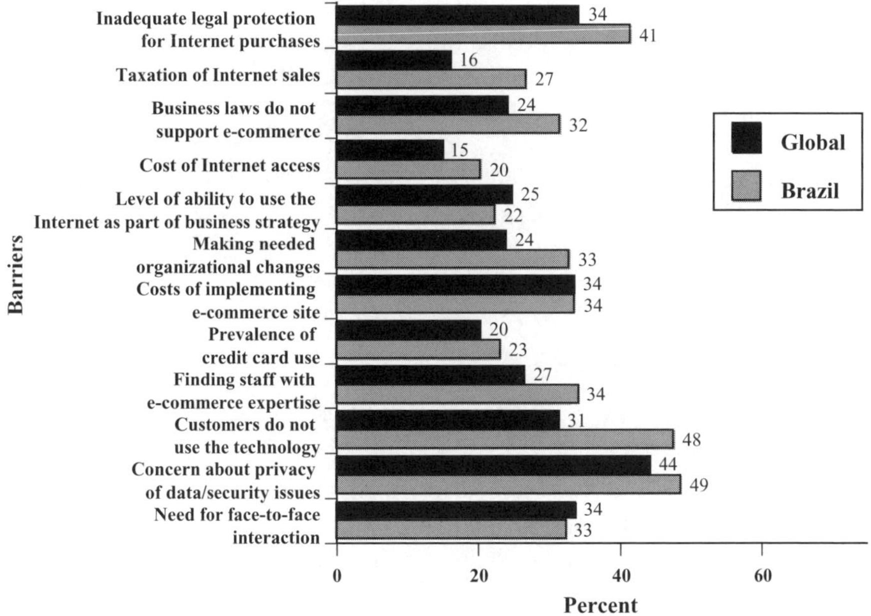

Figure 8.4 Barriers to Internet use for e-commerce
Source: CRITO GEC Survey, 2002

Table 8.6 shows that finding staff with e-commerce expertise is a problem affecting the distribution sector mainly. Traditionally, this sector pays lower salaries than both manufacturing and finance, and consequently it may face difficulties in attracting skilled people. It can be noted that there is a correlation between the relatively less advanced use of e-commerce in the distribution sector and its difficulty in finding qualified staff.

Since the problem of finding staff with e-commerce expertise is larger in Brazil (34%) than in the global sample (27%), we must also look at the country's educational levels and local readiness to engage in the use of information technologies. Given that Brazil had 3 million university-level students in 2002, a 43% increase over 1998 (INEP, 2003), the problem of skills shortage seems to be associated with insufficient on-the-job experience to develop and adapt information technologies to specific applications and business environments, rather than with the lack of basic skill levels. A positive indicator of the availability of IT and managerial capabilities is that the ability to use the Internet as part of business strategy is considered slightly less of a barrier in Brazil (22%) than in the global sample (25%).

As far as Internet costs are concerned, Table 8.6 shows that Brazilian firms attribute an equal weight to the cost of implementing an e-commerce site (34%) as do their global counterparts. The cost of Internet access is considered a larger problem in Brazil, but it seems to be restricted to SMEs and the distribution sector. Beyond Internet access cost, other considerations may be personnel or outside services needed to develop e-commerce.

Diffusion of e-commerce

E-commerce has grown rapidly in Brazil. From 1998 to 2000, electronic trade grew twenty fold, jumping from $100 million to nearly $2 billion, and by 2002 it had tripled to nearly $6 billion. In 2002, it represented 1.5% of GDP, with B2B transactions responsible for around 90% of total e-commerce (IDC, 2004).

Uses of the Internet

The financial sector leads in using the Internet for marketing, selling online, and after-sales service and support (Table 8.7). The manufacturing industry, meanwhile, leads in data exchange with suppliers, customers, and business partners. The distribution industry does not lead any particular applications, but all three sectors share a similar level of online purchasing.

Large firms are more intense e-commerce users in all applications. Overall, advertising and marketing is the largest application, followed by online purchasing (Figure 8.5). After-sales customer service and making sales online are the least common applications.

Online sales

These findings support our expectations that the financial sector would be the leader in using e-commerce and that large firms would be more aggressive than small ones. However, when we look at the actual volume of business conducted online, a somewhat different picture emerges. As Table 8.8 shows, SMEs are equally likely to sell online as large firms, and conduct about the same share of their consumer

Table 8.7 *Uses of the Internet*

Percent using the Internet for . . .	*Establishment size*		*Sector*			*Total*	
	SME	*Large*	*Mfg.*	*Distrib.*	*Finance*	*Brazil*	*Global*
Advertising and marketing purposes	59	59	74	51	91	59	58
Making sales online	28	32	13	34	43	28	30
After-sales customer service and support	23	40	26	21	38	23	44
Making purchases online	55	63	57	54	56	55	47
Exchanging operational data with suppliers	52	62	65	47	50	52	48
Exchanging operational data with business customers	49	56	57	46	49	49	51
Formally integrating business processes with suppliers or other business partners	49	48	54	46	51	49	34

Source: CRITO GEC Survey, 2002

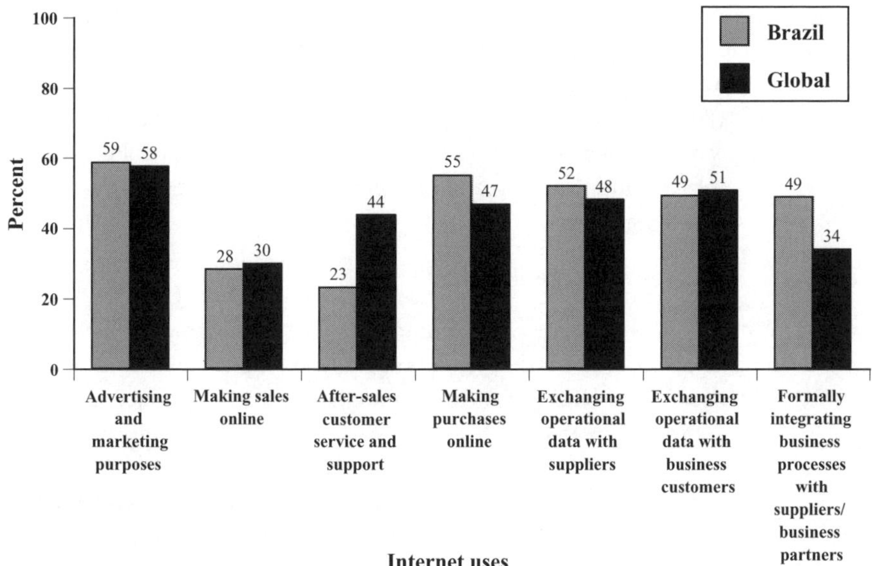

Figure 8.5 E-commerce adoption – types of use
Source: CRITO GEC Survey, 2002

Table 8.8 *Online sales, 2002*

	Establishment size		*Sector*			*Total*	
	SME	*Large*	*Mfg.*	*Distrib.*	*Finance*	*Brazil*	*Global*
Type of online sales (percent)							
B2B only	9	9	21	4	6	9	13
B2C only	9	10	0	13	16	10	7
Both B2B and B2C	19	17	12	21	30	18	15
Mean percent of total consumer sales conducted online (all establishments)	4	4	3	4	6	4	4
Mean percent of total business sales conducted online (all establishments)	4	4	9	1	6	4	4

Source: CRITO GEC Survey, 2002

and business sales online. Among the sectors, manufacturing firms are leaders in B2B sales volume, while finance is the leader in B2C sales.

Our interpretation is that financial firms are most likely to do business online and to sell online, but their actual sales activity is more modest. Manufacturers are less likely to sell online, but those that do so tend to emphasize B2B (not surprising given that their sales would mostly be to distributors or retailers) and do relatively large volumes of business online. The wholesale/retail distribution sector lags in participating in online selling and in volume of online sales.

Brazil's e-commerce industry

Whereas in the recent past e-commerce was dominated by new companies, traditional market leaders seem to be rapidly catching up. For instance, in the banking sector, Banco 1 was the most successful virtual company created, but it was soon taken over by an established financial institution.

Universo Online (UOL), a locally owned ISP, leads the Internet access market. Other large ISPs were taken over by telephone operators. These include IG (owned by Telemar) and Terra (a subsidiary of Telefonica). Many people see the links between telephone operators and ISPs as creating unfair competition by providing free services using cross-subsidies. In the ISP market, AOL failed to reproduce its worldwide success in Brazil. In the Internet content industry, however, some US companies were successful in adapting their content to the local language and building a customer base. Portals such as eBay, Google, and Yahoo! are very popular in Brazil.

In retail, Submarino is probably the most successful Brazilian-owned virtual shop. It was founded in 1999 and according to its website (www.submarino.com.br), it now holds 10% of the Brazilian B2C market. It sells sixteen categories of products online including books, CDs, DVDs, audio and video equipment, home goods, and tools. In 2001, Submarino handled more than 1.5 million orders and shipped over 3 million items. Among almost 5,000 locations to which it shipped products, 850 were outside the country. Over 720,000 people visit the site monthly. However, existing supermarkets and distribution chains (such as Americanas.com and Pão de Açucar) seem to be gradually gaining e-commerce markets.

For B2B, several new firms have also emerged. Mercosul Search (www.mercosulsearch.com.br) is a prize-winning website oriented to both B2B and B2C markets. It provides technical services and market information to small and medium-sized firms aiming at entering the Latin American and global markets. Its goal is to become a regional marketplace and to provide services and technology support for online business. It was created in 1996 as a local information site, but rapidly developed into the wider project of a Mercosur industrial marketplace. It now has about 5,000 clients.

In order to explore the rapidly growing e-commerce industry, many existing IT firms have shifted their focus to support online activities. Traditional IT firms such as IBM and Unisys took advantage of their large customer base and technical expertise to enter the e-commerce support market. IBM probably leads e-commerce software and support activities by providing turnkey solutions and data center management services. Its CRM system is reputed to be the best seller in Brazil, in a market fiercely disputed by local and foreign firms.

In addition, new firms have emerged in businesses such as data centers, web hosting, web development, web applications, and consulting. Two success stories deserve to be mentioned: Modulo Security Solutions and Everysystems Informatics. Not surprisingly, what they have in common is that they are oriented toward the Internet banking market, which is the most successful sector in Brazilian e-commerce development.

Modulo Security Solutions leads the growing market for securing information and financial transactions in Brazil. It also acts to secure the Brazilian electronic election system, a success story touted by Microsoft (www.microsoft.com/technet/archive/security/case/brzcase.mspx). Modulo has developed solutions for Internet tax collection in Panama, and is undertaking certification processes and legal procedures to start selling its security software to the US government.

Everysystems Informatics was founded in 1992 as a financial software development firm. Recently, it shifted to the Internet banking market and is now exporting software and services to twenty financial institutions in Latin America, Canada, and Japan. It claims that more than 900,000 people all over the world already use its solution. Everysystems is now focusing on the smart card segment of the market where a boom is expected through this means of online money transfer.

In general, we have observed that e-commerce pioneers are successful when they are able to innovate by creating services and business tools. Virtual firms oriented to traditional consumer markets such as books, CDs, and home appliances are gradually losing ground to pre-existing market leaders.

Impacts of e-commerce

Industry structure

One of the important phenomena of the last ten years has been the rapid growth of business networks. Although this process had started before the Internet was available for commercial use, e-commerce is expected to have important network impacts. Table 8.9 shows that over one-third of firms interviewed in Brazil reported an increase in network relationships such as number of suppliers (40%) and distribution channels (35%). The evidence shows that large firms are more likely to increase the number of distribution channels since they began using the Internet, suggesting again that they can achieve economies of scale from their e-commerce investments.

Going online also can expose firms to greater competitive pressure. Overall, Brazilian firms were about equally affected in terms of number

.9 Impacts of online business on industry structure

	Establishment size		Sector			Total	
Percent indicating . . .	*SME*	*Large*	*Mfg.*	*Distrib.*	*Finance*	*Brazil*	*Global*
Number of distribution channels							
Increased	35	48	27	38	57	35	40
No change	65	52	73	62	43	65	56
Decreased	0	0	0	0	0	0	4
Number of suppliers							
Increased	40	40	37	41	37	40	30
No change	60	54	61	59	62	59	64
Decreased	0	6	2	0	1	1	6
Number of competitors							
Increased	28	17	13	33	47	28	28
No change	66	79	86	59	53	66	67
Decreased	6	4	1	8	0	6	5
Intensity of competition							
Increased	38	30	13	47	51	38	42
No change	53	68	77	44	39	53	54
Decreased	9	2	9	9	10	9	4

Source: CRITO GEC Survey, 2002

of competitors and competitive pressure as the global sample. However, small firms were much more likely to report an increase in number of competitors and intensity of competition since going online, perhaps because doing business on the Internet exposed them to competition beyond their limited existing market area.

Among industry sectors, financial firms were most likely to increase their number of distribution channels and also faced the greatest increase in competition. The retail and wholesale distribution sector also showed strong increases in competitive pressure. Since the finance and distribution sectors both operate mostly within the domestic market, the increased pressure must be local rather than global. Interestingly, manufacturing saw much lower increases in competitive pressure, even though manufacturers are more likely to face global competition. This is consistent with the argument that e-commerce is mostly a local not a global phenomenon in Brazil.

Table 8.10 *Impacts of doing business online, 2002*

Percent indicating high impact	*Establishment size*		*Sector*			*Total*	
	SME	*Large*	*Mfg.*	*Distrib.*	*Finance*	*Brazil*	*Global*
Internal processes more efficient	32	53	39	30	57	33	34
Staff productivity increased	40	41	37	42	36	40	27
Sales increased	26	31	15	30	41	26	21
Sales area widened	27	41	6	36	39	28	31
Customer service improved	45	56	61	39	42	45	35
International sales increased	13	12	13	13	11	13	20
Procurement costs decreased	25	26	44	18	28	25	18
Inventory costs decreased	28	20	23	30	21	28	14
Coordination with suppliers improved	34	42	59	25	32	34	30
Competitive position improved	24	40	28	22	34	24	30

Source: CRITO GEC Survey, 2002

Firm performance

Table 8.10 shows the impacts of going online on business performance. Compared to the global sample, Brazilian firms reported similar impacts on most indicators, but were significantly higher in terms of increased staff productivity (40% versus 27%) and improved customer service (45% versus 35%). Large firms seem to be reaping more benefits than smaller firms in terms of increasing internal efficiency, widening sales areas, improving customer service, coordinating better with suppliers, and enhancing their competitive position. Small firms have an advantage only in inventory cost reduction. This is consistent with our expectation that the economies of scale enjoyed by large firms would enable them to reap greater benefits from e-commerce.

The finance sector benefits most in terms of improving internal efficiency, increasing sales, and widening sales areas. The manufacturing sector, in contrast, benefits most from enhancing customer services, improving coordination with suppliers, and reducing procurement costs. These differences are typical of the nature of business. While

, and other financial firms use the Internet primarily as a market- , tool, manufacturing firms are looking for better coordination of the ,upply chain. All sectors seek to improve internal efficiency through e-commerce, but the financial sector seems to enjoy more success in this area, possibly because it deals with information rather than physical products and can benefit more from automating its services.

Consistent with our expectation that e-commerce is more local than global in Brazil, only 13% of firms reported increased international sales since going online. The figure was very similar for large and small firms, and across the three sectors, showing that there is not even an identifiable segment of the economy that has used e-commerce to expand globally. In fact, much of Brazil's exports consist of agricultural and other primary products, which are not included in the survey and probably are not heavy users of e-commerce in any case.

Conclusion

The survey findings generally support the propositions developed in the three themes discussed earlier. In addition, the survey reveals interesting views on the role of government policy and the need for a better legal and regulatory environment to support e-commerce.

The finance sector is the leader in adoption, but the sectoral picture is mixed in terms of online sales volume and the impacts on performance. The survey results suggest that the financial sector has capitalized on its experience with IT in order to adopt e-commerce technologies and to integrate them with existing information systems. It also has found greater opportunities to use the Internet and has reaped more benefits in general, no doubt due to the information intensity of its activities. However, manufacturing and distribution firms are not far behind, and are actually ahead of finance on some indicators of adoption and impacts. For instance, manufacturers conduct a larger share of their sales volume online than the other sectors, even though they are less likely to sell online. This probably reflects the scope of some segments of the manufacturing sector, whose firms are using the Internet heavily to supply business customers both at home and abroad.

Local rather than global forces drive e-business. E-commerce in Brazil is strongly anchored in information-intensive sectors little affected by foreign transactions. Local forces seem to play a more influential role due to Brazil's inward orientation, large domestic economy, unique economic history, and government policies. Brazilian firms generally are not important global players, and using the Internet does not appear to be increasing their involvement in the global economy. This contradicts the technologically deterministic notion that e-commerce is an inherently globalizing force. But it is consistent with our expectation that e-commerce would be a more local than global phenomenon in Brazil's case, given the economic structure of the country.

Large firms are more active adopters of e-commerce and enjoy greater benefits. Large firms are clearly more active in implementing e-commerce technologies, and use the Internet more extensively for most applications. This is consistent with the notion that potential economies of scale and scope would provide greater incentive for adoption. Yet, 41% of large firms said that making needed organizational changes was an obstacle to doing business online, versus 33% for small firms. This may show that organizational inflexibility is a barrier that negates some of the advantages enjoyed by larger firms, or that the cost of making organizational changes is higher in large firms.

Large firms also report greater benefits from going online, mostly in terms of increased internal efficiency, increased sales, and better customer service. Smaller firms do as well or better on other variables. However, large firms are much more likely to report that their competitive position improved, so it would appear that there are advantages to leveraging e-commerce investments over a larger scale or scope of activities.

Lack of legal protection is a more important barrier than expected. The survey revealed that the absence of legal protection is considered a substantial barrier for e-commerce diffusion. It includes lack of business laws for e-commerce and inadequate legal protection for Internet purchases. These results do not support the proposition that governments play a more effective role by using the technology themselves and promoting private-sector adoption than by regulating and providing legal protection for e-commerce activities (Tigre & Dedrick, 2002). Although government may indeed play a role as promoter, especially for SMEs and the distribution sector, adequate legal protection is even more important for e-commerce diffusion.

We would argue that in developing economies such as Brazil, government policies should include "demonstration projects" aimed at attracting firms and individuals to use the Internet. Government online procurement can also bring more firms online, especially smaller firms otherwise might not be motivated to conduct e-commerce. However, the survey suggests that, at least in Brazil's case, the biggest impacts would likely come from promotion and enforcement of legal measures to protect businesses and consumers from online fraud and ensure privacy and security of data.

Lessons for other developing economies. Some aspects of the Brazilian case may not generalize to other developing economies, but our findings still can contribute to understanding the process of technology diffusion. Information technology is a powerful tool for increasing growth and productivity, but the technology itself will not determine economic outcomes. For example, in Latin America, most countries experienced high inflation during the 1970s and 1980s, but unlike Brazil they did not develop an "indexation culture" that required a highly automated banking system. Rather than relying on banks, assets holders in most high-inflation countries held hard currencies in order to protect themselves against local currency devaluation. Thus, the financial sector will not necessarily lead e-commerce progression in other developing economies, despite the strong incentives offered by its information-intensive nature.

Also, the importance of local and global factors as e-commerce drivers must be analyzed carefully as far as other developing economies are concerned. The small scale of local markets in most developing economies may give global factors a more prominent role as drivers of adoption than in a larger, inward-oriented country like Brazil. O'Connor's (2002) argument about the importance of competitive pressures for IT adoption seems to fit here. In the absence of strong domestic competition, IT adoption in developing economies may occur earliest in those sectors exposed to international competition.

The fact that large firms are clearly more active in implementing e-commerce technologies may have negative implications for developing economies. Since the vast majority of firms in the developing world are small, they may lack the incentives provided by scale and scope for e-commerce adoption.

Finally, it is likely that our findings about the importance of government regulation in creating a favorable environment for e-commerce will hold true for other developing economies. Given the costs and risks associated with doing business online, both firms and individuals in developing economies are likely to hesitate to engage in e-commerce in the absence of effective regulatory and legal institutions.

References

Boudreau, M. C., Loch, K. D., Robey, D., & Straud, D. (1998). Going Global: Using Information Technology to Advance the Competitiveness of the Virtual Transnational Organization. *Academy of Management Executive*, 12(4), 120–128.

Caselli, F. & Coleman II, W. J. (2001). Cross-Country Technology Diffusion: The Case of Computers. *The American Economic Review*, 91(2), 328–335.

Cavusgil, S. T. (2002). Extending the Reach of e-Business. *Marketing Management*, 11(2), 24–29.

Fundação Getulio Vargas de São Paulo (FGVSP) (2002). *Tecnologias da Informação: Cenários e Tendências.* 13 Pesquisa Anual. Panorama do uso nas empresas. Retrieved October 9, 2002, from www.fgvsp.br/academico/estudos/cia/index

Gazeta Mercantil Latino-Americana (2001). February 12–18, 26.

Globerman, S., Roehl, T. W., & Standifird, S. (2001). Globalization and Electronic Commerce: Inferences from Retail Brokering. *Journal of International Business Studies*, 32(4), 749–768.

Information Week (2002). *Business-Technology 500 Ranking.* September 23.

Instituto Brasileiro de Geografia e Estatística (IBGE) (2001). *Pesquisa Nacional de Amostra por Domicílio (PNAD) 2001.* Retrieved December 2002, from www.ibge.gov.br/pnad

Instituto Nacional de Estudos e Pesquisas Educacionais (INEP) (2003). *Sistema de Avaliação do Ensino Superior.* Censo 2000. Ministério da Educação. Retrieved February 14, 2003, from www.inep.gov.br/imprensa/noticias/censo

International Data Corporation (IDC) (2004). *Internet Commerce Market Model.* Framingham, MA.

International Planning and Research Corporation (IPR) (2003). *Eighth Annual Business Software Alliance (BSA) Global Software Piracy Study, Trends in Software Piracy 1994–2002.* Washington, D.C.: Business Software Alliance.

International Telecommunication Union (ITU) (2004). *World Telecommunication Indicators Database* (8th ed.). Geneva, Switzerland.

Mulligan, P. & Gordon, S. R. (2002). The Impact of Information Technology on Customer and Supplier Relationships in the Financial Services. *International Journal of Service Industry Management*, 13(1), 29–46.

Nord, W. R. & Tucker, S. (1987). *Implementing Routine and Radical Innovation.* Lexington, MA: Lexington Books.

O'Connor, D. (2002). E-Commerce for Development: Between Scylla and Charybdis. In Goldstein & O'Connor (Eds.), *Electronic Commerce for Development*. Development Centre of the OECD, 55–66.

Pohjola, M. (2002). The New Economy: Facts, Impacts and Policies. *Information Economics and Policy,* 14, 133–144.

Ruttan, V. W. (1997). Induced Innovation, Evolutionary Theory and Path Dependence: Sources of Technical Change. *The Economic Journal*, 107(444), 1520–1529.

Steinfield, C. & Klein, S. (1999). Local vs. Global Issues in Electronic Commerce. *Electronic Markets*, 9(1/2), 1–6.

Sturgeon, T. J. (2002). Modular Production Networks: A New American Model of Industrial Organization. *Industrial and Corporate Change*, 11(3), 451–496.

Tigre, P. & Dedrick, J. (2002). *Globalization and Electronic Commerce: Environment and Policy in Brazil.* Irvine, CA: Center for Research on Information Technology and Organizations. From www.crito.uci.edu/publications/pdf/GIT/GEC/Brazil_GEC2.pdf

Tornatzky, L. G. & Fleischer, M. (1990). *The Processes of Technological Innovation.* Lexington, MA: Lexington Books.

World Bank (2002). *World Development Indicators.* Washington, D.C.: World Bank.

Zhu, K., Kraemer, K., & Xu, S. (2002). *A Cross-Country Study of Electronic Business Adoption Using the Technology Organization Environment Framework*. Barcelona: International Conference on Information Systems.

9 Mexico: global engagement driving e-commerce adoption and impacts

JUAN J. PALACIOS

Introduction

After implementing a comprehensive economic liberalization program in the 1990s, Mexico has become one of the most open economies to foreign trade and investment, and has positioned itself among the ten largest economies in the world. The resulting substantial integration into the global economy has created both the conditions and the pressures for the business community in Mexico to adopt the Internet to improve coordination, expand markets, and cut costs to face a highly competitive environment in both national and international markets. Mexico has long been a major production platform for subsidiaries of numerous multinational corporations (MNCs), many of which operate as *maquiladoras*, a situation reinforced as it has become increasingly engaged in international trade. Those MNC subsidiaries, along with a small but growing echelon of internationally oriented domestic companies, account for a large share of the country's total exports, and are the most dynamic and technologically advanced business establishments in the Mexican economy. Accordingly, they have led in the use of information and communication technologies (ICTs) for commercial purposes.

Major improvements in the country's telecommunications infrastructure since the mid-1990s have facilitated and spurred the use of both personal computers and the Internet. Economic liberalization, along with aggressive promotion campaigns by trade and industry associations, have further paved the way for the adoption of e-commerce by large and small, domestic and foreign enterprises. This has occurred particularly in finance, distribution, and manufacturing, and largely in the country's main industrial hubs (Guadalajara, Monterrey, and Mexico City). The large presence of MNCs, the liberalization of the telecommunications industry, the creation of a basic legal framework for e-commerce, and the solid development of both e-banking and e-government have been key to the adoption of Internet-based business tools.

However, a number of inhibiting factors, common in most Latin American countries, has slowed the process. These include a large informal sector, an overwhelmingly large presence of micro and small enterprises, a highly skewed income distribution, a traditional shopping culture, a low technological and organizational development of businesses, and a predominantly informal business culture. Nevertheless, e-commerce has taken hold and thrived in Mexico, as substantial exposure to foreign competition and consistent implementation of promotion campaigns have driven firms to overcome those obstacles and adopt the Internet as a business tool.

The result has been a higher level of Internet and e-commerce adoption and use than might be expected for a developing country that otherwise lags most advanced economies on indicators such as wealth, education, income distribution, and overall use of ICTs, including the Internet. There is a common belief that Internet use and impacts among business enterprises in Mexico are narrow and limited, a view supported by estimates of e-commerce revenues at the national level. However, our study challenges that assumption by showing that Mexican firms in the GEC Survey are comparable to those in other, more advanced countries on many measures of e-commerce, particularly in usage and impacts. Likewise, surveys conducted by Mexico's leading IT market research firm estimated that Internet penetration in 2004 was between 50% and 70% in large enterprises, and between 38% and 60% in small businesses. The major remaining gap is in e-commerce transactions, as Mexican firms are more likely to use the Internet for marketing and coordination than for selling online.

Overall, one can say that Mexico's experience with e-commerce has been positive and promising so far. E-commerce practices by business enterprises have spread to a significant extent by developing country standards, and have had impacts similar to those observed in more advanced economies. While far from leading the flock, but also not lagging as much as commonly believed, the Mexican economy is poised for continued growth in e-commerce adoption. Internationally oriented firms are likely to lead this process, but there are signs that small and medium-sized enterprises will soon follow, helping to tap the large potential lying dormant in this segment of the Mexican economy.

With this general background, a summary of additional specific findings follows:

- *In Mexico, the finance sector leads in the adoption of e-commerce.* Financial firms and banking institutions turned out to be the most globalized and the ones that use Internet-based technologies most extensively and spend the highest proportions of their operating budget on information systems. Conversely, and contrary to expectations, manufacturing establishments generally tend to lag financial and distribution enterprises in most key areas of e-commerce adoption and use.
- *Large firms lead in the adoption of Internet technologies, including intranets, call centers, and electronic data interchange, as well as in overall e-commerce use.* These firms command a larger pool of financial and material resources, have more efficient and modern corporate structures, and remain more closely connected to global markets. SMEs are behind, as they lack resources, and many operate in the informal economy. Nonetheless, they are making solid progress given the flexibility allowed by their size and the possibilities opened up by options like application service providers (ASPs) and blogs. SMEs spend a significantly higher proportion of their revenues on information systems, suggesting that they are increasing their use of ICTs and the Internet at a faster pace than large firms.
- *Business-to-business e-commerce is much larger than business-to-consumer in terms of total transaction volume, accounting for 93% of online sales.* However, the gap is much smaller when looking at the number of firms conducting each type of activity, or the proportion of each type of online transaction. The difference is apparently in the scale of B2B versus B2C transactions.
- *Surveyed companies did not perceive government incentives and requirements as compelling factors for e-commerce adoption.* Instead, they deemed market factors such as improving coordination and communication with customers and suppliers, entering new markets and expanding existing ones, and reducing production costs as much more powerful drivers. Government policy has an indirect impact though, since the companies regarded telecommunications infrastructure and Internet connectivity as essential conditions that they take for granted when considering engaging in e-commerce. Yet, inadequate commercial policies may be a barrier to e-commerce. Surveyed firms reported legal and regulatory issues as the highest

Table 9.1 *Macroeconomic indicators, 1998–2002*

	1998	*1999*	*2000*	*2001*	*2002*
GDP in US$bn	421	480	580	624	637
GDP per capita US$	4,421	4,976	5,928	6,275	6,313
GDP growth (annual percent)	4.9	3.7	6.5	−0.1	0.7
GFDI (percent of GDP)	2.8	2.7	2.8	4.9	2.4
Trade (percent of GDP)	64	63	64	57	56
Income distribution: richest 20 percent: poorest 20 percent			16.5		

Source: World Bank, 2004

barriers to e-commerce, especially concerns about security and privacy of data and inadequate legal protection for online purchases. They also considered taxation of Internet sales and the perception that business laws do not sufficiently support e-commerce as significant barriers. These results suggest that the most useful roles for government are to provide a sufficient telecommunications infrastructure, set up an adequate legal framework, and maintain a healthy and favorable macroeconomic environment.

Country background: environment and policy

Traditionally a leader in Latin America given the size and maturity of its economy, Mexico has also been a leader in the adoption of ICTs, along with Brazil, Argentina, and Chile. Its proximity to the United States and the large presence in its economy of MNCs based in North America, Asia, and Europe have given Mexico an edge in the use of the Internet and the practice of e-commerce in the hemisphere.

Macroeconomic environment

Mexico is the world's ninth largest economy with a GDP that totalled $637 billion in 2002 and a per capita income of $6,313 for the same year (Table 9.1). Yet, Mexico presents a highly skewed income distribution, with the richest 20% of the population having an average income 16.5 times that of the poorest 20%. Such a marked income concentration implies limited possibilities for B2C e-commerce to spread,

Table 9.2 *Globalization indicators for business establishments in Mexico, 2002*

	Establishment size		*Sector*			*Total*	
	SME	*Large*	*Mfg.*	*Distrib.*	*Finance*	*Mexico*	*Global*
Percent of companies with establishments abroad	18	39	34	8	47	19	24
Percent of companies with headquarters abroad	10	14	11	7	32	10	8
Mean percent of total sales from abroad	15	14	22	8	42	15	12
Mean percent of total procurement spending from abroad	40	28	35	43	24	39	20
Degree affected by competitors abroad (percent)							
Low	61	58	25	86	38	61	68
Moderate	12	11	21	6	7	12	16
High	27	31	54	7	55	27	15

Source: CRITO GEC Survey, 2002

compared with economies such as the United States where the richest earn nine times as much as the poorest, or Japan where the richest earn only 3.4 times as much as the poorest (Table 1.3).

The Mexican economy boasts highly developed industry sectors made up of foreign multinational and domestic firms that compete successfully in global markets. It is an open, outward-oriented economy in which trade accounts for over 56% of GDP, compared with only 24% in the case of the United States. Over four-fifths of Mexico's trade is with the United States, while most of the rest is with Europe and Japan.

Table 9.2 shows the relatively high degree of internationalization in the Mexican economy. Mexican firms are roughly comparable to the global sample in the proportion of companies with headquarters or establishments abroad, and total sales abroad. However, they are much higher with regard to share of procurement spending abroad. This reveals a substantial reliance by these companies on imported inputs. The fact that Mexican firms are more highly affected by competition from abroad than the global sample reinforces this finding. Therefore, the results indicate that global factors, more than domestic ones, drive e-commerce.

The extent of globalization tends to grow with establishment size, except in the proportion of sales from abroad. As can be expected, large companies have more establishments and headquarters abroad, although a greater number of SMEs spend more on procurement in foreign countries. This interesting fact may be explained by the tendency for SMEs to import most of the parts and components they use for assembling products such as PCs, electronics goods, and auto parts in order to comply with the requirements of their larger clients.

From a sectoral perspective, finance and manufacturing are the most globalized sectors vis-à-vis distribution. Although finance leads manufacturing in most of the indicators in question, both sectors have a high proportion of companies with establishments and headquarters abroad, as well as sales from abroad, and accordingly are highly affected by foreign competitors. Distribution in turn leads in procurement from other countries, which suggests a high reliance on imported goods for wholesale and retail trade; a similar case appears in the case of manufacturing. International competition heavily affects financial firms due to the outright liberalization of the financial sector in the 1990s and early 2000s, which opened the doors for a number of foreign banks and financial institutions, largely from Spain, to buy their way into the Mexican economy.

Industrial organization

A distinguishing feature of Mexico's industrial structure is the overwhelmingly large proportion of micro and small businesses vis-à-vis large companies. According to the 1999 Economic Census, the private-sector company population in Mexico comprises 2.8 million business establishments, of which 95.7% are micro units,[1] 3.1% small businesses,[2] 0.9% medium-sized enterprises,[3] and only 0.3% large firms[4] (INEGI, 2000).

[1] Up to thirty employees in industry, up to five in commerce, and twenty in services.

[2] From thirty-one to one hundred employees in industry, six to twenty in commerce, and twenty-one to fifty in services.

[3] From 101 to 500 employees in industry, 21 to 100 in commerce, and 51 to 100 in services.

[4] Five hundred and one or more employees in industry, 101 or more in commerce, and 101 or more in services.

Micro, small, and medium-sized enterprises thus play an essential role in the Mexican economy. They generate six out of ten jobs in the formal sector, while their output accounts for 42% of GDP (El Financiero, 2004a), although they account for only 6.5% of total exports. According to the Industrial Chamber Confederation, only one out of ten have been awarded some form of quality certification, which means that most of them are unable to qualify as suppliers to the larger, more technologically advanced companies operating in Mexico (El Financiero, 2004b). This is illustrated by the fact that out of the 110 Mexican companies that supply parts and components to the Nissan plant in Aguascalientes, only 10 are located in the area, and most are family-run small businesses. This small participation by local companies occurs in spite of the fact that the Nissan plant has been there since 1980. The underlying reason is that Mexican SMEs have found it difficult to meet the quality standards Nissan requires from its suppliers (Chacón, 2004).

From a sectoral viewpoint, manufacturing, distribution, and services (finance, insurance, personal services, and transportation) account for 88% of GDP, with services alone making up 48% (INEGI, 2002b).

Manufacturing

Manufacturing has traditionally been one of the most dynamic sectors in the Mexican economy. One half of the establishments in this sector are in the food, tobacco, and beverages industries, and in the metallic products, machinery and equipment industries. These two industry clusters, together with that of textiles, apparel, and leather wares, jointly account for 69% of Mexico's industrial GDP (INEGI, 2000). At a more specific level, automobiles and electric – electronic products are the most dynamic industries, as they account for 28% and 20% of total manufacturing exports, respectively (INEGI, 2002a).

Advanced manufacturing is dominated by foreign multinationals that use Mexico as a production platform to cater to both the local and export markets, together with a handful of Mexican corporations which have gone multinational themselves in recent times. These firms are part of global production networks whose flagship companies make extensive use of ICTs and which pressure their suppliers and business partners to adopt such technologies as well. Therefore, manufacturing appears as one of the sectors most likely to engage in e-commerce transactions, specifically the B2B type which accounts for the overwhelmingly largest proportion of e-commerce activity in Mexico, as elsewhere. From this latter perspective, one might expect e-commerce to account for a larger proportion of commercial transactions in manufacturing firms than in other economic sectors. However, it turns out that this is not the case, as discussed below.

Financial services

The financial services sector is composed of more than 3,600 institutions and companies that employ over 230,000 people (INEGI, 2000). Banks are by far the largest and most important players in this sector. They account for 84% of financial establishments, followed by stock brokerage and insurance firms with 9% and 7%, respectively. Traditionally dominated by domestic firms since the mid-1990s, this sector has been penetrated by foreign interests from Spain, the United States, Canada, and Japan. This trend is likely to continue in the future.

In general, finance is the sector where e-commerce has developed most in Mexico. Since financial services are data intensive and do not require physical deliveries, the Internet is making it possible for "new entrants to build substantial businesses, go up the value chain, and compete on price" (Sato et al., 2001). This occurs particularly in the case of banking, as all major banks operating in Mexico have built comprehensive websites, with all the necessary resources to offer their customers this option. Multinational banking firms have been a major driving force in this process, as they have introduced Internet-based management practices that are leading to the development of true electronic banking in this country. For example, after Banamex was taken over by Citigroup, the priority was to gradually replace its existing branches with virtual service centers, and it created an e-banking arm called Artikos to coordinate the effort (Flores, 2002).

Distribution

Distribution (retail and wholesale) is highly skewed toward the retail side. As many as 92% of distribution establishments are in the retail business, most of which can be assumed to correspond to small shops. Yet, only 8% perform wholesale commercial activities and chiefly correspond to large companies (INEGI, 2000).

The entry of new competitors facilitated by the Internet is expected to force channel distributors to become more efficient and competitive, and thus to look for business solutions that can make such goals more feasible. A significant trend in this direction is the emergence of large wholesale distributors of electronic products, which also assemble PCs with their own brand – for example, Mexmal and its Alaska computers, which are among the top-selling domestic PCs in Mexico. Companies like this are now basing their strategies on web pages through which they deal both with other distributors and with final users, following the models of computer makers such as Dell and Gateway. Retailers are also going online to draw their customers into their e-commerce transactions.

Government policy and private-sector promotion

Government policy has played an important role in the development of e-commerce in Mexico. One of the most significant policy initiatives has been the liberalization of telecommunications markets carried out by the Salinas (1988–1994) and Zedillo (1994–2000) administrations. This liberalization created competition, brought new entrants into the market, and opened the way for the explosive growth of Internet access for both public and private users. It also spurred the rapid growth of personal computers in homes, businesses, and public offices.

Another policy that has been crucial for Internet penetration and e-commerce development is related to the development of telecommunications infrastructure. The number of both fixed and mobile phone lines has exploded since the late 1990s, thus expanding the use of the Internet for all purposes, including e-commerce (Palacios & Kraemer, 2003). Significant initiatives in this area include the so-called E-Mexico National System, which aims at building a vast nationwide broadband telecommunications network expected to spur the growth of commercial transactions over the Internet. Although this ambitious project has not met its goals, it has led to a significant enhancement of Internet connectivity and access in remote localities that otherwise would have remained unconnected.

Other policies that have improved the environment for e-commerce in Mexico include the Digital Economy Development Special Program implemented by the Ministry of the Economy to provide SMEs with the basic skills for the adoption of digital technologies. Likewise, Nacional Financiera, Mexico's main second-tier development bank, set up a Directorship for Electronic Products in 2002, which aims at facilitating the use of ICTs by SMEs so they can become suppliers to larger companies (Palacios & Kraemer, 2003).

Table 9.3 *Information infrastructure, 1998–2002*

	1998	*1999*	*2000*	*2001*	*2002*
Telecommunications					
Main phone lines per 1,000 pop.	104	112	125	137	147
Cell phone subscribers per 1,000 pop.	35	79	142	217	254
Cable subscribers per 1,000 pop.	17	20	23	25	24
Internet					
Internet hosts per 1,000 pop.	1	4	6	9	11
Internet users per 1,000 pop.	13	19	51	74	98
IT					
IT as percent of GDP	0.99	1.00	0.99	1.05	1.06
PCs per 1,000 pop.	37	44	58	69	85

Sources: IDC, 2003a; IPR, 2003; ITU, 2004; World Bank, 2004

A far more influential factor, though, has been the consistent work of a number of inter-sectoral working groups and private-sector organizations specifically devoted to the promotion of e-commerce practices, which includes members from both government branches and agencies, and industrial chambers and associations. The most important include the Mexican Association for Electronic Commerce Standards (AMECE), the Mexican Committee on Electronic Commerce (COMECE), the Electronics, Telecommunications and Informatics Industry National Chamber (CANIETI), the Mexican Association for the Information Technologies Industry (AMITI), and the Promotional Group on E-commerce Legislation (GILCE).

E-commerce readiness

Country-level information infrastructure

As pointed out above, the Mexican government has extended and significantly improved the country's telecommunications infrastructure over the past decade. To illustrate, the national fiber optic network increased from only 5,500 kilometers in 1992 to over 106,000 kilometers in 2001. Likewise, the number of fixed phone lines in operation increased steadily to 147 lines in 2002 (Table 9.3). By December 2002, 36.2% of private homes had at least one phone line installed, according to COFETEL (Mexico's Federal Telecommunications Commission).

The dynamism is even higher in the case of mobile telephony. The number of cellular phone subscribers per 1,000 people exploded from 35 in 1998 to 254 in 2002. By 2003, there were 27 million cell phones in use. The introduction of third-generation technologies should further propel the use of cell phones. There are projections that half of Mexico's e-commerce in 2006 will be conducted on mobile devices, and that the number of users of those devices will increase to 40 million in that year (AMECE, 2001).

The number of installed PCs increased from 37 per 1,000 people in 1998 to 44 in 1999, 58 in 2000, and 85 in 2002 (Table 9.3). Ten percent of Mexican homes had PCs in 2000, a rather low proportion compared with the 50% observed in the United States that year (Select-IDC, 2000). Over 70% of PCs installed in businesses had access to the Internet by January 2000 (Torres Chávez, 2000).

Firm-level use of e-commerce technologies

The surveyed companies in Mexico are fairly well equipped concerning technologies required for e-commerce (Table 9.4). They post figures similar to the averages for the global sample in most of the items examined, particularly with regard to websites, EDI, and call centers, but significantly higher with regard to EFT. In spite of operating in a developing country, these firms see the Internet as a useful instrument for conducting their business. They perceive EDI as a necessary complement, which is in fact used by more of them vis-à-vis intranets and extranets.

By sector, finance relies more on intranets and notably on extranets as these are powerful instruments for both providing services and communicating with customers. In turn, manufacturing and distribution emphasize the use of EDI, which is an essential part of B2B e-commerce, the kind that manufacturing and distribution firms practice more. Fewer of the former use email and extranets, but more of them have a website compared with those in finance and distribution. The explanation may lie in that distribution establishments have more direct contact with customers and final consumers (B2C) than manufacturing companies, while the latter tend to use their websites for conducting their dealings with suppliers and business partners (B2B).

Table 9.4 *Use of e-commerce technologies by business enterprises in Mexico, 2002*

	Establishment size		*Sector*			*Total*	
Percent using…	*SME*	*Large*	*Mfg.*	*Distrib.*	*Finance*	*Mexico*	*Global*
Email	98	100	95	100	100	98	99
Website	79	72	87	75	68	79	74
Intranet	50	74	51	51	55	51	64
Extranet	31	37	28	31	53	31	33
• accessible by suppliers/ business partners	23	22	17	25	39	23	21
• accessible by customers	16	21	18	13	46	16	18
EDI	58	68	53	63	48	58	43
• over private networks only	20	18	12	25	14	20	19
• Internet-based only	29	12	28	31	7	28	8
• both	9	38	13	7	27	10	16
EFT	70	80	66	74	67	71	43
Call center	44	60	52	38	61	44	32

Source: CRITO GEC Survey, 2002

The main finding is that financial firms and institutions do better on most items in comparison with manufacturing and distribution, supporting the observation that finance is the sector where e-commerce has developed most extensively. More generally, business establishments operating in Mexico have high confidence in electronic means for conducting commercial transactions, which provides grounds for arguing that a large potential for e-commerce growth exists in this country.

Enterprise integration

Business establishments in Mexico show lower levels regarding some key aspects of enterprise systems integration compared with other countries in the survey. Sixty percent of them have little to no integration of Internet applications with their internal information systems, and 82% have little to no external integration of Internet applications with those of suppliers and business customers, compared with 53% and 72% for the global sample. Nonetheless, the corresponding figures are much closer when it comes to the proportion of firms with a great deal of internal and external integration (Table 9.5, Figure 9.1).

Table 9.5 *Internal and external integration of enterprise systems and databases, 2002*

Extent to which Internet applications are electronically integrated with . . .	*Establishment size*		*Sector*			*Total*	
	SME	*Large*	*Mfg.*	*Distrib.*	*Finance*	*Mexico*	*Global*
Internal databases and information systems							
Percent little to none	61	44	68	56	36	60	53
Percent some	12	19	8	15	18	12	24
Percent a great deal	27	37	24	29	46	28	24
Those of suppliers and business customers							
Percent little to none	82	79	87	79	72	82	72
Percent some	9	15	1	14	18	10	18
Percent a great deal	9	6	12	7	10	9	10

Source: CRITO GEC Survey, 2002

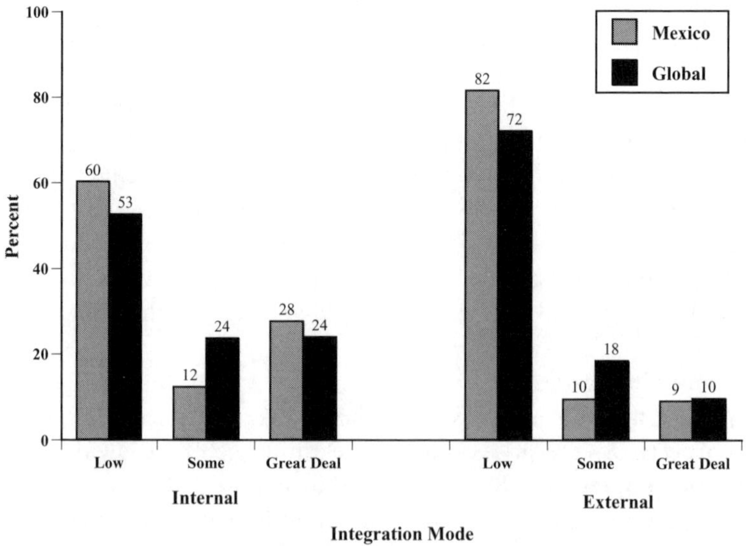

Figure 9.1 Integration mode
Source: CRITO GEC Survey, 2002

Those in the finance sector are ahead with internal integration, which is consistent with the high information intensity of this sector and with its focus on the consumer, wherein it is important to integrate all records. They outpace distribution companies, and are close to those in manufacturing with regard to the integration of Internet applications with those of suppliers and customers. Therefore, financial firms are said to be the most advanced in both respects, which is consistent with the fact that they are the best equipped with e-commerce technologies.

In contrast, manufacturing firms show a lower degree of internal integration, but are slightly higher in the integration of Internet applications with those of suppliers and customers. Again, this is consistent with the pattern of use of e-commerce technologies shown in Table 9.4. Although the pattern is mixed, distribution establishments tend to present lower levels of integration in general than either banking or manufacturing (Table 9.5).

Size does matter in this case, as large firms generally show higher degrees of system integration than SMEs, as the former tend to have more resources and a more developed business culture than the latter in an economic environment such as that of Mexico.

In sum, the extent of systems integration of business establishments in Mexico is still low, though not so distant from that prevailing in the other countries in the global sample. In any event, this finding signals a tendency for companies operating in Mexico to improve management systems and productivity tools supportive of e-commerce practices.

IT investment

At the country level, IT investment in Mexico is relatively low, as it amounted to only 1% of GDP in 2002, ranking lower than most other Latin American advanced nations, and of course lower in relation to Canada and the United States (Table 9.6). Total IT investment was estimated at $6.5 billion in 2002 (Ramírez, 2003).

At the firm level, average IT spending was found to top 10% of revenues, a figure higher than the global sample (Table 9.7). The number of PCs per employee in Mexico was the same as in the global sample. From a sectoral perspective, financial firms lead in information system spending vis-à-vis distribution and manufacturing, with the latter showing the lowest levels (Table 9.7). This is as expected, since banks

Table 9.6 *IT investment in selected countries in the Americas, 2002*

Country/region	*IT as percent of GDP*
Argentina	0.93
Brazil	2.49
Canada	3.29
Chile	1.73
Mexico	1.06
United States	3.89
Venezuela	1.27

Source: IDC, 2003b

Table 9.7 *Investment in IT by Mexican firms, 2002*

	Establishment size		*Sector*			*Total*	
Percent using...	*SME*	*Large*	*Mfg.*	*Distrib.*	*Finance*	*Mexico*	*Global*
PCs per employee	0.8	0.5	0.8	0.8	1.1	0.8	0.8
IT employees as percent of total employees	6.8	2.8	6.2	6.2	14.8	6.6	9.1
IS operating budget as percent of 2001 revenue	10.2	7.1	6.0	11.5	16.0	10.1	7.8
Web-based spending as percent of IS operating budget	19.1	22.8	22.4	16.7	24.8	19.2	14.9

Source: CRITO GEC Survey, 2002; weighted sample

rely most on Internet-based tools both internally and externally in providing services to their customers, as Palacios (2003) found.

Table 9.7 also supports the earlier observation that manufacturing firms tend to be highly focused in their use of e-commerce technologies, as they are mainly concerned with websites.

Contrary to expectations, size does matter in this case too, since the number of PCs per employee in SMEs is almost double that of larger establishments. Likewise, SMEs have more than twice the proportion of IT employees and spend a higher percentage of their revenues on IS than do larger firms. These results are most significant as they indicate that SMEs in Mexico are on their way to increasing the use of information systems and engaging in business practices that may include e-commerce. However, they spend a somewhat lower proportion on web-based applications, which may suggest that they are lagging larger companies in engaging in business practices related to e-commerce.

In summary, with a fairly sufficient telecommunications infrastructure, significant rates and promising patterns of investment in IT by businesses, and a sizable and growing number of Internet users, Mexico offers a favorable and enabling national environment for e-commerce activity to take hold and thrive. This is the result of the influence of particular barriers and drivers that have come into play to shape e-commerce diffusion in Mexico.

Drivers and barriers to e-commerce

Drivers

Mexico's progression into the Internet era in the early 1990s was largely influenced by the boom taking place in the United States next door, so the same combination of need and incentives motivated Mexico's firms to experiment with the Internet and e-commerce as a means of expanding existing markets or entering new ones. But an additional factor played a big part in Mexico, especially for firms that were part of global networks in the finance and manufacturing sectors. This was the need to improve coordination with suppliers and business partners in order to support expansion into new markets and to respond to pressures from international competition.

As mentioned earlier, foreign banks entered the local market, creating pressure on local banks to better integrate their internal operations and to engage in e-banking and other forms of B2C e-commerce. For the manufacturing sector, a major factor was multinational corporations putting pressure on their Mexican suppliers and business partners to engage in B2B e-commerce. In both instances, the drivers largely corresponded to market forces rather than to government policies. Other important enabling factors acting in Mexico's national environment have been the fact that all major banks have sophisticated portals through which they conduct a significant and increasing proportion of their dealings with their customers, and the existence of a legal framework that provides basic legal protection for electronic transactions (Palacios & Kraemer, 2003).

Table 9.8 *Drivers for Internet use by business enterprises in Mexico*

Percent indicating driver is a significant factor	*Establishment size*		*Sector*			*Total*	
	SME	*Large*	*Mfg.*	*Distrib.*	*Finance*	*Mexico*	*Global*
Customers demanded it	36	41	44	31	28	36	37
Major competitors were online	39	38	40	38	43	39	31
Suppliers required it	32	41	28	38	8	33	22
To reduce costs	58	56	45	68	35	58	36
To expand market for existing products or services	64	69	51	75	48	65	48
To enter new businesses or markets	65	74	51	74	53	65	42
To improve coordination with customers and suppliers	74	79	68	81	41	74	44
Required for government procurement	33	27	29	37	20	33	15
Government provided incentives	13	18	13	13	13	13	8

Source: CRITO GEC Survey, 2002

At the firm level, multiple factors act as incentives for businesses to engage in e-commerce. These range from government requirements, to customer demands, to productivity and market expansion goals. As illustrated in Table 9.8 and Figure 9.2, market expansion, entering new businesses, and improving coordination are the most significant drivers for companies in Mexico to use the Internet for doing business.

The quest to improve coordination and communication with customers and suppliers is by far the strongest driver for engaging in e-commerce, as 74% of the surveyed companies reported. This indicates that companies are responding to the need to attend closely to an increasingly personalized and sophisticated demand by staying in touch with their customers and to their suppliers in order to procure the required inputs. Entering new markets and expanding existing ones ranked second at 65% each, followed by the drive to reduce costs at 58%. However, it is intriguing that direct demands from both customers and suppliers are deemed far less important, given that this

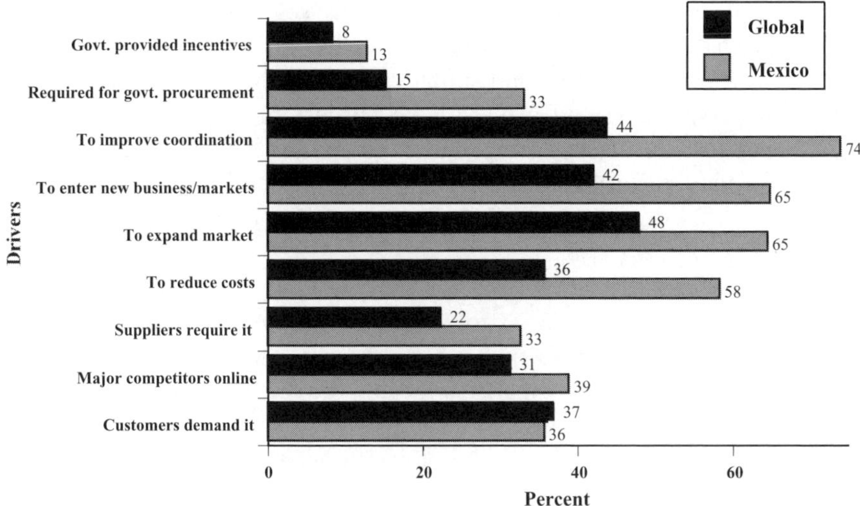

Figure 9.2 Drivers of e-commerce diffusion
Source: CRITO GEC Survey, 2002

contrasts with the intention of improving coordination with customers and suppliers.

What is clear is that government requirements and incentives are the least compelling drivers for using the Internet as a business tool. Nonetheless, the requirement to use e-commerce for government procurement is more than double in firms in Mexico than in other countries; this may indicate that it is more attractive to become a supplier to the government in Mexico than elsewhere. In turn, the fact that the figure is higher in the case of distribution establishments indicates that intermediaries – mainly wholesale distributors – tend to predominate among government suppliers.

In general, Mexico's figures are higher on virtually every count with respect to the global sample (Figure 9.2), which can be interpreted as reflecting the existence of greater competitive pressures in Mexico that are inducing businesses to engage in e-commerce. These pressures are surely the result of both the openness of its economy and its proximity to the world's largest market.

In this case, size does not make much difference, although SMEs tend to respond less to most of the drivers in question. From a sectoral point of view, it is no wonder that coordination with customers and suppliers is the most significant enabling factor for distribution establishments, given that their role as intermediaries hinges around direct relationships with both customers and suppliers more strongly than that of other sectors. Likewise, it makes sense that customer demand and market pressures seem more compelling as drivers for engaging in e-commerce for manufacturing firms.

Barriers

The various enabling factors considered above are counteracted by opposing forces present in Mexico's economic environment. At the national level, major barriers include the fact that over one-third of Mexican households do not have access to credit or other financial services, over two-fifths of the employed population works in the informal economy, and about half of the total population are under the poverty line. As a result, only a small slice of potential consumers have access to the Internet and engage in e-commerce, for most Internet users are less than thirty years old and have low purchasing power (Palacios & Kraemer, 2003).

Other forces influence e-commerce diffusion in another way. Select, Mexico's top domestic IT market research firm, reported that the main factors hampering the diffusion of B2C e-commerce in Mexico include lack of credit card use, the fact that consumers like to see products before buying, reservations about delivery services, and distrust in providing a credit card number over the Internet (Select, 2002). The latter is one of the main deterrents for consumers to shop over the web for the credit card is the instrument par excellence to buy over the web in Mexico and elsewhere.

Regarding B2B e-commerce, limiting factors include the fact that 96% of Mexico's companies are micro, small, and medium enterprises, and that many of these are in the informal sector. In addition, the still relatively limited extent of telecommunications infrastructure inhibits the growth of B2B, as Internet connectivity has reached only about 300 cities, although these are the largest ones and so account for the bulk of the country's economic activity (Palacios & Kraemer, 2003).

At the firm level, concerns about the legal framework rank highest among the barriers for companies in Mexico to engage in e-commerce

Table 9.9 ***Barriers to Internet use by business enterprises in Mexico***

Percent indicating statement is a significant obstacle	*Establishment size*		*Sector*			*Total*	
	SME	*Large*	*Mfg.*	*Distrib.*	*Finance*	*Mexico*	*Global*
Need for face-to-face customer interaction	26	26	29	25	8	26	34
Concern about privacy of data or security issues	58	52	53	62	41	58	44
Customers do not use the technology	39	41	41	38	28	39	31
Finding staff with e-commerce expertise	31	28	33	32	8	31	27
Prevalence of credit card use in the country	20	28	23	19	8	20	20
Costs of implementing an e-commerce site	36	19	33	37	27	35	34
Making needed organizational changes	32	31	37	31	14	32	24
Level of ability to use the Internet as part of business strategy	29	34	28	31	8	29	25
Cost of Internet access	3	18	8	1	8	4	15
Business laws do not support e-commerce	27	31	23	31	9	27	24
Taxation of Internet sales	21	26	17	26	1	22	16
Inadequate legal protection for Internet purchases	45	51	40	50	27	45	34

Source: CRITO GEC Survey, 2002

(Table 9.9, Figure 9.3). This holds more strongly in Mexico than in the other countries included in the global sample, which indicates that online fraud may be more likely to occur there and that businesses are more concerned about legal protection. These concerns are strongest in the case of distribution establishments, which are more engaged in e-commerce transactions than manufacturing. It is intriguing that financial firms are the least concerned about the legal framework when one considers that they deal with sensitive financial information.

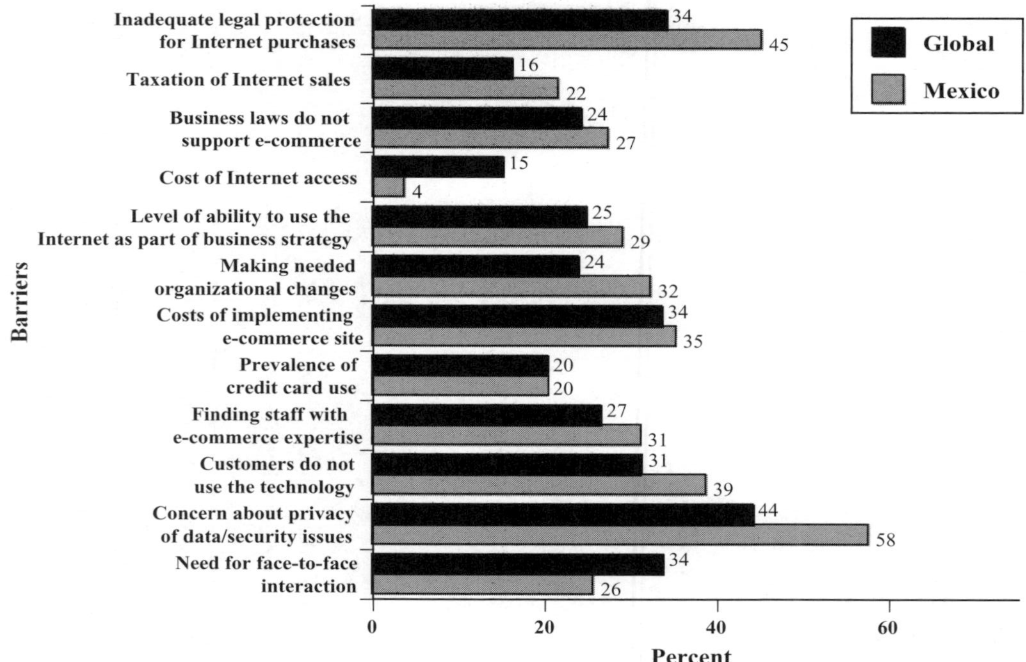

Figure 9.3 Barriers to e-commerce diffusion
Source: CRITO GEC Survey, 2002

Diffusion of e-commerce

Country-level pattern

E-commerce began in Mexico in 1993, when the first "com.mx" subdomain was created and put into operation (Palacios, 2003). A new era was born that year, when existing companies began to use the Internet as a new means for conducting business, and others were created expressly to do so.

E-commerce practices soon started to spread into the Mexican economy, and have made considerable progress thus far – IDC estimates that the total value of e-commerce transactions in Mexico reached 1.5% of GDP by 2003, which included online transactions by SMEs and large companies, as well as the government and education sectors (Vargas, 2004). The great bulk of those transactions corresponded to B2B e-commerce, with B2C accounting for a very small proportion. IDC estimates that B2B revenues accounted for 93% of Mexico's e-commerce in that year (IDC, 2003a). The total of $5.5 billion in e-commerce reached that year surpasses other Latin American countries except Brazil ($6.1 billion), but is way below Canada and the United States ($36 billion and $385 billion, respectively).

There are good indications, however, that e-commerce penetration in Mexico has reached a larger extent than that assessed on the basis of revenue measures. In its 2002 Community Survey on ICT Usage in Enterprises, the OECD reported that in 1999 Internet penetration in Mexico amounted to 54% in businesses with twenty-one or more employees. Likewise, a survey conducted by Select in 2004 reported that over half of business establishments in Mexico use the Internet for conducting their business (Figure 9.4). Although the proportion tends to increase with size – 70% in large firms of more than 5,000 employees – it is significant that in the case of micro shops with up to 15 employees it reaches 38%, and it gets up to 61% in establishments with up to 100 workers. This latter result is consistent with an earlier study in which Select reported that only 30% of SMEs had access to ICTs in Mexico (Select, 2003).

In sum, although e-commerce use in Mexico is limited thus far, there are signs that the process is spreading, so it is expected that the volume of commercial transactions online will continue to grow and the extent of its penetration will increase in the coming years.

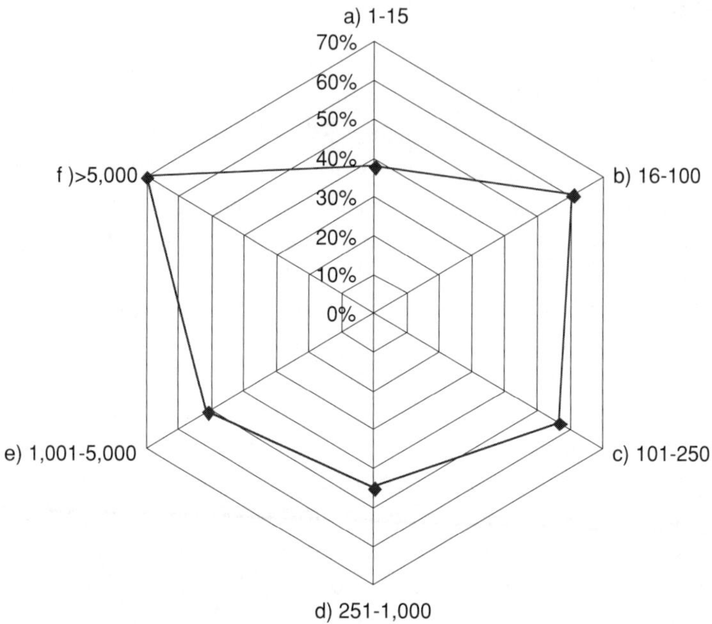

Figure 9.4 Internet penetration by firm size
Source: Select, 2004

Industry and firm level

E-commerce diffusion presents a different picture at the industry and firm levels. As Table 9.10 and Figure 9.5 illustrate, business enterprises in Mexico use the Internet most for advertising and marketing purposes, which may be explained by the fact that these are the least costly and the easiest to implement compared with full e-commerce solutions. Similarly, it is not surprising that making purchases online is the second most common use, as it is possible to make some types of purchases online simply by setting up an account with a supplier. Mexico also ranks favorably with other countries in terms of exchanging operational data with suppliers and customers and integrating business processes. It lags only in actually conducting sales online, possibly reflecting the cost of setting up an online transaction site and concerns about legal protection and security.

Although business establishments may direct advertising and marketing campaigns either to other companies or to individual consumers,

Table 9.10 *Uses of the Internet by business enterprises in Mexico*

Percent using the Internet for . . .	*Establishment size*		*Sector*			*Total*	
	SME	*Large*	*Mfg.*	*Distrib.*	*Finance*	*Mexico*	*Global*
Advertising and marketing purposes	73	55	50	87	73	73	58
Making sales online	12	20	8	13	21	12	30
After-sales customer service and support	40	35	33	44	48	40	44
Making purchases online	65	45	34	86	46	65	47
Exchanging operational data with suppliers	50	72	39	56	60	50	48
Exchanging operational data with business customers	46	70	59	38	54	47	51
Formally integrating business processes with suppliers or other business partners	55	48	25	74	46	55	34

Source: CRITO GEC Survey, 2002

it is more common that they aim at the latter. This indicates in principle that companies use the web mainly in the hopes of conducting B2C transactions. However, the fact that selling online is the least common use of the Internet in Mexico – at 12% versus 30% for the global sample – suggests that those hopes are not yet being realized. Moreover, since buying online is the second most common use, that result can suggest that B2B deals may be more numerous than B2C ones.

It is significant, however, that more than half of the surveyed firms used the Internet for coordination with suppliers and business partners in the form of exchanging operational data and integrating business processes for integrating their supply chains. This is consistent with both the results of Table 9.8 and the fact that 55% of the establishments report integrating their business processes with suppliers and business partners as a task for which they use the Internet.

What is intriguing is that a much higher proportion of the establishments is using the Internet to integrate with outside partners relative to the global sample. This is indicative of a rather mature perception of the potential of the Internet in Mexico, a feature expected to prevail

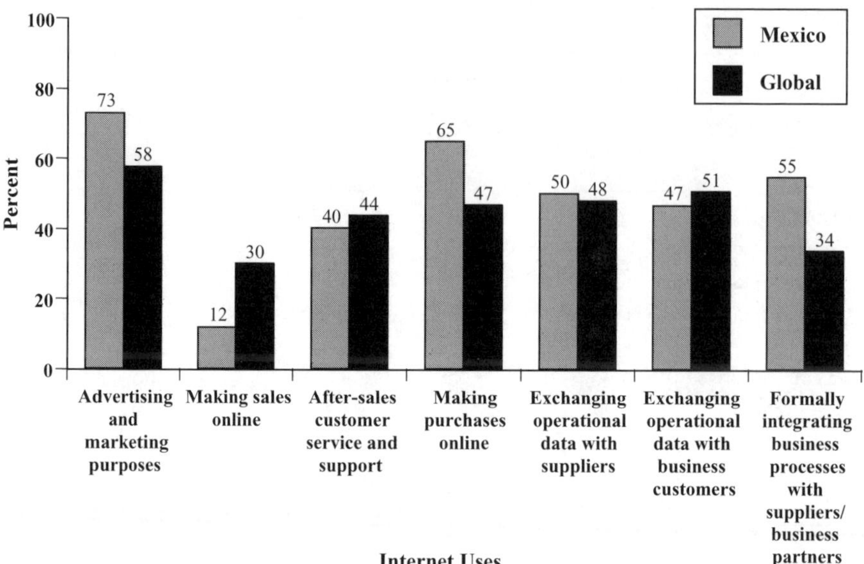

Figure 9.5 Use of the Internet
Source: CRITO GEC Survey, 2002

in the more advanced economies in the survey. One explanation may be that this kind of integration has been carried out already to a larger extent in other countries via EDI or other technologies.

Nature of use across sectors

The above trends are also visible in sectoral terms, with some particularities. Distribution establishments reported buying online (B2B) as a common use, as well as advertising and marketing, but followed closely by process integration. The picture is different in finance where, given the development of e-banking, data exchange with suppliers and business partners is next to advertising and marketing as the most important uses for the Internet. Manufacturing establishments have a similar perception, although data exchange with suppliers and, more significantly, process integration are much less influential.

Size does matter, as the two most important uses for the Internet – advertising and marketing, and buying online – are much more common for SMEs than for large firms. Differences also exist regarding data exchange and process integration, with data exchange with suppliers being the most influential purpose for large firms. These results point

Table 9.11 *Use of the Internet as a distribution channel*

Percent indicating Internet used to . . .	*Establishment size*		*Sector*			*Total*	
	SME	*Large*	*Mfg.*	*Distrib.*	*Finance*	*Mexico*	*Global*
Address new markets only	25	12	6	33	19	25	15
Address traditional distribution channels only	48	57	52	49	22	48	44
Compete directly with traditional distribution channels	9	16	21	1	57	9	27
Replace traditional distribution channels	18	15	21	17	2	17	13

Source: CRITO GEC Survey, 2002

to the conclusion that the smaller the firm, the higher the propensity for it to use the Internet as a commercial tool.

In terms of how the Internet is used with regard to the firms' distribution channels, surveyed establishments most commonly use the Internet to address traditional distribution channels (Table 9.11). The fact that competing with existing channels is the least common purpose indicates that firms in Mexico perceive there is still enough room for everyone in domestic markets, and so are not concerned about reinforcing their arsenal to compete with others in existing channels. The observation that addressing new markets is the second most important objective reinforces this conclusion.

The provision of mobile access, the exchange of data with business partners, and the use of the Internet in general depend on the extent to which private companies are aware of the existence and the benefits of electronic markets. In this respect, it is encouraging that most establishments in the survey (practically nine out of ten) already knew about trading communities as virtual places where they can not only buy and sell goods and services, but also exchange commercial information essential for decision-making (Table 9.12). Likewise, 50% of Mexican respondents reported participating in such communities as a buyer, a seller, or both, compared with only 36% of the global sample.

It is expected that manufacturing firms will increasingly conduct their business dealings through virtual markets, given that it is already

Table 9.12 *Extent of participation of business enterprises in Internet-based trading communities (percent)*

	Establishment size		*Sector*			*Total*	
	SME	*Large*	*Mfg.*	*Distrib.*	*Finance*	*Mexico*	*Global*
Have heard of the concept of an Internet marketplace	89	92	91	87	87	88	80
As a buyer only	20	23	6	28	29	20	7
As a seller only	7	12	6	7	16	7	12
As both a buyer and a seller	23	14	17	28	8	23	17

Source: CRITO GEC Survey, 2002

common for manufacturers to form groups that collectively buy inputs at convenient prices and conditions. Nonetheless, financial and distribution companies have participated in e-markets at higher levels, especially as buyers. Banks and insurance companies have used such marketplaces more intensely to sell their products and services, while distribution firms use them for both buying and selling.

Online sales by sector

While B2B transactions dominate total e-commerce at the national level, the survey data show that firms are equally likely to conduct either B2B or B2C e-commerce only (6%), while a larger share (18%) support both types (Table 9.13). The proportions are low for B2B only in comparison with the average for the global sample. In addition the proportions are low for the country as discussed earlier in this chapter. It appears that the difference between B2B and B2C e-commerce sales at the national level is driven by the volumes of transactions conducted, not by the number of firms doing one or the other.

Looking at sales volumes at the firm level, only 2% of consumer sales are conducted online versus 4% for business sales, or 10% versus 20% for those that actually conduct each type of sales online. This gap is significant but does not explain the national figures showing that 93% of e-commerce is B2B, except for the fact that these latter are based on revenue measures.

From a sectoral perspective, Table 9.13 confirms trends pointed out and observations made in previous sections. Distribution companies

Table 9.13 *Online sales*

	Establishment size		*Sector*			*Total*	
	SME	*Large*	*Mfg.*	*Distrib.*	*Finance*	*Mexico*	*Global*
Percent of firms conducting online sales							
B2B only	6	7	12	0	19	6	13
B2C only	6	3	5	7	1	6	7
Both B2B and B2C	18	21	6	27	14	18	15
Mean percent of total consumer sales conducted online (all establishments)	2	3	2	2	2	2	4
Mean percent of total business sales conducted online (all establishments)	4	4	3	5	8	4	4
Mean percent of total consumer sales conducted online (only those doing B2C sales online)	10	14	22	7	15	10	19
Mean percent of total business sales conducted online (only those doing B2B sales online)	20	16	21	19	29	20	15
Percent of websites that support online payment (only those doing online sales)	11	14	26	1	42	25	34

Source: CRITO GEC Survey, 2002

are the most actively engaged in the two modalities of e-commerce combined, and chiefly in B2C, given the predominance of retail over wholesale establishments in Mexico. The predominance of B2B over B2C sales in the case of financial firms, in turn, substantiates the fact that e-banking and other financial online services are provided primarily to other businesses more than to individual customers.

As expected, financial firms account for the highest proportion of establishments using websites to support online payments. A rather more unexpected result, given that distribution companies are supposed to have closer and more direct contact with customers, is that

Table 9.14 *Online services*

	Establishment size		*Sector*			*Total*	
	SME	*Large*	*Mfg.*	*Distrib.*	*Finance*	*Mexico*	*Global*
Type of online service							
B2B only	6	13	14	1	14	6	23
B2C only	5	23	13	1	14	6	13
both B2B and B2C	64	31	59	69	36	63	33
Mean percent of total consumer services conducted online	11	11	5	14	18	11	8
Mean percent of total business services conducted online	27	14	12	35	22	26	11

Source: CRITO GEC Survey, 2002

manufacturing establishments are next. Lastly, the fact that manufacturing companies account for the lowest proportion of online sales in the B2C and B2B modalities combined is in line with the finding that manufacturing is the sector showing the lowest proportion of firms using the Internet for doing business vis-à-vis distribution and finance.

Online services

The picture is different in the case of services provided online. The results summarized in Table 9.14 confirm the observation that business establishments in Mexico see the Internet as a tool for providing services much more than as a means for selling products. The proportion of services provided online to both consumers (B2C) and to other businesses (B2B) together (63%) is three-and-a-half times larger than in the case of online sales reported in Table 9.13 (18%). That proportion is almost twice that of the corresponding global sample (33%), which indicates that Mexico uses the Internet to provide services online twice as much as the countries in the global sample. By contrast, only 6% of Mexican firms provide either B2C or B2B services exclusively, compared with much larger percentages for the global sample. As in the case of online sales, the proportion of services provided online to consumers is less than half that of services provided to other businesses.

Table 9.15 *Online procurement*

	Establishment size		*Sector*			*Total*	
	SME	*Large*	*Mfg.*	*Distrib.*	*Finance*	*Mexico*	*Global*
Percent of establishments doing online purchasing	71	56	39	92	60	71	51
Mean percent of money spent for direct goods for production is ordered online (all establishments)	9	14	9	n. a.	n. a.	9	8
Mean percent of money spent on goods for resale is ordered online (all establishments)	19	8	n. a.	19	n. a.	19	7
Mean percent of money spent on supplies and equipment for doing business is ordered online (all establishments)	13	13	10	15	6	13	8

Source: CRITO GEC Survey, 2002

The conclusion that Mexico is not lagging in e-commerce is reinforced by the results presented in Table 9.15, which shows that Mexico has more respondents purchasing online than the global sample, and is conducting a higher volume of online purchases. In addition, SMEs are more likely to purchase online, and have a higher share of Internet purchases. This result suggests, prima facie, that there are proportionally more companies in Mexico that practice B2B e-commerce than in the other countries included in the study, which is not likely to be quite the case. Nevertheless, it does support the argument that e-commerce has extended more than revenue-based estimates convey.

Distribution appears as the sector where e-procurement is practiced most extensively, as could be expected, since wholesale establishments in particular are the ones that tend to use the Internet more regularly for purchasing their wares than manufacturing and financial firms. Conversely, manufacturing is the sector where online procurement shows the lowest proportion, which is not consistent with the fact that in practice it is the sector where procurement constitutes a central corporate function, far more than in finance and distribution.

In summary, Internet use in general and e-commerce in particular have spread over the Mexican economy to an overall limited extent, which is nonetheless not much different to that reached in more economically and technologically advanced countries. Moreover, the extent reached at the level of industry sectors and individual firms is much larger than that indicated by national estimates based on revenue measures.

Internet use is more common in the provision of services than in the sale of products. Here, too, the proportion reached in Mexico is twice that of the global sample. A similar case occurs with regard to online sales. This supports the idea that the Internet is evolving from a mere advertising tool into a new market weapon for competing with existing distribution channels.

Impacts of e-commerce

National impacts

As the foregoing discussion showed, e-commerce has spread into a significant number of companies in Mexico as a new way of doing business. This has induced important changes in the mindset of their executives and managers thanks to the possibilities offered by the Internet to expand their markets and business potential, and for making them more flexible, specialized, and efficient. As a result, some companies have extended their market reach while others have undertaken a thorough transformation of their production methods and organizational structures, thereby developing new and more efficient forms of both production and intermediation.

The above changes have taken place particularly in some of Mexico's largest corporations. For instance, Grupo Industrial Vitro, the country's top glass maker and one of its largest industrial conglomerates, signed an agreement with IBM in 2001 to reshape much of the company's business culture and operating processes through greater utilization of Internet applications and a redefinition of its e-business strategy. The initiative included the implementation of an entire e-procurement strategy with the aim of making Vitro "the first company in Latin America capable of sourcing 80% of its raw materials through the Internet" (Vitro, 2001).

Other companies are undertaking similar initiatives. Cemex, Mexico's top cement maker and another of its largest, multinational industrial conglomerates, launched its own e-business strategy in September 2000. To this end, Cemex created CxNetworks as a subsidiary responsible for developing an e-enabling strategy for the entire firm to extend its reach into marketplaces valuable for its core business (Cemex, 2000).

Impacts at the firm and industry levels

Looking at individual firms, the GEC Survey confirms that e-commerce has left a significant imprint on those that have adopted it as a new form of business practice. In general, there are grounds to assert that the Internet exerts a significant and positive influence on the companies that use it as a new tool for conducting business. The influence takes the form of both improved productivity and an enhanced flexibility to respond to demand signals, all this reflected in the expansion of sales and revenue volumes (Table 9.16).

The impacts have consisted of improvements in crucial company functions such as customer service, internal business processes, coordination with suppliers, and the companies' competitive position, in decreasing order. These impacts have been stronger in Mexico than among the global sample, which infers that the effects of e-commerce have been assimilated to a deeper extent in businesses operating in Mexico than in other countries in the survey.

The fact that one of the greatest impacts has been on the improvement of internal processes suggests that the Internet is being used not only as a marginal tool for making commercial deals but also as an internal instrument for upgrading corporate functions and processes. The improvement of coordination with suppliers ranks next, which indicates that use of the Internet has resulted in the improvement of the companies' communication mechanisms with such critical business partners as their suppliers.

It is relevant to point out that the changes have occurred largely irrespective of size in the case of the four areas where the impact of e-commerce has been strongest. This is at odds with the conclusion that the smaller the company, the more likely it is for new technologies and business models to induce changes in the organizational procedures and structures. The cases of Cemex and Vitro demonstrate that the impacts

Table 9.16 *Impacts of doing business online*

	Establishment size		*Sector*			*Total*	
	SME	*Large*	*Mfg.*	*Distrib.*	*Finance*	*Mexico*	*Global*
Internal processes more efficient	54	51	33	68	34	54	34
Staff productivity increased	37	45	37	37	40	38	27
Sales increased	37	14	26	43	34	36	21
Sales area widened	26	21	17	31	20	25	31
Customer service improved	55	55	43	62	60	55	35
International sales increased	20	16	31	13	20	20	20
Procurement costs decreased	20	29	22	19	20	20	18
Inventory costs decreased	14	22	16	13	7	14	14
Coordination with suppliers improved	51	55	34	62	40	51	30
Competitive position improved	45	40	38	50	40	45	30

Source: CRITO GEC Survey, 2002

of e-commerce can in effect be quite strong and comprehensive in large conglomerates.

Almost half of the surveyed establishments report that doing business online has resulted in an improvement in their competitive position, suggesting that their structures, processes, and managerial capabilities have improved due to e-commerce practices. The fact that this has occurred with more intensity than in other economies of the global sample endorses the observation made above, that the impacts of e-commerce have gone deeper in Mexico than in other GEC economies. This result can also be interpreted as revealing that e-commerce is not only making it possible for companies to expand markets and improve specific corporate functions but is also leading them to attain a more transcendental goal of competitive advantage more fully than in the global sample.

The other areas where the effects of e-commerce have been significant are in relation to the number of distribution channels and competitors, including the intensity of the competition faced by the companies interviewed in the survey (Table 9.17).

Table 9.17 *Changes in firms' environment since using the Internet*

Percent indicating . . .	Establishment size		Sector			Total	
	SME	*Large*	*Mfg.*	*Distrib.*	*Finance*	*Mexico*	*Global*
Number of distribution channels							
Increased	56	52	44	62	66	56	40
No change	37	43	56	25	34	37	56
Decreased	8	5	1	12	0	8	4
Number of suppliers							
Increased	51	58	42	56	57	51	30
No change	45	37	48	44	36	45	64
Decreased	4	5	10	0	7	4	6
Number of competitors							
Increased	38	36	29	44	33	38	28
No change	56	57	65	50	53	56	67
Decreased	6	7	6	6	13	6	5
Intensity of competition							
Increased	57	43	40	68	41	56	42
No change	39	53	60	26	40	39	54
Decreased	5	3	0	6	19	4	4

Source: CRITO GEC Survey, 2002

The use of the Internet for commercial purposes in Mexico has led, above all, to the intensification of competitive pressures for companies and to an increase in the number of distribution channels, in both instances much more than in the ten countries in the GEC Survey taken as a whole. This confirms the notion that the Internet generally leads to a reduction of entry barriers, thus opening the way for new competitors to enter existing and new markets, as it provides access to information on existing products and services, as well as to information on producers and providers on a global scale.

In sum, the impacts of e-commerce in Mexico have been significant in themselves and in reference to the corresponding figures in the other countries of the global sample. This means that this new way of doing business is delivering the expected benefits, such as improving key company functions like customer service, internal business processes, coordination with suppliers, as well as the companies' entire competitive position. Therefore, in Mexico, these results show that the Internet is fulfilling its purpose of providing business enterprises with access to information on products and markets, and that of reducing entry barriers for new competitors in all markets. Nevertheless, the results also show that doing business online can expose firms to greater competitive pressure, which acts as a positive incentive for them to improve on efficiency, productivity, and productive capabilities.

Conclusion

The survey results and other data discussed in this chapter have shown that e-commerce has spread into a sizable and growing number of companies of all sizes across Mexico's major industry sectors. Moreover, the evidence supports the assertion that the process has spread more extensively than that expressed by conventional estimates based on revenue measures, as indicated by estimates made by the OECD and Mexico's premier IT market research firm. These results thus come to define the substance and direction of Mexico's experience with e-commerce as the case of a country that is not a leader, but also not quite the laggard it was once perceived to be.

This is further supported by the fact that the extent and nature of diffusion as well as the impacts of e-commerce have been similar to and even greater in several key respects than in other more advanced economies, including, for instance:

- the extent of systems integration
- the number of PCs per employee
- the use of the Internet for coordinating with suppliers and customers and for procuring inputs
- the provision of services online
- the deployment and operation of EDI networks
- the volume of sales via the web conducted by companies doing B2B
- the improvement of coordination with business partners
- the improvement in businesses' competitiveness, efficiency, and productivity.

Another major result is that finance is the most advanced sector in e-commerce adoption and development in Mexico vis-à-vis distribution and manufacturing. Financial firms lead in the integration of Internet applications with internal information systems, in information system spending, in the use of the Internet for expanding markets, and in the use of websites to support online payments. They are also the most globalized companies in Mexico, and the ones that make the highest use of Internet-based technologies like email and extranet. Although no clear, definite pattern was found, distribution companies tend to rank next in most areas of e-commerce adoption and use, while manufacturing establishments tend to rank third.

In turn, although there is not a regular pattern across all the sectors and all the aspects of e-commerce diffusion and impacts, it is clear that the size of establishments matters in most of those respects. Exceptions include the proportion of IS budgets spent on web-based technologies, where size makes no significant difference. The other exception concerns the use of e-commerce technologies where it makes a mixed difference. The main finding, though, is that SMEs have great potential for the adoption and practice of e-commerce. This is based on the fact that they outperform large companies in many important respects, including that they:

- invest more in ICTs and information systems
- are twice as likely to use the Internet to probe into new markets
- participate more as both buyers and sellers
- use the Internet more to purchase inputs and equipment
- have twice the number of PCs per employee
- spend more on IT
- use the Internet more for advertising, marketing, and buying online than large firms do.

Moreover, SMEs have felt greater impacts from e-commerce in the intensity of competition and the number of competitors, suggesting that going online has exposed these smaller firms to new competitive forces. The prospects for SMEs to use the Internet may further increase as new services and technologies become available. For instance, application service providers offer access to Internet-based business applications at a low cost, and blogs are proving to be a powerful, simple, and cheap tool for marketing and other business functions that are already in use by a significant proportion of SMEs in the United States. It would be sound, therefore, to make small and micro businesses a top-priority target of government policies and private-sector campaigns, given the immense potential for e-commerce growth in what is overwhelmingly the largest segment of Mexico's company population.

What is required, though, is for both SMEs and larger businesses to fully realize that the benefits of using the Internet cannot be reaped by just adopting it as a new, marginal tool, but rather by using it fully to tap the large business development potential it offers. They also have to realize that it is not enough to set up a website and wait for profits and success to come along; instead it will be necessary for them to undertake a thorough transformation of their organizational structures and business outlook and culture. It is encouraging that the results discussed in this chapter show that progress has been made in these directions.

The adoption of e-commerce solutions and strategies is in fact having a substantial impact on both the corporate structure and the levels of efficiency and productivity of some of Mexico's top industrial conglomerates. This is not only projecting a strong demonstration effect over the rest of the country's business population, but also contributing to induce smaller suppliers and business partners to follow suit as a condition for keeping their place in the value chain. As observed above, SMEs are investing more in information systems and are thus progressing rapidly in the adoption of Internet-based business solutions. Pointing in the same direction is the fact that the highest impacts of e-commerce practices have been in the improvement of the companies' competitive position and in the efficiency of their internal processes, which implies that the Internet has allowed them to create unique advantages in products, content, and processes.

Looking to the future, the development and eventual maturation of e-commerce will require broadening conventional views about what this expression means, with an eye to widening the concept and thinking of e-business instead. Only in this way will companies of all sizes take all the required steps to effectively transform their structures, strategies, and organizational practices, and go beyond the limited tactic of simply setting up a website and buying inputs online.

In the same way, it will require the implementation of aggressive promotion and information campaigns by both the public and the private sectors about the benefits of Internet use. They will have to make clear to businesses of all sizes that although it is nothing more than a technology, the Internet can become a powerful instrument that will enable them to improve their entire corporate structure, resources, and organizational practices, and make them more competitive and able to generate value more efficiently. As Porter (2001: 6) put it, "The creation of true economic value once again becomes the final arbiter of business success."

Finally, and drawing further on Porter (2001), it can be said that the Internet is still a source of advantage in Mexico, since only a relatively limited number of companies use it so far, although this advantage will tend to disappear as more businesses embrace the technology. But this advantage should be made clear so that managers and entrepreneurs become aware of the benefits of adoption, especially for those who get in early.

References

Asociación Mexicana de Estándares para el Comercio Electrónico (AMECE) (2001). Telefonía Celular para el Comercio Electrónico en México, June 21, from www.amece.com.mx/emexico

Cemex (2000). Cemex Launches E-business Strategy. Press release, September 13, from www.cemex.com

Chacón, L. (2004). Aumentan en México Usuarios de Internet. *Mural*, September 30.

Comisión Federal de Telecomunicaciones (COFETEL) (2003). Área Económica, Estadísticas, from www.cofetel.gob.mx

El Financiero (2004a). Revisar el Modelo, PUNTO Y APARTE. *El Financiero en linea*, October 19, from www.elfinanciero.com.mx

El Financiero (2004b).Corta Visión de Pymes para hacer Negocios, *El Financiero en linea*, June 10, from www.elfinanciero.com.mx

Flores, E. (2002). Verdadera Estrategia. *Empresa-E*, February–March, 42–44.

Instituto Nacional de Estadística Geografía e Informática (INEGI) (2000). *Censos Económicos 1999. Resumen.* Aguascalientes, Ags., from www.inegi.gob.mx

Instituto Nacional de Estadística Geografía e Informática (INEGI) (2002a). *Banco de Información Económica.* Aguascalientes, Ags., from www.inegi.gob.mx

Instituto Nacional de Estadística Geografía e Informática (INEGI) (2002b). *Sistema de Cuentas Nacionales.* Aguascalientes, Ags., from www.inegi.gob.mx

International Data Corporation (IDC) (2003a). *Internet Commerce Market Model v.8.3.* Framingham, MA.

International Data Corporation (IDC) (2003b). *EIM-Country View.* Framingham, MA.

International Planning and Research Corporation (IPR) (2003). *Eighth Annual Business Software Alliance (BSA) Global Software Piracy Study, Trends in Software Piracy 1994–2002*. Washington, D.C.: Business Software Alliance.

International Telecommunication Union (ITU) (2004). *World Telecommunication Indicators Database* (8th Ed.). Geneva, Switzerland.

Palacios, J. J. (2003). The Development of E-Commerce in Mexico: A Business-led Passing Boom or a Step toward the Emergence of a Digital Economy? *The Information Society*, 19(1), 69–79.

Palacios, J. J. & Kraemer, K. L. (2003). Globalization and E-Commerce IV: Environment and Policy in Mexico. *Communications of the Association for Information Systems*, 10(5), 129–185.

Porter, M. E. (2001). Strategy and the Internet. *HBR OnPoint*, Product number 6358. *Harvard Business Review*, March.

Ramírez, A. (2003). Presente Duro, Futuro Incierto. *Empresa-e*, no. 12 (December 2002–January 2003), 50–55.

Sato, S., Hawkins, J., & Berentsen, A. (2001). E-Finance: Recent Developments and Policy Implications. In S. Cohen and J. Zysman (Eds.), *Tracking a Transformation: E-Commerce and the Terms of Competition in Industries*, 64–91.

Select (2002). 15.9% de los Cibernautas Mexicanos han Comprado en la Red. *Tecnología y Negocios*, no. 85, December.

Select (2003). 70% de la MPyME aún sin tecnificar, *Tecnología y Negocios*, no. 91, April.

Select (2004). Penetración de Internet por Tamaño de Empresa. Internal report, October.

Select-IDC (2000). 50 Percent de las Oportunidades de Negocios con el Usuario Final se Ubican Fuera del Distrito Federal, Guadalajara y Monterrey. *Tecnología y Negocios*, no. 29, October 23.

Torres Chávez, L. (2000). Nivel de Automatización en las Empresas. *Negocios y Web*, no. 10, January 31.

Vargas, A. (2004). Comercio Electrónico Real. *El Economista*, August.

Vitro (2001). Vitro Signs a Framework Agreement with IBM to Enhance Internet Initiative. Press release, February 11, from www.vitro.com.mx

World Bank (2004). *WDI Online*. From http://publications.worldbank.ord/WDI/

10 *Global convergence and local divergence in e-commerce: cross-country analyses*

KEVIN ZHU, SEAN XU,
KENNETH L. KRAEMER, AND
JASON DEDRICK

Introduction

The Internet and e-commerce are recent examples of ongoing information technology innovations credited with driving the productivity revival of the past decade. Established firms such as Dell, Cisco, General Electric, IBM, and Wal-Mart, along with firms "born on the Internet," such as Amazon and eBay, have shown the potential of IT and e-commerce to enhance customer services, streamline internal operations, and improve B2B coordination. Today, Internet use is almost universal among firms in the industrialized countries, and is growing rapidly in the developing world as well. Thus, there is global convergence in the continuing trend toward e-commerce diffusion.

Yet, technology diffusion is rarely a smooth and linear process. Many firms fail to achieve deep usage beyond initial adoption. Prior studies show that an e-commerce innovation must be integrated into a firm's value chain before it can generate significant business value. E-commerce integration encompasses using the Internet for selling, buying, and coordinating both internal and external business processes. We would expect firms that are more advanced – that integrate the Internet most extensively – would reap the greatest benefits. And because firms in developed and developing countries may be at different stages of the diffusion process, we would expect there to be divergence in the relative importance of the factors that influence each stage.

Indeed, as with the earlier chapters in this book, we find that there is both global convergence and local divergence in e-commerce diffusion. Firms in developed countries have reached a more advanced stage than those in developing countries. There are common factors that influence firms in all countries, such as technological capabilities, competition, trading partner readiness, and regulatory environment.

However, the relative importance of these factors differs depending on the firm's stage of development and its national environment. Developing countries are still in the process of achieving widespread adoption of Internet technologies and creating the regulatory environment to support e-commerce. Developed countries have passed that stage and are involved in expanding the breadth and depth of their online activities, and integrating their e-commerce technologies internally and with their trading partners. Not surprisingly, firms in developed countries generally report greater impacts on their performance as a result of using the Internet for business.

Focus of this chapter

This chapter presents findings from the GEC project that specifically address the relationships among e-commerce adoption, use, and impacts, and the various factors that influence each of these stages of the diffusion process. The previous chapters have analyzed e-commerce diffusion in individual countries. In this chapter, we conduct cross-country analyses to examine the global diffusion of e-commerce. Three major benefits come from such cross-country analyses. First, using data from multiple countries allows us to identify common features of e-commerce diffusion in the global environment. As the Internet supports global connectivity, it is important to understand the *convergence*, i.e., common drivers and effects in the global diffusion of e-commerce, as well as the *country divergence* discussed in previous chapters.

Second, despite global convergence at the firm level, cross-country differences may still exist in e-commerce diffusion. As we said in Chapter 1, the GEC Survey covers both developed and developing countries. Relationships identified in the context of mature economies need to be re-examined in the context of developing countries, because these countries may have different economic and regulatory environments. Yet, most of the existing research on e-commerce has been focused on a single country, usually the United States. It is important to examine whether or not innovation theories can be generalized and empirical findings are applicable in different economic contexts. To fill this gap, this chapter analyzes e-commerce diffusion in different countries, which might represent different stages of e-commerce evolution.

Third, pooling data from multiple countries increases the size of the sample used for data analyses. The large sample enables analyses that are statistically more rigorous. These statistical analyses complement the qualitative and descriptive analyses performed in the previous chapters. We tease out scientific findings beyond the nuances and results based on descriptive statistics.

In addition to the cross-country analyses, this chapter develops a process-oriented model to investigate e-commerce diffusion at the firm level. Innovation diffusion is not limited to one-shot adoption decisions. Instead, the *process* of innovation diffusion consists of multiple stages from a firm's adoption to its use and finally to impacts on firm performance (Zhu et al., 2006). Drawing upon the innovation diffusion literature (Rogers, 1995; also see Fichman, 2000 for a review), we define e-commerce diffusion in a firm as a process from the firm's initial adoption of e-commerce to full-scale use when e-commerce becomes an integral part of the value chain activities. We go further still to look also at the impacts of e-commerce on the firm's performance. Thus, by providing empirical evidence of e-commerce adoption, use, and impacts, we advance understanding of the whole process of e-commerce diffusion. This is different from prior studies that have treated these stages separately.

Further, as discussed in Chapter 1, one of the major goals of the GEC project is to identify drivers for and barriers to e-commerce diffusion (see Figure 1.1). Along this line, the current chapter analyzes specific drivers and barriers that firms confront in the process of e-commerce diffusion. Furthermore, our process orientation brings forth an interesting question: Is the role of a driver or barrier the same throughout the diffusion process? Or, can a factor act as a driver at an earlier stage but become a barrier later? For instance, industry competition has long been considered as a factor driving innovation adoption (Kamien & Schwartz, 1982). Yet the influence of competition at post-adoption stages (use and impacts) remains an under-researched topic. Similarly, large firms are more likely to adopt a new technology (Rogers, 1995), but are they more likely to use the technology more extensively and create value from its use? Our process-oriented model is designed to tackle these kinds of questions.

Specifically, three questions frame the research reported in this chapter:

1. What factors (drivers and barriers) affect e-commerce diffusion in firms?
2. How do their effects differ in different environments across developed and developing countries?
3. How do their effects vary at different stages of e-commerce diffusion (adoption, use, and impacts)?

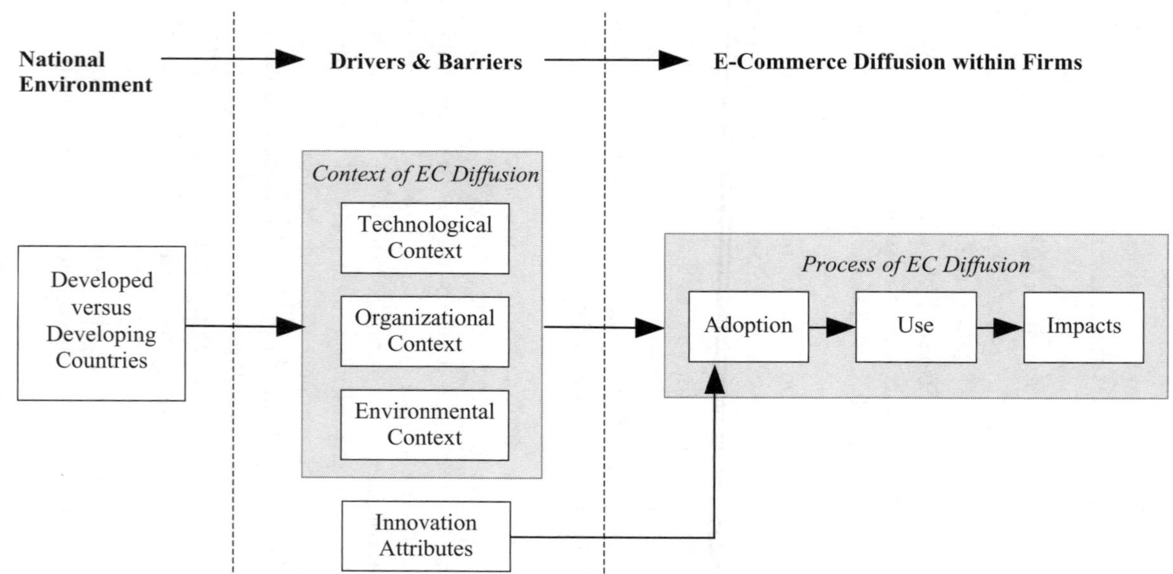

Figure 10.1 Conceptual model

To better understand these questions, we develop a conceptual model (Figure 10.1) based on synthesis of several perspectives in the innovation literature. The next section presents this model. Then, we discuss specific findings from three streams of our own research. Finally, we summarize major conclusions based on these findings.

Theory and conceptual model

Theory

Viewing e-commerce as a technological innovation, we draw upon multiple theories in the innovation literature to study the three research questions identified above. First, based on the innovation adoption and use literature, we propose a three-stage model for the process of e-commerce diffusion. Then, we integrate two theoretical views – the theory of diffusion of innovations (Rogers, 1995) and the technology–organization–environment framework (Tornatzky & Fleischer, 1990) – to identify factors that influence the three-stage diffusion model.

The process of e-commerce diffusion

E-commerce diffusion starts with adoption. We define e-commerce adoption as making the decision to use the Internet for conducting or supporting value chain activities (i.e., allocating resources and physically acquiring the technology). This stage is a necessary step toward technology usage.

Yet, adoption does not always lead to widespread use of the technology within the enterprise. After a new information technology innovation is adopted, it needs to be accepted, adapted, routinized, and institutionalized into the organization (Zhu et al., 2006). Hence, adoption and use are two distinct stages. We define e-commerce use as the stage where e-commerce is widely used as an integral part of the firm's value chain activities.

Finally, we are interested in the consequences of e-commerce use, i.e., its performance impacts. We define e-commerce impacts as the extent to which a firm improves its performance in value chain activities by using e-commerce. We expect a significant relationship between innovation use and performance impacts, because technology must become a routinized element of a firm's value chain before it can exhibit any significant business value.

Theory of diffusion of innovations

According to the theory of diffusion of innovations (DOI), technological innovations possess attributes, and these attributes have systematic effects on the diffusion of the innovations. Rogers (1995) highlighted five such attributes:

1. *Relative advantage*, the degree to which an innovation can help improve organizational performance.
2. *Compatibility*, the degree to which an innovation is consistent with a potential adopter's current practices, existing technologies, and value systems.
3. *Complexity*, the degree to which an innovation is difficult to implement and use.
4. *Observability*, the degree to which the results of an innovation are observable.
5. *Trialability*, the degree to which an innovation may be experimented with before adoption.

Among these, relative advantage and compatibility, as well as the cost of deploying an innovation, were found to be the most frequently identified influential factors in the innovation literature (Tornatzky & Klein, 1982).

Yet, a model based solely on the DOI theory is unlikely to be a strong model for predicting diffusion of complex information systems at the firm level. Rogers's (1995) theory was initially developed for studying diffusion of innovations among individual members in the population. Hence, additional variables representing specific diffusion contexts should be incorporated if the phenomenon of interest is complex technological innovations at the organizational level (Zhu et al., 2005). Because we are interested in the whole process of diffusion of complex IT innovations (e-commerce), the DOI theory needs to be enriched by other theoretical views.

The technology–organization–environment framework

Focused on general technological innovations, the technology–organization–environment (TOE) framework posits three aspects of a firm's context that influence the process by which it adopts, implements, and uses a technological innovation:

1. *Technological context* describes the existing technologies in use and relevant technical skills.

2. *Organizational context* typically refers to organizational attributes such as size and scope.
3. *Environmental context* is the external arena in which the firm conducts its business – competitors, trading partners, and the government (Tornatzky & Fleischer, 1990; Zhu et al., 2006).

We use the TOE framework because it addresses what has been generally neglected in the DOI theory – specific technological and environmental circumstances of an organization. Internet technologies can be used in a variety of value chain processes, and their use often requires changes to existing IT systems and integration of those systems with the new Internet-based infrastructure. E-commerce diffusion also may be affected by organizational variables such as the size and scope of the firm. Moreover, the external environment, such as trading partners, competitors, and policy context, may also affect e-commerce diffusion. Hence, we expect the three contexts proposed in this framework to be significant factors.

Conceptual model

Based on the above theoretical views, we develop a conceptual model (Figure 10.1) that is consistent with the framework proposed in Chapter 1 (see Figure 1.1). According to that framework, e-commerce diffusion is affected by a set of drivers and barriers whose existence and magnitude may depend on the national environment. In the same vein, the conceptual model developed in this chapter includes the following: the national environment in developed versus developing countries; drivers and barriers influencing e-commerce diffusion by firms; and e-commerce diffusion within firms.

The model in Figure 10.1 has its unique features, though. First, based on the process orientation, this model identifies three stages of e-commerce diffusion – adoption, use, and impacts – as dependent variables.

Second, the model draws upon the two theoretical views, DOI and TOE, to identify drivers and barriers for e-commerce diffusion. The model first posits a set of e-commerce innovation attributes as independent variables, which represent the characteristics of e-commerce as a technological innovation. These attributes may be significant factors at the adoption stage; but, to understand firm-level variations at the post-adoption stages (use and impacts), we incorporate technological,

Table 10.1 *Conceptual model*

Concepts	*Variables*
1. E-commerce diffusion	
Adoption	Adoption decisions
Use	Breadth, volume of use
Impacts	Impacts on sales, internal operations, and coordination
2. Drivers and barriers	
Technological context	Technology readiness, front-end functionality, back-end integration
Organizational context	Firm size, global scope
Environmental context	Competition intensity, trading partner readiness, consumer readiness, regulatory environment
Innovation attributes	Relative advantage, compatibility, adoption costs, security concern
3. National environment	
Country-level factors	IT investment/GDP, GDP per capita, e-commerce volume/GDP

organizational, and environmental contexts. These three dimensions capture firm-specific effects in the e-commerce diffusion process.

Third, the model postulates that the national environment will shape the context in which firms operate, and that the impacts of various drivers and barriers may be different in developed versus developing countries. Together, these concepts (the process of e-commerce diffusion, the context of e-commerce diffusion, e-commerce innovation attributes, and the national environment) form a coherent model for studying the diffusion and impacts of e-commerce by firms in multiple countries.

Based on this model, we next propose specific variables affecting the diffusion process. We list these variables in Table 10.1 and discuss them in detail below.

The process of e-commerce diffusion

We define e-commerce adoption as whether or not a firm has made the decision to use the Internet to conduct business. We define use as the extent to which the Internet is actually deployed, measured by the breadth and volume of use. Breadth refers to the diffusion of e-commerce across value chain activities, which include marketing, sales, customer service, procurement, information exchange, and coordination with suppliers or business partners. Volume refers to the percentage of each of these value chain activities that is conducted on the Internet. Finally, we study how a firm uses e-commerce to improve productivity and internal efficiency, reduce operational and inventory costs, improve coordination with suppliers, and increase customer service quality. We thus define e-commerce impacts as a multidimensional variable to describe performance improvements related to Internet use, including impacts on sales, internal operations, and coordination with suppliers and partners.

Innovation attributes

To identify specific variables for e-commerce innovation attributes, we consider the salient features of e-commerce. To begin with, conducting e-commerce requires firms to commit substantial financial resources. Managers understand these costs, and their assessments of the costs and the potential payoff to e-commerce spending may have significant influence on e-commerce diffusion (Zhu et al., 2005).

Second, e-commerce needs to be integrated with core business processes, as it supports a variety of mainstream business activities. In this regard, e-commerce is different from EDI, which mainly supports the exchange of structured transaction documents. Internet-based e-commerce can enable customer personalization, improve after-sales services, and enhance business-to-business coordination, such as sharing demand forecasts, coordinating production plans, and facilitating joint product design (Zhu & Kraemer, 2002). Hence, e-commerce has the potential to show both strategic and operational benefits, both of which should be considered when evaluating its relative advantage.

Third, as e-commerce represents new approaches to managing value chain activities, not all firms may deem it compatible with their technology base, current business processes, distribution channels, and corporate culture. To overcome the possible incompatibility, senior management, business executives, and IS managers are collectively responsible for shaping e-commerce initiatives and organizational features. The necessary interactions among these managers are more intensive compared with previous technologies. This suggests that the degree to which e-commerce is compatible with existing technologies and practices will be a significant factor affecting firms' adoption decisions.

Finally, firms may have significant concerns about e-commerce security. Internet technologies are based on open data standards (e.g. XML). Hence, firms involved in Internet-based e-commerce generally have less control over data standards and data access, compared with less open systems such as EDI. Thus, firms and customers would have greater concerns about unauthorized access to data, which jeopardizes information security and privacy. Further, e-commerce is integrated in value chain activities, and thus involves transferring funds and exchanging critical corporate data, increasing the importance of security. In addition, e-commerce is still relatively new, so e-commerce users face a less mature institutional framework regarding contracts, financial transactions, and privacy protection (Gibbs et al., 2003).

Based on the above considerations, we propose to study relative advantage, compatibility, adoption costs, and security concerns as e-commerce innovation attributes. We define these variables as follows:

- Relative advantage refers to the potential benefits of e-commerce, including both strategic benefits and operational benefits.
- Compatibility refers to the degree to which e-commerce is compatible with a firm's business processes, distribution channel, corporate culture, and value system.
- Adoption costs refer to the costs of implementing necessary technologies and firms' efforts devoted to organizational restructuring and process reengineering.
- Security concerns refer to the degree to which the Internet platform is deemed insecure for exchanging data and conducting online transactions.

The context of e-commerce diffusion

We identified four contextual variables that were consistently found by prior studies to affect IT diffusion. Within the technological context, technology readiness (infrastructure, relevant systems, and technical skills) is an important factor for the adoption and use of IT innovations. We conceptualize technology readiness as consisting of technology infrastructure and IT human resources. Technology infrastructure refers to existing technologies that enable Internet-related businesses, and IT human resources refer to IT professionals possessing the knowledge and skills to implement Internet-related applications.

Within the organizational context, we identify two organizational features – firm size and scope. Theories about IT and organizational attributes highlight the role of these two variables in IT diffusion. Hence, we place firm size and global scope within the organizational context. Firm size is defined as the total number of employees in a firm. Global scope is defined as the geographical extent of a firm's operations in the global market. This definition of scope is consistent with the international perspective of our research and our emphasis on globalization of e-commerce.

Within the environmental context, we include competition intensity, which is defined as the degree to which a firm is affected by competitors in the same industry. This variable has consistent empirical support from the diffusion literature (Zhu & Kraemer, 2005). Besides these variables, we next consider what other factors should be incorporated to reflect the unique features of e-commerce.

As a technological innovation, e-commerce leverages the characteristics of Internet technologies – open standards (e.g., TCP/IP, XML) and public network (the Internet). In this chapter, we investigate e-commerce functionalities that make use of these characteristics for conducting value chain activities. We classify these e-commerce functionalities into two types: front-end functionality provides product information to consumers on the Internet, facilitates transaction processing, and enables customization and personalization; back-end integration connects web-based applications with back-office databases and facilitates information exchange with suppliers.[1]

These characteristics of the Internet have another implication. The Internet supports global connectivity and its open standards make information exchange easier. This is different from EDI, which is based on private networks and uses less open data standards. The trading partner base of EDI is typically limited to large firms, while e-commerce can be used by firms with more limited financial and IT resources. Certain XML-based standards also enable indexing and searching unknown trading partners. E-commerce has the potential to connect previously separated market segments and help firms reach new trading partners who have the capability to do business online. We thus incorporate trading partner readiness as an environmental factor, which is defined as the degree to which trading partners have systems in place for transactions on the Internet.

[1] Because back-end integration facilitates the integration of individual technologies (web applications, software, databases, etc.), this chapter uses the two terms – "back-end integration" and "technology integration" – interchangeably.

Similarly, the potential of e-commerce to expand the current consumer segment is substantial. To fully realize this potential, it is necessary for consumers to be willing and ready to purchase on the Internet (Zhu et al., 2003). We define consumer readiness as a combination of consumer willingness and Internet penetration. Consumer willingness reflects the extent to which consumers engage in online shopping; Internet penetration measures the diffusion of PCs and the Internet in the population. Consumer readiness is an important factor because it reflects the potential market volume, and thereby determines the extent to which e-commerce adoption can be translated into profits.

Finally, the open-standard nature of the Internet brings unique issues regarding business law, security, credit card use, and online transactions between parties that have no prior relationship, which in turn puts substantial demands on the legal and regulatory system (Shih et al., 2005). In addition, governments can stimulate Internet use both directly (by requiring it for government procurement) and indirectly by not taxing Internet sales as a stimulus for its use (Gibbs et al., 2003). Thus, regulatory environment is another critical factor that should be examined within the environmental context.

In summary, reviewing the existing literature suggests four variables with consistent support – technology readiness, firm size, global scope, and competition intensity. Considering the salient features of e-commerce leads us to add five additional variables – front-end functionality, back-end integration, trading partner readiness, consumer readiness, and regulatory environment. Together these nine variables capture the technological, organization, and environmental context wherein e-commerce diffuses.

Cross-country effects: developed vs. developing countries

Extending the environmental context of the TOE framework, we want to understand cross-country differences regarding e-commerce adoption, use, and impacts. Developed and developing countries differ in terms of the level of IT investment, the degree of IT diffusion, and the economic return to technologies. Moreover, the extent of technology usage and performance impacts depends on a variety of economic, social, and political factors, including income, education, technology policies, cultural norms, and access to formal and informal communication networks. In the case of e-commerce, the Asia-Pacific region,

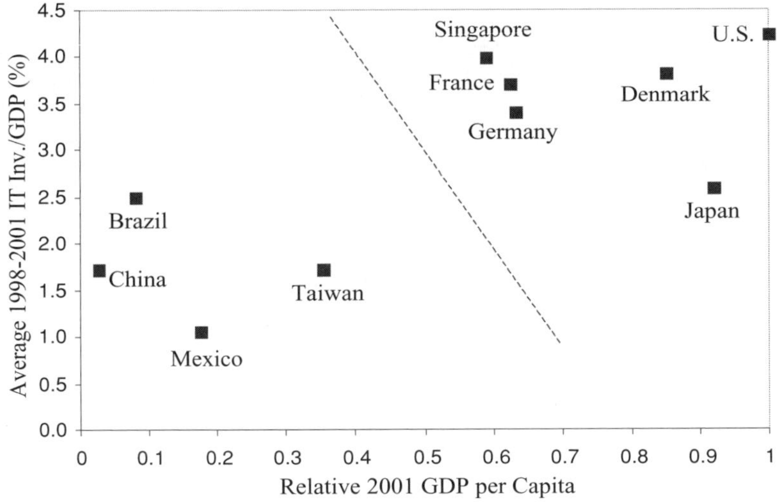

Figure 10.2 Developed vs. developing economies
Source: CRITO GEC secondary database

Latin America, and Eastern Europe have been experiencing rapid e-commerce adoption but very low volumes of transactions, while North America and Western Europe account for the vast majority of world-wide e-commerce transactions. In particular, e-commerce has evolved into deeper stages for information sharing, revenue generation, supply chain coordination, and business process optimization in developed countries. Developing countries also face significant barriers to e-commerce diffusion – especially less developed IT infrastructure and less mature institutional frameworks (Xu et al., 2004). Based on these considerations, we expect variables identified above to have different effects, moderated by economic environments.

Chapter 1 analyzed the economic environments using two variables: e-commerce sales as a percentage of GDP, and GDP per capita. In this chapter, we add another variable – the national IT investment as a percentage of GDP. Figure 10.2 shows the scatter plot of this variable against GDP per capita for the ten economies in our study. As shown in the scatter plot, the countries included in the GEC Survey can be categorized into two groups: (1) developed economies (Denmark, France, Germany, Japan, Singapore, and the USA), and (2) developing economies (Brazil, China, Mexico, and Taiwan). As shown later,

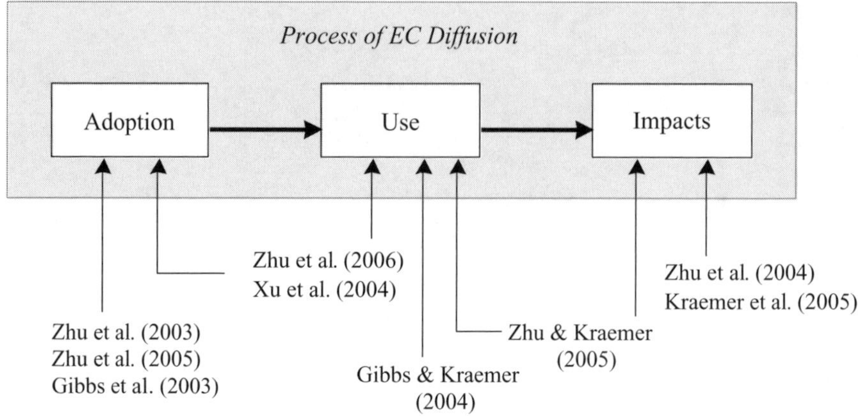

Figure 10.3 Research of e-commerce diffusion

we test the process of e-commerce diffusion and the associated drivers and barriers in the two groups. The cross-country analyses show different effects of the same factors between developed and developing economies. In the next section, we discuss in detail the cross-country differences.

Findings

To test the conceptual model for e-commerce diffusion as proposed in Figure 10.1, primary data collected via the GEC Survey and secondary data from the ECATT and eBusiness Watch studies (see Appendix I) were analyzed (for detailed descriptions of these data sources, please see Chapter 1). Studies reported in this chapter fall into three streams of research, categorized by stages of the e-commerce diffusion process. These include: (1) research of e-commerce adoption; (2) research of the process from adoption to use; and (3) research of the process from use to impacts. Together these three streams of research investigate the whole process of e-commerce diffusion. Given the different foci, these three streams have different dependent variables. Figure 10.3 illustrates these studies framed by the three-stage diffusion model. Table 10.2 summarizes major findings of these studies, which are discussed in detail next.

Table 10.2 ***Research on e-commerce diffusion***

Study	Research methodology	Key findings
		Research stream I: e-commerce adoption
Zhu et al. (2003)	• ECaTT survey • Eight European countries • Manufacturing, retail/wholesale, financial services • Logic regression	E-commerce adoption is significantly affected by contextual factors (technological, organizational, and environmental). In countries with high e-commerce intensity, e-commerce is no longer a phenomenon dominated by large firms, and the readiness of consumers (for online purchasing) and the readiness of trading partners (for B2B online transactions) becomes a less significant factor.
Zhu et al. (2005)	• eWatch survey • Eight European countries • Manufacturing, retail/wholesale, financial services • Logic regression	Effects of TOE factors on e-commerce adoption are confirmed. Further, e-commerce adoption is affected by innovation attributes of e-commerce (relative advantage, compatibility, adoption costs, and security concerns). Among the four innovation attributes, compatibility turns out to be the strongest factor, and security concerns represent a unique feature of e-commerce. Overall, this study suggests that e-commerce adoption by firms is better understood by the *combination* of innovation attributes and adoption contexts.
Gibbs et al. (2003)	• GEC Survey • Ten countries in the GEC Survey • Manufacturing, retail/wholesale, financial services • Multiple case studies	Specific factors shaping B2B e-commerce and B2C e-commerce vary considerably. B2B e-commerce seems to be driven by global forces whereas B2C e-commerce seems to be more of a local phenomenon. In terms of policy, the case studies suggest that enabling policies such as trade and telecoms liberalization are likely to have the biggest impact on e-commerce diffusion.

(*cont.*)

Table 10.2 (*cont.*)

Study	Research methodology	Key findings
	Research stream II: from e-commerce adoption to use	
Zhu et al. (2006)	• GEC Survey • Ten countries in the GEC Survey • Manufacturing, retail/wholesale, financial services • Structural equation modeling	Contextual factors (e.g., competition intensity and firm size) may have *differential effects* across stages (adoption versus use). Regarding cross-country effects, this study finds that in developing countries, the strongest factor affecting e-commerce use is the acquisition of fundamental technologies, while in developed countries technology integration emerges as the key factor affecting e-commerce use.
Xu et al. (2004)	• GEC Survey • China and the USA • Manufacturing, retail/wholesale, financial services • ANOVA and structural equation modeling	This study finds a series of China–USA differences: (1) Chinese firms lag in using interorganizational technologies; (2) fewer Chinese firms are using the Internet for selling, offering services, purchasing, and exchanging data with business partners; (3) government plays a far more critical role in encouraging e-commerce use in China; and (4) Chinese firms fall behind significantly in B2B online procurement.
Gibbs & Kraemer (2004)	• GEC Survey • Ten countries in the GEC Survey • Manufacturing, retail/wholesale, financial services • Multiple regression	A firm's technology readiness and organizational attributes are key determinants not just of adoption but of the breadth of e-commerce use in its business activities. This study also confirms the importance of government policy, particularly legislation. Government promotion through incentives and procurement requirements are also important, although they have less of an effect.

	Research stream III: from e-commerce use to impacts	
Zhu et al. (2004)	• GEC Survey • Ten countries in the GEC Survey • Financial services • Structural equation modeling	Among contextual factors proposed for studying e-commerce impacts, technology factors (technology readiness and technology integration) emerge as the strongest factors, firm size shows a negative effect, while competition intensity turns out to be insignificant. Regarding cross-country differences, firm size and regulatory environment play different roles between developing and developed countries.
Zhu & Kraemer (2005)	• GEC Survey • Ten countries in the GEC Survey • Retail/wholesale • Structural equation modeling	E-commerce use is shown to be a significant mediating construct in the path from the initial adoption to performance impacts. This study further investigates two types of e-commerce functionalities: front-end functionality and (back-end) technology integration. Although both have the potential to facilitate use and impacts, back-end integration tends to have a stronger effect than front-end functionality.
Kraemer et al. (2005)	• GEC Survey • Ten countries in the GEC Survey • Manufacturing, retail/wholesale, financial services • Multiple regression	Global firms use Internet technology more extensively, engaging in a wider variety of e-commerce activities than less global firms. This study also finds a different picture for B2B and B2C e-commerce, with global firms more likely to engage in the former and local firms in the latter. Although globalization has a negative effect on B2C, firms derive most of their performance benefits from B2B rather than B2C. Thus the net effect of globalization on firm performance seems to be positive.

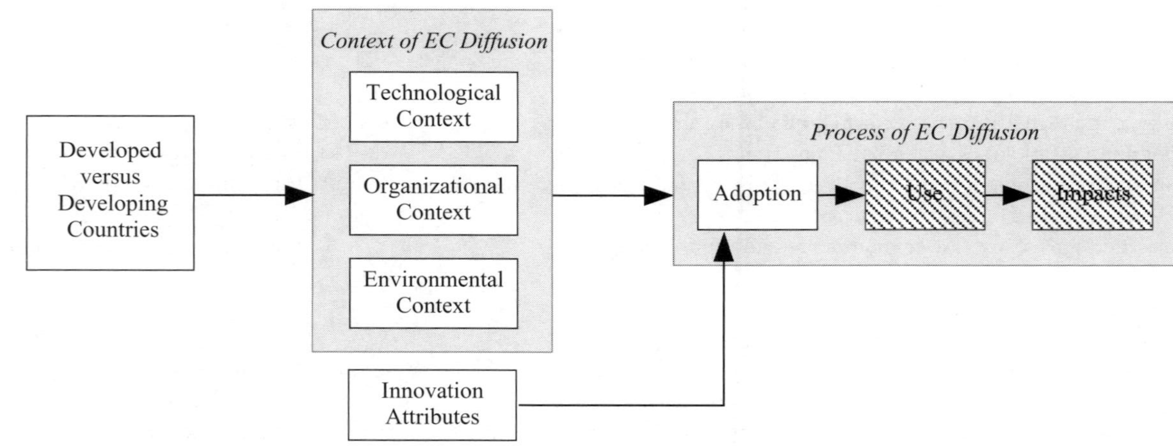

Concepts not tested in this stream of research

Figure 10.4 Research stream I: e-commerce adoption

Research stream I: e-commerce adoption

This stream of research studies shows how e-commerce adoption is affected by innovation attributes and contextual factors, which may be moderated by the environments of different economies (Figure 10.4). The studies show cross-country differences in the impacts of these two dimensions on e-commerce adoption. Findings from these studies are discussed in turn below.

Contextual factors affecting e-commerce adoption

Zhu et al. (2003) found that firms with higher technology readiness, larger size and broader scope, and facing greater competition intensity are more likely to adopt e-commerce, while firms are less likely to adopt if they confront low levels of partner readiness for doing e-commerce.

This study further analyzes differences in e-commerce adoption across countries. The authors use three indices to measure e-commerce intensity: (1) annual online consumer spending per capita; (2) e-commerce adoption rate by firms; and (3) the ratio of e-commerce volume over GDP. The three indices measure e-commerce intensity at three levels – consumers, firms, and the economy – and data analysis indicates high correlations among them. Based on them, the eight European countries involved in this study are split into two groups: Finland, Denmark, and the UK are grouped together, while the remaining five countries (Germany, Ireland, France, Spain, and Italy) are clustered into the other group. Each of the three indices in the first group has significantly higher value than the second group. Thus, in the context of this study, the first group is considered as "high EC-intensity countries" and the second group "low EC-intensity countries."

The authors analyze a series of country-level factors that might have resulted in the imbalance of e-commerce development, which is reflected in this sample split. At the time of the survey, high EC-intensity countries (Denmark, Finland, and the UK) enjoyed greater levels of diffusion of information and telecommunication technologies including PC, cell phone, and the Internet than low EC-intensity countries. In addition to technology infrastructure, government policies may play a role in stimulating e-commerce diffusion. For instance, the Danish government centered its e-commerce strategy on rapid adoption, implementation, and exploitation of e-commerce in all sectors of the economy (Andersen et al., 2003).

As well as different adoption levels, this study finds that as e-commerce intensity increases, two environmental factors – consumer readiness (for online purchasing) and trading partner readiness (for B2B online transactions) – become less important, while competitive pressure becomes the only significant environmental factor. The authors argue that as more customers and competitors adopt e-commerce, firms in the high EC-intensity countries tend to regard it as a long-run strategic necessity, while consumer readiness, which reflects the potential return in the short run, becomes a less important factor. Accordingly, firms tend to choose adoption to avoid competitive decline, which is consistent with the finding that, in the high EC-intensity environment, competitive pressure is the only significant environmental adoption facilitator. Trading partner readiness becomes an insignificant factor, possibly because in high EC-intensity countries it is much easier to find online partners as more firms have adopted e-commerce.

Joint effects of contextual factors and innovation attributes

Zhu et al. (2005) extended the study above by considering the joint effects of context and innovation attributes on e-commerce adoption. They confirm the significant effects of contextual factors and reveal impacts of innovation attributes on firms' adoption decisions. Most importantly, they find that the adoption of e-commerce is better understood by the combination of innovation attributes and adoption context.

Among the innovation attributes, relative advantage and compatibility are found to encourage e-commerce adoption, while adoption costs and security concerns discourage adoption. The strongest factor is compatibility between new and previous innovations, for example between EDI and Internet-based e-commerce. The study's findings are consistent with diffusion of innovation studies (Rogers, 1995; Tornatzky & Klein, 1982), yet shed new light on the nature of e-commerce and the relative importance of innovation attributes.

Finally, the study investigated one factor that few prior studies had examined, which are unique to e-commerce: security concerns. The empirical results indicate that security is a more significant barrier to e-commerce than adoption costs. This finding is new and not considered in previous IT adoption literature (e.g., Chau & Tam, 1997; Ramamurthy et al., 1999).

Impact of global forces and national policies on e-commerce adoption
Gibbs et al. (2003) investigated two particular dimensions of the environmental context: (1) global forces, i.e., environmental factors associated with firm globalization, and (2) national policies and regulations on e-commerce. This study finds that the specific factors shaping business-to-business and business-to-consumer e-commerce vary considerably. For B2B e-commerce, competitive forces are the greatest driver of adoption. Global competitive pressure is driving greater convergence in business practices through global integration of production networks and supply chains. B2C diffusion seems to be less affected by global forces and more affected by local variables which are specific to the national and local environment, such as consumer preferences, retail structure, and local language and cultural factors. The authors find that consumer preference for valuable content and concerns for security and privacy are the most significant factors.

The authors conclude that B2B e-commerce seems to be driven by global forces, whereas B2C seems to be more of a local phenomenon. A preliminary explanation for this difference is that B2B is driven by MNCs that "push" e-commerce to their global suppliers, customers, and their own subsidiaries. This in turn creates pressure on local companies to adopt e-commerce to stay competitive. In the process, business practices become more standardized across borders. Business education and imitation of best practices reinforce this convergence; as innovation occurs in theory or practice, firms adopt it rapidly in order to be competitive. It is this continual "push" of innovation and imitation that leads to global convergence in B2B e-commerce.

In terms of policy, this study finds that enabling policies such as trade and telecoms liberalization are likely to have the biggest impact on e-commerce, by making ICTs and Internet access more affordable to firms and consumers, and increasing pressure on firms to adopt e-commerce to compete. Promotional efforts can also have an impact, especially if carried out in partnership with the private sector. Specific e-commerce legislation appears not to have as big an impact, although concerns in some countries about inadequate protection for e-commerce suggest the need to develop proper mechanisms to increase firms' and consumers' confidence in doing business online.

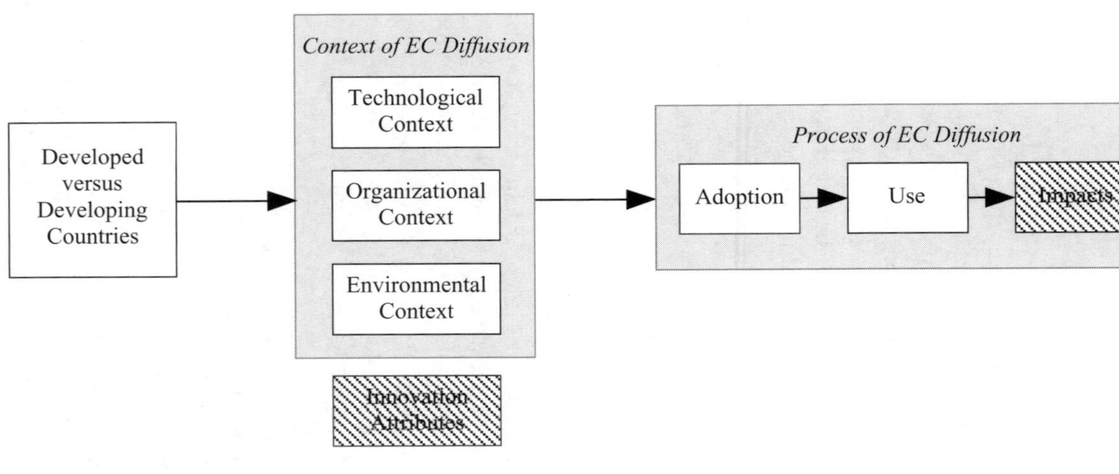

Figure 10.5 Research stream II: from e-commerce adoption to use

Research stream II: from e-commerce adoption to use

Zhu et al. (2006), Xu et al. (2004), and Gibbs and Kraemer (2004) proceeded to study both adoption and use (Figure 10.5). Here, TOE contexts become the major focus when the dependent variable is e-commerce use. Findings from these studies are discussed in turn below.

Contextual factors affecting the process from e-commerce adoption to use

Zhu et al. (2006) investigate the role of TOE contexts in the progression from e-commerce adoption to e-commerce use. This study confirms the usefulness of the TOE factors (technology readiness, technology integration, firm size, global scope, competition intensity, and regulatory environment) for understanding e-commerce diffusion. Further, the authors find that contextual factors, such as competition intensity and firm size, may play different roles at different stages of the diffusion process (i.e., adoption versus use).

This study finds a positive relationship of competition intensity with e-commerce adoption but a negative relationship with use. The authors argue that this finding is consistent with the rationale that competition drives firms to adopt innovations to maintain a competitive edge. Based on Internet technologies, e-commerce applications can help firms improve market responsiveness and increase operational efficiencies. Thus, competition is likely to drive firms to adopt e-commerce. This rationale is consistent with previous research on IT and competition (Porter & Millar, 1985).

However, the effect of competition on use is different. To efficiently use a complex technology, firms need profound technical and managerial skills that are acquired mainly through a learning-by-using process. Yet, firms in a more competitive environment are often driven by competitive pressure to leap rapidly from one technology to the next. As a result, firms are less likely to undergo a gradual, careful, and sustained process to develop skills for efficient use. E-commerce is particularly prone to this pattern. This finding suggests that too much competition is not necessarily a good thing for technology use. This finding challenges the conventional wisdom about competition and innovation diffusion (Kamien & Schwartz 1982; Williamson, 1983).

Another factor with differential effects across stages is firm size. This study finds that firm size is positively related with e-commerce adoption, but negatively related with e-commerce use. The authors explain that this finding suggests a tension of resource advantages and structural inertia. On the one hand, large firms are more likely to adopt because they tend to enjoy resource advantages. On the other hand, large firms may face structural inertia, a negative factor for innovation use. E-commerce use requires adopting firms to adapt existing information systems, redesign business processes, and adjust organizational restructure. In general, large firms may have more fragmented legacy information systems, which tend to increase the complexity and costs of systems adaptation. Moreover, in large firms, changes in structures and processes may be further complicated by the entrenched organizational structure and hierarchical decision making. These factors would translate into structural inertia that may retard e-commerce use. In this regard, the authors argue that small firms may enjoy advantages, as they require less communication, less coordination, and less influence to gather support. Thus, small firms are more likely to diffuse e-commerce into more value chain activities, and achieve a deeper use in each activity.

In addition, this study identifies different relationships across countries. It finds that, in developing countries, technology readiness is the most critical factor among all variables affecting e-commerce use. This suggests that basic technology infrastructure is still highly important in these countries. In contrast, technology integration becomes the strongest factor in developed countries. Firms in developed countries tend to be more advanced in using information technologies, and as common technologies become "strategic necessities," firms need to pursue deeper usage of IT. One example of such deeper usage is to integrate disparate systems and reduce incompatibility between existing IS applications.

A comparison of a developed country and a developing country

Grounded in the TOE framework, Xu et al. (2004) conducted an in-depth comparison of a developed country and a developing country in terms of firms' use of e-commerce. The United States, the largest developed economy, was chosen as a representative of developed countries, while China, the largest developing economy, was chosen as a representative of developing countries.

Analyzing GEC data about e-commerce adoption and use (both breadth and volume), this study finds that Chinese firms lag in using e-commerce-related technologies, especially interorganizational technologies such as EDI and EFT. Fewer Chinese firms are using the Internet for selling, offering services, purchasing, and exchanging data with business partners, compared with US firms. Further, this study finds that government plays a far more critical role in promoting e-commerce use in China than in the United States, perhaps due to the fact that China lacks a legal and institutional environment to support e-commerce. Finally, this study suggests that Chinese firms may be able to catch up by taking advantage of newer technologies. The GEC Survey seems to suggest that advanced Chinese firms are using e-commerce proactively. Yet, Chinese firms significantly fall behind in B2B online procurement, partly due to the imbalance of e-commerce diffusion in China. An implication from this result is that Chinese government needs to promote wider diffusion of e-commerce in the economy; once the diffusion reaches a certain level of critical mass, network effect will kick in to speed up e-commerce diffusion.

Determinants of the breadth of e-commerce use

Focused on the breadth of e-commerce use, Gibbs and Kraemer (2004) investigated the determinants of this particular use dimension. This study confirms that a firm's technology readiness and organizational attributes are key determinants not just of adoption but of the breadth of e-commerce use. Further, this study finds significant country differences. US firms use e-commerce more extensively than comparable firms in other countries. This result is consistent with findings by Xu et al. (2004) as discussed above.

This study also confirms the importance of government policy, particularly legislation, in firms' e-commerce use. Lack of a supportive regulatory environment for e-commerce is found to have a significant negative effect on the breadth of use. Policy factors such as lack of legal protection, inadequate business laws supporting e-commerce, and Internet taxation are likely to inhibit the breadth of e-commerce use. Government promotion through incentives and procurement requirements are also marginally significant in increasing use, although they have less of an effect.

Research stream III: from e-commerce use to impacts

The third stream of research (Zhu et al., 2004; Zhu & Kraemer, 2005; Kraemer et al., 2005) proceeds to investigate performance impacts of

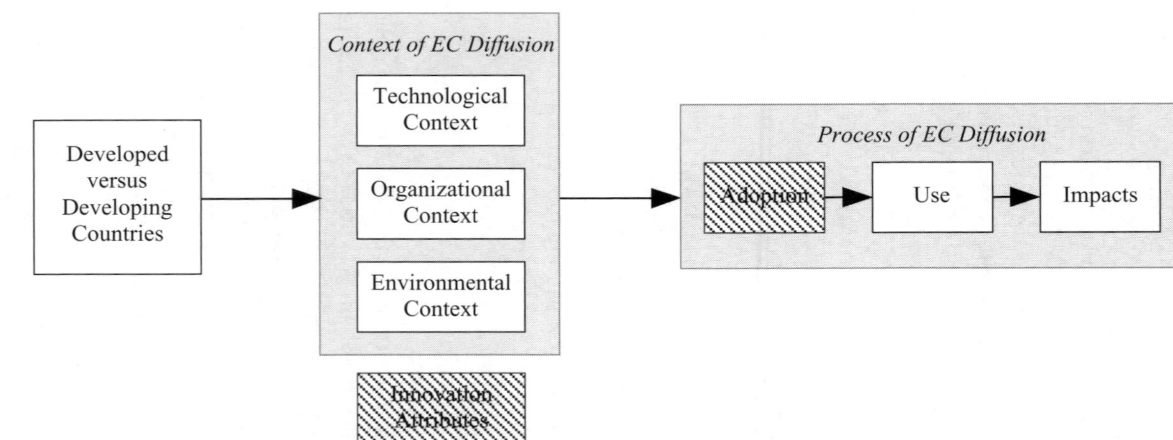

Figure 10.6 Research stream III: from e-commerce use to impacts

e-commerce (Figure 10.6). Findings from these studies are summarized below.

Contextual factors affecting e-commerce impacts

Zhu et al. (2004) found that, within the TOE framework, technology readiness and technology integration were the strongest factors associated with e-commerce impacts, while global scope and regulatory environment also contributed. Financial firms with stronger technological capability are more likely to realize e-commerce value. In addition, wider scope allows financial firms to capture more benefits from the connectivity of the Internet. Finally, regulatory support is found to facilitate value creation in e-commerce.

Consistent with the relationship between firm size and e-commerce use discussed above, this study finds that large firms are less likely to realize the value of e-commerce than small firms. This finding shows that the structural inertia associated with large firms plays a role not only at the use stage but also at the impacts stage of the e-commerce diffusion process.

Another finding consistent with the research of use (Zhu et al., 2006) is that competition intensity turns out to be insignificant for e-commerce impacts. As discussed above, competition is an important factor driving firms to adopt a new technology, and is even more so in the e-commerce domain as many firms jumped onto the Internet bandwagon driven by competitive pressure. Yet, the extent to which e-commerce actually improves firm performance tends to be less tied to competition intensity. E-commerce value originates more from internal organizational resources and technological capability than from external pressure.

Finally, Zhu et al. (2004) found a stronger effect of regulatory support on e-commerce impacts in developing countries than in developed countries. This cross-country difference highlights the greater importance of regulations and policies for firms in developing countries, through the whole process of e-commerce diffusion (adoption, use, and impacts).

The relationship between e-commerce use and impacts

Zhu and Kraemer (2005) investigated the relationship between use and impacts. They found a significant effect of the level of e-commerce use on the degree of e-commerce impacts. This result suggests that e-commerce use is an important mediating stage in the path from the initial adoption to performance impacts, as technology cannot improve firm performance unless used effectively.

The authors analyze the rationale underlying this relationship. They argue that, by using e-commerce for customer-facing activities, a firm can obtain richer information about markets, increase its responsiveness to demand changes, reach new customers, and improve customer relationships, thereby enhancing revenue generation. Inside the firm, e-commerce has the potential to streamline business processes through better data exchange, hence increasing operational efficiency and staff productivity. By using e-commerce to support supplier-facing activities, the firm can improve information flow and strengthen online integration with suppliers and business partners, thus reducing coordination costs and increasing inventory turnover. These effects lead to a positive relationship between e-commerce use and e-commerce impacts on firm performance, as empirically validated by the GEC Survey.

This study also investigates the effects of front-end functionality and back-end technology integration. Front-end functionality helps firms deliver real-time information to customers, better understand market demand, allow customers to track delivery status, and provide customer support, thereby promoting e-commerce use along the value chain. Back-end integration is critical for e-commerce systems to function in the back office. Information systems often include legacy systems built over years. These pre-Internet systems are frequently isolated from each other, and thus data re-entry is often needed, increasing costs and errors. In this regard, the Internet helps eliminate or reduce the incompatibility. By integrating incompatible technologies with the Internet protocol, firms can build an integrated infrastructure that may facilitate e-commerce automation within a firm and streamline workflow along the value chain.

This study further finds that, although both have the potential to facilitate use and impacts, back-end integration is much more important than front-end functionality. Front-end functionality is public and open on the Internet, and thus could be easily observed and imitated by competitors. The process of back-end integration is far more difficult to imitate, because its success requires complementary resources (Zhu & Kraemer, 2002). In addition, the integration process is often tailored to a firm's strategic context and is woven into the organization's fabric, which is not transparent to competitors. Therefore, back-end integration emerges as a more significant factor to differentiate firms in their use of e-commerce.

Globalization and e-commerce use and impacts

Kraemer et al. (2005) focus on the impact of a specific organizational factor – a firm's global scope – on the use and impacts of e-commerce. Global scope is measured by geographic global scope (with headquarters and establishments abroad), trading globalization (international sales and procurement), and global competition (pressure from international competitors). This research shows that the relationship between globalization and e-commerce is complex and varied. Among firms that use the Internet to conduct business, more global firms use the technology more extensively, engaging in a wider variety of e-commerce activities than less global firms. However, when e-commerce is broken down in terms of the type of business relationship involved, the authors find a different picture for B2B and B2C e-commerce, with global firms more likely to engage in the former and local firms in the latter. The findings provide empirical support for Porter's (1986) thesis that upstream activities, which involve B2B transactions, are more global in nature, while downstream activities, involving B2C interactions, are more local.

Although globalization has a negative effect on B2C, firms derive most of their performance benefits from B2B rather than B2C. Thus, the authors argue that the net effect of globalization seems to be a positive one on firm performance. Local firms do appear to be benefiting from e-commerce though, especially B2C services, which drive increased sales. Global firms get more performance improvements from e-commerce than local firms, as they tend to adopt B2B, which has greater impacts across a broader range (downstream sales, internal efficiency, and upstream coordination) than B2C. Global firms also get more direct impacts from e-commerce, presumably as they have greater resources and scope to use it better.

Summary and conclusions

With the rapid development of network technologies and open standards, and the associated reduction of communication costs, firms are migrating toward the Internet-based digital platform that holds the promise of significant performance improvements. The adoption, use, and impacts of e-commerce stand out as an important research topic. In this chapter, we have developed a conceptual model for e-commerce diffusion (Figure 10.1). The model incorporates specific variables to study drivers and barriers for e-commerce diffusion; it also considers how these drivers and barriers are moderated by the economic environments in developed versus developing countries. The model is consistent with the overall framework of the GEC project discussed in Chapter 1; yet, it is more specific than that. The model presented in this chapter is particularly designed to study the process and the context of e-commerce diffusion at the firm level. Another major difference from other chapters is that the model has been tested by a series of cross-country studies. Distilling findings from these studies, we identify four key themes: (1) the critical role of technology usage; (2) global convergence at the firm level; (3) cross-country differences; and (4) differential effects along the diffusion process.

The critical role of technology usage

Our analyses provide significant evidence that usage is a key factor linking adoption and impacts. We find that firms with a higher degree of technology usage tend to achieve greater value from e-commerce. This sheds new light on why e-business investment does not always lead to improved firm performance, and thus helps move the research focus from simple, direct relationships between investment and performance to intermediate links such as usage. Our mediation model shows that the effect can be indirect. The middle stage requires more study because less is known about it.

All firms surveyed by the GEC project have adopted e-commerce, but they have taken very different paths with different outcomes after adoption. Firms vary significantly in their ability to use e-commerce, which further affects the benefits they achieve from going online. After the burst of the dot.com bubble, IT and e-commerce managers have been struggling to justify investments in Internet technologies. Our research shows that adoption of e-commerce and investments in Internet technologies have significant economic payoffs when e-commerce is used extensively. We have further shown that the effect of usage is more significant in developed countries than in developing countries, suggesting the increasing importance of usage as e-business diffuses in an economy.

There are two managerial implications of these analyses. First, to derive greater business value of e-commerce, managers should achieve wide use of e-commerce in the various value chain activities. In other words, they should achieve greater breadth of use. Second, managers should promote deeper usage (e.g., greater volume of use) in each value chain activity as well. The value chain activities to be addressed include marketing, sales, customer services, procurement, operations, information sharing, and value chain coordination. Which activities should come first is a strategic issue, and there is no one answer for all firms. For firms where customer relationships are strategic, emphasis should be placed on customer-facing activities as a matter of relative emphasis. For firms where operational excellence is strategic, emphasis should be placed on operations and value chain coordination. For firms where new products and services are strategic, emphasis should be placed on information sharing and fulfillment from new product development to market introduction (Tallon & Kraemer, 2004).

We provide the following insights to explain the critical role of use. When e-commerce diffuses internally across a wider scope of business activities and is used more extensively for each of them, the fixed development costs of e-commerce systems can be spread more widely, thus increasing cost effectiveness. Further, as diversified business activities are conducted over the Internet-enabled, open-standard platform, firms are more likely to connect various systems supporting a variety of business activities, thus improving the degree of process automation and reducing coordination costs among these activities. In addition, with a greater proportion of each business activity conducted on the Internet, the economies of specialization may lead to more skills for managing e-commerce. It has been noted that technical and managerial skills for effective use of IT innovations are mainly acquired through learning by using. Thus, firms having used e-commerce on a wider base of applications likely have developed critical technical and managerial skills. As technologies per se tend to become a strategic necessity, such skills become a major differentiator of e-commerce adopters. Collectively, these effects lead to a positive impact of e-commerce use on the degree to which firms can improve their performance by adopting e-commerce.

This also shows that actual usage may be the "missing" link to IT payoffs. That is, focusing on use as the intermediate stage in IT value creation is likely to be a promising approach to understanding the payoffs from IT, rather than focusing solely on IT capital investment, which is just the first stage in the diffusion process.

Global convergence at the firm level

As presented in the introduction section, one of our research questions is what factors affect the process of e-commerce diffusion. We have reported a series of findings from our analyses in order to answer this question (see Table 10.2). Our studies suggest global convergence in e-commerce diffusion. First, we find that e-commerce diffusion is indeed a multistage process, as shown by the survey data from both developed and developing countries. The significant relationship between e-commerce use and e-commerce impacts commonly exists in these countries.

Second, we find common factors for firms in developed and developing countries within the technological, organizational, and environmental context influencing e-commerce diffusion. Within the technological context, we find that firms need to possess technology infrastructure and human resources to adopt and use e-commerce; more importantly, firms need to achieve technology integration in order to facilitate e-commerce use and derive e-commerce benefits.

Within the organizational context, we find that large firms are more likely to adopt e-commerce, but less likely to achieve deeper usage and realize e-commerce benefits. This suggests that structural inertia is a common barrier to e-commerce use for all firms. Another important organizational factor is global scope. Although global firms in general conduct more business online than local firms, there is no significant difference in terms of selling, purchasing, and coordination. Global firms are more likely to engage in B2B e-commerce and local firms in B2C e-commerce. Since firms derive most of their performance benefits from B2B rather than B2C, the net effect of globalization on firm performance seems to be positive.

Within the environmental context, the legal and regulatory structure is an important factor for e-commerce diffusion. This is consistent with case studies reported in other chapters in this book. In addition, we find that the readiness of trading partners significantly facilitates e-commerce diffusion, suggesting that the network nature of e-commerce seems to be true in the global environment.

Cross-country differences

Although factors and effects suggesting global convergence have been identified, they may differ in magnitude between developed versus developing countries. We have reported differences between developed and developing countries in terms of drivers, barriers, and e-commerce diffusion.

We find that e-commerce use has a more significant relationship with e-commerce impacts in developed countries than in developing countries. In contrast, investment in e-commerce is more important for realizing benefits in developing countries. This is consistent with the conventional wisdom that firms in developing countries lack financial resources for IT investment. Further, developed and developing countries seem to be at different phases of e-commerce evolution, and e-commerce has achieved higher levels of diffusion in developed countries, as indicated by macro-level statistics (UNCTAD, 2002) and by our own survey. As more firms have adopted and invested in e-commerce, investment by itself is unlikely to serve as a differentiator. Instead, value comes increasingly from use.

We also find cross-country differences regarding factors within the TOE context. Within the technological context, we find that technology readiness is the strongest factor facilitating e-commerce diffusion in developing countries, while technology integration is the strongest in developed countries. This difference suggests that as e-commerce evolves, the key determinant of its diffusion shifts from accumulation of individual technologies to integration of these technologies (Zhu et al., 2006).

Within the environmental context, the importance of partner readiness differs between developed and developing countries. Relative to firms in developed countries, firms in developing countries consider partner readiness to be more critical (Xu et al., 2004). This finding is consistent with case studies in other chapters showing that, in developing countries, e-commerce has not been adopted as extensively as in developed countries. Thus, firms in developing countries often run into difficulty in finding partners that are digitally ready. As a result, the technology readiness of business partners is more important in developing countries. Another factor with differing significance is regulatory environment. E-commerce legislation (e.g., digital signatures, privacy, and consumer protection) is less comprehensive in developing countries. Hence, firms in developing countries tend to consider a supportive regulatory framework to be more critical.

Based on the above findings, we conclude that a digital divide in e-commerce exists between developed and developing countries. This digital divide results from cross-country differences in consumers and firms. On the side of consumers, the degree of Internet penetration is significantly higher in developed countries than in developing countries. In addition, different consumer behaviors may influence e-commerce development. For instance, consumers in the USA are more familiar with long-distance shopping (such as purchase via catalog, phone, or TV) and are more willing to pay in advance by credit card. The high Internet penetration and great consumer willingness to purchase online lead to the actual consumer "readiness" for e-commerce.

On the side of firms, limited IT infrastructure and shorter experience using IT are major barriers in developing countries. As indicated by the GEC Survey, building technology infrastructure still seems to be the most critical task for those firms to achieve deeper use and derive e-commerce benefits. Yet, firms in developing countries also may catch up by taking advantage of newer technologies. For instance, more advanced Chinese, Mexican, and Brazilian firms are using e-commerce pro-actively. In developed countries, many firms invested in pre-Internet technologies such as EDI for inter-firm information exchange. Although they likely have acquired skills for managing B2B technologies through the EDI experience, the substantial investment may create switching costs for the adoption of the newer Internet technologies. Further, the previous digital platform such as EDI may result in dedicated buyer–supplier relationships. As a result, firms have to progress in "waves" to move from the old technology to the new Internet platform.

How do we interpret the findings of global convergence with cross-country differences in firm-level adoption, use, and impacts of e-commerce? We see the diffusion of e-commerce as an evolutionary process, with firms in developed countries having reached a more advanced stage than those in developing countries. There are common factors that influence firms in all countries, such as technological capabilities, competition, trading partner readiness, and regulatory environment. However, the relative importance of these factors differs depending on the firm's stage of development and its national environment. Developing countries are still in the process of achieving widespread adoption of Internet technologies and creating the regulatory environment to support e-commerce. Developed countries have passed that stage and are involved in expanding the breadth and depth of their online activities and integrating their e-commerce technologies internally and with their trading partners. Not surprisingly, firms in developed countries generally report greater impacts on their performance as a result of using the Internet for business.

While these findings are true for firms in general, they do not imply that there is no room for firms in either environment to improve their prospects through managerial action. For instance, while developing countries might be at an earlier stage of e-commerce evolution, there are some industry sectors that are much more advanced, such as finance in Brazil and some manufacturing sectors in Mexico and China. Firms in those industries may find a favorable environment to use e-commerce aggressively without waiting for the whole country to catch up. Those doing business globally likewise can benefit by developing electronic linkages with MNCs, as we have seen in Taiwan's electronics industry. In less advanced sectors, larger firms can provide incentives and assistance to their trading partners to help prepare them to use e-commerce, thereby driving the diffusion of e-commerce and the emergence of a larger, industry-specific network. Smaller firms in these sectors can invest in basic infrastructure and experiment with basic applications such as email, informational websites, and buying simple goods online. If e-commerce diffusion is a global process, then firms in the earlier stages can benefit from the experiences of those which have gone before them, and be ready for the opportunities that will arise.

Relative to developing countries, e-commerce has been adopted and used more extensively in developed countries. As a result, it is unlikely that firms in developed countries will gain competitive advantages by simply adopting e-commerce. They need to deploy technologies in a deeper way, for instance integrating systems, databases, and applications based on the Internet platform.

Our results also have implications for governments. For instance, our analyses have highlighted how firms in developing countries confront significant barriers to e-commerce diffusion, such as lacking fundamental technologies and the difficulty of finding e-commerce partners. Thus, governments in developing countries need to focus on providing useful information about e-commerce diffusion in specific industry sectors, and providing incentives for adopting and using e-commerce such as offering technical support, training, and funding for e-commerce.

Differential effects along the diffusion process

We have found that the factors influencing the process of e-commerce diffusion may show different effects as the diffusion evolves to a deeper stage. Firm size may drive e-commerce adoption, since large firms enjoy the so-called "resource advantages"; yet, firm size is shown to have a negative effect on both e-commerce use and e-commerce impacts. We have explained these results using the notion of "structural inertia." That is, large firms tend to face greater complexity in organizational changes, including redesigning organizational restructures, re-engineering business processes, and aligning e-commerce with the overall business strategy. In contrast, although small firms have limited resources, they may have greater control over implementation and be able to use e-commerce more intensively, and, therefore, achieve greater benefits.

Another factor showing differential effects along the diffusion process is competition. Consistent with the common wisdom, competition intensity may drive e-commerce adoption, but the effect of competition becomes negative at post-adoption stages. It is likely that competition drives firms to leap quickly from one technology to another. As a result of the quick technology changes, these firms do not have enough time to adapt, use, and routinize existing technologies and applications. Also, in a highly competitive environment, any productivity improvements from adopting e-commerce may simply be passed on to consumers rather than providing a sustained advantage for firms.

These findings shed new light on influential factors along the diffusion process. The extant innovation literature did not study factors from a process perspective, and thus did not identify such process-related, differential relationships. This chapter contributes to the innovation diffusion research by highlighting the need to probe deeper into contextual factors at different stages of diffusion.

These findings have several managerial implications. First, the differential effects of firm size (structural inertia in organizational changes) at different stages in the diffusion process suggest that managers need to pay special attention to change management issues at each stage.

For example, a large firm will face structural inertia during the use stage, whereas a small firm will face limited capabilities in the adoption stage. These differences suggest that managers in small firms need to develop capabilities internally and then focus on the most critical processes and partners in the firm's value chain. The large firm faces path dependencies from legacy systems, more departmentalized structures, and problems of scale. It will need to focus on a product, plant, or geography where it can conduct a controlled demonstration to show the benefits and discover the change management practices that will help overcome resistance to greater use.

Second, as these differences between large and small firms illustrate, managers need to pay attention to the change model that they use to effect diffusion. The literature identifies two key models – the traditional three-stage, planned change model of "unfreezing, change, and refreezing" (Lewin, 1952; Markus & Benjamin, 1997), and a more improvisational model of "iterative experimentation, use and learning over time" (Orlikowski & Hofman, 1997). The planned change model is appropriate for well-understood technologies and for organizations whose environments and functionality are relatively stable such that a systematic and structured approach is possible. The improvisational model may be more appropriate for the current stage of e-commerce evolution as it is best used for technologies that are more open-ended and for organizations in uncertain environments where assimilation requires a fast and flexible approach. Improvisation requires setting up a special team(s) with decentralized authority, a charter to experiment, and focus on a defined area (activity, product, plant, or geography). If the experiment is shown to be successful, it can be driven into other areas of the firm using a planned change approach. An appropriate change model then involves a period of improvisation followed by anticipated change, and then more improvisation, and so on in order to spread e-commerce use across activities, divisions, and geographies.

Third, managers need to recognize that the issues change with the level of economic development in a country. In developing countries, the key issue is getting firms interconnected via the Internet. This is critical because the network usually is not large enough to achieve network benefits, and therefore it is critical to grow the network to "critical mass." As illustrated in the chapters on China, Mexico, and Taiwan, industry associations and government agencies can play major roles by providing information, training, standardization efforts, and cooperation within a few key industry sub-sectors. In developed countries, most firms are already connected, so the key issue is how to get firms and their value chain partners more deeply integrated, and to push integration to third- and fourth-level value chain partners. Major firms within industry sub-sectors can take the lead or industry consortia can be formed to provide leadership, as has been the case with RosettaNet in the global electronics industry.

In conclusion, we have shown that e-commerce diffusion is both similar to and different from earlier technologies, and that the differences are at least as important as the similarities. In particular, many of the same technical and organizational factors shape diffusion from the standpoint of the individual firm. But, because e-commerce increasingly takes place on the global, open-standard platform of the Internet and involves customers, suppliers, and partners in the firm's value chain, diffusion is strongly shaped by these players in the firm's environment, and increasingly by the national environments and policies in the countries in which the firms do business. We have shown that while e-commerce is a slow-growing global force in all countries of the study, firms, industries, and countries are taking different paths to Internet-based e-commerce. We therefore urge managers and policymakers to carefully study the insights and lessons highlighted in this book.

References

Andersen, K. V., Bjorn-Andersen, N., & Dedrick, J. (2003). Governance Initiatives Creating a Demand-Driven E-Commerce Approach: The Case of Denmark. *The Information Society*, 19(1), 95–105.

Chau, P. Y. K. & Tam, K. Y. (1997). Factors Affecting the Adoption of Open Systems: An Exploratory Study. *MIS Quarterly*, 21(1), 1–21.

Fichman, R. G. (2000). The Diffusion and Assimilation of Information Technology Innovations. In R. W. Zmud (Ed.), *Framing the Domains of IT Management: Projecting the Future Through the Past.* Cleveland, OH: Pinnaflex Publishing, 105–127.

Gibbs, J. & Kraemer, K. L. (2004). A Cross-Country Investigation of the Determinants of Scope of E-Commerce Use: An Institutional Approach. *Electronic Markets*, 14(2), 124–137.

Gibbs, J., Kraemer, K. L., & Dedrick, J. (2003). Environment and Policy Factors Shaping Global E-Commerce Diffusion: A Cross-Country Comparison. *The Information Society*, 19(1), 5–18.

Kamien, M. & Schwartz, N. (1982). *Market Structure and Innovation.* Cambridge: Cambridge University Press.

Kraemer, K. L., Gibbs, J., & Dedrick, J. (2005). Impacts of Globalization on E-Commerce Use and Firm Performance: A Cross-Country Investigation. CRITO working paper.

Lewin, K. (1952). Group Decision and Social Change. In E. Newcombe & R. Harley (Eds.), *Readings in Social Psychology.* New York: Henry Holt, 459–473.

Markus, M. L. & Benjamin, R. I. (1997). The Magic Bullet Theory of IT-Enabled Transformation. *Sloan Management Review*, 38(2), 55–68.

Orlikowski, W. J. & Hofman, J. D. (1997). An Improvisational Model of Change Management: The Case of Groupware Technologies. *Sloan Management Review*, 38(2), 11–21.

Porter, M. E. (1986). *Competition in Global Industries.* Boston, MA: Harvard Business School Press.

Porter, M. & Millar, V. (1985). How Information Gives You Competitive Advantage. *Harvard Business Review*, 63(4), 149–160.

Ramamurthy, K., Premkumar, G., & Crum, M. R. (1999). Organizational and Interorganizational Determinants of EDI Diffusion and Organizational Performance: A Cause Model. *Journal of Organizational Computing and Electronic Commerce*, 9(4), 253–285.

Rogers, E. M. (1995). *Diffusion of Innovations* (4th Ed.). New York: Free Press.

Shih, C. F., Dedrick, J., & Kraemer, K. L. (2005). Rule of Law and the International Diffusion of E-Commerce. *Communications of the ACM*, 48(11), 57–62.

Tallon, P. P. & Kraemer, K. L. (2004). *The Impact of IT Capabilities on Firm Performance: Perspectives on the Mediating Effects of Strategic Alignment.* Irvine, CA: Center for Research on Information Technology and Organizations, UC Irvine.

Tornatzky, L. G. & Fleischer, M. (1990). *The Processes of Technological Innovation.* Lexington, MA: Lexington Books.

Tornatzky, L. G. & Klein, K. (1982). Innovation Characteristics and Innovation Adoption-Implementation: A Meta-Analysis of Findings. *IEEE Transactions on Engineering Management*, 29(1), 28–45.

United Nations Conference on Trade and Development (UNCTAD) (2002). *E-Commerce and Development Report 2002.* New York and Geneva.

Williamson, O. E. (1983). Organizational Innovation: The Transaction Cost Approach. In J. Ronen (Ed.), *Entrepreneurship*, Lexington, MA: Lexington Books, 101–133.

Xu, S., Zhu, K., & Gibbs, J. (2004). Global Technology, Local Adoption: A Cross-Country Investigation of Internet Adoption by Companies in the United States and China. *Electronic Markets*, 14(1), 13–24.

Zhu, K. & Kraemer, K. L. (2002). E-Commerce Metrics for Net-Enhanced Organizations: Assessing the Value of E-Commerce to Firm Performance in the Manufacturing Sector. *Information Systems Research*, 13(3), 275–295.

Zhu, K. & Kraemer, K. L. (2005). Post-Adoption Variations in Usage and Value of E-Business by Organizations: Cross-Country Evidence from the Retail Industry. *Information Systems Research*, 16(1), 61–84.

Zhu, K., Kraemer, K. L., & Xu, S. (2003). E-business Adoption by European Firms: A Cross-country Assessment of the Facilitators and Inhibitors. *European Journal of Information Systems*, 12(4) 251–268.

Zhu, K., Kraemer, K. L., Xu, S., & Dedrick, J. (2004). Information Technology Payoff in E-Business Environments: An International Perspective on Impacts of E-Business in the Financial Services Industry. *Journal of Management Information Systems*, 21(1), 17–54.

Zhu, K., Kraemer, K. L., Xu, S., Korte, W., & Gareis, K. (2005). Extending the Theory of Diffusion of Innovations to Explain E-Business Adoption by Firms – Innovation, Context, and Fit. CRITO working paper.

Zhu, K., Kraemer, K. L., & Xu, S. (forthcoming, 2006). Assimilation of Electronic Business by Firms in Different Countries: A Technology Diffusion Perspective. *Management Science*.

Appendix I Data collection and survey instrument

This appendix describes the Global E-Commerce Survey (GEC Survey) – the primary data source used for the country case studies – including objectives, instrument construction, survey administration, sampling methodology, and response rates.

Objective

The GEC Survey was designed to benchmark the state of e-commerce diffusion in firms, industries, and countries, and to determine whether the Internet and e-commerce are making some more competitive than others. Specifically, the survey focuses on six areas: 1) globalization of firms and markets; 2) use of e-commerce technologies (EDI, Internet, extranet, etc.); 3) drivers for Internet use; 4) barriers to conducting business on the Internet; 5) prevalence of online sales and online service offerings; and 6) benefits from e-commerce use. Each country chapter uses the GEC Survey as the primary data source. Country cases may also employ secondary data sources, and authors were encouraged to supplement GEC data as needed.

Countries and time period

Data were collected via telephone interviews in ten economies: Brazil, China, Denmark, France, Germany, Japan, Mexico, Singapore, Taiwan, and the United States. Interviews were conducted during the period 18 February 2002 to 5 April 2002. A total of 2,139 companies were interviewed.

Instrument design

The questionnaire was designed by researchers at the University of California, Irvine and reviewed and critiqued by International Data

Corporation's Global Research Organization and its global subsidiaries in the countries studied. The questionnaire was translated into Spanish, Portuguese, Chinese, French, German, Japanese, and Danish; translations were reviewed by the country academic experts, by IDC in-country experts, and by CRITO researchers.

Survey administration

CRITO partnered with IDC, located in Framingham, MA, to plan, organize, and conduct the survey. With the exception of Japan, all surveys were conducted by Market Probe (subcontracted and managed by IDC). For Japan, Adams Communications conducted the surveys.

Sampling method

The establishment (site) was the sampling unit and is the unit of the database. An establishment is defined as a physical location of a company. Thus, it may be a full company, a subsidiary, or a branch of a company.

The sampling was a stratified random sample. Stratification was by size (large: 250 or more employees; small: between 25 and 249 employees) and by industry (manufacturing: Standard Industrial Classification [SIC] 20–39; wholesale/retail distribution: SIC 50–54, 56–57, 59; and banking and insurance: SIC 60–65). A stratified sampling method without replacement was used, with sites selected randomly within each vertical/size cell.

The sample frame was obtained from a list source representative of the entire local market, regardless of computerization or web access. Dun & Bradstreet was used for the United States, Denmark, France, and Germany. Kompas was used for Brazil, Mexico, Taiwan, and Singapore. The Census of Enterprises and Yellow Pages was used for China. The Teikoku Data Bank was used for Japan.

A predetermined number of interviews was completed in each establishment size and industry category to ensure an adequate sample to report on for each country at the 95% confidence interval. Interviews were conducted only with those companies that were using the Internet in conducting their business at the time of the study – 2002. That is, all respondents were asked the following question: "Does your

Table A1.1 *GEC Survey – number of observations by country*

	Manufacturing			*Retail/Wholesale*			*Banking/Insurance*			
	SME	*Large*	*Total*	*SME*	*Large*	*Total*	*SME*	*Large*	*Total*	*TOTAL*
Brazil	34	34	68	34	34	68	30	34	64	**200**
China	34	35	69	35	33	68	33	34	67	**204**
Denmark	35	34	69	33	34	67	32	32	64	**200**
France	34	34	68	31	33	64	36	33	69	**201**
Germany	33	35	68	34	32	66	35	33	68	**202**
Japan	41	54	95	37	29	66	46	20	66	**227**
Mexico	34	35	69	33	36	69	30	33	63	**201**
Singapore	34	34	68	34	33	67	37	30	67	**202**
Taiwan	35	34	69	33	33	66	34	33	67	**202**
United States	50	50	100	53	47	100	52	48	100	**300**
TOTAL	**364**	**379**	**743**	**357**	**344**	**701**	**365**	**330**	**695**	**2,139**

Note: Cells represent counts of responses for each population subset

establishment use the Internet to buy, sell, or support products or services?" If they said "yes," the interview was continued; if not, it was terminated.

Target completion counts were a minimum of 200 interviews per country (but 300 in the USA). The interviews were to be equally divided by size (large; small) and industry sector: manufacturing, distribution (wholesale and retail), and finance (banking and insurance).

A "national" sampling approach was used in data collection for all countries except China. In national sampling, all sites were selected regardless of geographic location within the country. In China (PRC), sites were selected from the following cities: Beijing, Shanghai, Guangzhou, and Chengdu. We were advised by people knowledgeable about China that this would be the only way to get a useful response.

Results of the sampling approach are displayed in Table A1.1. Each country comprises roughly 200 firms, with Japan (227) and the USA (300) being outliers. On average, there are slightly more large firms (379) than SMEs (364) in manufacturing. In contrast, there are more SMEs in retail/wholesale (357) than large firms (344), as well as

Table A1.2 *GEC Survey – distribution by respondent type (percent)*

	SME (N = 1,086)	*Large (N = 1,053)*	*Total (N = 2,139)*
Business executives (CEO, COO, CFO, president, owner)	21	12	16
Other business unit management	4	2	3
IS unit executives (CIO, CTO, IS Director/VP of IS)	50	56	52
Other IS unit management	23	27	25
Other	3	3	3
Total	**100**	**100**	**100**

Source: CRITO GEC Survey, 2002

more SMEs in banking (365) than large firms (330). These differences partly reflect differences in sectoral representation of small versus large firms.

Despite these minor differences, within each economy stratification is very balanced across the two dimensions of size and sector. As an example, Mexico contains 34 SMEs versus 35 large firms in manufacturing, 33 versus 36 in retail wholesale, and 30 versus 33 in banking. Summing all firms across all countries leads to a total count of 2,139 firms in the GEC database.

Respondents

Eligible respondents were the individuals at each site best qualified to speak about the site's overall computing activities. For medium/large sites, the respondent was more likely to be the CIO, an IT director, or IT manager. For small sites, there was a higher percent of business-level executives, although overall more than three-quarters of the respondents were from IT (see Table A1.2).

Response rates

Response rates varied across countries, from a low of 8% in Germany and the USA to a high of 39% in China (Table A1.3). The mean response rate across all countries was 13%.

Table A1.3 *GEC Survey – response rate by country*

	Response rate (percent)
Brazil	15
China	39
Denmark	18
France	9
Germany	8
Japan	10
Mexico	12
Singapore	27
Taiwan	38
United States	8
Total	13

Note: response rate is calculated by dividing the total number completed by the total number qualified of those contacted

UCI GLOBAL E-COMMERCE SURVEY

Introduction

[READ:] Hello. My name is _____ and I'm calling on behalf of the University of California. We would appreciate a few minutes of your time to help us understand your business's use of the Internet for an academic research study targeting all regions of the world.

All responses will be used for research purposes only and are kept strictly confidential. We are not selling anything. In return for your time and help, we will send you an executive summary of our research findings.

May I speak with the person at your site who is most qualified to answer questions about your site's use of the Internet and other technologies?

[Wait for referral. Repeat intro and move to QA]

This will take twenty minutes or less. I'd like to begin by getting some background information.

QA **ALL.** What is your current title?

[Read as needed. Single response]

1 President, Owner, Managing Director, CEO

2 Chief Information Officer/Chief Technology Officer/VP of Information Systems
3 IS Manager, Director, Planner
4 Other manager in IS department
5 Business Operations Manager, COO
6 Administration/Finance Manager, Controller, CFO
97 Other [specify in QAO, length = 30]

Respondent selection/filter

Q1 **ALL.** Which industry best represents your site's primary business?
[Read. Single response]
1 Manufacturing
2 Retail or wholesale distribution [includes e-retail]
3 Banking, insurance or other finance
97 Other [specify in Q1O, length = 30]

Q2 **ALL.** An establishment is defined as a physical location. Does your organization have one or more than one establishment?
[Interviewer: an establishment is a single building]
1 One establishment
2 More than one establishment

Q3 **ALL.** How many employees work at this establishment?
[Note to translators: employee means those with a work contract]
[Note: collect actual response. Ranges are not acceptable for this question. "Don't know" not acceptable response. All respondents must respond. Establishment is defined as that physical location where the respondent is based]

Q4 **If Q2 = 2.** Approximately, how many employees does your organization have in this country?
[Programmer: Q4 can't be less than Q3. Code "don't know/refused" as –9]

Q5 **ALL.** Does your establishment use the Internet to buy, sell, or support products or services?
1 Yes
2 No

If Q1 (industry) = 1, 2, 3 and Q3 (estab size) greater than 24 employees and Q5 (conduct business on the Internet) = 1, continue with survey interview. [Programmer – Q1, Q3, and Q5 used to fill quotas. Please record responses to Q1 through Q5 for all respondents, even if they do not qualify]

Globalization of firm

Q6A **If Q2 = 2.** Does your organization have any establishments outside your country?

1 Yes
2 No
99 Don't know/not answered

Q6B **If Q6A = 1.** Approximately, how many employees does your organization have in total including all branches, divisions, and subsidiaries?

[Interviewer: if exact value is not known, ask for rough estimate]
[Programmer: Q6B can't be less than Q4. Code "don't know/refused" as –9. If cannot say, go to Q6C. Organization may be defined as the company or enterprise, the highest level of the entire worldwide entity]

Q6C **If cannot say.** Is it:

1 Less than 250
2 250–999
3 1,000 to 9,999
4 10,000+
99 Don't know

Q7 **If Q6A = 1.** Does your organization have its headquarters outside your country?

1 Yes
2 No
99 Don't know/not answered

If Q2 = 2. READ: For the rest of this survey, we would like you to consider only this establishment when answering questions about your organization

Globalization of markets/sourcing

Q8 **ALL.** Does your establishment generate revenue from sales of products and/or services?
1 Yes
2 No
99 Don't know/refused

Q9 **If Q8 = 1.** With the total equal to 100%, what percent of your establishment's sales are to business customers, including commercial, government, and education establishments, versus consumers?

[Interviewer: if exact value is not known, ask for rough estimate. Less than 1% should be recorded as 1%. Enter 0 where appropriate]
[Programmer: total must sum to 100%; label variables as Q9A, Q9B]

A. Percent to business, government, education
B. Percent to consumers
Total = 100%

Q10 **If Q8 = 1.** What percent of your establishment's total sales are from outside your country?

[Interviewer: if exact value is not known, ask for rough estimate. Less than 1% should be recorded as 1%. Enter 0 where appropriate]
[Programmer: record actual value. Code "don't know" as –9]

Q11 **ALL.** What percent of your establishment's total procurement spending is from outside your country?

[Interviewer: if exact value is not known, ask for rough estimate. Less than 1% should be recorded as 1%. Enter 0 if they do not procure from outside the country]
[Programmer: record actual value. Code "don't know/refuse" as –9]

Q12 **ALL.** Using a 5-point scale, where 5 is significantly affected and 1 is not at all affected, please tell me how much your establishment is affected by competitors in your local area, inside your country, and outside your country.

[Scale: 1 = not at all affected, 5 = significantly affected. Code "don't know/refuse" as 99. Label variables as Q12A, Q12B, etc. Read all three options before recording any answers]

A. Competitors in your local area
B. Competitors inside your country
C. Competitors from outside your country

Use of e-commerce technologies

End-user devices

Q13 **ALL.** Approximately how many personal computers are currently in use at your establishment? Again, establishment refers to this physical location. Please include both desktop and portable personal computers.

[Record actual value. Code "don't know/refuse" as –9]
[Question 14 eliminated in the pilot stage of the survey]

Access to email

Q15 **ALL.** Does your establishment use email?
1 Yes
2 No
99 Don't know/not answered

Access to website

Q16 **ALL.** Does your organization have a website that is accessible by the public?
1 Yes
2 No
99 Don't know/not answered

Access to intranet/extranet

Q17 ALL. An intranet is a private, internally accessible website that provides information about the firm to employees. Does your establishment use an intranet?
1 Yes
2 No
99 Don't know/not answered

Q18 **ALL.** An extranet is a private website accessible by external organizations such as clients, business partners, and suppliers, but not by the general public. Does your establishment use an extranet?

1 Yes
2 No
99 Don't know/not answered

Q19 **If Q18 = 1.** Is this extranet accessible by . . .
[1 = Yes, 2 = No, 99 = "don't know"]
A Suppliers or business partners?
B Customers?

Access to EDI

Q20 **ALL.** Does your establishment use EDI, that is, electronic data interchange?
[Interviewer: if in doubt, quote definition: EDI involves information transfers between computers of different enterprises using a standardized format]

1 Yes
2 No
99 Don't know/not answered

Q21 **If Q20 = 1.** Is this standard EDI over private networks or Internet-based EDI or both?

1 EDI over private networks
2 Internet-based EDI
3 Both
99 Don't know/not answered

Access to EFT

Q22 **ALL.** Does your establishment use EFT, that is, electronic funds transfer?

1 Yes
2 No
99 Don't know/not answered

Access to call center

Q23 **ALL.** Does your establishment use a call center, that is, a unit whose primary purpose is sales, technical support, or services to customers?

1 Yes
2 No
99 Don't know/not answered

Uses of the Internet

Q24 **ALL.** Does your establishment use the Internet for . . .
[Read. Rotate. Scale: 1 = Yes, 2 = No, 99 = don't know/refused. Label variables as Q24A, Q24B, etc.]

A. Advertising and marketing purposes?
B. Making sales online?
C. After-sales customer service and support?
D. Making purchases online?
E. Exchanging operational data with suppliers?
F. Exchanging operational data with business customers?
G. Formally integrating the same business processes with suppliers or other business partners?

Q25A **ALL.** Have you ever heard of the concept of an Internet marketplace, exchange, or trading community, through which multiple businesses buy and sell goods and services?

1 Yes
2 No
99 Don't know/not answered

Q25B **If Q25A = 1.** Does your establishment participate as a buyer, a seller, or both in such an Internet-based trading community?

1 Buyer
2 Seller
3 Both
4 No
99 Don't know/not answered

Q26 **If Q24B = 1 or Q25B = 2 or 3.** Which of the following statements best characterizes how you are using the Internet to sell products and services?
[Single response]
1 Addresses new markets only
2 Addresses our traditional distribution channels only
3 Competes directly with our traditional distribution channels
4 Replaces our traditional distribution channels
99 Don't know

Q27 **ALL.** Today it is possible to access content or services from various mobile devices such as cell phones and handhelds such as Palms or pocket PC devices. Does your organization provide or plan to provide content or services that mobile customers can access?
[Single response]
1 Already available
2 Plan to add mobile access within the next year
3 No, we have no current plans
99 Don't know

Drivers for Internet use

Q28 **ALL.** Using a 5-point scale, where 5 is "a very significant factor" and 1 is "not a factor at all," please rate how significant each of the following was to your organization's decision to begin using the Internet for business. How significant was . . .
[Rotate. Scale: 1 = not a factor at all, 5 = a very significant factor, 99 = don't know/refused. Label variables as Q28A, Q28B, etc.]
A. Customers demanded it
B. Major competitors were online
C. Suppliers required it
D. To reduce costs
E. To expand market for existing product/services
F. To enter new businesses or markets
G. To improve coordination with customers and suppliers
H. Required for government procurement
I. Government provided incentives

Barriers/difficulties to doing business on the Internet

Q29 **ALL.** Using a 5-point scale, where 5 is "a very significant obstacle" and 1 is "not an obstacle," please rate how significant the following obstacles are to your establishment's ability to do business online.

[Rotate. Scale: 1 = not an obstacle, 5 = a very significant obstacle, 99 = don't know/refused. Label variables as Q29A, Q29B, Q29C, etc.]

A. Need for face-to-face customer interaction to sell our products
B. Concern about privacy of data or security issues
C. Customers do not use this technology
D. Finding staff with e-commerce expertise
E. Prevalence of credit card use in the country
F. Costs of implementing an e-commerce site
G. Making needed organizational changes
H. Our level of ability to use the Internet as part of our business strategy

Q30 **ALL.** Using the same 5-point scale, how much do the following obstacles affect your establishment's ability to do business online?

[Rotate. Scale: 1 = not an obstacle, 5 = a very significant obstacle, 99 = don't know/refused. Label variables as Q30A, Q30B, Q30C, Q30D]

A. Cost of Internet access
B. Business laws do not support e-commerce
C. Taxation of Internet sales
D. Inadequate legal protection for Internet purchases

Impacts of doing business online

Q31 **ALL.** Using a 5-point scale, where 5 is "a great deal" and 1 is "not at all," please rate the degree to which your establishment has experienced the following impacts since it began using the Internet for business?

[Rotate. Scale: 1 = not at all, 5 = a great deal, 99 = don't know/refused. Label variables as Q31A, Q31B, Q31C, etc.]

A. Internal processes more efficient
B. Staff productivity increased

C. Sales increased
D. Sales area widened
E. Customer service improved
F. International sales increased
G. Procurement costs decreased
H. Inventory costs decreased
I. Coordination with suppliers improved
J. Our competitive position improved

Q32 **ALL.** Please indicate whether the following have increased, decreased, or stayed the same in your establishment since it began using the Internet for business.
[Rotate. Scale: 1 = decreased, 2 = stayed the same, 3 = increased, 99 = don't know/refused. Label variables as Q32A, Q32B, etc.]
A. Number of distribution channels
B. Number of suppliers
C. Number of competitors
D. Intensity of competition

Online sales

Online Sales section asked if Q24B = 1 or Q25B = 2, 3, else skip to Online Services section (Q37A)

[READ:] Now, turning to a few more questions regarding your establishment's online sales.

Q33 Are these online sales to other businesses, or to consumers, or to both?
[Single response]
1 Businesses
2 Consumers
3 Both
99 Don't know/refused

Q34 **If Q33 = 2, 3.** What percent of your establishment's total consumer sales is conducted online?

[If exact value is not known, ask for rough estimate. Enter 0 where appropriate. Less than 1% should be recorded as 1%. Code "don't know" as −9]

Q35 **If Q33 = 1, 3.** What percent of your establishment's total business-to-business sales are conducted online?

[If exact value is not known, ask for rough estimate. Enter 0 where appropriate. Less than 1% should be recorded as 1%. Code "don't know" as −9]

Q36 Does the website support online payment?
1 Yes
2 No
99 Don't know/not answered

Online services

Q37A **If Q1 = 1 and Q16 = 1 (Manufacturing).** Does your organization's website support any of the following services?
[Rotate. Scale: 1 = yes, 2 = no, 99 = don't know/refused. Label variables as Q37AA, Q37AB, etc.]
A. Product configuration
B. Order tracking
C. Service and technical support
D. Product specification
E. Account information

Q37B **If Q1 = 2 and Q16 = 1 (Retail or Distribution).** Does your organization's website support any of the following services?
[Rotate. Scale: 1 = yes, 2 = no, 99 = don't know/refused. Label variables as Q37BA, Q37BB, etc.]
A. Gift certificates and/or registry
B. Product catalog
C. Product reviews
D. Individual customization
E. Account information

Q37C **If Q1 = 3 and Q16 = 1 (Finance, Insurance).** Does your organization's website support any of the following services?

[Rotate. Scale: 1 = yes, 2 = no, 99 = don't know/refused. Label variables as Q37CA, Q37CB, etc.]

A. Online services such as filing applications, filing claims, paying bills, transferring funds
B. Access to account information
C. Online tools such as research tools, planning tools, etc.

Q38 **If any Q37AA–AE = 1 or any Q37BA–BE = 1 or any Q37CA–CC = 1.** Are these online services to other businesses, or to consumers, or to both?

1 Businesses
2 Consumers
3 Both
99 Don't know/refused

Q39 **If Q38 = 2, 3.** What percent of your establishment's total services to consumers is conducted online?

[If exact value is not known, ask for rough estimate. Enter 0 where appropriate. Less than 1% should be recorded as 1%]
[Programmer: record actual value. Code "don't know" as −9]

Q40 **If Q38 = 1, 3.** What percent of your establishment's total services to businesses is conducted online?

[If exact value is not known, ask for rough estimate. Enter 0 where appropriate. Less than 1% should be recorded as 1%]
[Programmer: record actual value. Code "don't know" as −9]

Online procurement

Online Procurement section asked if Q24D = 1 or Q25B = 1, 3, else skip to Enterprise Application Strategy section

Q41 **If Q1 = 1.** What percent of the money your establishment spends on direct goods for production, such as parts and components, is ordered online?

[Interviewer: if exact value is not known, ask for rough estimate. Less than 1% should be recorded as 1%. Enter 0 if they do not buy direct goods for production, such as parts and components, online. Enter –9 if they don't know]
[Programmer: record actual value]

Q42 **If Q1 = 2.** What percent of the money your establishment spends on goods for resale is ordered online?

[Interviewer: if exact value is not known, ask for rough estimate. Less than 1% should be recorded as 1%. Enter 0 if they do not buy goods for resale online. Enter –9 if they don't know]
[Programmer: record actual value]

Q43 What percent of the money your establishment spends on supplies and equipment for doing business is ordered online?

[Interviewer: if exact value is not known, ask for rough estimate. Less than 1% should be recorded as 1%. Enter 0 if they do not buy supplies and equipment for doing business online. Enter –9 if they don't know]
[Programmer: record actual value]

Enterprise application strategy

Q44 **If Q16 = 1 or Q18 = 1.** Using a 5-point scale, where 5 is "a great deal" and 1 is "not at all," please rate the extent to which your Internet applications are electronically integrated with your internal databases and information systems.

[Scale: 1 = not at all, 5 = a great deal, 99 = don't know/refused]

Q45 **If Q16 = 1 or Q18 = 1.** Using a 5-point scale, where 5 is "a great deal" and 1 is "not at all," please rate the extent to which your company's databases and information systems are electronically integrated with those of your suppliers and business customers.

[Scale: 1 = not at all, 5 = a great deal, 99 = don't know/refused]

Spending

[Ask Q46A. Record Q46B if "calendar year" is difficult for respondent to answer]

Q46A **ALL.** What was your establishment's total revenue in calendar year 2001?

[Interviewer: if exact value is not known, ask for rough estimate (or range, if needed, to be entered verbatim)]
[Code "don't know/refuse" as −9]

Q46B **ALL.** What was your establishment's total revenue in fiscal year 2001?

[Interviewer: if exact value is not known, ask for rough estimate (or range, if needed, to be entered verbatim)]
[Code "don't know/refuse" as −9]

Q47 **ALL.** What would you estimate was your establishment's total IS operating budget as a percent of your establishment's revenue in 2001?

[Code "don't know/refuse" as –9. Cannot be >100%. Note: includes internal and external spending]

Q48 **ALL.** What percent of your establishment's IS operating budget in 2001 was devoted to web-based, that is, Internet, extranet, and intranet initiatives, including systems, software, IT services, consulting, and internal staff?

[Code "don't know/refuse" as –9. Cannot be >100%. Enter 0 if no web spending. Note: includes internal and external spending]

Q49 **ALL.** How many IT professionals are located in this establishment?
[Code "don't know/refuse" as –9. Can't be greater than Q3]

Q50 Finally, I want to emphasize again that all responses will be used for academic research purposes only and are kept strictly confidential. Would you be willing to allow us to provide the name of your establishment to the researchers at the University of California? [If necessary, explain that the data will be linked to additional data obtained from public sources such as annual reports on your company.

Your organization's name would only be used in aggregated analysis and at no time would your responses be reported by itself, nor would your company be identified]

1 Yes

2 No

[Obtain email address of those who want exec summary]

Appendix II GEC Survey measures by sector and size

The tables contain the weighted survey responses in the ten countries combined, what is referred to in the chapters as the "global sample," broken down by size of establishment and sector. The responses were weighted based on the total number of establishments by employee size within the three sectors in each country.

Table A2.1 ***Globalization indicators, 2002***

	Establishment size		*Sector*			
	SME	*Large*	*Mfg.*	*Distrib.*	*Finance*	*Global*
Percent of companies with establishments abroad	23	37	28	22	23	24
Percent of companies with headquarters abroad	8	13	12	6	11	8
Mean percent of total sales from abroad	12	13	15	11	8	12
Mean percent of total procurement spending from abroad	21	12	24	21	5	20
Degree affected by competitors abroad (percent)						
Low	69	57	47	77	83	68
Moderate	15	22	21	14	8	16
High	16	21	32	9	9	15

Source: CRITO GEC Survey, 2002

Table A2.2 *Use of e-commerce technologies, 2002*

	Establishment size		*Sector*			
Percent using . . .	*SME*	*Large*	*Mfg.*	*Distrib.*	*Finance*	*Global*
Email	98	99	96	100	99	99
Website	73	83	80	70	82	74
Intranet	62	78	64	63	66	64
Extranet	32	42	31	33	32	33
• accessible by suppliers/business partners	20	33	19	22	22	21
• accessible by customers	17	25	18	17	21	18
EDI	44	41	43	45	42	43
• over private networks	35	35	30	39	30	35
• Internet-based	24	22	28	22	28	24
EFT	44	39	41	42	62	43
Call center	32	37	33	31	39	32

Source: CRITO GEC Survey, 2002

Table A2.3 *Enterprise integration strategy, 2002*

	Establishment size		*Sector*			
Extent to which Internet applications are electronically integrated with . . .	*SME*	*Large*	*Mfg.*	*Distrib.*	*Finance*	*Global*
Internal databases and information systems						
Percent little to none	53	44	60	50	39	53
Percent some	23	30	24	24	21	24
Percent a great deal	24	26	16	26	40	24
Those of suppliers and business customers						
Percent little to none	73	64	73	73	66	72
Percent some	17	29	19	18	16	18
Percent a great deal	10	7	8	9	18	10

Source: CRITO GEC Survey, 2002

Table A2.4 *Content/services to mobile customers, 2002*

Percent providing or planning to provide mobile content or services	*Establishment size*		*Sector*			
	SME	*Large*	*Mfg.*	*Distrib.*	*Finance*	*Global*
Already available	13	19	14	13	21	14
Plan to add within the next year	19	15	18	18	19	18

Source: CRITO GEC Survey, 2002

Table A2.5 *Drivers for Internet use, 2002*

Percent indicating driver is a significant factor	*Establishment size*		*Sector*			
	SME	*Large*	*Mfg.*	*Distrib.*	*Finance*	*Global*
Customers demanded it	37	40	35	38	37	37
Major competitors were online	31	37	31	29	48	31
Suppliers required it	22	28	26	21	13	22
To reduce costs	35	43	43	32	34	36
To expand market for existing product or services	47	54	51	46	53	48
To enter new businesses or markets	42	46	39	44	36	42
To improve coordination with customers and suppliers	43	54	51	40	40	44
Required for government procurement	15	17	19	14	11	15
Government provided incentives	8	11	10	7	7	8

Source: CRITO GEC Survey, 2002

Table A2.6 ***Barriers/difficulties in Internet use, 2002***

Percent indicating statement is a significant obstacle	*Establishment size*		*Sector*			
	SME	*Large*	*Mfg.*	*Distrib.*	*Finance*	*Global*
Need for face-to-face customer interaction	34	31	32	34	40	34
Concern about privacy of data or security issues	44	45	47	40	62	44
Customers do not use the technology	32	27	30	33	23	31
Finding staff with e-commerce expertise	28	15	24	29	20	27
Prevalence of credit card use in the country	21	16	22	20	15	20
Costs of implementing an e-commerce site	34	32	33	35	28	34
Making needed organizational changes	24	24	24	25	18	24
Level of ability to use the Internet as part of business strategy	25	25	28	24	21	25
Cost of Internet access	15	13	14	16	13	15
Business laws do not support e-commerce	24	27	28	23	23	24
Taxation of Internet sales	17	12	14	19	8	16
Inadequate legal protection for Internet purchases	34	34	37	34	26	34

Source: CRITO GEC Survey, 2002

Table A2.7 *Uses of the Internet, 2002*

	Establishment size		*Sector*			
Percent using the Internet for . . .	*SME*	*Large*	*Mfg.*	*Distrib.*	*Finance*	*Global*
Advertising and marketing purposes	57	64	56	57	68	58
Making sales online	30	33	25	32	33	30
After-sales customer service and support	43	53	48	41	48	44
Making purchases online	48	39	43	48	52	47
Exchanging operational data with suppliers	48	54	50	48	42	48
Exchanging operational data with business customers	50	57	53	49	52	51
Formally integrating the same business processes with suppliers or other business partners	34	38	27	28	34	34

Source: CRITO GEC Survey, 2002

Table A2.8 *Participation in an Internet-based trading community, 2002*

	Establishment size		*Sector*			
	SME	*Large*	*Mfg.*	*Distrib.*	*Finance*	*Global*
Percent who have heard of the concept of an Internet marketplace	80	86	84	78	79	80
Percent participating as a buyer only	7	6	5	8	9	7
Percent participating as a seller only	12	15	17	10	11	12
Percent participating as both a buyer and a seller	17	16	13	19	9	17

Source: CRITO GEC Survey, 2002

Table A2.9 *How establishments use the Internet to sell products and services, 2002*

Percent indicating Internet used to . . .	*Establishment size*		*Sector*			
	SME	*Large*	*Mfg.*	*Distrib.*	*Finance*	*Global*
Address new markets only	16	11	23	12	13	15
Address traditional distribution channels only	45	37	39	48	33	44
Compete directly with traditional distribution channels	26	41	26	26	42	27
Replace traditional distribution channels	13	11	12	14	12	13

Source: CRITO GEC Survey, 2002

Table A2.10 *Online sales, 2002*

	Establishment size		*Sector*			
	SME	*Large*	*Mfg.*	*Distrib.*	*Finance*	*Global*
Type of online sales						
B2B only	13	11	16	12	7	13
B2C only	7	10	4	8	14	7
both B2B and B2C	15	15	11	17	16	15
Mean percent of total consumer sales conducted online (all establishments)	4	3	2	4	5	4
Mean percent of total business sales conducted online (all establishments)	4	5	3	4	4	4
Percent of websites that support online payment (only those doing online sales)	33	43	25	37	37	34

Source: CRITO GEC Survey, 2002

Table A2.11 *Online services, 2002*

	Establishment size		*Sector*			
	SME	*Large*	*Mfg.*	*Distrib.*	*Finance*	*Global*
Type of online service						
B2B only	23	26	34	19	10	23
B2C only	13	15	7	14	31	13
both B2B and B2C	32	40	36	32	35	33
Mean percent of total consumer services conducted online	8	8	7	7	12	8
Mean percent of total business services conducted online	11	12	15	9	9	11
Percent of manufacturing websites which support						
Product configuration	55	52	55			55
Order tracking	22	20	22			22
Service and technical support	53	60	54			54
Product specification	79	82	80			80
Account information	16	23	17			17
Percent of wholesale/retail distribution websites which support						
Gift certificates and/or registry	20	39		21		21
Product catalog	70	75		70		70
Product reviews	48	60		49		49
Individual customization	20	43		21		21
Account information	21	33		22		22
Percent of banking and insurance websites supporting						
Online services such as filing applications, filing claims, paying bills, transferring funds	53	62			54	54
Access to account information	56	71			57	57
Online tools such as research tools, planning tools, etc.	51	58			52	52

Source: CRITO GEO Survey, 2002

Table A2.12 *Online procurement, 2002*

	Establishment size		*Sector*			
	SME	*Large*	*Mfg.*	*Distrib.*	*Finance*	*Global*
Percent of establishments doing online purchasing	52	43	46	52	56	51
Mean percent of money spent for direct goods for production is ordered online (all establishments)	9	5	8			8
Mean percent of money spent on goods for resale is ordered online (all establishments)	7	4		7		7
Mean percent of money spent on supplies and equipment for doing business is ordered online (all establishments)	8	7	6	9	14	8

Source: CRITO GEC Survey, 2002

Table A2.13 *Impacts of doing business online, 2002*

	Establishment size		*Sector*			
Percent indicating high impact	*SME*	*Large*	*Mfg.*	*Distrib.*	*Finance*	*Global*
Internal processes more efficient	33	42	38	32	34	34
Staff productivity increased	27	30	26	28	30	27
Sales increased	20	30	19	22	20	21
Sales area widened	30	43	34	30	31	31
Customer service improved	34	43	41	31	40	35
International sales increased	19	28	24	18	9	20
Procurement costs decreased	17	24	24	15	14	18
Inventory costs decreased	13	20	16	13	13	14
Coordination with suppliers improved	29	38	33	29	25	30
Competitive position improved	29	43	34	28	31	30

Source: CRITO GEC Survey, 2002

Table A2.14 *Changes in firms' environment since using the Internet, 2002*

	Establishment size		*Sector*			
Percent indicating . . .	*SME*	*Large*	*Mfg.*	*Distrib.*	*Finance*	*Global*
Number of distribution channels increased	40	45	37	42	40	40
Number of suppliers increased	29	41	38	26	30	30
Number of competitors increased	27	33	29	27	29	28
Intensity of competition increased	42	40	40	42	42	42

Source: CRITO GEC Survey, 2002

Appendix III GEC Survey measures by country

The tables contain the weighted survey responses in the ten countries and what is referred to in the chapters as the "global sample." The responses were weighted based on the total number of establishments by employee size within the three sectors in each country. The unweighted survey responses for each country are: United States (n = 300), Mexico (n = 201), Brazil (n = 200), Denmark (n = 200), France (n = 201), Germany (n = 202), China (n = 204), Taiwan (n = 202), Singapore (n = 202), Japan (n = 227), global (n = 2,139).

Table A3.1 *Globalization indicators, 2002*

	Americas			*Europe*			*Asia*				
	USA	*Mexico*	*Brazil*	*Denmark*	*France*	*Germany*	*China*	*Taiwan*	*Singapore*	*Japan*	*Global*
Percent of companies with establishments abroad	23	19	4	41	23	40	25	42	57	19	24
Percent of companies with headquarters abroad	5	10	3	14	7	12	12	21	31	3	8
Mean percent of total sales from abroad	5	15	4	23	15	15	15	51	39	5	12
Mean percent of total procurement spending from abroad	8	39	10	29	21	23	28	30	45	13	20
Degree affected by competitors abroad (percent)											
Low	78	61	89	67	71	65	54	35	34	82	68
Moderate	10	12	4	17	17	15	25	39	31	9	16
High	12	27	7	16	12	20	21	26	35	9	15

Source: CRITO GEC Survey, 2002

Table A3.2 *Use of e-commerce technologies, 2002*

	Americas			*Europe*			*Asia*				
Percent using . . .	*USA*	*Mexico*	*Brazil*	*Denmark*	*France*	*Germany*	*China*	*Taiwan*	*Singapore*	*Japan*	*Global*
Email	100	98	100	100	98	100	96	100	100	100	99
Website	80	79	71	96	54	92	70	57	83	73	74
Intranet	56	51	38	84	68	84	61	51	67	81	64
Extranet	29	31	33	40	15	22	36	30	32	50	33
• accessible by suppliers/business partners	17	23	11	30	12	14	29	19	24	26	21
• accessible by customers	16	16	16	23	11	12	22	23	20	22	18
EDI	43	58	37	69	43	68	25	23	33	64	43
• over private networks only	17	20	8	16	30	31	10	10	17	34	19
• Internet-based only	8	28	7	20	5	10	4	7	10	8	8
• both	16	10	22	32	8	27	10	5	6	22	16
EFT	63	71	52	74	30	87	26	20	43	8	43
Call center	41	44	46	27	22	30	21	19	24	40	32

Source: CRITO GEC Survey, 2002

Table A3.3 *Enterprise integration strategy, 2002*

Extent to which Internet applications	*Americas*			*Europe*			*Asia*				
are electronically integrated with . . .	*USA*	*Mexico*	*Brazil*	*Denmark*	*France*	*Germany*	*China*	*Taiwan*	*Singapore*	*Japan*	*Global*
Internal databases and information systems											
Percent little to none	53	60	58	23	49	56	47	43	40	57	53
Percent some	15	12	12	24	19	17	36	25	37	29	24
Percent a great deal	32	28	30	53	32	27	17	32	23	14	24
Those of suppliers and business customers											
Percent little to none	67	82	89	58	81	72	63	62	48	81	72
Percent some	16	10	9	27	14	11	29	26	28	17	18
Percent a great deal	16	9	2	15	5	17	8	12	24	2	10

Source: CRITO GEC Survey, 2002

Table A3.4 ***Content/services to mobile customers, 2002***

Percent providing or planning to provide mobile content or services	*Americas*			*Europe*			*Asia*				
	USA	*Mexico*	*Brazil*	*Denmark*	*France*	*Germany*	*China*	*Taiwan*	*Singapore*	*Japan*	*Global*
Already available	15	7	4	29	8	18	15	18	12	16	14
Plan to add within the next year	16	46	31	12	14	12	16	10	16	15	18

Source: CRITO GEC Survey, 2002

Table A3.5 *Drivers for Internet use, 2002*

Percent indicating driver is a significant factor	*Americas*			*Europe*			*Asia*				
	USA	*Mexico*	*Brazil*	*Denmark*	*France*	*Germany*	*China*	*Taiwan*	*Singapore*	*Japan*	*Global*
Customers demanded it	36	36	45	52	15	25	45	48	52	37	37
Major competitors were online	33	39	27	38	22	43	33	40	40	19	31
Suppliers required it	19	33	24	14	10	8	28	32	31	26	22
To reduce costs	33	58	61	56	18	20	40	41	47	27	36
To expand market for existing product or services	50	65	59	46	22	58	55	47	58	24	48
To enter new businesses or markets	39	65	54	37	20	46	43	54	54	34	42
To improve coordination with customers and suppliers	42	74	61	51	41	42	38	50	68	33	44
Required for government procurement	9	33	25	15	15	2	22	23	32	5	15
Government provided incentives	3	13	14	3	9	2	12	28	30	2	8

Source: CRITO GEC Survey, 2002

Table A3.6 *Barriers/difficulties in Internet use, 2002*

Percent indicating statement is a significant obstacle	*Americas*			*Europe*			*Asia*				
	USA	*Mexico*	*Brazil*	*Denmark*	*France*	*Germany*	*China*	*Taiwan*	*Singapore*	*Japan*	*Global*
Need for face-to-face customer interaction	42	26	32	34	46	12	31	37	38	43	34
Concern about privacy of data or security issues	47	58	49	23	20	25	45	66	48	55	44
Customers do not use the technology	27	39	48	27	31	24	33	31	27	30	31
Finding staff with e-commerce expertise	24	31	34	15	20	41	20	27	20	29	27
Prevalence of credit card use in the country	16	20	23	5	14	22	30	18	24	9	20
Costs of implementing an e-commerce site	32	35	34	13	22	32	29	40	45	53	34
Making needed organizational changes	14	32	33	14	22	31	22	18	38	28	24
Level of ability to use the Internet as part of business strategy	21	29	22	19	16	14	31	24	22	31	25
Cost of Internet access	11	4	20	6	6	2	22	24	34	24	15
Business laws do not support e-commerce	8	27	32	15	24	5	41	28	35	22	24
Taxation of Internet sales	15	22	27	9	20	2	19	18	28	15	16
Inadequate legal protection for Internet purchases	12	45	41	12	39	21	54	49	44	21	34

Source: CRITO GEC Survey, 2002

Table A3.7 ***Uses of the Internet, 2002***

	Americas			*Europe*			*Asia*				
Percent using the Internet for . . .	*USA*	*Mexico*	*Brazil*	*Denmark*	*France*	*Germany*	*China*	*Taiwan*	*Singapore*	*Japan*	*Global*
Advertising and marketing purposes	64	73	59	89	26	78	52	48	61	53	58
Making sales online	43	12	28	47	12	57	23	32	30	21	30
After-sales customer service and support	56	40	23	57	16	53	55	41	39	25	44
Making purchases online	73	65	55	68	24	61	31	27	29	33	47
Exchanging operational data with suppliers	43	50	52	56	36	60	47	42	45	52	48
Exchanging operational data with business customers	54	47	49	40	40	52	52	46	50	53	51
Formally integrating the same business processes with suppliers or other business partners	36	55	49	44	24	48	30	24	41	16	34

Source: CRITO GEC Survey, 2002

Table A3.8 *Participation in an Internet-based trading community, 2002*

	Americas			*Europe*			*Asia*				
	USA	*Mexico*	*Brazil*	*Denmark*	*France*	*Germany*	*China*	*Taiwan*	*Singapore*	*Japan*	*Global*
Percent who have heard of the concept of an Internet marketplace	72	89	84	95	62	87	88	82	85	73	80
Percent participating as a buyer only	14	20	11	3	5	1	7	4	4	1	7
Percent participating as a seller only	32	7	10	8	8	14	10	18	5	14	12
Percent participating as both a buyer and a seller	45	23	7	6	6	20	22	21	18	0	17

Source: CRITO GEC Survey, 2002

Table A3.9 *How establishments use the Internet to sell products and services, 2002*

	Americas			*Europe*			*Asia*				
Percent indicating Internet used to . . .	*USA*	*Mexico*	*Brazil*	*Denmark*	*France*	*Germany*	*China*	*Taiwan*	*Singapore*	*Japan*	*Global*
Address new markets only	8	25	26	4	39	7	24	25	1	12	15
Address traditional distribution channels only	45	48	60	57	31	76	10	34	37	22	44
Compete directly with traditional distribution channels	29	9	10	36	25	17	49	20	47	37	27
Replace traditional distribution channels	18	17	4	4	6	0	17	21	14	29	13

Source: CRITO GEC Survey, 2002

Table A3.10 *Online sales, 2002*

	Americas			*Europe*			*Asia*				
	USA	*Mexico*	*Brazil*	*Denmark*	*France*	*Germany*	*China*	*Taiwan*	*Singapore*	*Japan*	*Global*
Type of online sales											
Percent B2B only	16	6	9	16	7	34	9	15	8	7	13
Percent B2C only	14	6	10	15	4	12	3	9	6	1	7
Percent both B2B and B2C	18	18	18	23	4	18	14	14	17	13	15
Mean percent of total consumer sales conducted online (all establishments)	5	2	4	8	0	9	1	4	2	5	4
Mean percent of total business sales conducted online (all establishments)	6	4	4	5	0	8	2	6	6	3	4
Mean percent of total consumer sales conducted online (only those doing B2C sales online)	17	10	13	22	4	31	9	21	12	36	19
Mean percent of total business sales conducted online (only those doing B2B sales online)	18	20	13	15	0	16	10	24	32	15	15
Percent of websites that support online payment (only those doing online sales)	38	25	33	50	52	42	13	33	25	73	34

Source: CRITO GEC Survey, 2002

Table A3.11 *Online services, 2002*

	Americas			*Europe*			*Asia*				
	USA	*Mexico*	*Brazil*	*Denmark*	*France*	*Germany*	*China*	*Taiwan*	*Singapore*	*Japan*	*Global*
Type of online service											
B2B only	20	6	8	23	8	39	28	21	20	30	23
B2C only	22	6	8	19	16	22	4	6	14	19	13
Both B2B and B2C	35	63	48	53	19	30	34	27	47	15	33
Mean percent of total consumer services conducted online	8	8	20	11	2	5	6	8	14	8	8
Mean percent of total business services conducted online	11	10	11	14	2	13	14	16	16	12	11
Percent of manufacturing websites which support:											
Product configuration	51	54	51	23	56	40	61	41	38	57	55
Order tracking	20	20	4	10	20	37	21	50	35	19	22
Service and technical support	56	21	23	53	41	45	74	54	32	39	54
Product specification	81	82	69	67	58	66	92	88	76	60	80
Account information	16	20	4	22	10	11	22	31	31	10	17

Percent of wholesale/retail distribution websites which support:											
Gift certificates and/or registry	23	9	29	8	15	16	22	16	31	24	21
Product catalog	61	82	85	68	69	91	76	76	90	38	70
Product reviews	55	20	71	41	53	45	56	28	50	39	49
Individual customization	37	20	36	31	16	16	16	9	15	13	21
Account information	36	19	22	15	15	16	22	33	10	13	22
Percent of banking and insurance websites supporting:											
Online services such as filing applications, filing claims, paying bills, transferring funds	53	35	81	51	29	72	70	80	51	30	54
Access to account information	62	76	38	59	18	62	72	71	27	35	57
Online tools, e.g. research tools, planning tools, etc.	63	43	62	58	12	54	52	80	43	19	52

Source: CRITO GEC Survey, 2002

Table A3.12 ***Online procurement, 2002***

	Americas			*Europe*			*Asia*				
	USA	*Mexico*	*Brazil*	*Denmark*	*France*	*Germany*	*China*	*Taiwan*	*Singapore*	*Japan*	*Global*
Percent of establishments doing online purchasing	74	71	61	68	25	62	40	36	37	33	51
Mean percent of money spent for direct goods for production is ordered online (all establishments)	11	9	16	17	3	7	4	7	7	20	8
Mean percent money spent on goods for resale is ordered online (all establishments)	11	19	14	14	3	7	5	3	4	0	7
Mean percent of the money spent on supplies and equipment for doing business is ordered online (all establishments)	19	13	13	13	3	7	3	4	7	0	8

Source: CRITO GEC Survey, 2002

Table A3.13 *Impacts of doing business online, 2002*

	Americas			*Europe*			*Asia*				
Percent indicating high impact	*USA*	*Mexico*	*Brazil*	*Denmark*	*France*	*Germany*	*China*	*Taiwan*	*Singapore*	*Japan*	*Global*
Internal processes more efficient	28	54	33	39	38	42	31	42	35	29	34
Staff productivity increased	31	38	40	16	26	19	24	28	40	24	27
Sales increased	24	36	26	25	9	19	26	26	31	1	21
Sales area widened	36	25	28	20	19	32	48	33	47	3	31
Customer service improved	40	55	45	45	24	36	37	44	45	11	35
International sales increased	9	20	13	4	13	28	33	33	42	5	20
Procurement costs decreased	12	20	25	18	7	11	30	25	32	4	18
Inventory costs decreased	11	14	28	12	4	6	21	24	21	5	14
Coordination with suppliers improved	29	51	34	27	24	14	29	26	44	34	30
Competitive position improved	33	45	24	30	12	23	41	38	50	10	30

Source: CRITO GEC Survey, 2002

Table A3.14 *Changes in firms' environments since using the Internet, 2002*

	Americas			*Europe*			*Asia*				
Percent indicating . . .	*USA*	*Mexico*	*Brazil*	*Denmark*	*France*	*Germany*	*China*	*Taiwan*	*Singapore*	*Japan*	*Global*
Number of distribution channels increased	45	56	35	42	20	63	41	35	33	20	40
Number of suppliers increased	34	51	40	17	16	25	34	31	33	12	30
Number of competitors increased	29	38	28	18	11	18	43	32	38	10	28
Intensity of competition increased	38	56	38	48	34	45	49	51	46	27	42

Source: CRITO GEC Survey, 2002

Index